EYEWITNESS *TRAVEL GUIDES*

LOIRE VALLEY

EYEWITNESS *TRAVEL GUIDES*

LOIRE VALLEY

Main contributor: JACK TRESIDDER

DORLING KINDERSLEY

LONDON • NEW YORK • STUTTGART • MOSCOW

A DORLING KINDERSLEY BOOK

Produced by Duncan Baird Publishers
London, England

PROJECT EDITOR Stephanie Driver
EDITOR Slaney Begley
EDITORIAL ASSISTANT Joanne Levêque
DESIGNERS Paul Calver, Jill Mumford
DESIGN ASSISTANT Christine Keilty
MANAGING EDITOR Louise Bostock Lang
MANAGING ART EDITOR David Rowley

PICTURE RESEARCH Jill De Cet, Michèle Faram
RESEARCHER Caroline Mackenzie
DTP DESIGNER Alan McKee

Dorling Kindersley Limited
SENIOR EDITOR Fay Franklin
SENIOR MANAGING ART EDITOR Gillian Allan
DEPUTY EDITORIAL DIRECTOR Douglas Amrine
DEPUTY ART DIRECTOR Gaye Allen
MAP CO-ORDINATORS Michael Ellis, David Pugh
PRODUCTION David Proffit

MAPS
Jane Hanson, Jennifer Skelley (Lovell Johns Ltd, Oxford)

PHOTOGRAPHERS
John Heseltine, Paul Kenward, Kim Sayer

ILLUSTRATORS
Joanna Cameron, Roger Hutchins, Robbie Polley,
Pat Thorne, John Woodcock
•
Film outputting bureau Creative Text Limited (London)
Reproduced by Colourscan (Singapore)
Printed and bound by G. Canale & C. (Italy)

First published in Great Britain in 1996
by Dorling Kindersley Limited
9 Henrietta Street, London WC2E 8PS

Copyright 1996 © Dorling Kindersley Limited, London

A CIP CATALOGUE RECORD IS AVAILABLE FROM THE BRITISH LIBRARY.

ISBN 0-7513-0252-X

•
Every effort has been made to ensure that the information in this
book is as up-to-date as possible at the time of going to press.
However, details such as telephone numbers, opening hours, prices,
gallery hanging arrangements and travel information are liable to
change. The publishers cannot accept responsibility for any
consequences arising from the use of this book.

We would be delighted to receive any corrections and suggestions
for incorporation in the next edition. Please write to: Deputy
Editorial Director, Eyewitness Travel Guides,
Dorling Kindersley
9 Henrietta Street, London WC2E 8PS.

CONTENTS

Statue in La Lorie

INTRODUCING THE LOIRE VALLEY

King Louis XIV portrayed as
Jupiter, conquering La Fronde

The town of Argenton-sur-Creuse

Manoir du Grand-Martigny

Stained-glass portrait of Agnès Sorel

Young boys fishing at Pornichet marina in Loire-Atlantique

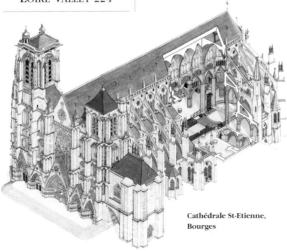

Cathédrale St-Etienne, Bourges

HOW TO USE THIS GUIDE

THIS GUIDE will help you get the most from your stay in the Loire Valley. It provides both expert recommendations and detailed practical information. *Introducing the Loire Valley* maps the region and sets it in its historical and cultural context. *The Loire Valley Area by Area* describes the important sights, with maps, photographs and illustrations. Suggestions for food, drink, accommodation, shopping and activities are in *Travellers' Needs*, and the *Survival Guide* has tips on everything from the French telephone system to getting to the Loire and travelling around the region.

THE LOIRE VALLEY AREA BY AREA

In this guide, the Loire Valley has been divided into six regions, each of which has its own chapter. A map of these regions can be found inside the front cover of the book. The most interesting places to visit in each region have been numbered and plotted on a *Pictorial Map*.

Each area of the Loire Valley can be quickly identified by its colour coding.

1 Introduction
The landscape, history and character of each region is described here, showing how the area has developed over the centuries and what it has to offer the visitor today.

A locator map shows the region in relation to the whole of the Loire Valley.

Exploring Touraine

2 Pictorial Map
This gives an illustrated overview of the whole region. All the sights are numbered, and there are also useful tips on getting around by car and public transport.

Features and story boxes highlight special or unique aspects of a particular sight.

3 Detailed information on each sight
All the important towns and other places to visit are described individually. They are listed in order, following the numbering on the *Pictorial Map*. Within each town or city, there is detailed information on important buildings and other major sights.

4 Major Towns
An introduction covers the history, character and geography of the town. The main sights are described individually and plotted on a Town Map.

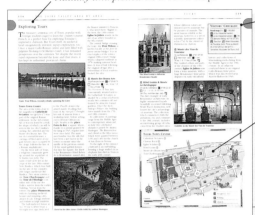

A Visitors' Checklist gives contact points for tourist and transport information, plus details of market days and local festival dates.

The town map shows all major through-roads as well as minor streets of interest to visitors. All the sights are plotted, along with the bus and train stations, parking, tourist offices and churches.

5 Street-by-Street Map
Towns or districts of special interest to visitors are shown in detailed 3D, with photographs of the most important sights, giving a bird's-eye view of the area.

A suggested route for a walk covers the most interesting streets in the area.

6 Top Sights
These are given two or more pages. Important buildings are dissected to reveal their interiors.

For all the top sights, a Visitors' Checklist provides the practical information you will need to plan your visit.

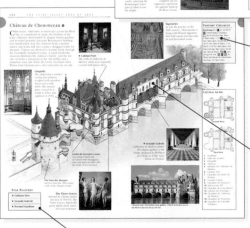

Stars indicate the works of art or features that no visitor should miss.

INTRODUCING
THE
LOIRE VALLEY

Putting the Loire on the Map

THE LOIRE VALLEY lies in central France, bordered by the regions of Brittany, Normandy and the Ile de France to the north, the Massif Central and Poitou to the south, Burgundy to the east, and the Atlantic Ocean to the west. The river itself, the longest in France, flows for 1,020 km (634 miles) from its source in the Cévennes to the Atlantic Ocean just south of Nantes at St-Nazaire. The region covers an area of 71,228 sq km (27,500 sq miles) and has a population of about 5.2 million.

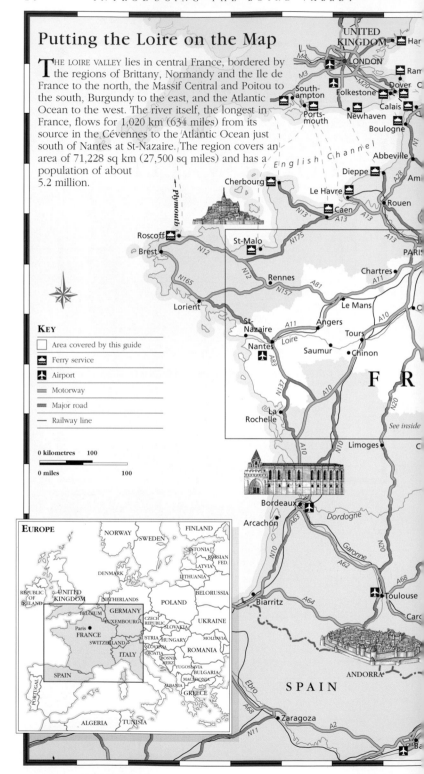

KEY

- Area covered by this guide
- Ferry service
- Airport
- Motorway
- Major road
- Railway line

0 kilometres   100

0 miles   100

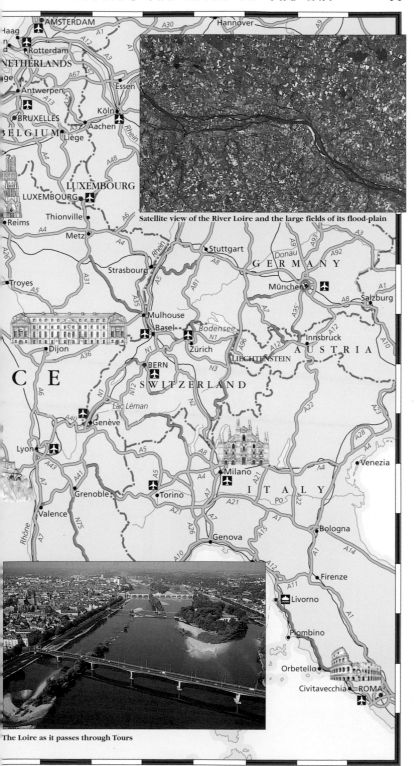

Satellite view of the River Loire and the large fields of its flood-plain

The Loire as it passes through Tours

A PORTRAIT OF THE LOIRE VALLEY

THE LOIRE VALLEY, *world-famous for its beautiful châteaux, has long been described as exemplifying* la douceur de vivre*: it combines a leisurely pace of life, a mild climate, mellow wines and the gentle ways of its inhabitants. The overall impression conveyed by the region is one of an unostentatious taste for the good things in life.*

In this central region of France, the people have neither the brisk, sometimes brusque, demeanour of their northern counterparts, nor the excitable nature of the southern provinces. They get on peacefully with their lives, benefiting from the prosperity generated not only by the region's centuries old popularity with French and foreign visitors alike, but also by a fertile soil and a favourable climate, which rarely succumbs to extremes of heat or cold.

The Loire as a region is far from being a cultural and historical anachronism, although the wealth of well-preserved historical monuments harks back to the past. Many local people are surprisingly proud of the nuclear power stations at Avoine-Chinon and at St-Laurent-des-Eaux near Beaugency, both symbols of the region's role in the technological revolution. The well-publicized (and successful) campaign in the mid-1980s to have the high-speed TGV train rerouted was based not on any intrinsic dislike of new-fangled schemes, but on alarm at the potential damage to the bottles of wine stored in their underground cellars close to the planned track.

Cyclist on the Ile de Noirmoutier causeway

The bridge across the Loire at Blois, one of several historic bridges in the region

◁ Berry village in the evening

Folk dancers in costume at the Château de Blois

The many fairs, fêtes and festivals devoted to local wines and produce – garlic, apples, melons or even chitterling sausages – bear witness to the large part, even by French standards, that food and drink play in the social life of these old provinces.

They also play a major role in the region's economy: around 12 per cent of the local population is involved in agriculture or the food industry in some way. Many a *primeur* (early fruit or vegetable) in the markets and restaurants of Paris has been transported from the fertile fields and orchards beside the Loire, and the region's melons and asparagus are sold all over the country. So, too, are the button mushrooms, known in French as *champignons de Paris* (Paris mushrooms), grown in abandoned tufa quarries near Saumur and elsewhere – the region produces some 75 per cent of France's mushrooms.

Colourful summer display

Yet the way of life in the Loire Valley remains largely anchored to the traditional values of *la France profonde*, the country's conservative heartland – seeking to perpetuate a way of life that has proved its worth over the centuries. This is particularly true of the Berry, the easternmost region of the Loire covered in this guide. It is the geographical centre of the country – several villages claim the honour of being situated at "the heart of France" – and it seems to the visitor charmingly off the beaten track. It comes as no surprise to discover that folk traditions and, some say, witchcraft are still part of everyday life in some of these timeless villages.

Although some local wines are reputed not to travel well, many of them do so very successfully, not only in France but also abroad, adding to the region's prosperity. In terms of the volume of production, the

The Loire at Amboise, dotted with sandbanks

LOCAL ATTRACTIONS

The opportunity to stay in a private château is one of the many treats for visitors to the Loire Valley, where hospitality is a serious business. Even in Orléans, whose proximity to Paris has led to its reputation as a dormitory town, a warm welcome in hotels and restaurants is assured. And in the towns and villages of Touraine and Anjou, conviviality is everywhere apparent.

A walk along a river bank at Rochefort-sur-Loire, one of many country pursuits to enjoy

region ranks fifth in France and, although production is on a smaller scale than the famous wine giants of Bordeaux and Burgundy, the quality and popularity of Loire wines are both increasing. Sancerre and Muscadet are probably the best known, but others, such as Vouvray and Bourgueil, are also much in demand.

The restaurants and hotel dining rooms of the Loire Valley take full advantage of the excellent produce available locally – no wonder so many Parisian families have been attracted to the area. Just as once the nobility of France established their châteaux and stately homes in the area, now wealthy Parisians are flocking to the Loire Valley to buy *résidences secondaires*. The influx has been swelled in recent years with the advent of the TGV, which takes less than an hour to reach the region from Paris.

VINS DE PROPRIETE
Dégustation
Vente

Sign offering wine-tastings

RECENT DEVELOPMENTS
In the west of the region, Nantes has adapted to changing economic times. The closure of its once-flourishing shipyards has led to a new focus on advanced technology and international

business. In the mid-1980s a science park, the Technopole Atlantique, was built on the banks of the River Erdre, an electronic research institute opened and the city acquired a World Trade Centre (*Centre Atlantique du Commerce International*). Yet here, too, the broad streets and avenues (formerly water-courses) create a feeling of spaciousness that helps to perpetuate the mood of *douceur de vivre* beside the new economic dynamism. In the same way, Tours' chic new conference centre in the heart of the city does not seem to have detracted from the bustle of streets often thronged with foreign students. They have come to learn to speak what is alleged to be the purest French in France. By "pure", the experts mean well-modulated speech devoid of any strong accent – a fine symbol for a populace admired for being pleasant and relaxed.

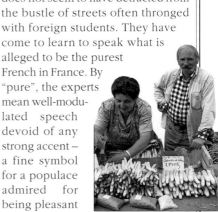

Locally grown asparagus

From Defence to Decoration

OVER THE CENTURIES, châteaux in the Loire Valley gradually developed from feudal castles, designed purely as defensive fortresses, into graceful pleasure palaces. Once the introduction of firearms put an end to the sieges that medieval castles were built to withstand, comfort and elegance became key status symbols. Many defensive elements evolved into decorative features: watchtowers became fairy-tale turrets, moats served as reflecting pools and crenellations were transformed into ornamental friezes. During the Renaissance, Italian craftsmen added features such as galleries and formal gardens, and carved decoration became increasingly intricate.

Château d'Angers in 1550, before its towers were lowered

Slate and stone walls

Fortifications with pepper pot towers removed

Angers (see pp74–5) *was built between 1220 and 1240 as a mighty clifftop fortress, towering over the River Maine. Along its curtain wall were spaced 17 massive round towers. These would originally have been 30 m (98 ft) high before their pepper pot towers were removed in the 16th century.*

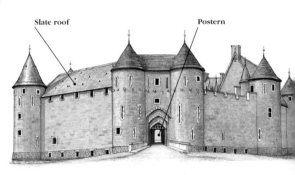

Slate roof

Postern

Ainay-le-Vieil (see p148), *dating fr the 12th century, contrasts two style An octagonal walled fortress, with nine massive towers topped by pepp pot turrets and lit by arrow slits, wa entered through a huge medieval postern gate across a drawbridge th crossed the moat. Inside, however, there is a charming, early 16th-century Renaissance home.*

Ainay-le-Vieil's delightful living quarter hidden inside an octagonal fortress

Circular tower, formerly defensive

Corbelled walkways, once useful in battle

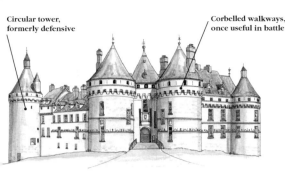

Chaumont (see p128) *stands on the site of a 12th-century fortress, destroyed in 1465 by Louis XI to punish its owners for disloyalty. The château was rebuilt from 1498 to 1510 in the Renaissance style. Although it has a defensive appearance, with circular towers, corbelled walkways and a gatehouse, these features have been lightened with Renaissance decoration.*

Chaumont's walls are carved with the crossed Cs of Charles II d'Amboise, whose family rebuilt the château.

Decorated turret

Renaissance carved windows

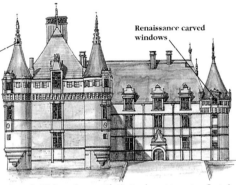

Decoration on the north façade of Azay-le-Rideau

Azay-le-Rideau (see pp96–7), *its elegant turrets reflected in a peaceful lake, was built from 1518 to 1527 and is considered one of the best-designed Renaissance châteaux. Its interior staircase, behind an intricately decorated pediment with three storeys of twin bays, is very striking.*

Dormer window

Cylindrical tower

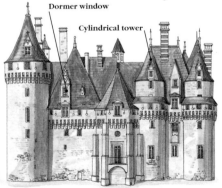

Ussé (see p101) *was built in 1462 as a battlemented fortress. Later, the walls overlooking the main court-yard were modified during the Renaissance, with dormer windows and pilasters. In the 17th century the north wing was replaced by terraced gardens.*

Château d'Ussé, once a fortress, now an aristocratic château

Inside the Châteaux

Stone carving on staircase

THE TYPICAL LOIRE VALLEY château boasted several large, lavishly furnished reception rooms, adorned with luxurious tapestries and paintings and featuring decorative panelling and ceilings. The main rooms included the Grand Salon, often with an imposing fireplace, and an elegant dining room. The gallery was a focal point for host and guests to meet to discuss the events of the day, admire the views over the grounds or the paintings displayed on the gallery walls. The châtelain's private rooms, and those reserved for honoured (particularly royal) guests, were grouped in a separate wings, while servants were housed in the attics.

Apartments in one wing were for private use.

Grand Escalier (Grand Staircase)

Chairs *were often spindly – elegant but uncomfortable. The more comfortable models with armrests might be covered with precious tapestries, as with this one from Cheverny, upholstered in Aubusson.*

The Grand Salon, mostly used for entertaining, had a majestic marble fireplace carved with the owner's coat of arms, emblem or inter-twined initials.

The Grand Escalier, *or Escalier d'Honneur (grand staircase), had richly carved balustrades and an elaborately decorated ceiling, such as this magnificent Renaissance staircase at Serrant (see p69). The staircase led to the owner's private suites, as well as to state guest bedrooms and rooms used on special occasions, such as the armoury.*

Main entrance

Galleries*, like this one at Beauregard (see pp130–31), were where owners and guests met to converse or to be entertained. They were often hung with family and other portraits.*

State dining rooms, *for receiving important visitors, were as sumptuously furnished and decorated as the other main reception rooms. This one in Chaumont* (see p128) *features Renaissance furniture.*

Château rooms *were filled with costly tapestries, paintings and fine furniture, and attention was paid to detail. Decorative features, such as this French Limoges enamel plaque, or intricately carved wooden panelling were common. Even the tiles on stoves that heated the huge rooms were often painted.*

The Salle d'Armes, or armoury, displayed suits of armour and weapons beside fine tapestries and furniture.

The east wing was reserved for important guests.

Dining Room

King's Bedroom

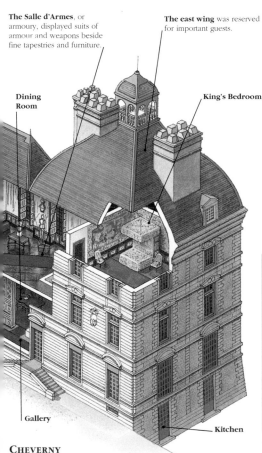

The King's Bedroom *was kept permanently ready for a royal visit. Under the droit de gîte (right of lodging), château owners were bound to provide accommodation to the king in return for a building permit. This room, at Cheverny* (see p130), *was used frequently.*

Gallery

Kitchen

CHEVERNY

A dignified Classical building in white tufa, Cheverny *(see p130)* has scarcely been altered since it was built between 1620 and 1634. The central section, containing the staircase, is flanked by two symmetrical wings, each consisting of a steep-roofed section and a much larger pavilion with a domed roof. The interior is decorated in 17th-century style.

Kitchens *were in the cellars, or separately housed. Huge spits for roasting whole carcasses were worked by elaborate mechanisms. Though often dark, the kitchens gleamed with an array of copper pots and pans, like these at Montgeoffroy* (see p71).

Churches and Abbeys

THE LOIRE VALLEY is well-endowed with medieval
ecclesiastical architecture, ranging from tiny
Romanesque village churches to major Gothic cathedrals like Chartres and Tours. In the early Middle
Ages, the Romanesque style predominated, character-
ized by straightforward ground plans, round arches
and relatively little decoration. By the 13th century,
the rib vaulting and flying buttresses of Gothic architecture had emerged, enabling builders to create taller,
lighter churches and cathedrals. The Late Gothic style
in France, often referred to as Flamboyant Gothic,
features window tracery with flowing lines licking
upwards like flames.

LOCATOR MAP

① Romanesque architecture

⑨ Gothic architecture

ROMANESQUE FEATURES

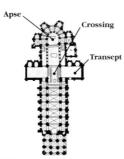

**The plan of St-Benoît-
sur-Loire** *is typical of
Romanesque architecture,
with its cross shape and
rounded apse.*

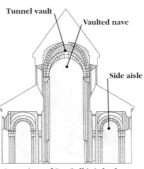

**A section of La Collégiale de
St-Aignan-sur-Cher** *shows
Romanesque tunnel vaulting.
The vaulted side aisles provide
added support for the high nave.*

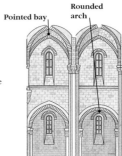

**The round arches of
St-Aignan** *are typically
Romanesque, while the
pointed nave bays
predict the Gothic style.*

GOTHIC FEATURES

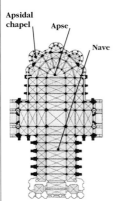

**The plan of Chartres
Cathedral** *shows its very
wide nave, and its apse
ringed with chapels.*

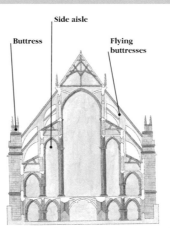

A section of St-Etienne *in Bourges reveals
its five divisions with two aisles on either
side of the nave. The building also has five
portals rather than the usual three.*

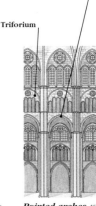

Pointed arches *wit
stand greater stress a
allow large windows
in the nave at Bourg*

WHERE TO FIND ROMANESQUE ARCHITECTURE

① St-Maurice, Angers *pp72–3*
② L'Abbaye St-Vincent, Nieul-sur-l'Autise *pp182–3*
③ Notre-Dame, Cunault *p79*
④ L'Abbaye de Fontevraud *pp86–7*
⑤ St-Maurice, Chinon *pp98–9*
⑥ La Collégiale, St-Aignan-sur-Cher *p129*
⑦ St-Eusice, Selles-sur-Cher *pp24–5*
⑧ La Basilique de St-Benoît-sur-Loire *p140*

WHERE TO FIND GOTHIC ARCHITECTURE

⑨ St-Etienne, Bourges *pp152–3*
⑩ St-Louis, Blois *pp124–5*
⑪ St-Hubert, Amboise, *p110*
⑫ St-Gatien, Tours *pp116–17*
⑬ La Trinité, Vendôme *p123*
⑭ Notre-Dame, Chartres *pp172–5*
⑮ St-Julien, Le Mans *p166*
⑯ Asnières-sur-Vègre *p163*

The west façade of Notre-Dame *at Cunault is simply decorated. Its machicolations and lateral towers give it a fortified appearance.*

Bell-tower, Machicolations, Tympanum

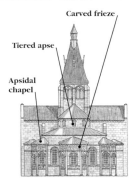

The east end of St-Eusice *in Selles-sur-Cher, with its three apsidal chapels, is decorated with friezes of carved figures.*

Carved frieze, Tiered apse, Apsidal chapel

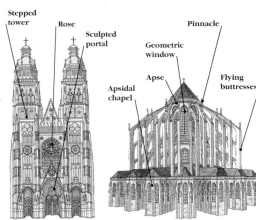

The west façade *of St-Gatien in Tours has richly carved, Flamboyant Gothic portals.*

Stepped tower, Rose, Sculpted portal

The east end *of St-Julien cathedral in Le Mans has a complex arrangement of paired flying buttresses, each topped by pinnacles.*

Pinnacle, Geometric window, Apse, Flying buttresses, Apsidal chapel

TERMS USED IN THIS GUIDE

Basilica: Early church with two aisles and nave lit from above by clerestory windows.

Clerestory: A row of windows illuminating the nave from above the aisle roof.

 Rose: Circular window, often stained glass.

Buttress: Mass of masonry built to support a wall.

 Flying buttress: An arched support transmitting thrust of the weight downwards.

Portal: Monumental entrance to a building, often decorated.

 Tympanum: Decorated space, often carved, over a door or window lintel.

Vault: Arched stone ceiling.

Transept: Two wings of a cruciform church at right angles to the nave.

Crossing: Centre of cruciform where transept crosses nave.

Lantern: Turret with windows to illuminate interior, often with cupola (domed ceiling).

Triforium: Middle storey between arcades and the clerestory.

Apse: Termination of the church, often rounded.

Ambulatory: Aisle running round east end, passing behind the sanctuary.

Arcade: Set of arches and supporting columns.

Rib vault: Vault supported by projecting ribs of stone.

 Gargoyle: Carved grotesque figure, often a water spout.

Tracery: Ornamental carved stone pattern within Gothic window.

Flamboyant Gothic: Carved stone tracery resembling flames.

 Capital: Top of a column, usually carved.

Writers and Artists of the Loire Valley

THE VALLEY OF THE River Loire is well known for its agricultural fertility, and it has also proved to be productive ground for literature, too. Over the centuries, internationally famous writers such as François Rabelais, the great lyrical poet Pierre de Ronsard and the novelists Honoré de Balzac and George Sand have lived close to the mighty river, often drawing inspiration from their native soil. Perhaps strangely, however, the pure light that so appeals to visitors to the region does not seem to have inspired as many of the country's greatest painters, although Claude Monet spent a fruitful period in the peaceful Creuse Valley.

Novelist Honoré de Balzac

Writer Marcel Proust, in a late 19th-century portrait by Jacques-Emile Blanche

WRITERS

ONE OF THE earliest authors to write in the "vulgar" French tongue was born in Meung-sur-Loire in the mid-13th century. Jean Chopinel, better known as Jean de Meung, produced the second part of the widely translated and influential *Roman de la Rose*, a long, allegorical poem about courtly love. While the first half of the poem focuses delicately on two young lovers and their affair, Jean de Meung's sequel undermines the idealistic conventions of courtly love, taking a more cynical view of the world.

During the Hundred Years' War, a century and a half later, aristocratic poet Charles, Duc d'Orléans was

Illumination from the *Roman de la Rose*

imprisoned by the English for 25 years. While in prison he was able to develop his considerable poetic skills. On his return he made his court at Blois a key literary centre. He invited famous writers and poets, among them François Villon, a 15th-century poet as renowned for the skill of his writing as for his highly disreputable lifestyle. While he was in Blois, Villon won a poetry competition with his work, *"Je Meurs de Soif auprès de la Fontaine"* ("I am Dying of Thirst by the Fountain").

François Rabelais, the racy 16th-century satirist and humanist, was born in 1483 near Chinon *(see pp98–9)* and educated at Angers. He became famous throughout Europe upon the publication of his *Pantagruel* (1532) and *Gargantua* (1535), huge, sprawling works full of bawdy humour and learned discourse in equal measure.

Pierre de Ronsard, born near Vendôme 30 years after Rabelais, was the leading

George Sand, the 19th-century novelist

French Renaissance poet, perhaps best known for his lyrical odes and sonnets to "Cassandre", "Hélène" and "Marie" (an Anjou peasant girl). Court poet to Charles IX and his sister Marguerite de Valois, he lived and died at St-Cosme Priory near Tours. Ronsard was also at the head of the Pléiade, a group of seven poets who were determined to revolutionize French poetry through the study of the classics. In the same group was Joachim du Bellay, an Anjou aristocrat and keen advocate of French literature. His *Defence and Illustration of the French Language* (1549) was a prose manifesto of Pléiade doctrine.

Another famous native of the Loire Valley spearheaded a 17th-century intellectual revolution. Mathematician and philosopher René Descartes, born in Touraine and educated at the Jesuit college in La Flèche *(see p167)*, developed a new method of philosophical inquiry involving the simultaneous study of all the sciences. Starting with the celebrated "I think, therefore

I am," he developed the rationalist doctrine known as Cartesianism in his most famous work, the *Discourse on Method*.

France's most prolific 19th-century novelist, Honoré de Balzac, often referred to his native Touraine as his favourite province. Tours, Saumur and the Château de Saché feature as settings for some of his best-known novels, all of which are keenly observant of 19th-century French mores. The work of Balzac's contemporary, George Sand (the masculine pen name of Aurore, Baroness Dudevant), is rooted in the landscapes of her native Berry, which also inspired Alain-Fournier's magical *Le Grand Meaulnes*, a romantic vision of his childhood in the region.

The hawthorn hedges and peaceful villages near Chartres provided the unforgettable setting for the early passages of Marcel Proust's impressive sequence of novels, *Remembrance of Things Past*. At the mouth of the Loire, the city of Nantes saw the birth, in 1826, of the ever-popular Jules Verne *(see pp192–3)*, whose pioneering works of science fiction have been enormously influential.

ARTISTS

IN 1411, THE THREE Limbourg brothers became court painters to the Duc de Berry in Bourges. He commissioned them to paint some 39 miniatures for *Les Très Riches Heures du Duc de Berry*. This Book of Hours was to become the jewel in the duke's fabled manuscript collection and remains one of the finest achievements of the International Gothic style. Some of these intricate illustrations depict scenes from life in the Loire Valley.

Jehan Fouquet, born in Tours in about 1420, was officially appointed royal painter in 1475. His portraits

A miniature from *Les Très Riches Heures du Duc du Berry*

include the famous image of the royal mistress Agnès Sorel *(see p104)* posing as the Virgin Mary.

A century after Fouquet's birth, François I persuaded the elderly Leonardo da Vinci to settle in the manor house of Cloux (now called Le Clos-Lucé, *see pp110–11*) near the royal château of Amboise. Aged 65, Leonardo was no longer actively painting, although he is known to have made some sketches of court life which have not survived. However, he was engaged in scientific investigations and inventions, the results of which can be seen in a museum in the basement of the château.

At about the time of Leonardo's death in 1519, François Clouet was born in

Henri Rousseau, in a self-portrait that typifies his naïve style

Tours. He succeeded his father, Jean, as court painter to François I and produced a string of truly outstanding portraits. His sitters included François I himself, Elizabeth of Austria and Mary, Queen of Scots. François Clouet's style, which was typical of the French Renaissance, was perpetuated by the artists and artisans in his workshop.

Anjou's most celebrated sculptor is David d'Angers, who was born in 1789. His works include busts and medallions of many of the major historical figures of his day, including a memorial to the Marquis de Bonchamps, which can be found in the church at St-Florent-le-Vieil *(see p57)*.

François Clouet's portrait of Mary, Queen of Scots

Exactly a century later, the Impressionist painter Claude Monet spent several weeks in the village of Fresselines in the Creuse Valley, painting the river as it passed through a narrow gorge *(see p147)*. One of these canvases, *Le Pont de Vervit*, now hangs in the Musée Marmottan in Paris.

Henri Rousseau, the quintessential naïve painter, was born in the town of Laval in 1844. Although he never left France, his best-known works are stylized depictions of lush jungles, home to all manner of wild animals. Part of the château in Laval has been converted into a Museum of Naïve Art *(see p160)* in honour of the artist.

Themed Tours of the Loire Valley

FOR THOSE WHO WISH to travel independently of tour companies, or who have a special interest in the region, themed tours provide an attractive alternative. Local tourist offices produce information on routes visitors can travel in order to see the best sights on a given theme – including wine, churches, châteaux, and historical buildings and beautiful botanical gardens and arboretums. Illustrated brochures and tourist maps describing each route, often in languages other than French, are available, and some of the routes are signposted along the way. Tourist office staff are also able to customize a route for your particular needs.

A la Recherche des Plantagenêts *traces the lives of Henry Plantagenet, his wife, Eleanor of Aquitaine, and their sons (see p50). The evidence of their remarkable lives, including this fortress in Loches, can be seen throughout the region.*

The Route Touristique du Vignoble (Wine Route) *guides the traveller through some of the region's prettiest wine country, including the Coteaux de la Loire. Further information is available from the tourist offices in Angers, Nantes and Saumur.*

La Flèche

Angers

Champtoceaux   St-Cosr

Nantes   St-Florent-   Chalonnes   Bour
le-Vieil   Cunault   Saumur

Clisson   Montreuil-Bellay

Vouvant
Fontenay
Luçon   le Comte
Nieul-sur-
Autise
Maillezais

The Route de la Vallée des Rois *takes motorists to many former royal residences, such as Azay-le-Rideau, as well as to cathedrals and churches along the part of the Loire known as the Valley of the Kings. Information is available from tourist offices in Saumur, Blois, Gien and Orléans.*

The Circuit Sud-Vendéen au Pays de la Fée Mélusine *takes in the attractions of the south Vendée, including the Marais Poitevin, to give a selection of the varied sights in this area. The tourist office at La-Roche-sur-Yon provides details.*

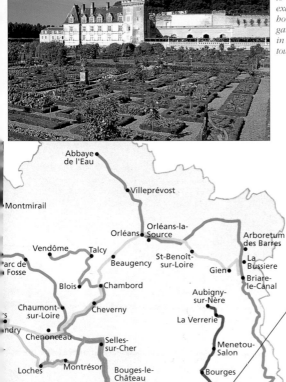

The Route Historique des Parcs et Jardins takes visitors to Villandry and many other exquisite châteaux and manor house gardens, contemporary gardens, parks and arboretums in the region. Contact the tourist office in Tours.

The Route Jacques Cœur leads motorists through some picturesque towns as well as to memorable châteaux, including the Château de Maupas and the Palais Jacques-Cœur in Bourges (see p151), the former home of the wealthy merchant who gives the tour its name. Some of the private châteaux on the route take paying guests (see pp200–201). The tourist office in Bourges provides details of the route.

| 0 kilometres | 50 |
| 0 miles | 50 |

The Route Historique François I explores the châteaux, such as Valençay, constructed during the reign of François I (see p54), who held court in Chambord and Blois during the 16th century. Information is available from the tourist office in Romorantin-Lanthenay.

KEY

— Circuit Sud-Vendéen

— Route Historique des Parcs et Jardins

— A la Recherche des Plantagenêts

— Route Historique François I

— Route Jacques Cœur

— Route de la Vallée des Rois

— Route Touristique du Vignoble

Walking in the Loire Valley

T HE BEST WAY to follow the "most sensual river in France", as Flaubert called it – to appreciate the transformation of the river as it flows through the Sologne forests, carves out the Valley of the Kings, and finally rushes into the ocean – is on foot. The *Grande Randonnée 3* (GR 3) is one of the longest marked walks in France, accompanying the Loire from its source at Gerbier de Jonc to its mouth. The route occasionally strays from the river bank in order to follow the most picturesque paths. For walks lasting a few hours, or several days, ramblers can follow a part of the *Grande Randonnée* or try the region's many shorter, often circular, routes. A Topo-Guide *(see p224)* is a useful companion for detailed information about your walk.

KEY

— Recommended walk
— Grande Randonnée de Pays
— Grande Randonnée

In the charming Alpes Mancelles, in the Parc Régional Normandie-Maine, there are four- to seven-day walks in the valleys of the Sarthe, the Mayenne and the Orne. *(Topo-Guide 039)*

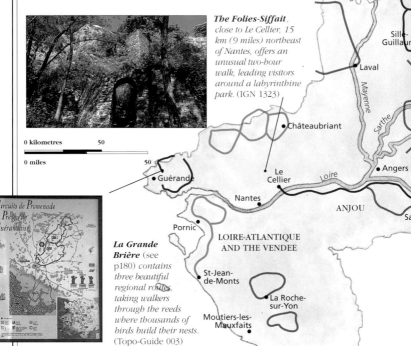

The Folies-Siffait, *close to Le Cellier, 15 km (9 miles) northeast of Nantes, offers an unusual two-hour walk, leading visitors around a labyrinthine park.* (IGN 1323)

0 kilometres 50
0 miles 50

La Grande Brière (see p180) *contains three beautiful regional routes, taking walkers through the reeds where thousands of birds build their nests.* (Topo-Guide 003)

ROUTE MARKERS

All the walking routes are marked *(balisé)* with symbols painted onto trees or rocks along the paths. The different colours of the symbols indicate which kind of route you are taking. A red and white mark denotes a *Grande Randonnée* (GR) route, yellow and red are used for a regional route *(Grande Randonnée de Pays),* and local routes *(Petites Randonnées)* are marked in a single colour (usually yellow).

	Grande Randonnée	Grande Randonnée de Pays	Petite Randonnée
Straight on			
Change direction			
Wrong way			

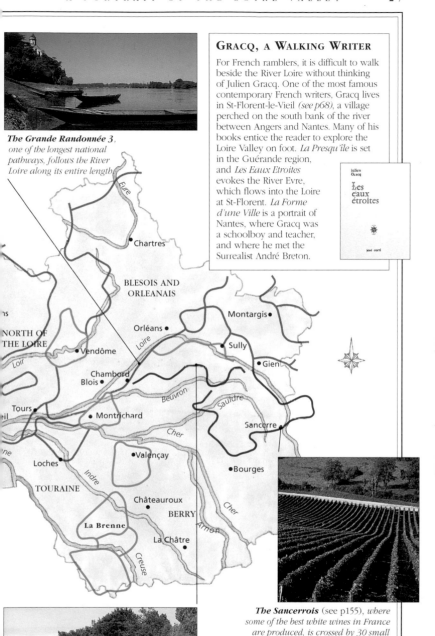

The Grande Randonnée 3, *one of the longest national pathways, follows the River Loire along its entire length.*

GRACQ, A WALKING WRITER

For French ramblers, it is difficult to walk beside the River Loire without thinking of Julien Gracq. One of the most famous contemporary French writers, Gracq lives in St-Florent-le-Vieil *(see p68)*, a village perched on the south bank of the river between Angers and Nantes. Many of his books entice the reader to explore the Loire Valley on foot. *La Presqu'île* is set in the Guérande region, and *Les Eaux Etroites* evokes the River Evre, which flows into the Loire at St-Florent. *La Forme d'une Ville* is a portrait of Nantes, where Gracq was a schoolboy and teacher, and where he met the Surrealist André Breton.

The Sancerrois (see p155), *where some of the best white wines in France are produced, is crossed by 30 small walks (Petites Randonnées) of between 9 and 32 km (5–20 miles) passing through Sancerre's vineyards.* (Topo-Guide 064)

The Sologne *is on the route of the GR 3C, a variation of the GR 3. The path leaves the Loire between Gien and Chambord and takes walkers on a five-day journey through this mysterious forest (see p141).* (Topo-Guide 362)

The Natural History of the Loire Valley

European grey wolf

Fᴿᴬɴᴄᴇ's ʟᴏɴɢᴇsᴛ ʀɪᴠᴇʀ is fed by a number of tributaries, including the Loir, the Mayenne, the Sarthe, the Cher, the Indre, the Vienne, the Creuse and the Beuvron. Within easy reach of the central Loire Valley are four park areas *(Parcs Naturels Régionaux)*: Brière, Normandie-Maine, Marais Poitevin and La Brenne. The region is dotted with lakes and ponds that shelter birds and other wildlife, and the woods, forests, hills and plains are crossed with trails known as *Grandes Randonnées (see p26)*, ideal for walkers and cyclists.

Kᴇʏ

- Regional natural park
- Forest and woodland
- Lake
- Major river

0 kilometres   50

0 miles   50

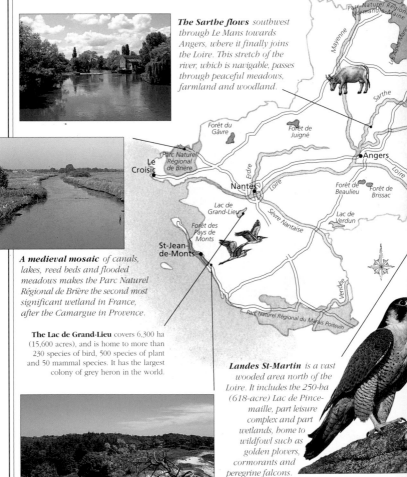

The Sarthe flows southwest through Le Mans towards Angers, where it finally joins the Loire. This stretch of the river, which is navigable, passes through peaceful meadows, farmland and woodland.

A medieval mosaic of canals, lakes, reed beds and flooded meadows makes the Parc Naturel Régional de Brière the second most significant wetland in France, after the Camargue in Provence.

The Lac de Grand-Lieu covers 6,300 ha (15,600 acres), and is home to more than 230 species of bird, 500 species of plant and 50 mammal species. It has the largest colony of grey heron in the world.

Landes St-Martin is a vast wooded area north of the Loire. It includes the 250-ha (618-acre) Lac de Pince-maille, part leisure complex and part wetlands, home to wildfowl such as golden plovers, cormorants and peregrine falcons.

The Forêt des Pays de Monts consists of mixed woodland bordering golden Atlantic beaches.

Parc Naturel Régional Normandie-Maine
Mayenne
La Sarthe Mar
Sarthe
Forêt du Gâvre
Forêt de Juigné
Forêt de Beaulieu
Forêt de Brissac
Angers
Loire
Parc Naturel Régional de Brière
Le Croisic
Erdre
Nantes
Loire
Lac de Grand-Lieu
Sèvre Nantaise
Lac de Verdun
Forêt des Pays de Monts
St-Jean-de-Monts
Vendée
Parc Naturel Régional du Marais Poitevin

Magnificent oaks, some more than 300 years old, flourish alongside horse chestnuts, pines and beech in the Futaie des Clos (see p168) part of the Forêt de Bercé. Bounded by the Veuve, Dinan and Loir rivers, the forest has seven straight "rides".

The Forêt d'Orléans is the second largest in France at 50,000 ha (124,000 acres). It is bisected by the canal d'Orléans and is rich in wild boar, deer and other game. Agricultural scenery alternates with wild woodland and pools.

Containing a wealth of botanical treasures, including orchids and alpine plants, the 300-ha (740-acre) Vallée de la Grande Pierre de Marolles et de Vitain lies 10 km (6 miles) north of Blois.

The Parc de Chambord is a game reserve covering 5,500 ha (13,600 acres) and surrounded by 33 km (21 miles) of wall, making it the largest "walled garden" in Europe. It is possible to observe resident wildlife (including deer, wild boar and badger) from viewing platforms.

The park area between the rivers Indre and Creuse is known as the Pays des Mille Etangs, after its 1,270 lakes and pools. Two unusual residents are pond tortoises and the wolves housed in a wildlife reserve in the Forêt de Preuilly, about 4 km (2½ miles) northwest of Azay-le-Ferron.

A little off the beaten track, the Sologne (see p141) covers 490,000 ha (1.2 million acres). The wooded landscapes of silver birch, oak, larch, spruce pine and fir blend with marshland and heath. Its lakes attract many species of bird and other wildlife including pine marten, roe deer, and the black and yellow salamander.

Winemaking and Vineyards

Caricature of
a wine maker
in "costume"

THE IMPORTANCE OF WINE to life in the Loire
Valley is immediately apparent. Fields of
vines stretch along both banks of the
river, and roadsides are lined with signs
offering *dégustations*, or wine tastings *(see
p212)*. Stretching 300 km (186 miles) from
Nantes to Pouilly-sur-Loire, the Loire Valley
is the fifth largest wine-producing area by
volume in France and offers an unprece-
dented range of wine styles. The white
Sancerres have an excellent reputation
(see p155), as do some of the rosé wines
of Anjou, the sweet and sparkling Vouvrays, the full-bodied reds of Chinon and
Bourgueil, and the superb, dry *méthode champenoise*
wines of Saumur. There are many more modest wines
available, including Muscadet and its younger cousin
Gros Plant, which are best served chilled.

Traditional vineyard cultivation

The great sweet wine of the
Côteaux du Layon, Quarts de
Chaume, is little known outside
France.

Muscadet designated
sur lie *has greater
flavour because of a
special ageing process.*

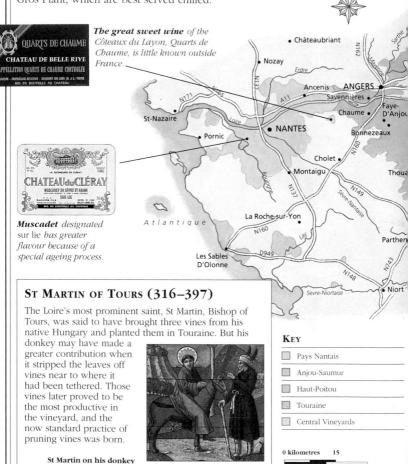

ST MARTIN OF TOURS (316–397)

The Loire's most prominent saint, St Martin, Bishop of
Tours, was said to have brought three vines from his
native Hungary and planted them in Touraine. But his
donkey may have made a
greater contribution when
it stripped the leaves off
vines near to where it
had been tethered. Those
vines later proved to be
the most productive in
the vineyard, and the
now standard practice of
pruning vines was born.

St Martin on his donkey

KEY

- Pays Nantais
- Anjou-Saumur
- Haut-Poitou
- Touraine
- Central Vineyards

0 kilometres 15

0 miles 15

KEY FACTS ABOUT LOIRE WINES

 Grape Varieties
The Muscadet grape makes simple, dry whites. The Sauvignon Blanc produces gooseberryish, flinty dry whites. Chenin Blanc is used for the dry and medium Anjou, Vouvrays, Savennières and Saumur, and the famous sweet whites, Vouvray, Quarts de Chaume and Bonnezeaux. Summery reds are made from the Gamay and the Cabernet Franc.

 Good Producers (west to east)
Muscadet: Château de la Bretesche, Marquis de Goulaine, Château de Chasseloir. *Anjou* (red): Domaine de Ste-Anne. *Anjou* (rosé): Robert Lecomte-Girault. *Anjou* (dry white): Domaine Richou. *Saumur* (sparkling): Bouvet-Ladunay, Ackerman-Laurance, Gratien & Meyer. *Saumur* (red): Château de Villeneuve. *Saumur* (white): Domaine des Nerleux,

Château de St-Florent. *Bourgueil* (red): Clos du Vigneau. *Chinon* (red): Domaine Réné Couly, Clos de la Dioterie. *Touraine* (white): Domaine Joel Delaunay. *Vouvray*: Clos du Bourg, Le Haut-Lieu, Chevreau-Vigneau, Alain Ferraud, Sylvain Gaudron. *Sancerre*: Domaine de St-Pierre, Domaine des Villots, Domaine Paul Prieur. *Crémant de Loire* (sparkling white): Château de Midouin, Perry de Maleyrand.

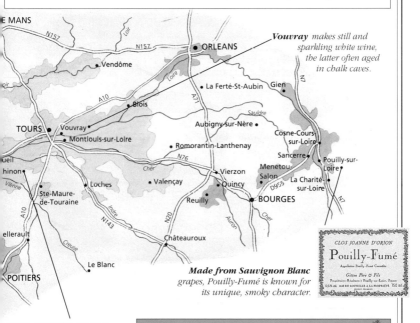

Vouvray makes still and sparkling white wine, the latter often aged in chalk caves.

Made from Sauvignon Blanc grapes, Pouilly-Fumé is known for its unique, smoky character.

Couly-Dutheil's Clos de l'Echo *is a beautiful, bright ruby wine made from Cabernet Franc grapes. The AOC wines of Chinon have an attractive, spicy aroma and age well.*

The Clos de l'Echo vineyard

A VIEW OF THE RIVER LOIRE

A NATURAL HIGHWAY to the centre of France, the Loire was travelled from the earliest days. The remains of prehistoric canoes have been found along the river; later evidence shows that Celtic tribes and the Romans used the river extensively as a major trade route. In fact, until the development of the railway network during the 19th century, the river was a key transportation route. The growth of the French canal network from the 17th to 19th centuries, connecting the port of Nantes with Paris and the north, enhanced the Loire's importance. **See pages 34–5**

See pages 36–7

The River Loire can be unpredictable and sometimes dangerous, and it was one of the first rivers that man tried to control. There is evidence that embankments were being built as early as the 12th century – and work continues – but the river remains essentially wild and is still subject to floods, freezes, shifting sands and dangerous currents. Today, the river is no longer used for commerce, except by tour boats giving visitors a unique view of the surrounding landscape. This makes an exploration of the River Loire all the more pleasant.

Sailing boats, with their typical square sails, often travelled in groups of three or more.

Steamers would use powerful winches to dip their smoke-stacks, enabling them to pass under low bridges.

Amboise's bridge traverses the river and the Ile St-Jean.

Château d'Amboise is set on a promontory above the river, safe from possible flooding.

VUE D'AMBOISE
This painting by Justin Ouvrié, which now hangs in the Musée de la Poste in Amboise (see p110), was painted in 1847. The bustling river scene, which includes several types of vessel, gives an indication of the importance of the Loire to life and trade in the region, before the railways came to dominate transportation later in the century.

Barges, known in French as *chalands*, did not always have sails – sometimes they were rowed.

Everyday objects were often decorated with river scenes, such as this 19th-century plate from the Musée de la Marine de Loire in Châteauneuf-sur-Loire.

◁ **Orléans, with the imposing Cathédrale Ste-Croix, seen from across the river**

River View: St-Nazaire to Montsoreau

A pleasure barge on the River Loire

AS THE RIVER LOIRE leaves Touraine and heads through Anjou and the Loire Atlantique, it widens and flows faster, as though rushing towards the Atlantic Ocean. Its waters are also swelled by many tributaries. Some flow alongside, creating a multitude of islands big and small; other tributaries flow north and south through the surrounding countryside. This land is rich in ancient monuments, including the Bagneux dolmen, the largest Neolithic construction of its kind, as well as fortresses built during the Middle Ages.

Champtoceaux
The village of Champtoceaux, on a cliff 80 m (260 ft) above the river, offers panoramic views. A private Renaissance château now occupies the lower part of the bluff, where a medieval citadel once stood.

St-Nazaire
At the mouth of the River Loire, where it flows into the Atlantic Ocean, St-Nazaire (see p190) is the site of a major French industrial zone. Its graceful bridge is the westernmost river crossing.

Nantes' Cathédrale
St-Pierre et St-Paul is built in the Flamboyant Gothic style.

Anc

Nantes
Nantes was a prosperous port during the 18th and 19th centuries (see pp190–193), the meeting point between the ocean and the inland river transportation channels.

0 kilometres   20
0 miles   20

Péage Fortifié du Cul-du-Moulin
This toll station was one of many constructed in the 13th century to collect revenue from passing vessels. This is one of the few remaining river toll stations in France.

THE BRIDGES OF THE LOIRE
There have long been bridges across the River Loire – there was one at Orléans as early as AD 52, which was later destroyed by Julius Caesar's army. Now, with so many options for places to cross the river, it is difficult to imagine what it was like during the Middle Ages, when there were only five, or during the 15th century, when there were just 13. The bridges crossing the river today tell the story not only of the development of bridge building, but also of the region itself, its history and relationships.

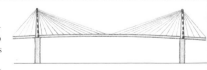

St-Nazaire
At 3,356 m (11,000 ft), St-Nazaire is the longest bridge in France. The central, suspended section is 404 m (1,300 ft) long. It opened for traffic in 1975. Before then, the estuary was crossed by ferry, and the nearest bridge was at Nantes.

St-Florent
Once the church of a Benedictine monastery, the abbey on the promontory was the site of dramatic events during the Vendée Uprising (see p68). More than 40,000 Royalist troops and their supporters crossed the river here.

Montsoreau
Montsoreau, at the confluence of the Loire and Vienne rivers, has a 15th-century turreted château (see p85)

The **Château d'Angers**, with its massive towers and curtain walls, is on the River Maine, north of the Loire.

Angers
The Apocalypse Tapestries (see pp76–7), masterpieces of the 14th century, are displayed in the Château d'Angers.

Cunault
The impressive Romanesque church in Cunault (see p79) is home to this painted 15th-century statue of St Catherine.

Les Rosiers

Saumur
Saumur is famous for its cavalry school, whose fallen cadets are honoured by this memorial.

The **Château de Saumur** (see p82) rises above the town like a fairytale castle.

Ile Béhuard
This island (see p69) was once a pilgrimage site for sailors, who prayed to a sea goddess to help them navigate the sometimes treacherous waters of the River Loire. The present church was built by Louis XI who had nearly drowned here.

Chinon
Above the River Vienne, Chinon (see pp98–100) was home to Henry Plantagenet in the 12th century.

Ancenis
The suspension bridge at Ancenis opened in 1953, replacing one destroyed in 1940. As the town is at the border of Brittany and Anjou, two coats of arms adorn either end of the bridge, one with the three lilies of Anjou and one with the ermine of Brittany.

Les Rosiers
The bridge at Les Rosiers is one of the two that cross the Loire at this point. The river is particularly wide here and has an island in the middle. The island is connected to the banks at the towns of Les Rosiers and Gennes by two bridges.

River View: Tours to Nevers

Stained glass in Gien

THIS IS TRULY the royal Loire Valley. As the river flows through the regions of Touraine, Blésois and Orléanais, it passes beside many Renaissance châteaux. Some, like Chaumont, Amboise and Gien, show their fortress-like exteriors to the river, often concealing courtyard gardens and highly decorated façades. Others, like Sully, glory in their luxury. Throughout Touraine, vineyards gently slope towards the river, while in the west, the lands bordering the river are taken up by the forests that were once the hunting grounds of kings and princes.

Beaugency's massive keep *(see p136)* dates from the 10th century.

Beaugency

Langeais
In the town of Langeais, (see p92) high above the river, there is a massive 15th-century château, still furnished in keeping with its period.

Château d'Amboise
(see p110) is a 15th-century château, built by Charles VIII.

Blois
On the north bank of the Loire, Blois (see pp124–7) was the seat of the counts of Blois, and then the residence of François I, whose salamander emblem decorates one fireplace.

Pagode de Chanteloup
All that remains of a once-lovely château, this strange pagoda (see p111) is 44 m (145 ft) tall.

Tours
In the heart of the Loire Valley region, Tours (see pp112–17) was always a significant crossing point on the river. The lively place Plumereau, lined with 15th-century buildings, is in the Old Town.

Château de Chaumont
The great fortress of Chaumont (see p128) is softened by Renaissance touches and offers impressive views from its terrace.

Tours
When Tours' original 18th-century bridge was built, the rue Nationale, which links it to the centre of the city, became the major thoroughfare, in place of the road between the cathedral and the Old Town.

Blois
The bridge at Blois was built between 1716 and 1724, replacing a medieval bridge destroyed when a ship crashed into it. It was built to a very high standard, enabling it to survive floods and freezes.

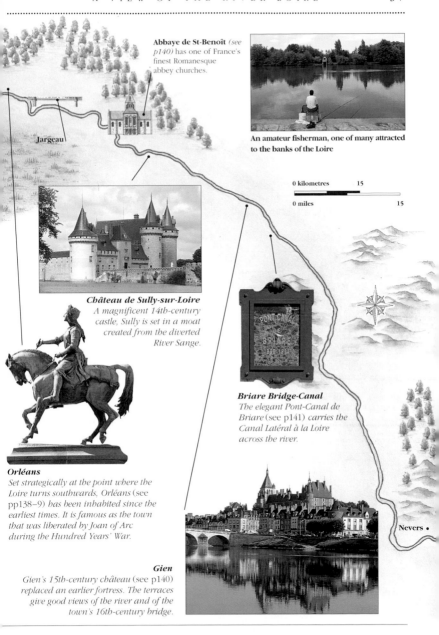

Abbaye de St-Benoît (*see p140*) has one of France's finest Romanesque abbey churches.

An amateur fisherman, one of many attracted to the banks of the Loire

Jargeau

| 0 kilometres | 15 |
| 0 miles | 15 |

Château de Sully-sur-Loire
A magnificent 14th-century castle, Sully is set in a moat created from the diverted River Sange.

Briare Bridge-Canal
The elegant Pont-Canal de Briare (see p141) carries the Canal Latéral à la Loire across the river.

Orléans
Set strategically at the point where the Loire turns southwards, Orléans (see pp138–9) has been inhabited since the earliest times. It is famous as the town that was liberated by Joan of Arc during the Hundred Years' War.

Nevers •

Gien
Gien's 15th-century château (see p140) replaced an earlier fortress. The terraces give good views of the river and of the town's 16th-century bridge.

Beaugency
Beaugency's bridge is built in several different styles, because sections of the original 12th-century wooden structure were gradually replaced with stone. The earliest date from the 14th century.

Jargeau
The original bridge was replaced by a wooden suspension bridge in the 19th century. A steel bridge, built in the 1920s, was hit in World War II. The current bridge dates from 1988.

THE LOIRE VALLEY
THROUGH THE YEAR

SPRING AND EARLY SUMMER are often particularly beautiful in the regions bordering the River Loire. But it should not be forgotten that this is the "Garden of France", and that successful gardens need plentiful watering in the main growing season, so be prepared for showery days. In the sultry, humid heat of July and early August, the Loire is usually reduced to a modest trickle between glistening sand banks. The châteaux can be very crowded in the high summer months. Perhaps the most pleasant season is the autumn,

Spring asparagus

when the forests gleam red and gold in the mild sunshine, the restaurants serve succulent local game and wild mushrooms, and the grape harvest is celebrated in towns and villages with many colourful festivals. Music festivals are also very popular in the region. Concerts are staged all year round at the Abbaye de Fontevraud *(see pp86–9)*, and Amboise *(see p110)* holds its Summer Organ Festival between June and August. For more information about any of these festivals, contact the local tourist office *(see p227)*.

SPRING

MARCH SEES the reopening of many châteaux after their winter closure, often on the Palm Sunday weekend that marks the beginning of the influx of visitors from the rest of France and abroad. The spring flowers in the meadows, the flowing waters of the Loire and other rivers, swollen by winter rains, and the spring migrations of birds are particularly appreciated by nature lovers.

MARCH

Foire à l'Andouillette *(Palm Sunday)*, Athée-sur-Cher (nr Chenonceau). This is one of many celebrations of local produce, in this case chitterling sausages.
Foire aux Vins *(first weekend)*, Bourgueil (nr Chinon).

Wine fairs bring together many local producers to display their latest vintages, but drinking as well as tasting is the order of the day.

APRIL

Concours Complet International *(last week)*, Saumur *(pp80–82)*. This international horse-riding competition also signals the beginning of the famous Cadre Noir tattoo and equestrian displays, which continue until September.
Foire à la Brocante *(second week)*, Saint-Cyr-sur-Loire (nr Tours). Popular in France, bric-à-brac fairs provide good opportunities to find bargains.
Le Printemps de Bourges *(third week)*, Bourges *(pp150–51)*. This contemporary music festival starts off the long concert season in this music-loving region.

Horse and rider from Saumur's Cadre Noir display team

MAY

Fête de Jeanne d'Arc *(week of 8 May)*, Orléans *(pp138–9)*. One of France's oldest fêtes, begun in 1435 to celebrate the routing of the English in 1429, this festival takes the form of a huge, colourful costume pageant.
Carnaval de Cholet *(first week)*, Cholet *(p69)*. Cholet's grand carnival culminates in a night-time parade of multi-coloured floats on the first Saturday of the month.
Le Printemps des Arts *(May and Jun)*, Nantes *(pp190–93)* and surrounding area. A Baroque dance and music festival, with concerts and shows held in churches and historic buildings in Nantes, Angers and other towns in the western Loire.

Farm workers in the fields around Bourgueil

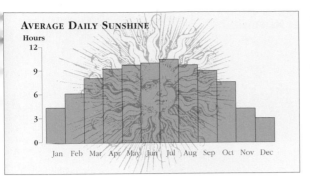

AVERAGE DAILY SUNSHINE

Hours

Sunshine Chart
*The summer months
are generally hot, with
the hottest period in
July. On the Atlantic
coast, cool sea
breezes often bring
welcome relief from
the heat but do not
mean that sun-
bathers are less likely
to burn. In the spring
and autumn, river
areas can be misty in
the mornings.*

SUMMER

FRANCE's traditional mid-
summer celebrations take
place on or around the Feast
of John the Baptist on 24
June, with fireworks, bonfires,
live music and dancing. Towards the end of the month,
most of the famous son et
lumière *(see pp42–3)* performances begin again, although
the long, light evenings of
June and July are the peak
time for these special events.
Many of the small towns and
villages hold local fêtes in July
and the first half of August,
the height of the French
tourist season.

JUNE

Les 24 Heures du Mans
(third weekend), Le Mans
(pp164–7). One of France's
major sporting events, this
world-famous, international
car race always attracts
enormous crowds.
Foire aux Escargots *(last
weekend)*, Loché-sur-Indrois
(nr Azay-le-Rideau). Snails, a
delicacy in the Loire Valley,
are served with local wines in
an open-air restaurant, with
live music and dance.
Les Dimanches Animés
(each Sun), Cunault *(p79)*.
Popular craft and local
produce markets are held all
summer long in the square
outside the abbey church.
Fêtes Musicales de Touraine
(two or three weekends), Tours
(pp112–17). Started by Svia-
toslav Richter in 1964, this
international festival of chamber music is held in a superb
medieval tithe barn, the
Grange de Meslay.

The beach at the popular Atlantic
resort, Les Sables d'Olonne

JULY

Bastille Day *(14 Jul)*.
The celebrations for the Fête
Nationale, commemorating
the Storming of the Bastille in
1789, are the high point of
the year in many small communities, when visitors can
join in the dancing, firework
displays and wine-quaffing.
Foire aux Champignons,
(first Sun), Ports-sur-Vienne
(nr Richelieu). This fair
celebrates mushrooms, a
local speciality that
contributes to the
region's economy.
**Foire au Vin, au
Fromage et au
Boudin** *(last Sun)*,
Richelieu
(pp102–3). The
fair associates local
cheeses and wine
with *boudin*, one
of the many
delicious pork
products of the
region.
Foire au Basilic et à l'Ail
(26 Jul), Tours. The basil and
garlic fair is held on the Feast
of St Anne *(p117)*.

Folk dancers at a festival

Festival d'Anjou *(all month)*,
Angers *(pp72–3)*. Plays are
staged within the walls of the
Château d'Angers.
**Festival International
d'Orgue** *(Sun in Jul and
Aug)*, Chartres Cathedral
(pp171–5). Famous organists
come from all over the world
to participate in this prestigious organ festival.

AUGUST

Marché Médiéval *(first
weekend)*, Chinon *(pp98–
100)*. A lively market takes
over the whole of the little
town, with stallholders
dressed in period costume
and medieval dishes served in
outside taverns.
Foire aux Vins *(on or
around 15 Aug)*, Montlouis-
sur-Cher, Vouvray and other
major wine-producing centres.
The Feast of the Assumption
is marked by numerous local
festivities, with wine events
predominating in the vine-
growing areas.
Foire aux Sorcières *(first
Sun)*, Bué (nr Sancerre). The
Berry is often said to
be a centre of witch-
craft and sorcery.
Children dressed as
witches or ghosts
parade through the
village to a nearby
field where crowds
play games and
watch folk groups
performing.
**Festival de
Musique Baroque**
(last weekend),
Sablé-sur-Sarthe
(p162). Over a period of four
days, musicians perform in
churches and manor houses
around Sablé.

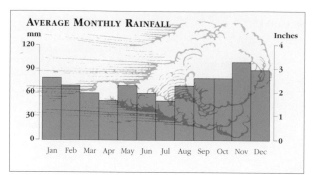

AVERAGE MONTHLY RAINFALL

Rainfall Chart
*Spring and autumn
are the wettest times,
with the amount of
rainfall occasionally
causing the River Loire
and its many tribu-
taries to break their
banks. As you head
inland from the coast,
precipitation tends to
increase. During the
summer, rains and
violent storms are
common at night.*

AUTUMN

THE GOLDEN DAYS of autumn
attract large numbers of
Parisians to the region for
shooting weekends, espe-
cially to the forested eastern
areas. This is also the season
for the *vendanges*, or grape
harvest, and the events and
festivities associated with it,
and for fairs celebrating the
new season's produce.

SEPTEMBER

Fête du Pain *(second Sat)*,
Montreuil-en-Touraine (nr
Amboise). The humble bread
loaf, often decorated with
nuts and leaves to celebrate
the arrival of autumn, becomes
a work of art in the skilful
hands of local bakers.
Foire aux Melons *(second
Sat)*, Bléré. The fields around
Bléré near Chenonceau are
bright with golden and orange
melons in autumn.
Foire aux Rillons *(29 Sep)*,
St-Michel-sur-Loire (nr

Langeais). The Feast of St
Michael is celebrated with a
festival devoted to a delicacy
of Touraine *(see p210)*.
Journées du Patrimoine
(second or third weekend).
For one weekend in the year,
châteaux and other historic
buildings that are not normally open to the public can be
visited, and concerts, exhibitions and other cultural events
are staged.
**Festival International de
Musique et Folklore** *(second
weekend)*, Angers *(pp72–3)*.
Folk-music groups from many
countries perform in the streets
and squares of Angers during
this four-day festival. The highlight is a concert held in the
modern Centre des Congrès.

OCTOBER

Foire aux Pommes *(second
Sat)*, Le Petit-Pressigny (nr Le
Grand-Pressigny). The Loire's
apple orchards yield their fruit
this month, filling the markets
with a wide variety of often
misshapen but delicious

**High-quality local produce on sale
at the Saturday market in Saumur**

apples. Azay-le-Rideau holds
its own Apple Fair during the
last weekend of October.
Foire à la Bernache *(last
Sun)*, Reugny (nr Tours).
Although it may be an
acquired taste, the *bernache*
(unfermented new wine) is
very popular with the locals.
**Festival International de
Cinéma Européan** *(early
Oct)*, La Baule *(p180)*. This
chic resort on the Atlantic
coast stages an annual
Festival of European Cinema
lasting for a week.
Foire aux Marrons *(last
Tue)*, Bourgueil (nr Chinon).
Chestnuts are the traditional
accompaniment to new wine,
and for this reason they
feature during this fair.
Concerts d'Automne *(each
Sun)*, Saint-Cyr-sur-Loire (nr
Tours). Autumn concerts are
held in the Salon Ronsard in
the Hôtel de Ville. Of the four
events, three are recitals of
chamber music, while the
fourth may feature a more
contemporary style of music,
such as jazz.

Wine-tasting at Kerhinet in La Grande Brière

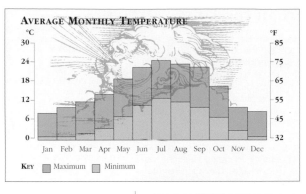

AVERAGE MONTHLY TEMPERATURE

KEY — ▉ Maximum   ▉ Minimum

Temperature Chart
It is rare for winter temperatures to fall below freezing in the Loire Valley. In the west, the sea moderates the climate, keeping it mild. Elsewhere, summer temperatures can reach over 30° C (86° F) in the middle of the day, but the evenings are usually cooler and perfect for eating outside on terraces by the river.

WINTER

WINTER IS THE QUIET season in the Loire Valley, when a damp chill rather than a frosty cold sets in, and many of the châteaux are closed. A few Christmas markets are held, but in general this is a time when local people prefer the pleasures of home.

DECEMBER

Foire de St-Nicolas *(Sat closest to 6 Dec)*, St-Nicolas-de-Bourgueil (nr Chinon). The Feast of St Nicolas marks the beginning of the Christmas season, celebrated with fairs and markets selling toys and festive decorations.
Foire de Noël *(third weekend)*, Richelieu *(p102–3)*. This Christmas market sells gifts, decorations and seasonal food. In the evening, there is a son et lumière performance.
Festival des Chants de Noël *(first weekend)*, Château de Brissac *(p78)*. The members of the audience process through the château while carols are sung.

An old windmill in the Anjou countryside

JANUARY

Foire des Rois *(second Mon)*, Richelieu *(pp102–3)*. Epiphany is celebrated with a large craft and food market. The arrival of the Three Kings is celebrated here and throughout France with the *galette des rois*, a flat, round, flaky pastry confection filled with almond paste and containing a *fève*, a tiny gilt or ceramic figure.

FEBRUARY

Foire aux Vins *(first weekend)*, Vouvray (nr Tours). Through the region, the winter period is enlivened by wine fairs. Another is held in Azay-le-Rideau on the last weekend of the month.

PUBLIC HOLIDAYS
New Year's Day (1 Jan)
Easter Sunday and Monday
Ascension (sixth Thursday after Easter)
Whit Monday (second Monday after Ascension)
Labour Day (1 May)
VE Day (8 May)
Bastille Day (14 Jul)
Feast of the Assumption (15 Aug)
All Saints' Day (1 Nov)
Remembrance Day (11 Nov)
Christmas Day (25 Dec)

A concert at the Abbaye de Fontevraud

Son et Lumière in the Loire

THE LOIRE VALLEY was the birthplace of son et lumière (literally "sound and light") shows, and some of the world's finest examples can be found here. The first performances, staged at Chambord in 1952, combined lighting effects and a soundtrack to emphasize the beauty of the building and to conjure up important historical figures. Today many of the shows use lasers and dramatic fireworks, as well as a cast of hundreds (often amateur actors drawn from the local community), to create a spectacular pageant. The following list includes the main regular shows, but it is worth keeping an eye open for posters advertising one-off events. Performance times may vary.

Actor at Amboise

Lighting effects bringing drama to the Château d'Azay-le-Rideau

TOURAINE

Amboise At the Court of King François (1½ hours). 🔲 47 57 14 47. 🕐 late Jun–Jul: 10:30pm Wed, Sat; Aug: 10pm Wed, Sat. 📖 book in advance. **Translations** Eng.

This is a celebration of the life of François I, held at his favourite royal château (see p110). The show is enacted by local residents and re-creates the court, with its sumptuous costumes, thrilling hunts, pleasure gardens and elaborate festivities.

Azay-le-Rideau The Fantasy of Azay-le-Rideau (1 hour). 🔲 47 45 42 04. 🕐 mid-May–Jul: 10:30pm nightly; Aug–mid-Sep: 10pm nightly. 📖 under 12s free.

During this fascinating promenade production, all the spectators walk around the grounds of this elegant château (see pp96–7), as they observe a succession of stage, sound and lighting effects.

Chenonceau In the Days of the Ladies of Yesteryear (45 minutes). 🔲 47 23 90 07. 🕐 late-Jun–early-Sep: 10:15pm nightly. 📖

The history of Chenonceau is the history of a series of remarkable women who in turn designed, improved and restored this beautiful royal residence (see pp106–9). In the château's son et lumière production, a light show takes place in the garden designed by Diane de Poitiers, while a commentary tells the story of her life and that of the wife she usurped, Catherine de Médicis.

Loches La Peau d'Ane (1½ hours). 🔲 47 59 07 98. 🕐 Jul: 10:30pm Fri, Sat; Aug: 10pm Fri, Sat. 📖 book in advance. **Translations** Eng, Ger, Ital.

In this musical dramatization of La Peau d'Ane (The Donkey Skin) by Charles Perrault, a small orchestra accompanies the cast of 170 actors dressed in stunning costumes. At the same time, images of fairy-tale landscapes are projected onto the imposing walls of the château (see p104).

BLÉSOIS AND ORLÉANAIS

Blois The Story of Blois (45 minutes). 🔲 54 78 72 76. 🕐 Jun–Jul: 10:30pm nightly; Aug: 10pm nightly; early Sep: 9:30pm nightly. 📖 under 7s free. **Translations** Eng, Ger, Ital, Span.

Key moments in the history of the château (see pp126–7) are related through images projected onto its façade. Included are the visit of Joan of Arc in 1429, the poetry contest between Charles of Orléans and François Villon, and the assassination of the Duc de Guise. Spectators watch the show while standing in the château's courtyard.

Cheverny The Course of Time (1½ hours). 🔲 54 42 69 03. 🕐 early Jul–mid-Jul: 10:30pm Sat; mid-Jul–Aug 10:30pm Fri, Sat. 📖 book in advance. **Translations** Eng.

This show tells the story of the River Loire, starting from the Vikings and moving to the present day. It is performed by 900 participants, clothed in more than 2,000 costumes. Staged in front of the château (see p130), lighting and water effects provide a stunning backdrop to the story.

Faces from the past projected onto the walls of Château de Blois

Fireworks reflected in the water during Le Lude's spectacular show

Meung-sur-Loire The Blue Bird (2 hours). 📞 38 44 32 28. 🕐 Jul: 10:30pm Fri, Sat. 📧 Advance booking requested.

A cast of all ages, numbering more than 100, enact a fantasy about the search for a magical blue bird, which possesses the secret of happiness, set against the backdrop of the château in Meung-sur-Loire (see p136). Local volunteers organize the special effects and costumes.

BERRY

Valençay Esclarmonde (1½ hours). 📞 54 00 04 42. 🕐 mid-Jul–Aug: 10pm Fri, Sat. 📧 book in advance. **Translations** Eng, Ger, Ital, Span.

More than 900 local actors in elaborate costumes gather at the château (see p146) to tell the tale of the beautiful princess, Esclarmonde, and her suitor, Roland. The show's highlights include a firework display and a medieval joust.

NORTH OF THE LOIRE

Le Lude The Enchanted History (1½ hours). 📞 43 94 62 20. 🕐 mid-Jun–Jul: 10:30pm Fri, Sat; Aug: 10pm Fri, Sat. 📧 book in advance. **Translations** Eng.

The history of the château (see p167) is re-created by over 350 actors. Water jets add to the impact of huge images projected onto a 200-m (650-ft) wall.

LOIRE ATLANTIQUE AND THE VENDÉE

Le Puy-du-Fou Jacques Maupillier: a Peasant from the Vendée (1 hour, 50 minutes). 📞 51 64 11 11. 🕐 Jun–Jul: 10:30pm Fri, Sat; Aug–early Sep: 10pm Fri, Sat. 📧 book in advance. **Translations** Eng.

The Château du Puy-du-Fou (see p188) hosts the Cinéscénie, which is the largest permanent water and light show in Europe. More than 700 professional actors, 2,000 volunteers from the region, 50 horsemen and various spectacular technical effects combine to trace the turbulent history of the Vendée from the Middle Ages to the present day. The music for the show was composed by Georges Delerue.

THE MAGICIAN OF THE NIGHT

The master of the modern son et lumière in France is Jean-Claude Baudoin, who is also known as "le magicien de la nuit". Since 1966 he has created the sets for more than 150 musical productions, held at the châteaux of Blois, Loches, Chambord and Valençay, as well as in St-Aignan-sur-Cher, Les Sables d'Olonnes and Chartres.

Producer Jean-Claude Baudoin

The history of the Vendée re-enacted in the Cinéscénie at Le Puy-du-Fou

THE HISTORY OF THE LOIRE VALLEY

THE LOIRE'S central role in French history is splendidly displayed in the breadth of its architectural styles, ranging from megalithic structures to royal and ducal châteaux.

Imposing prehistoric monuments testify to the existence of thriving Neolithic cultures as early as the third millennium BC. By the 1st century BC, the conquering Romans found sophisticated Celtic communities already established. Later, as Christianity spread, the ancient Celtic towns at Angers, Bourges, Chartres, Orléans and Tours became well known as centres of learning, and they remain vibrant cultural centres today.

Fleur-de-lys, the royal emblem

A long period of territorial conflict began in the 9th century, first among local warlords and later between France and England, when Henry Plantagenet, count of Anjou and duke of Normandy and Aquitaine, inherited the English crown in 1154. Major battles between the two countries were fought in the region during the Hundred Years' War. The Loire also saw bloodshed during the fierce 16th-century Wars of Religion, which took place between the Catholics and the Protestant Huguenots. Later, the Vendée Uprising of 1793 was the most serious civil threat to the French republic after the 1789 Revolution.

Yet the Loire was also the scene of outstanding cultural achievements and the preferred home of many French kings. By the 17th century, France's political focus had shifted to Paris, although the River Loire remained a key transportation route until the advent of the railway in the late 19th century.

In the 20th century, the impressive architectural evidence of this rich history has led to the growth of the Loire's tourist industry. This balances with a diverse, well-established industrial base and thriving agriculture to make the valley one of the most economically stable regions of France.

16th-century views of Tours, with its cathedral, and Angers, with quarries of *ardoise* slate

◁ A portrait of François I, the Renaissance king (reigned 1515–47), attributed to Jean Clouet

Rulers of the Loire

IN THE COURSE of the Loire's history, the power of the local nobility often rivalled that of the French throne. The dukedoms of Anjou and Blois were established when Charlemagne's territory was divided among his sons upon his death in 814. Henry Plantagenet, count of Anjou, duke of Normandy and king of England, could trace his lineage to Charlemagne. The French monarchy did not consolidate its authority until Charles VII moved from the Loire back to Paris in 1437. Another local family, the royal house of Orléans, saw two of its sons become kings.

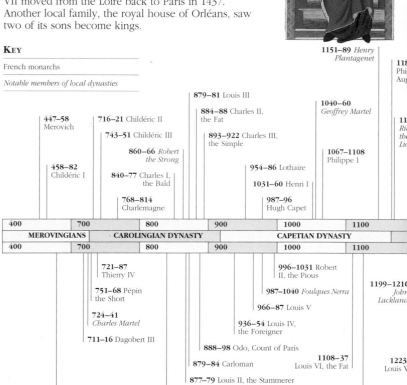

1151–89 *Henry Plantagenet*

KEY

French monarchs

Notable members of local dynasties

879–81 Louis III

884–88 Charles II, the Fat

893–922 Charles III, the Simple

1040–60 *Geoffrey Martel*

447–58 Merovich

716–21 Childéric II

743–51 Childéric III

860–66 *Robert the Strong*

954–86 Lothaire

1067–1108 Philippe I

458–82 Childéric I

840–77 Charles I, the Bald

1031–60 Henri I

768–814 Charlemagne

987–96 Hugh Capet

400	700	800	900	1000	1100	
MEROVINGIANS	CAROLINGIAN DYNASTY			CAPETIAN DYNASTY		
400	700	800	900	1000	1100	

721–87 Thierry IV

751–68 Pépin the Short

996–1031 Robert II, the Pious

987–1040 *Foulques Nerra*

966–87 Louis V

724–41 *Charles Martel*

936–54 Louis IV, the Foreigner

711–16 Dagobert III

888–98 Odo, Count of Paris

879–84 Carloman

1108–37 Louis VI, the Fat

877–79 Louis II, the Stammerer

814–40 Louis I, the Pious

1199–1216 *John Lackland*

1223 Louis V...

482–511 Clovis I

1137–80 Louis VII

1422–61
Charles VII,
the Victorious

1270–85 Philippe III

1285–1314 Philippe
IV, the Fair

1314–16 Louis X

1316–22
Philippe V,
the Tall

1322–28
Charles IV,
the Fair

1328–50
Philippe VI

1483–98
Charles VIII,
the Affable

1498–1515 Louis XII,
Father of the People

1515–47 François I

1547–59 Henri II

1559–60
François II

1643–1715 Louis
XIV, the Sun King

1774–92 Louis XVI

1804–14
Napoléon I

1300	1400	1500	1600	1700	1800

VALOIS DYNASTY   **BOURBON DYNASTY**

1300	1400	1500	1600	1700	1800

1350–64
Jean II,
the Good

1430–80
*René I of
Anjou*

1461–83
Louis XI, the
Spider

1560–74
Charles IX

1575–89 Henri III

1814–24
Louis XVIII

1824–30
Charles X

1830–48
*Louis-Philippe I,
Duc d'Orléans,
King of the French*

1715–74
Louis XV

1852–70
Napoléon III

1226–70
Louis IX
(St Louis)

1364–80
Charles V,
the Wise

1380–1422
Charles VI,
the Fool

1589–1610 Henri IV

1610–43 Louis XIII

Neolithic and Roman Loire

NEOLITHIC CULTURE produced some of France's largest prehistoric tombs and sacred sites. Their builders had Central European roots, as did the Celts who established cities along the Loire in the Bronze and Iron Ages. Julius Caesar's conquest of the valley in 51 BC left the Celtic tribes under a light Roman rule, the basis of peace and prosperity for the next 300 years. The spread of Christianity coincided with Rome's military decline and the rise of kingdoms ruled by Visigoths to the south and Germanic Franks to the north. The Frankish king Clovis I converted to Christianity and took power in 507 by routing the Visigoths.

Baptism of Clovis
Frankish chieftain Clovis converted to Christianity at the start of the 6th century to legitimize his rule.

The entrance porch is a distinctive feature of Angevin dolmens.

Palaeolithic Remains
Flint tools made in the Loire basin were traded by Palaeolithic tribes at least 50,000 years ago.

Celtic Art
Celtic art was not dominated by the naturalistic ideals of the occupying Romans. This bronze statuette of a young woman dates from the 1st–2nd century AD.

BAGNEUX DOLMEN
This 5,000-year-old chamber tomb in Saumur is 21 by 7 m (69 by 23 ft). The nine massive uprights were levered onto loose stones, dragged to the site, tilted and sunk into ditches 3 m (10 ft) deep.

TIMELINE

c.2500 Loire dolmens with porches set new style of Neolithic burial chamber

c.800 Celtic Carnutes found settlements at Blois, Chartres and Orléans

57–6 Romans conquer western Loire tribes

51 Julius Caesar ends Gaulish uprising that began in Orléans

Julius Caesar, first to unite Gaul

2500 BC		100 BC	AD 1	AD 100

c.1200 Loire region exports bronze weapons made using local tin resources

Celtic helmet

31 Roman emperor Augustus sets framework for 300 years of Pax Romana (peace and prosperity) in the Loire

50 Loire Valley flourishes as border link between two Gallo-Roman provinces, Lugdenunsis and Aquitania

Celtic Armour
The warlike Celts were skilled armourers, as this bronze breastplate of 750–475 BC shows. The Romans found them formidable opponents.

WHERE TO SEE NEOLITHIC AND ROMAN LOIRE

Anjou is rich in Neolithic sights, mostly on the south bank of the Loire. The largest are at Saumur *(see pp82–3)* and Gennes *(p78)*. Gennes' amphitheatre and the walls at Thésée *(p129)* are two of the few surviving Gallo-Roman monuments. Museums at Orléans *(pp138–9)* and Tours *(pp114–15)* have major Gallo-Roman collections.

Gennes Amphitheatre
Roman gladiatorial combats were held in the amphitheatre at Gennes.

An inner pillar, perhaps part of a wall, helps support a 40-tonne capstone.

Gallo-Roman Art
This beaten bronze stallion, displayed in the archeology museum in Orléans, was dedicated to Mars, bringer of war and god of agriculture.

Orthostats (walls) were sunk in holes 3 m (10 ft) deep and filled with sand, which was then dug out.

Fresh Water by Aqueduct
Roman pillars near Luynes supported a 2nd-century aqueduct which carried spring water to baths in Caesarodunum (Tours).

Gatien, Bishop of ...rs, among the first ...ristian evangelists in the Loire | **313** Emperor Constantine makes Christianity official Roman religion | **372** Martin, Bishop of Tours, leads monastic growth | **507** After converting to Christianity, Clovis defeats Visigoths near Poitiers | **498** Clovis I takes Orléans | **511** Clovis I dies; his sons divide his lands

200 ... Romans build ...heatre at Gennes | **300** *St Martin, Bishop of Tours* | **400** **451** Visigoth kingdom of Toulouse helps repel Attila the Hun at Orléans | **500**

275 Emperor Aurelian gives Orléans independent status | *Wine: an early Loire export* **473** Visigoths capture Tours | **c.550** First record of wine production in the Loire region

The Early Middle Ages

Royal seal of Henry II

IN RAISING the massive keep at Loches, Foulques Nerra of Anjou was typical of the warlords who took power in the Loire after the 9th century. The chains of citadels they built laid the foundations for the later châteaux. The Plantagenets, who followed Nerra as rulers of Anjou, also claimed territory from Normandy to Aquitaine and then inherited the English throne. It was not until the 13th century that the French King Louis IX brought Anjou back under direct control of the crown. Throughout this period the Church was a more cohesive power than the French crown. Its cathedrals and monastic orders established schools and *scriptoria* (where manuscripts were copied and illuminated), and it was to the Church rather than the throne that feudal warlords turned to mediate their brutal disputes.

THE LOIRE AROUND 1180

| | French royal domain |
| | Other fiefs |

Gregory I codified the liturgical music sung during his reign as pope (590–604).

St Louis
Popularly called St Louis for his piety, Louis IX (1214–70) was the first Capetian monarch to inherit a relatively stable kingdom. A brave crusading knight and just ruler, he forced England to abandon claims to the Loire.

us inte confi do non cru be
irrideant me inimici m
uniuersi qui te expe dant

TIMELINE

687 Pépin II establishes the power of the "mayors" of the Carolingian dynasty, ancestors of Charlemagne, over Merovingian kings	**732** Charles Martel drives Moors back from the Loire in decisive battle south of Tours	**850** Normans lay waste to Loire Valley	**866** Robert the Stron ancestor of Capetiar killed by Normans i
			911 Chartres re Norm
600	**700**	**800**	
Charlemagne, the Frankish king	**768–84** Charlemagne conquers Brittany and all Loire		
	796 Charlemagne's mentor, Alcuin, makes Tours a centre of Carolingian art	*Coinage of Charles the Bold*	

Carolingian Ivory

Ivory plaques, reliquaries and book covers are among the most beautiful Frankish decorative objects to survive Norman destructions of the 10th century. Carolingian art usually served a religious or utilitarian purpose.

Medieval musical notation showed variations in pitch (high and low notes). The length of each note depended on the natural rhythm of the text.

Monastic Arts

The development of the Caroline Miniscule style of calligraphy was led by the monks of Tours' Basilique St-Martin in the 9th century.

Fine Craftsmanship

Many of the finest surviving pieces of medieval craftsmanship are worked in metal. This 13th-century funerary mask was cast in copper from the effigy of a woman and then gilded.

ILLUMINATED MANUSCRIPT

This manuscript is the first page of a 13th-century gradual, a book of plainsong sung during mass. It is typical of the style of illuminated manuscripts that were produced by the abbeys of the Loire Valley. This collection of Gregorian chant was compiled by monks of the strict Cistercian Order *(see p149).*

WHERE TO SEE EARLY MEDIEVAL LOIRE

Early churches such as the one at Cunault *(see p79)* are charged with medieval atmosphere, as are abbeys such as Noirlac *(p149)* or at Solesmes *(p162)* and Fontgombault *(p146)*, where you can hear Gregorian chant. Fortress châteaux such as the one at Loches *(p104)* and ruined towers at Lavardin *(p122)* or Montrichard *(p128)* tell grimmer feudal stories.

Romanesque Capitals
This Romanesque sculpture is on a capital in Cunault church.

Hugh Capet of Orléans

Hugh, depicted here being handed the keys to Laon, was elected king in 987, ending the Carolingian dynasty. He set a precedent for kings to seek refuge in the Loire in troubled times.

1101 Founding of Abbaye de Fontevraud

1096 First Crusade launched

gh Capet of
ns becomes
rst Capetian
g of France

1128 Marriage in Le Mans of Geoffrey Plantagenet and Matilda, daughter of Henry I of England

1189 Henry II's death leaves his son, Richard the Lionheart, as the Angevin rival to the French king

1000	1100	1200

Foulques Nerra

992 Bretons driven out of Anjou by Foulques Nerra

1154 Henry Plantagenet accedes to the English throne as Henry II

1125 Thibaut IV of Blois and Champagne rivals Capetian power

1214 Angevin empire ends with defeat of King John at Angers

The Hundred Years' War

T HE DESTRUCTIVE CLIMAX of the Middle Ages was war between the French and English crowns, flaring intermittently from 1337 to 1453. When the English besieged Orléans in 1428, the Loire region became the focus for a struggle that seemed likely to leave France partitioned between England and its powerful ally, Burgundy. Instead, the teenage heroine, Joan of Arc, inspired Orléans to fight off the English and brought the dauphin Charles VII out of hiding in Chinon. Her martyrdom in 1431 helped to inspire a French recovery. In spite of marauding soldiery and the more widespread disaster of the plague known as the Black Death, the Loire knew periods of peace and prosperity, during which medieval court life flourished.

14th-century knight

THE LOIRE VALLEY IN 1429

☐ *French territory in the Loire*

▨ *English possessions*

The English longbow was a powerful weapon, requiring strong, skilled archers.

Charles VII
Joan of Arc's dauphin, often portrayed as a weakling, was in fact a crafty man in a difficult situation. Disinherited by the French royal family in 1420, he used Joan's charisma to rally support. However, he distrusted her political judgment.

Cannons could fire stone balls that weighed as much as 200 kg (440 lb).

Jousting Tournament
The sumptuous trappings of their warlike recreations display the wealth of the ruling class in the early 15th century. Jousting was dangerous – Henri II died from a lance blow.

TIMELINE

1341 English support John of Montfort against Charles of Blois in War of Brittany Succession

1346 English longbows defeat French knights at Crécy

1352 Loire begins recovery from four years of plague

Black Death depicted in a 15th-century illuminated manuscript

1325	1350	1375

1337 Philippe VI, first Valois king, confiscates English lands in Guyenne, starting Hundred Years' War

Portrait of Philippe VI

1360 Anjou becomes a duchy

Apocalypse
War and the plague made the end of the world a preoccupation of 15th-century art. In this tapestry from Angers (see pp76–7), St John hears the clap of doom.

WHERE TO SEE THE LOIRE OF THE 14TH AND 15TH CENTURIES

Guérande (p180) is a well-preserved, 15th-century walled town. Many others, such as Chinon (pp98–100), have half-timbered houses. Orléans (pp138–9) has a replica of the house in which Joan of Arc lodged. Le Plessis-Bourré (p70) exemplifies the shift towards more graceful lifestyles after the end of the Hundred Years' War.

The halberd was a typical infantryman's weapon.

Siege tower

Château de Chinon
This château is strategically positioned on a cliff above the River Vienne.

Joan of Arc
Although shown here in feminine attire, the real Joan (see p137) wore men's dress into battle.

René, Duke of Anjou
René I (1409–80) loved tournaments but was also a painter, scholar and poet. To his people he represented the ideal 15th-century ruler.

THE SIEGE OF ORLÉANS

The English first besieged Orléans in November 1428, and they quickly established their position and built major siegeworks. In February 1429, a French attempt to cut English supply lines was defeated, and it was not until 30 April that Joan of Arc's troops were able to enter the city. Within a week the English were forced to abandon the siege.

1409 Birth of René I, Duke of Anjou

1417–32 English occupy Chartres

1418 Charles VI burns Azay-le-Rideau

1429 Joan of Arc visits the dauphin Charles at Chinon, ends English siege of Orléans and crowns him King Charles VII at Reims

1453 War ends without a treaty, with English retaining only Calais

1461 Louis XI begins his reign

400   1425   1450

2 Louis, Duke [Or]léans, [acqu]ires Blois

1415 Crushing English victory at Agincourt leads to alliance between England and Burgundy

1428 English besiege Orléans

1435 Charles VII makes peace with Burgundy. Army reforms lead to French victories

1438 Jacques Cœur of Bourges becomes court banker and reorganizes France's tax system

15th-century sporting crossbow

1470 Silk weaving in Tours begins

Renaissance Loire

Catherine de Médicis (1519–89)

THE ITALIAN WARS of Charles VIII, Louis XII and François I between 1494 and 1525 gave all three kings a taste for Italian art and architecture. At Amboise, Blois and Chambord they made the Loire a centre of court life, establishing the culture of the French Renaissance. François I patronized countless artists and craftsmen who worked in the Italian style, setting an example imitated by the aristocracy throughout France. The Loire suffered nearly 40 years of warfare when his son's widow, Catherine de Médicis, could not persuade Catholics, led by the Guise family, to live in peace with Protestants during the reigns of her sons, Charles IX and Henri III.

Fortress of Faith
The pope is besieged by Protestants in this portrayal of the Wars of Religion.

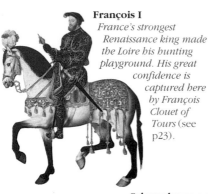

François I
France's strongest Renaissance king made the Loire his hunting playground. His great confidence is captured here by François Clouet of Tours (see p23).

Colonnades were a feature of the Classical Renaissance style.

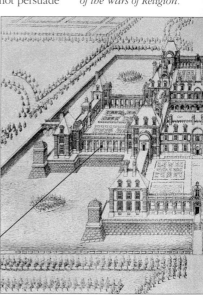

The First Tank Design
Leonardo spent his last years fêted at Le Clos-Lucé (see p111). This tank is a model of one of the inventions he worked on there.

THE IDEAL CHÂTEAU

From Charles VIII (1483–98) onwards, French Renaissance kings dreamt of creating the ideal château. The symmetrical vistas of this plan by Androuet du Cerceau display a late-Renaissance stylistic move towards Classical grandeur.

TIMELINE

Charles VIII, France's first Renaissance king

Cellini's salt cellar for François I (1515–47)

1484 Etats Généraux, a national assembly, meets at Tours	**1493** Charles VIII redesigns his birthplace, the Château d'Amboise, in Italian style	**1498** Duke of Orléans is crowned Louis XII and marries Anne of Brittany		**1515** François I conquers Milan and invites Italian artists to the Loire
				1532 Treaty binds Britt and Nantes to Fra
1475		**1500**		**1525**
		1508 Louis XII remodels Blois as Renaissance royal capital		**1519** François I begins building Chambord. Leonardo da Vinci dies at Le Clos-Lucé *(see p111)*
	1491 Marriage of Charles VIII to Anne of Brittany links autonomous Brittany to French crown			

Henri IV
Brave, astute and likeable, Henri IV of Vendôme and Navarre skilfully reasserted the authority of the crown over a disintegrating kingdom within 10 years of his accession in 1589. Rubens (1577–1640) shows him receiving a betrothal portrait of Marie de Médicis.

WHERE TO SEE RENAISSANCE LOIRE

Fine Renaissance buildings can be seen throughout the region. Older châteaux that reflect the Italian influence include Amboise *(p110)* and Blois *(pp126–7)*. The most delightful achievements of the French Renaissance are Chenonceau *(pp106–9)* and Azay-le-Rideau *(pp96–7)*. Smaller examples, such as Beauregard *(pp130–1)*, are widespread. Undoubtedly the most spectacular is Chambord *(pp132–5)*.

Château de Chambord
This impressive château sits on the banks of the River Cosson.

High roofs and dormers show the persisting French influence.

Anne of Brittany's Reliquary
By marrying successively Charles VIII and Louis XII, Anne of Brittany, whose reliquary is in Nantes (see p191), welded her fiercely independent duchy to France.

An arcaded central courtyard formed the basis of 15th-century palaces in the Italian style.

Diane de Poitiers
The mistress of Henri II was flatteringly portrayed as Diana, the Roman goddess of the hunt.

1559 Death of Henri II begins power struggle between his widow, Catherine de Médicis, and Protestant followers of the Duc de Guise

1572 Court moves to Fontainebleau after St Bartholomew's Day massacre of Protestants

1576 Henri, Duc de Guise, founds pro-Catholic Holy League. Meeting of Etats Généraux at Blois fails to find a peace formula

1598 Edict of Nantes establishes Protestant rights of worship

1550

1575

1547 Henri II begins reign and gives Chenonceau to his mistress, Diane de Poitiers

1562 Wars of Religion start with major battles and massacres along the Loire

1588 Holy League virtually takes over government. Henri III has Duc de Guise and his brother murdered at Blois

Coin of Henri IV "the Great"

1594 Henri IV crowned at Chartres after becoming a Catholic to end the Wars of Religion

Growth and Prosperity

THE LOIRE LOST ITS CENTRAL ROLE in French politics when the focus of court life moved to the Paris region at the end of the 16th century. The Vendée, however, was the centre during the French Revolution of a violent popular uprising against Republican excesses, including rising taxes, the persecution of priests and conscription. River trade remained important, especially for the increasingly wealthy port of Nantes. In the 17th century, work had begun on canals to connect Nantes and the Loire directly with Paris, of which Eiffel's bridge-canal at Briare was the aesthetic high point. Although industry grew slowly, the region remained predominantly agricultural.

19TH-CENTURY WATERWAYS

— *Rivers*

— *Canals built before 1900*

Cardinal Richelieu
As Louis XIII's chief minister between 1624 and 1642, Cardinal Richelieu helped to establish orderly government in France.

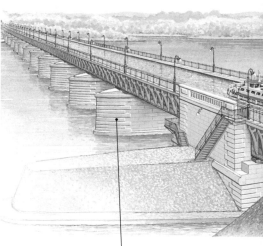

The 15 granite piers supporting the structure were bedded using early compressed-air techniques.

Winemaking in the Loire
Winemaking in the 18th century remained a pastime for the idle rich, who used badly paid peasants to harvest and press the grapes.

TIMELINE

1610–16 Regency of Henri IV's widow, Marie de Médicis, over Louis XIII

1617 Louis XIII banishes his mother to Blois. They are reconciled by Richelieu in 1620

1631 Richelieu starts building planned village and château in Touraine

1720s Loire again becomes a centre of country life for the nobility

1600

1650

1700

Louis XIII

1648–53 La Fronde: a series of French civil wars

17th-century watch made in Blois

1685 Saumur and other cities lose Huguenot population as these terrorized Protestants flee after the revocation of the Edict of Nantes

Vendée Hero
Bonchamps' plea to spare Republican prisoners (see p187) was depicted in stone by David d'Angers.

Loire "Inexplosibles"
Faced by competition from the railways, 19th-century steamboats were a last attempt to maintain the Loire's role as France's greatest trade route.

Graceful lamps above the wide pavements provide a Parisian boulevard touch.

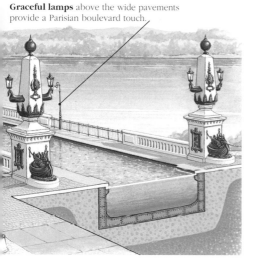

Passage Pommeraye
The elegance of this 19th-century shopping arcade reflected the wealth of Nantes.

Briare Bridge-Canal

Gustave Eiffel designed this 662-m (725-yd) bridge to carry canal traffic safely across the Loire. Opened in 1896, it completed a grand waterway system begun in the 17th century linking the Seine and Rhône rivers. The metal structure used new steel technology.

Steam Omnibus
In 1873, Amédée Bollée's l'Obéissante was the first car to be built in Le Mans.

The Modern Era

Aᴸᴛʜᴏᴜɢʜ ꜱʜɪᴘ-ʙᴜɪʟᴅɪɴɢ reached a peak at Nantes and St-Nazaire in the 1920s, and light industry expanded steadily around Orléans, Le Mans and Angers, the region did not become prosperous until after World War II. Its larger cities were occupied by the Germans in 1940 and many were bombed in 1944. Since the 1960s, when the recovery gathered momentum, booming tourism has supplemented the Loire's traditional strength as the "Garden of France". Private châteaux have been opened to the public, and the state has funded several major restoration schemes, as at the Abbaye de Fontevraud.

Fruits of the Loire Valley

Wilbur Wright
The pioneer US flying ace galvanized European aviation when he demonstrated this commercial prototype near Le Mans in 1908.

Dramatic fireworks light up the night sky.

TGV Links
With stops at Vendôme, Tours, Angers and Nantes, the Loire is well served by France's TGV (Train à Grande Vitesse) network.

Orléans, 1944
Bridges across the River Loire were prime bombing targets at both the beginning and the end of World War II.

Sᴏɴ ᴇᴛ Lᴜᴍɪèʀᴇ
Puy-du-Fou's Cinéscénie laser spectacle updates a tradition begun at Chambord in 1952 by Robert Houdin, son of a famous Blois magician. Evening performances draw thousands to Blois, Chenonceau, Cheverny and other great châteaux (see pp42–3).

TIMELINE

1905 Loire farming in decline as falling wheat prices follow damage to vines from phylloxera

1908 Wilbur Wright stages test flights at Auvours near Le Mans

1920 Cheverny opens to the public

Cheverny (see p130), a privately-owned château

1900	1910	1920	1930	194

Alain-Fournier (1886–1914)

1914 World War I begins. Among the first dead is the writer Alain-Fournier (see p23)

1923 First 24-hour race at Le Mans

1929 Town of La Baule builds promenade and becomes one of France's top beach resorts

1936 Renault opens Le Mans factory

1940 German advance forces temporary government to move from Paris to Tours

Earth Day Ecology Protests on the Loire
Environmentally-aware locals are committed to preserving the rich natural resources of the great river.

Nuclear Power
The Loire was an early resource for cooling nuclear reactors. Avoine, near Chinon, opened in 1963.

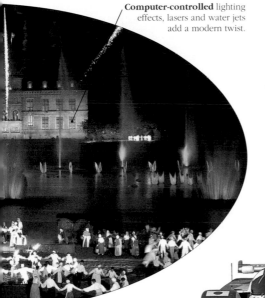

Computer-controlled lighting effects, lasers and water jets add a modern twist.

More than 2,000 local residents volunteer as performers, security patrols and guides at each Cinéscénie evening.

Le Vinci
The sensitive modernization of Tours city centre shows how old and new architectural styles can be combined.

Le Mans
The renowned 24-hour race at Le Mans attracts motor enthusiasts from around the world.

1950	1960	1970		1980	1990

...iberation ...e cities ...our-year ...n ...ation

1963 First French nuclear power station at Avoine near Chinon

1970s Loire wine exports, especially of Muscadet, soar

1994 Government dismantles dam at Maisons Rouges on the River Vienne to allow salmon to reach spawning grounds

1952 First son et lumière performance at Chambord

1959 André Malraux made Minister of Cultural Affairs. He speeds up restoration work on Loire monuments

Muscadet, produced east of Nantes

1989–90 Inauguration of TGV Atlantique high-speed services brings Angers within 90 minutes of Paris

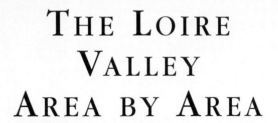

THE LOIRE VALLEY AREA BY AREA

The Loire Valley at a Glance

RICH IN HISTORY AND ARCHITECTURE, the Loire Valley is best known for its sumptuous Renaissance châteaux, such as Chambord and Chenonceau. But the region has also retained the wealth of earlier ages, from Bronze Age dolmens to medieval keeps, such as the Château d'Angers, and an impressive heritage of religious architecture, including the Gothic marvels of Chartres and Bourges cathedrals. Visitors who desire a break from the past can revel in the beauty of the landscape, which contains natural surprises such as the lush Marais Poitevin. In a region packed with delights, those shown here are among the very best.

The Gothic spires of Chartres Cathedral, which tower over an attractive town *(see pp172–5)*

NORTH OF
THE LOIRE

The Château d'Angers, protected by its formidable curtain walls *(see pp74–7)*

Angers •

ANJOU

• Nantes

• Cholet

LOIRE-ATLANTIQUE
AND THE VENDÉE

La Roche-
sur-Yon •

Abbaye de Fontevraud, the largest medieval abbey complex in France *(see pp86–7)*

0 kilometres   50

0 miles   50

The Marais Poitevin, a labyrinth of shady canals contrasting with rich fields of painstakingly reclaimed land *(see pp182–5)*

The memorable François I Renaissance staircase of the Château de Blois *(see pp126–7)*

Chambord, the largest royal residence in the Loire *(see pp132–5)*

Bourges Cathedral, a Gothic masterpiece *(see pp152–3)*

Chartres

Orléans

BLESOIS AND ORLEANAIS

Blois

rs

RAINE

BERRY

Bourges

Châteauroux

Chenonceau, stretching languidly across the River Cher *(see pp106–9)*

The graceful symmetry of Azay-le-Rideau *(see pp96–7)*

Villandry's spectacular reconstructed Renaissance gardens *(see pp94–5)*

ANJOU

THE LANDSCAPE OF ANJOU *is as gentle and pleasant as its climate and its people. The region's rolling plains are intersected by a network of rivers, which help to irrigate the already fertile land. North of the city of Angers, the confluence of the Sarthe, Mayenne and Loir rivers forms a great flood-plain in the winter months and is a regular port of call for thousands of migrating birds.*

The creamy limestone, or tufa, used to build the great châteaux of Anjou, combines with grey roof slates to give Angevin architecture its distinctive look. Tufa quarrying has created hundreds of caves. Many are now used for growing mushrooms, and others have been transformed into troglodyte dwellings, some of which are open to visitors.

Some of the Loire Valley's finest fruits and vegetables are grown here. Trees and flowers also flourish: white magnolias, mimosas and palms decorate the region's parks, and the rose gardens of Doué are legendary. The region's vines produce the sparkling wines of Saumur and St-Cyr-en-Bourg. Visitors can see the complicated process of the *méthode champenoise* firsthand by visiting the major wine houses around Saumur.

Anjou is steeped in the history of the powerful rival dynasties of medieval France. Then, as now, Angers, dominated by its barrel-chested fortress, was the centre of the region. The city was the feudal capital of the Plantagenets, among them Henry of Anjou, who became Henry II of England. Fifteen of the family, including Henry II, his wife, Eleanor of Aquitaine, and their sons, Richard the Lionheart and John Lackland, are buried at Fontevraud Abbey. Nearby, Saumur's château formed the fairy-tale backdrop to the "September" miniature in the 15th-century masterpiece, *Les Très Riches Heures du Duc de Berry*. Other impressive châteaux in this region include Brissac, the tallest château in the Loire, and Le Plessis Bourré, a charming pre-Renaissance château.

Château de Saumur, towering above the town and the River Loire

◁ **Cattle resting in an Anjou meadow**

Exploring Anjou

NORTHERN ANJOU IS CROSSED by the Mayenne, Sarthe and Loir rivers, flowing southwards to their convergence in the River Maine. Angers, the geographical and administrative centre of the region, straddles the Maine 8 km (5 miles) before it flows into the Loire. Anjou's most famous châteaux, antiquities and troglodyte sites are located around Angers and Saumur, 50 km (30 miles) up the Loire. But there are also dozens of lesser-known châteaux, clustered around Segré in the northwest and Baugé in the northeast.

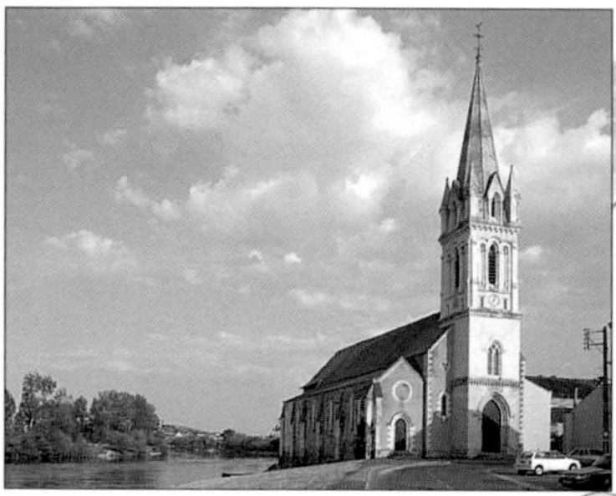

**Eglise St-Maurille,
Chalonnes-sur-Loire**

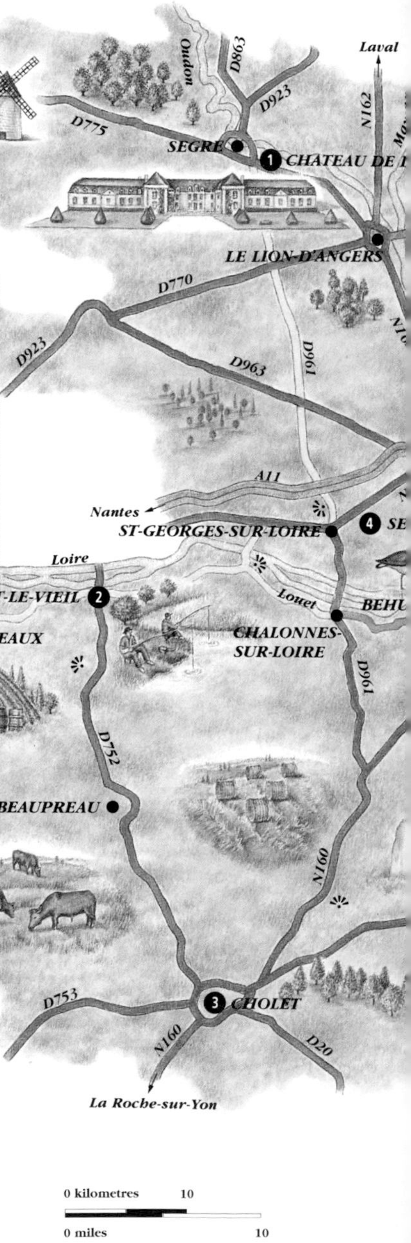

SIGHTS AT A GLANCE

0 kilometres   10

0 miles   10

The Loire in full flood in Anjou

GETTING AROUND

Angers is 90 minutes from Paris by TGV. *L'Océane* autoroute (A11) via Le Mans is the fastest road access from Paris. Between Tours and Angers, the D766 via Baugé is reasonably quick. The D751 from Saumur follows the south bank of the Loire and is the most pleasant drive towards Angers. It continues as the Corniche Angevine, providing splendid views of the Loire on the road to Champtoceaux. Leisurely boat cruises are available on the Oudon and Mayenne tributaries.

KEY

▬	Motorway
▬	Major road
▬	Minor road
▬	Scenic route
≈	River
☆	Viewpoint

One of Angers' lively pavement cafés

St-Florent-le-Vieil's 18th-century church, on a hill above the old town

Château de la Lorie ❶

Road map B3. 🚌 *Segré, then taxi.*
📞 *41 92 10 04.* 🕐 *Jul–mid-Sep:*
Wed–Mon; Easter–Oct: groups by
appt. 🏛

ELEGANT GARDENS in the 18th-century French style introduce this private, dry-moated château, 2 km (1 mile) southeast of the old town of Segré on the River Oudon.

The original building, which is embellished by a statue of the Roman goddess Minerva over the central door, was built during the 17th century by René le Pelletier, provost-general of Anjou.

A century later, two wings were added to form a court-yard, together with an ornate marble ballroom. This *pièce de résistance* is crowned with a musicians' gallery located in an overhead rotunda. It was completed by Italian craftsmen in 1779, only a few short years before the French Revolution put an end to these types of extravagant shows of wealth and personal power.

St-Florent-le-Vieil ❷

Road map B3. 🏘 *2,650.* 🚉 🚌
ℹ *Pavillon de la Mairie (41 72 62 32).*
🏪 *Fri pm.* 🎵 *Festival de Musique*
(Jun–Jul).

A WALK THROUGH the narrow streets of the old town, lined with buildings dating from the 16th to the 18th centuries, ends atop a hill on which stands a large, 18th-century church, the scene of dramatic events during the Vendée Uprising. The Uprising began in the square outside the church in March 1793, with a mass revolt against conscription into the Republican army.

Seven months later, the Royalist army, beaten at Cholet, crossed the Loire here with 40,000 troops and at least as many supporters. They planned to kill more than 4,000 Republicans held in the church, but were stopped by one of their leaders, the Marquis de Bonchamps, who cried, "Spare the prisoners," as he lay dying.

THE CORNICHE ANGEVINE

One of the most scenic routes in the region, the Corniche Angevine (D751) curves along the cliffs above the south side of the Loire, offering lovely views of the islands that break up the river in this area, and of the opposite bank, with its fertile vineyards and beautiful manor houses. The road is never more than hilly and has a pleasantly rural feel as it runs alongside the Louet (a tributary of the Loire), passing though villages and flanked by vineyards and fields.

Chalonnes-sur-Loire, at the western end, is an ancient village with a graceful church, the Eglise St-Maurille, parts of which date back to the 12th century. The quay beside the church is a good place to stop for a picnic. Further along, La Haie Longue has particularly pretty views across the river. At the eastern end of the Corniche Angevine, the town of Rochefort-sur-Loire has a 15th-century bell-tower and a square of old turreted houses. Powerful fortresses once stood on outcrops of rock below the village, and the ruins of some of them can be explored.

The view across the river at La Haie Longue

Among those saved was the father of sculptor David d'Angers, whose marble statue of Bonchamps was placed in the church in 1825 *(see p57)*. Stained-glass windows in the chancel tell the story, as does the **Musée d'Histoire Locale et des Guerres de Vendée**.

🏛 **Musée d'Histoire Locale et des Guerres de Vendée**
Place J et M Sourice. 📞 *41 72 62 32, 41 72 50 20.* ⭕ *Jul–mid-Sep: daily, pm only; Easter–Jun & mid-Sep–Oct: Sat, Sun & public hols, pm only.* 📷

Emile Boutigny's 1899 depiction of the Vendée Uprising in Cholet

Cholet ❸

Road map B4. 🏘 *58,000.* 🚉 🚌
ℹ *pl de Rougé (41 62 22 35).*
📅 *Sat.* 🎭 *Festival de l'Arlequin (Apr); L'Eté Cigale (Jun–Sep); L'Aqua Festival (Jul).*

CAPITAL OF THE Mauges region and second city of Anjou, Cholet was a thriving town until it lost half its population in the Vendée Uprising. Its subsequent revival was testimony to the strength of the textile industry in the area. Cholet's distinctive red

The tomb of the Marquis de Vaubrun in Serrant's chapel

handkerchiefs with white borders are souvenirs of a crucial battle fought near here in the year 1793. The Vendée Uprising is commemorated in a remarkable range of portraits, battle scenes and models in the city's **Musée d'Art et d'Histoire**.

🏛 **Musée d'Art et d'Histoire**
27 av de l'Abreuvoir. 📞 *41 49 29 00.*
⭕ *Wed–Mon.* ⚫ *public hols.*

Château de Serrant ❹

Road map B3. 🚉 *Angers, then taxi*
📞 *41 39 13 01.* ⭕ *Apr–Jun, Sep–Oct: Wed–Mon; Jul–Aug: daily.* 📷

THE MOST WESTERLY of the great Loire châteaux, the privately-owned Serrant was begun in 1546 and developed in an entirely harmonious style over the next three centuries. Its pale tufa and dark schist façades, with massive corner towers topped by cupolas, create an air of formal dignity. Inside, the central pavilion contains one of the most beautiful Renaissance staircases to be found in the region. The château also has a fine collection of 18th-century furniture and Flemish

tapestries, and a library of some 12,000 books.

Serrant's most famous owner was the Marquis de Vaubrun, whose death in battle (1675) is commemorated by a magnificent tomb in the chapel, sculpted by Antoine Coysevox. The Irish Jacobite family of Walsh, shipowners at Nantes, owned Serrant in the 18th century, and the château displays a painting of Bonnie Prince Charlie bidding farewell to Anthony Walsh, whose ship took the prince to Scotland.

In 1830 Serrant became the property of the Duc de La Trémoille, one of whose descendants owns it today.

A statue of the Madonna, set in the church wall at Béhuard

Béhuard ❺

Road map C3. 🚉 *Savennières, then taxi.* ℹ *Angers (41 23 51 11).*

THE NARROW LANES of the medieval village on this delightful island in the Loire were made not for cars but for pilgrims visiting a tiny church fitted into an outcrop of rock. Since pagan times, prayers have been offered on this site for the safety of sailors navigating the often treacherous river.

The church, moving in its simplicity, was built during the 15th century under the protection of Louis XI, who was himself saved from shipwreck on the Loire. The aisle that bisects the little nave is hollowed from the rock.

The south façade of Château de Serrant, with huge corner towers

Château du Plessis-Bourré ❻

Road map C3. 🚆 *Angers, then taxi.*
🎫 *41 32 06 01.* ⏰ *Mar–Jun,
Sep–Oct: Thu pm–Tue; Jul–Aug: daily;
Nov & Feb: Thu–Tue, pm only.*
🔲 ♿ *grd flr only.*

S ET IN A MOAT so wide it
looks more like a lake,
Château du Plessis-Bourré,
with its silvery-white walls
and dark slate roofs, seems
to float on the water. Built in
five years from 1468, this is
the least altered and perhaps
most perfect work of Jean
Bourré, whose home it was.

As advisor and treasurer to
the king of France, Bourré

also oversaw the creation of
Langeais *(see p92)* and Jarzé
and was influential in the
transformation of Loire castles
from fortresses into pleasure
palaces. The Château du
Plessis-Bourré is well
defended, but its fortifications
do not interfere with a design
that is orientated towards
gracious living. Its wonderful
condition stands as a testament to the quality of the
materials used in its construction and to the skills of the
craftsmen who created it.

After crossing a long, seven-
arched bridge, visitors enter
the château's arcaded courtyard by one of two working
drawbridges. The owner still

Ceiling of the Salle des Gardes

shuts these each night, using
a beautifully balanced
mechanism. The state rooms
are surprisingly light and airy,
with finely-carved stone
decoration. In the Salle des
Gardes, a magnificent painted
ceiling depicts many allegorical and alchemical scenes,
including a representation of
the demon-wolf Chicheface,
emaciated because she could
eat only wives who always
obeyed their husbands. Some
furniture, mainly dating from
the 18th century, is displayed.
During the French Revolution,
coats of arms on the library
fireplace were defaced, and
graffiti can still be seen.

Château du Plessis-Bourré, set in its wide moat

BIRD-WATCHING IN THE BASSES VALLÉES ANGEVINES

At the confluence of the Sarthe, Loir and
Mayenne rivers, some 4,500 ha (11,100 acres)
of land, the Basses Vallées Angevines, are
flooded between October and May each year.
Thousands of migrating birds visit the area,
making it an exceptional bird-watching site.

Perhaps the rarest visitor is the elusive
corncrake, which arrives in the grasslands
during March. There are more than 300

breeding pairs in the area – more than anywhere else in Europe. Protection of this
species is aided by enlightened local farming
methods, such as late hay harvests.

Insects in the meadows, ditches and rivers
attract swifts, hobbys, whinchats and yellow
wagtails. In early summer the Basses Vallées
resound with birdsong and in the evenings the
strange call of the corncrake can be heard.

The flood-plains of Anjou at twilight

Château de Montgeoffroy **⑦**

Road map C3. 🚉 *Angers or Saumur, then taxi.* ☎ *41 80 60 02.* ◯ *Palm Sunday–Oct: daily.* 🖼 ♿

MONTGEOFFROY is an understated masterpiece of late 18th-century style, built for the Maréchal de Contades by the architect Nicolas Barré between 1773 and 1775, and beautifully preserved by his descendants. Visitors are struck by the balance and lightness of the château with its subtle blue and grey harmonies of stone and paintwork, its tall French windows and its lovely park.

The central building is flanked by flat-roofed pavilions, which connect two side wings to the main house. The wings are both rounded off with towers built in the 16th century. One tower houses a harness room smelling of fresh Norwegian spruce, leading to magnificent stables and a fine display of carriages. The chapel in the opposite wing is also 16th-century.

The symmetrical façade of the Château de Montgeoffroy

Hérault de Séchelles by Hubert Drouais

Next to the main house, the kitchen has a collection of 260 copper and pewter pots. The charming principal rooms are alive with pictures, tapestries and furniture made especially for the château. An innovation in the dining room is a porcelain stove fashioned in the shape of a palm tree, brought from Strasbourg where the *maréchal* (marshal) was governor. His crossed batons are used as a decorative motif in the superbly positioned Grand Salon. The marshal's "friend", Madame Hérault, had her own rooms, where a portrait of their "natural" grandson, Marie-Jean Hérault de Séchelles, can be seen.

Montgeoffroy's stables, where the collection of carriages is housed

Snipe

Lapwing

BIRD SPECIES

Resident ducks, cormorants and coots can be seen all year round. In winter, they are joined by geese and swans at the margins and golden plovers in the fields. February sees the arrival of 30,000 black-tailed godwits. Pintail ducks, greylag geese, lapwings and black-headed gulls also appear for a time, as do waders such as ruff, snipe, redshank and dunlin.

Golden plover

BIRD-WATCHER'S CHECKLIST

Road map C3. 🚉 *Angers, then taxi or hire car.* ℹ *Ligue pour la Protection des Oiseaux, 84 rue Blaise Pascal, Angers (41 44 44 22).* 🌐 *Mar–Jun: day, night and weekend outings including special trips for children.* 🖼 *Reservations are required for LPO programmes.*

Best viewing area (Feb–late Jul): confluence of Loir and Sarthe rivers, southwest of Briollay. Take the D107 from Angers to Cantenay-Epinard. Turn right just before the village and follow signs for Le Vieux Cantenay. Return to the D107 via Vaux. Continue north to Noyant, where all of the little roads across the meadows lead to the River Sarthe. Return to Noyant and head for Les Chapelles and Soulaire-et-Bourg. Then take the D109 to Briollay if the road is passable.

Angers

Sɪᴛᴜᴀᴛᴇᴅ ᴏɴ ᴛʜᴇ River Maine, only 8 km (5 miles) before it joins the Loire, Angers was once the power base for Foulques Nerra *(see pp50–51)* and the other notorious medieval counts of Anjou. By the 12th century, under the rule of the Plantagenets, Angers became the regional capital of an empire stretching as far as Scotland. Today, it is a thriving university town, with wide boulevards, beautiful public gardens and narrow older streets evocative of its long history.

Angers Cathedral carving

Exploring Angers

Angers is divided into two sections by the River Maine. The oldest part is on the left bank of the river, guarded by the fortress-like 13th-century **Château d'Angers** *(see pp74–5)*. Shielded inside the château's massive walls are the Apocalypse Tapestries, the oldest and largest of France's tapestries, dating from the 14th century *(see pp76–7)*. The **Cathédrale St-Maurice** is just a short walk from the château.

Angers has 46 timber-framed houses, most of them found in the old streets near the cathedral. The best of these is the **Maison d'Adam**, at No. 1 place Ste-Croix. This 15th-century merchant's house is decorated with carved wooden figures of sirens, musicians and lovers tucked into every angle. The extravagant decoration was a display of the owner's prosperity. Maison d'Adam is now a centre for the textile industry, but its exterior is its principal charm.

On the right bank of the River Maine, the old quarter

of **La Doutre** (*"d'outre Maine"*, or "the other side of the Maine") is well worth a visit. Formerly an area of tradesmen's establishments, inhabited only by the poor, the district has now been restored and contains a number of well-preserved timber-framed buildings.

A rewarding stroll from rue Gay-Lussac to place de la Laiterie passes many of La Doutre's historic buildings. Included among them are the elegant **Hôtel des Pénitentes** (once a refuge for reformed prostitutes), a 12th-century **apothecary's house** and the restored church of **La Trinité**, which adjoins the ruins of Foulques Nerra's Romanesque **Abbaye du Ronceray** – a Benedictine abbey reserved for daughters of the nobility.

⛪ Cathédrale St-Maurice
Parvis de la Cathédrale.
📞 41 87 58 45. ⏲ daily.
This striking cathedral was built at the end of the 12th century, although the central lantern tower was added during the Renaissance period. The façade's Gothic

Maison d'Adam, the best of Angers' timber-framed houses

sculptures are still impressive, although they have become heavily worn over the years and are shell-pocked.

The elegant Angevin vaulting in the nave and the transept is one of the best, and earliest, examples of its kind, and gives a rounded, dome-like shape to the high ceiling. The interior of the cathedral is lit through glowing stained glass, which includes a beautiful 15th-century rose window in the northern transept.

🏛 Musée des Beaux Arts
10 rue du Musée. 📞 41 88 64 65.
⏲ mid-Jun–mid-Sep: daily; mid-Sep–mid-Jun: Tue–Sun. 🈺
The municipal art collection of Angers is housed in a fine 15th-century mansion, the Logis Barrault. There is an intriguing display of religious antiquities on the first floor, including a lapidary Cross of Anjou; a beautiful 13th-century copper-gilt mask, taken from the effigy of a woman; and sceptres from the abbeys at Toussaint and Fontevraud *(see pp86–7)*.

Among the paintings in the upper galleries are a number of portraits, including one of Agnès Sorel, mistress of Charles VII *(see p104)*; still lifes by Jean-Baptiste Chardin; *Les Génies des Arts*, a vast and amusing work by François Boucher; and Jean-Auguste-Dominique Ingres' *Paolo Malatesta and Francesca da Rimini*, which illustrates a scene from Dante's *Inferno*.

One of the many beautiful public gardens in Angers

COINTREAU

Angers, the city of Cointreau, produces some 30 million bottles of the famous liqueur every year. The distillery was founded in 1849 by the Cointreau brothers, local confectioners well known around Angers for their exotic, curative tonics. But it was Edouard, the son of one of them, who created the original recipe. The flavour of this unique colourless liqueur is artfully based on sweet and bitter orange peels.

VISITORS' CHECKLIST

Road map C3. 🏛 200,000.
🚉 pl de la Gare. 🚌 pl Molière.
ℹ pl Kennedy (41 23 51 11).
🛒 Tue–Sun. 🎭 Festival d'Anjou (Jul).

🏛 Galerie David d'Angers

37 bis, rue Toussaint. **(** 41 87 21 03.
○ mid-Jun–mid-Sep: daily; mid-Sep–mid-Jun: Tue–Sun. ● public hols. 🎫
The glassed-over ruins of the 13th-century abbey church of Toussaint is filled with plaster casts of the work of local sculptor Pierre-Jean David (1788–1856), known as David d'Angers. His idealized busts and figures were much in demand as memorials for people such as the Marquis de Bonchamps *(see p57)*. With their flowing lines, enhanced by the attractive, well-lit setting of the gallery, they are forceful examples of Academic art.

Sculpture by David d'Angers

🏛 Hôpital St-Jean (Musée Jean Lurçat)

4 bd Arago. **(** 41 87 41 06.
○ mid-Jun–mid-Sep: daily; mid-Sep–mid-Jun: Tue–Sun. ● public hols. 🎫 ♿
A Gothic masterpiece in La Doutre, this graceful building functioned as a hospital until 1875, the oldest surviving one in France. It was founded in 1175 by Henry II of England, and the Plantagenet coat of arms is displayed with the Anjou heraldry just inside the entrance to the delightful grounds. A reconstruction of the dispensary occupies one corner of the Salle des Malades, and a chapel and 12th-century cloisters can be reached through a door at the far end of the gallery. The Hôpital St-Jean now houses the Musée Jean Lurçat, which displays a collection of the vivid, 20th-century tapestries of that renowned artist who inspired a renaissance in the art form *(see p77)*.

🏛 Espace Cointreau

Bd des Brétonnières. 🚌 **(** 41 43 25 21. ○ mid-Jun–mid-Sep: Mon–Fri, Sat & Sun: pm only; mid-Sep–mid-Jun: Sun, public hols (pm only), weekdays by appt 🎫
At this, the only Cointreau distillery, situated in Angers' St-Barthélémy district, visitors can observe the production process from raw ingredients to the bottled liqueur. The scale of the operation is formidable, with 19 copper stills and a vast bottling plant. After the tour, visitors can taste the famous orange-flavoured liqueur and look around the adjacent museum, where the development of Cointreau is related through documents, memorabilia and an audiovisual presentation.

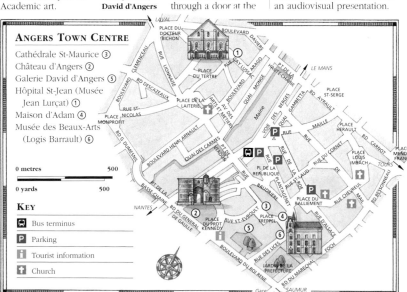

ANGERS TOWN CENTRE

Cathédrale St-Maurice ③
Château d'Angers ②
Galerie David d'Angers ⑤
Hôpital St-Jean (Musée
 Jean Lurçat) ①
Maison d'Adam ④
Musée des Beaux-Arts
 (Logis Barrault) ⑥

0 metres   500
0 yards   500

KEY

🚌 Bus terminus

🅿 Parking

ℹ Tourist information

✝ Church

Château d'Angers

One of the deer living in the dry moat

THE HUGE DRUM TOWERS and curtain walls of this powerful feudal fortress were built on the site of Count Foulques Nerra's stronghold between 1230 and 1240. The work was begun at the behest of Blanche of Castille, the mother of Louis IX and regent during his youth. Within the 650-m (2,100-ft) perimeter, later nobles developed a château lifestyle in almost playful contrast to the forbidding schist and limestone towers. The last duke of Anjou, King René I, added charming buildings, gardens, aviaries and a menagerie. After several centuries as a prison, the citadel-château now houses France's most famous tapestries.

The Logis du Gouverneur was built in the 15th century and modified in the 18th century.

Moat gardens

★ Moat Gardens
The dry moat, which is 11 m (36 ft) deep and 30 m (98 ft) wide, is now filled with geometric flower beds.

Fortress Towers
The 17 towers rise up to 60 m (200 ft) in height. They lost their pepper pot roofs and were shortened as a delaying tactic, following royal orders to demolish them completely during the 16th century.

Formal gardens have been planted in the great courtyard.

The drawbridge leading to the Porte de la Ville (Town Gate) is the entrance to the château.

TIMELINE

Henry III

1230–40 Fortress built on a rocky spur, where counts of Anjou had built older castles

1410 Louis II and Yolande of Aragon reconstruct chapel and Logis Royal

1945 Allied bombers damage fortress, in use as a German munitions base

1648–52 Louis XIV turns fortress into a prison

1200	1300	1400	1500	1600	1700	1800	1900

1360 Louis I of Anjou cuts doors and windows to relieve the grimness of the walls

1450–65 René I renovates interior, adding gardens and new buildings

1585 Fortress taken by Huguenots. Henri III wants towers demolished but governor merely lowers them

1875 Declared a historic monument

1952–54 Bernard Vitry builds gallery to house Apocalypse Tapestries

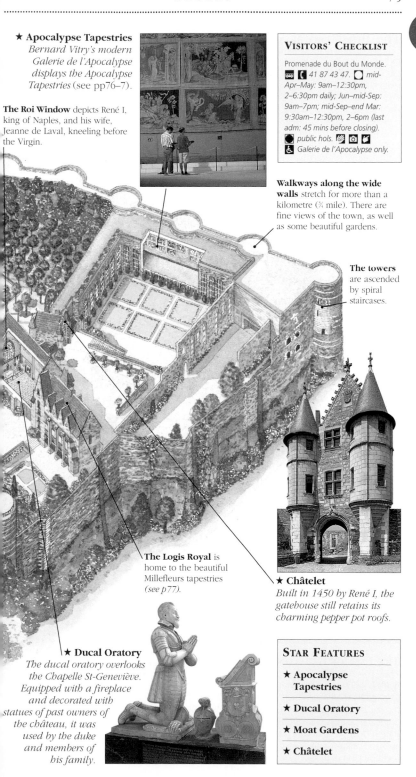

★ **Apocalypse Tapestries**
*Bernard Vitry's modern
Galerie de l'Apocalypse
displays the Apocalypse
Tapestries (see pp76–7).*

The Roi Window depicts René I,
king of Naples, and his wife,
Jeanne de Laval, kneeling before
the Virgin.

VISITORS' CHECKLIST

Promenade du Bout du Monde.
📠 📞 *41 87 43 47*. ⏰ *mid-
Apr–May: 9am–12:30pm,
2–6:30pm daily; Jun–mid-Sep:
9am–7pm; mid-Sep–end Mar:
9:30am–12:30pm, 2–6pm (last
adm: 45 mins before closing).*
🌑 *public hols.* 📷 📹
♿ *Galerie de l'Apocalypse only.*

**Walkways along the wide
walls** stretch for more than a
kilometre (¾ mile). There are
fine views of the town, as well
as some beautiful gardens.

The towers
are ascended
by spiral
staircases.

The Logis Royal is
home to the beautiful
Millefleurs tapestries
(see p77).

★ **Châtelet**
*Built in 1450 by René I, the
gatehouse still retains its
charming pepper pot roofs.*

★ **Ducal Oratory**
*The ducal oratory overlooks
the Chapelle St-Geneviève.
Equipped with a fireplace
and decorated with
statues of past owners of
the château, it was
used by the duke
and members of
his family.*

STAR FEATURES

★ **Apocalypse
Tapestries**

★ **Ducal Oratory**

★ **Moat Gardens**

★ **Châtelet**

The Tapestries at Angers

THE APOCALYPSE TAPESTRIES, made in the 14th century for Duke Louis I of Anjou, illustrate the visions of St John from the Book of Revelation. In the turmoil of the French Revolution, the tapestries were thrown out, cut up and used for anything from bed canopies to horse blankets. Restoration began in the mid-19th century. Acclaimed as a masterpiece, the surviving sections of this work stretch for 103 m (338 ft) along a specially-built gallery in the Château d'Angers. Nearly 600 years after their creation, they inspired Jean Lurçat to design his own tapestry sequence, called *Le Chant du Monde*.

Detailed Work
Each of the devils devouring Babylon has a distinct character. The tapestries were woven so skilfully that the front and the back are almost mirror images.

St John appears as the narrator of each vision.

An angel dictates to St John in one of the best-preserved scenes. Elsewhere, the green textiles have faded to beige.

THE FALL OF BABYLON

The Apocalypse Tapestries were woven in 1375–83 in Parisian workshops. Designed by Hennequin de Bruges, who was inspired by Carolingian manuscript illuminations, they depict the end of the world and the coming of a New Jerusalem. The original 90 panels were arranged in 6 chapters, each with an introductory panel and 14 scenes. Scene 66 depicts the Fall of Babylon: "Babylon the Great is fallen, is fallen, and is become the habitation of devils" (Rev. 18:2).

Water is changed to poisonous wormwood at the blowing of the third trumpet in this cataclysmic scene.

Mille Fleurs Tapestries
*Displayed in the Logis Royal,
these late 15th-century
Flemish tapestries are still
vibrantly coloured.*

Le Chant du Monde

Jean Lurçat (1892–1966)

THE VAST, VAULTED INTERIOR of the Musée Jean Lurçat *(see p73)* provides a stunning background to *The Song of the World*. This piece, which stretches for 79 m (260 ft) around three sides of the hall, was Lurçat's response to the Apocalypse Tapestries, which he saw for the first time in 1937. The ten panels are 4 m (13 ft) high and were woven from wool at workshops in Aubusson between 1957 and 1966. Thematically, the images move from the horrors of Nazi genocide and the bombing of Hiroshima to the conquest of space, conceived as the dawning of a new age.

"Ornamentos Sagrados" from Lurçat's *Le Chant du Monde* tapestry

THE ART OF TAPESTRY

In medieval times, tapestries were a symbol of luxury, commissioned by royal and noble families to adorn châteaux and churches. Hung on the thick stone walls, they helped to keep the vast rooms warm by preventing drafts.

Medieval tapestry weaver

Paris and Flanders were the centres of tapestry work in the 14th century, where highly skilled weavers followed an artist's full-size drawing, called a "cartoon". Threads were stretched vertically (the warp) on a loom to the length of the finished piece, then coloured threads (the weft) were woven horizontally across them.

Tapestry-making declined from the 16th century, but the 20th century has seen a revival, with artists such as Pablo Picasso and Henri Matisse experimenting in the medium.

The tumbling towers
of Babylon reveal a
nest of demons.

Blue backgrounds alternate
with red, providing continuity
through the series.

Coloured tapestry threads at the Manufacture St-Jean in Aubusson

Brissac's wine cellars

Château de Brissac **9**

Brissac-Quincé. **Road map** C3.
🚆 Angers, then taxi. 🚌
📞 41 91 22 21. 🕐 Apr–Jun,
mid-Sep–Oct: Wed–Mon; Jul–mid-
Sep: daily. 🚫

T HE CHATEAU of the dukes of
Brissac, towering above
the River Aubance 18 km (11
miles) southeast of Angers, is
the tallest of those along the
Loire, and is perhaps the
grandest still in private hands.
Ownership has passed down
a line going back to Charles
de Cossé, governor of Paris
and marshal of France. His
death in 1621 halted the
completion of a vast palace
set upon the ruins of an
earlier fortress.

On the entrance façade, an
ornate, 17th-century, domed
pavilion soars to 37 m (120 ft)
between two 15th-century
towers. Ten of the château's
150 rooms are open to the
public and are filled with
furniture, paintings, tapestries
and other treasures. Among
the most striking is the Salle
des Gardes, which is 32 m
(105 ft) long and is decorated
with Aubusson tapestries and
gilded ceilings. The room is
superbly lit through the
distinctive paned windows
that are a feature of architect
Jacques Corbineau's work.

Other memorable rooms
are Louis XIII's bedroom and
an 1883 opera theatre, still
used for concerts. In the
château's picture gallery hangs
a 19th-century portrait of
Madame Clicquot, matriarch of
the famous champagne house
and a distant ancestor of the
present duke. At the end of
the visit, the duke's own
wines can be tasted in cellars
dating from the 11th century.

Gennes **10**

Road map C3. 🚶 1,900. 🚆 Les
Rosiers-sur-Loire. 🚌 🛈 square de
l'Europe (41 51 84 14). 🕐 Tue.

D URING THE Gallo-Roman
period (see pp48–9) the
pleasant village of Gennes
(then known as Genina Loca),
on the south bank of the River
Loire, was an important religious and commercial centre.
The largest **amphitheatre** in
western France was built on a
hillside here more than 1,800
years ago and was used from
the 1st to the 3rd centuries for
gladiatorial contests. A restoration project, started in 1985, has
revealed the sandstone walls
and brick tiers of a stadium
that seated at least 5,000 spectators and included changing
rooms and an efficient drainage system. In front of the
arena, which measures 2,160
sq m (2,600 sq yds), marshlands on the Avort river were
probably flooded for aquatic
combats and displays.

The area around Gennes is
also very rich in Neolithic
sites. Among the 20 ancient
burial chambers and menhirs
nearby is the **Dolmen de la
Madeleine**, one of the largest
in France. Used as a bakery

**The medieval Eglise St-Vétérin in
the town of Gennes**

until recently, it can be found
1 km (1100 yds) east, past
Gennes' medieval **Eglise St-
Vétérin** on the D69.

An excellent panoramic
view can be seen from the
tower of **St-Eusèbe**, a ruined
church dating from the 11th
to the 15th centuries, sited
on a knoll above the village.
Beside the old nave is a
moving memorial to cadets of
the Saumur cavalry school
(see p83) who died in an
attempt to prevent the German army crossing the Loire
in June 1940.

A bronze statue of Mercury
has been discovered on the
hill, and this seems to suggest
that a temple to the Roman
god may have stood here in
the Gallo-Roman period.

🏛 **Amphithéâtre**
📞 41 51 83 33. 🕐 Jul–Aug: daily;
Apr–Jun & Sep: Sun & public hols pm.
🚫
🏛 **Dolmen de la Madeleine**
📞 41 39 12 01. 🕐 daily. 🚫

The Neolithic Dolmen de la Madeleine, near Gennes

ENVIRONS: At L'Orbière, 4 km (2½ miles) from Gennes, the sculptor Jacques Warminsky has created a monumental work, named *L'Hélice Terrestre* (*The Earth's Helix*). Occupying a surface area of 875 sq m (1,050 sq yds), this spiralling labyrinth has been cut into the soft limestone hillside. Warminsky and his assistants have carved out a series of galleries, some reaching 14 m (46 ft) below the surface, which expand or contract into organic and mineral forms.

The helix continues its path out to the exterior, where it becomes a spiral assemblage of reversed forms. The two spaces are complementary and represent the universal philosophy of the artist.

Artist Jacques Warminsky at work on *L'Hélice Terrestre*

🏛 **L'Hélice Terrestre**
L'Orbière, St-Georges-des-Sept-Voies. **Road map** C3. 🚉 *Les Rosiers-sur-Loire, then taxi.* 🚌 *Gennes, then taxi.* 📞 *41 57 95 92.* ⏰ *May–Sep: daily; Oct–Apr: daily, pm only.* ♿

Cunault ⑪

Road map C3. 🚶 *1,000.* 🚉 *Les Rosiers-sur-Loire, then taxi.* ℹ️ *pl Victor Daillaut (41 67 92 55).* 🎵 *Les Heures Musicales (Jul–Aug).*

CUNAULT'S pale limestone priory church, the **Eglise Notre-Dame**, has rightly been called the most majestic of all the Romanesque churches in Anjou, if not the whole of the Loire Valley. In the 12th century, Benedictine monks from Tournus in Burgundy built the church in this small village on the south bank of the Loire. They incorporated the sturdy bell-tower, dating from the 11th century, from an earlier building, and a short spire was added in the 15th century.

Cunault is the longest Romanesque church without a transept in France. Inside, the first impression is of simplicity and elegance. The height of the pillars is impressive; they are topped with 223 carved capitals, decorated with fabulous beasts, demons and religious motifs, and are placed high enough so as not to interfere with the pure architectural lines. Binoculars are needed to see details.

Three aisles of equal width were made to accommodate the crowds of pilgrims who travelled to the church to see its relics, which include one revered as the wedding ring of the Virgin Mary, and the floor is deeply worn beside a 12th-century marble stoup at the foot of the entrance steps. Towards the chancel, the ambulatory is floored with scalloped terracotta tiles. Traces of 15th-century frescoes remain, including a figure of St Christopher.

Other notable treasures in the church include furniture in oak and ash, a 13th-century carved wooden reliquary and a painted 15th-century statue representing St Catherine.

The central aisle of Cunault's majestic 12th-century church

CULTIVATED MUSHROOMS

Around 75 per cent of French cultivated mushrooms come from Anjou. The damp, dark caves in the tufa cliffs along the Loire are the perfect environment for the *champignons de Paris*, so called because they were first cultivated in disused quarries in the Paris region before production began in the Loire Valley in the late 19th century. Today, mushroom cultivation is a thriving business, employing around 5,000 people in the region. Growers have been diversifying in recent years, cultivating more exotic mushrooms such as *pleurottes* and *shiitake*, in response to demand from food-lovers.

Oyster mushrooms, known as *pleurottes*

Street-by-Street: Saumur ⓬

THE STORYBOOK CHATEAU is set on a hill high above the town, making it easy for visitors to locate Saumur's old quarter, which lies mainly between the château, the river and the main street running straight ahead from the central bridge over the Loire. The twisting streets that wind up and down the hill on which the château is built merit exploration. Saumur's modest size, which suits sightseeing on foot, is only one of the many charms of this friendly town.

Theatre
Saumur's theatre, which opened in the late 19th century, was modelled on the Odéon in Paris.

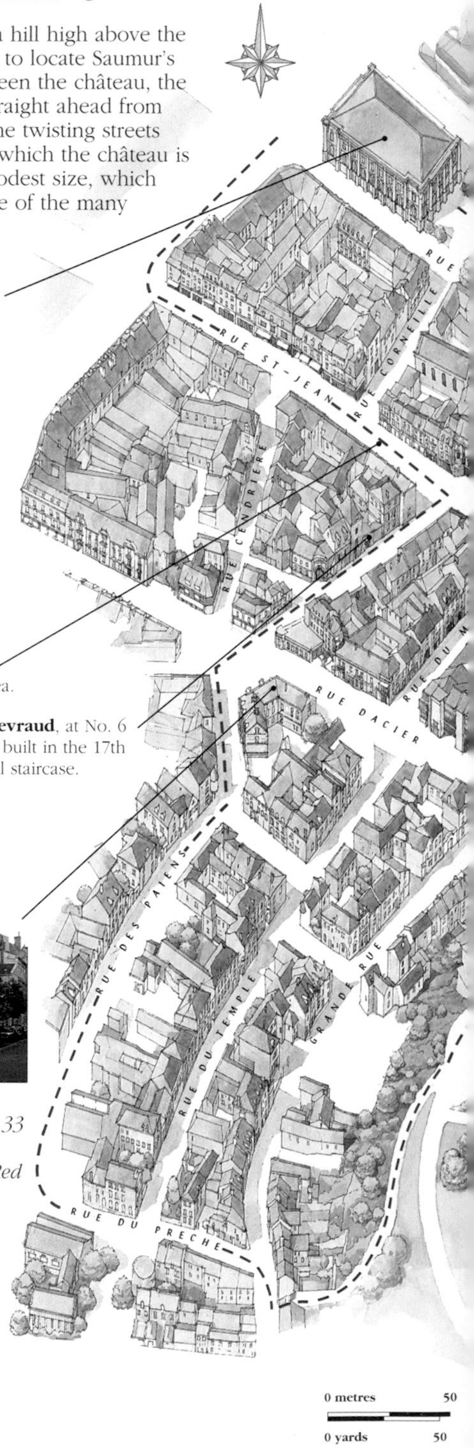

Rue St-Jean is the heart of Saumur's main shopping area.

The Hôtel des Abbesses de Fontevraud, at No. 6 rue de l'Ancienne-Messagerie, was built in the 17th century and has a marvellous spiral staircase.

Maison du Roi
This pretty Renaissance building at No. 33 rue Dacier once housed royalty but is now the headquarters of the Saumur Red Cross. In the courtyard is a plaque to the much-loved René I of Anjou, who often held court at Saumur.

STAR SIGHTS

★ Château de Saumur

★ Eglise St-Pierre

---

0 metres   50

0 yards   50

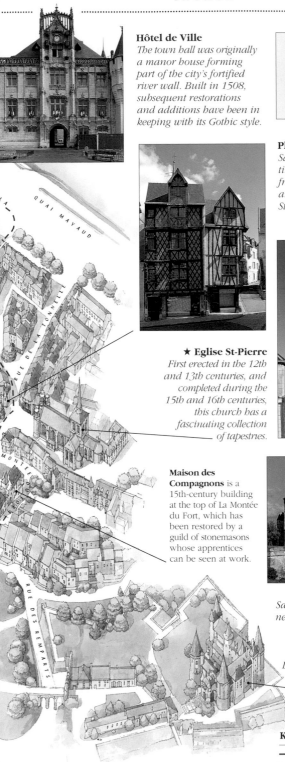

Hôtel de Ville
The town hall was originally a manor house forming part of the city's fortified river wall. Built in 1508, subsequent restorations and additions have been in keeping with its Gothic style.

Place St-Pierre
Saumur's oldest half-timbered houses, dating from the 15th century, are situated in place St-Pierre (Nos. 3, 5 and 6).

★ Eglise St-Pierre
First erected in the 12th and 13th centuries, and completed during the 15th and 16th centuries, this church has a fascinating collection of tapestries.

Maison des Compagnons
is a 15th-century building at the top of La Montée du Fort, which has been restored by a guild of stonemasons whose apprentices can be seen at work.

★ Château de Saumur
Saumur's château is situated next to the Butte des Moulins, a small hill that was once covered with windmills. Views of the town and the Loire and Thouet rivers can be seen from the top of the watchtower.

KEY

− − − Suggested route

Exploring Saumur

TODAY, SAUMUR is best known for its sparkling wines, mushrooms and fine horse riders. It was once an important port and a centre of Protestant scholarship in the 16th and 17th centuries, until the revocation of the Edict of Nantes in 1685 forced many Protestants to leave. This rich legacy is easy to see during a walk through the attractive streets of the old quarter.

Panel from the 15th-century choir stalls in the Eglise St-Pierre

The old quarter

At the heart of Saumur's old quarter stands the **Eglise St-Pierre**, which was built in the late 12th century. Sadly, the front entrance was destroyed by lightning in 1674, but on the south side a Romanesque door survives from the original building. The treasures of the church include the beautifully carved wooden stalls in the choir, which date from the 15th century. There are also some magnificent 16th-century tapestries illustrating the lives of St Peter and St Florent. The latter is an influential figure in the monastic history of the region. He is depicted being rescued from Roman persecution, slaying a dragon and founding a monastery.

Nearby, the **Grande Rue**'s limestone and slate houses reflect Saumur's prosperity in the late 16th century under Protestant rule. The "Huguenot Pope", Philippe Duplessis-Mornay, who governed the town between 1589 and 1621, owned the house at No. 45.

The oldest church in Saumur, **Notre-Dame de Nantilly**, was the town's principal place of worship for centuries. Its severe lines date from the beginning of the 12th century. In the 14th century Louis XI ordered a Gothic aisle and a royal oratory to be built. The church has a collection of 16th- and 17th-century tapestries. But perhaps more interesting are the carved capitals and an epitaph composed by the poet-king René I (see p53) to his childhood nurse inscribed on the third pillar on the south side of the nave.

The façade of the Eglise Notre-Dame de Nantilly

Skyline of the Château de Saumur

stacks and pinnacles was later simplified to a more sturdy skyline of shortened pencil towers, but the shape of the château remains graceful. In the ducal apartments, the window bays have romantic views of the River Loire. The powerful-looking outbuildings that surround the château recall its later, although less pleasant, roles as a Protestant bastion, state prison and finally army barracks.

The château houses two very different museums. The **Musée des Arts Décoratifs** is a collection formed by Count Charles Lair, a native of Saumur, who left it to the château in 1919. It includes paintings, many fine tapestries, furniture, statuettes and ceramics that date from the 13th up to the 19th century.

Statuette from the Musée des Arts Décoratifs

Horse-lovers will find a great deal to delight them in a second museum, the **Musée du Cheval**, housed beneath the timbered ceilings of the château's attics. Founded by a veterinarian at Saumur's cavalry school, its exhibits trace the development of the horse and its relationship with man from prehistoric times to the present day. They include a wonderful Russian carved sleigh and the skeleton of the unbeaten Flying Fox, winner of the 1899 Epsom Derby and sire of 20th-century French champions. There is also a collection of beautiful saddles from all around the world.

⚜ Château de Saumur

🗺 41 51 30 46. ⬤ Jun–Sep: daily; Oct–May: Wed–Mon. ⬤ 1 Jan, 25 Dec. 🖼

The famous miniature of this château in *Les Très Riches Heures du Duc de Berry (see p23)* shows a white fairy-tale palace. The château was built by Louis I, Duke of Anjou, in the second half of the 14th century. It was constructed on the base of an earlier fortification. The glittering mass of chimney

🏛 Musée des Blindés

1043 rte de Fontevraud. **[** *41 53 06 99.* ○ *daily.* ● *1 Jan, 25 Dec.*

This barn-like museum houses hundreds of tanks. Owned by the Cavalry and Armoured Vehicles School, it has on display more historic tanks and armoured personnel carriers in working order than any other international military collection.

A 1917 Renault tank in the collection of the Musées des Blindés

Beginning with a FT 17 Renault dating from 1917 and moving through the German World War II panzers to the monsters produced today, the museum offers a chance to see at close quarters these veterans of many conflicts.

🏛 Bagneux Dolmen

56 rue du Dolmen, Bagneux. **[** *41 50 23 02.* ▦ ○ *5 Jan–20 Dec: daily.*

Saumur's main street (N147) leads directly to the suburb of Bagneux. Here, in the strange setting of the garden of a bar, stands one of the biggest and most impressive Neolithic burial chambers in Europe. Visitors can sip drinks in the garden, absorb the impact of the dolmen and marvel at the massive sandstone slabs, some weighing 40 tonnes, that were dragged, tilted and wedged into position some 5,000 years ago *(see p48–9).*

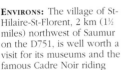

A signpost for the Bagneux dolmen

ENVIRONS: The village of St-Hilaire-St-Florent, 2 km (1½ miles) northwest of Saumur on the D751, is well worth a visit for its museums and the famous Cadre Noir riding school. It also has a number of wine cellars where visitors can taste and buy the famous Saumur Brut, a sparkling wine that is produced by the *méthode champenoise.* The chalky tufa stone, contained in the soil on which local grapes are grown, is said to add to the wine's natural tendency to sparkle.

🏛 Musée du Champignon

D751, St-Hilaire-St-Florent. **[** *41 50 31 55.* ○ *mid-Feb–mid-Nov: daily.*

This unique museum takes visitors through a network of limestone caves. Displays show how mushrooms that are grown from spores in bagged or boxed compost thrive in the high humidity and constant temperature of this environment *(see p79).* The museum has an excellent collection of live mushroom species, as well as of fossils found during quarrying. On offer, and worth tasting, is a local speciality, *gallipettes farcies.* These are large mushrooms, stuffed with a variety of fillings.

🏛 Musée du Masque

Rue de l'Abbaye, St-Hilaire-St-Florent. **[** *41 50 75 26.* ▦ ○ *Easter–mid-Oct: daily; mid-Oct–mid-Dec: Sat–Sun.*

Saumur is a leading producer of masks, and this little museum, attached to the Jules César mask factory in St-Hilaire-St-Florent, is a delight. Specializing in masks of film stars, royalty and political figures, the company produces both caricatures and portraits. On display in the museum are fantasy tableaux showing costumed models in circus, carnival, stage and film masks, some dating from the 1870s.

Tintin in the Musée du Masque

🏛 Ecole Nationale d'Equitation

Terrefort, St-Hilaire-St-Florent. **[** *41 53 50 60.* ○ *Apr– Sep: Mon pm–Sat am (also Jun–Aug: Sat pm). Mornings: show and buildings; afternoons: buildings only.*

The National Riding School, founded in 1814, is world famous for its team, known as the Cadre Noir because of the riders' elegant black and gold ceremonial uniforms. The Cadre Noir's horses are trained in a distinctive style of dressage, which was first practised in the 19th century. They are taught perfect balance and control and learn to perform choreographed movements that show their natural grace.

During the summer months, visitors can enter the academy team's quarters and watch a training session. There are also regular performances of the spectacular show.

The 5,000-year-old Bagneux dolmen near Saumur

Montreuil-Bellay ⑬

Road map C4. ☗ *4,300.* ☐ ☐
ℹ️ *Apr–Sep: pl du Concorde (41 52
32 39); Oct–Mar: mairie (41 40 17
60).* ☐ *Tue, Sun (summer only).*

COMBINING an ancient
village and a fascinating
château, Montreuil-Bellay,
18 km (11 miles) south of
Saumur, is one of the most
attractive towns in Anjou. The
château complex occupies a
site first fortified in the 11th
century by Foulques Nerra
and besieged by Geoffrey
Plantagenet during the following century. In the 13th
century it was surrounded by
strong walls, with a grand
towered entrance (known as
the Château-Vieux) and 11
other towers. Inside the
ramparts is a collection of
mainly late 15th-century

**Frescoes in the oratory of the
Château de Montreuil-Bellay**

buildings, which look down
on landscaped terraces falling
to the pretty River Thouet.
The Château-Neuf is an
elegant Renaissance-fronted
building, begun in the late

15th century. The turret was
made famous by the beautiful
and scandalous French noble-
woman, Anne de Longueville
(1619–79), who once rode her
unfortunate horse to the top
of its spiral staircase.
The interior of the château
is superbly furnished and has
a number of fireplaces in the
Flamboyant style as well as
splendid painted and carved
ceilings. Frescoes dating from
the 15th century, depicting
the Crucifixion and angelic
musicians, adorn the touch-
ingly beautiful, small oratory.
The medieval kitchens are
said to be modelled on those
of the earlier Fontevraud
Abbey *(see pp86–7).*

♠ **Château de
Montreuil-Bellay**
☑ *41 52 33 06.* ☐ *Apr–Oct:
Wed–Mon.* 🖼

Troglodyte Tour ⑮

CAVES, CUT INTO THE TUFA cliffs beside
the Loire and other limestone-rich
areas in Anjou, are used as dovecotes,
chapels, farms, wine cellars and even
homes. These so-called "troglodyte"
dwellings are extremely old, with some
dating back to the 12th century, and
have hardly changed over the
centuries. They are now
fashionable again as
résidences secondaires for
wealthy Parisians. Life in
and among these caves
is the subject of this
fascinating tour.

```
0 kilometres        3
0 miles             3
```

Dénézé-sous-Doué ⑥
In these underground
caves, carved by
Protestant stonemasons
during the 16th-century
Wars of Religion, more
than 400 figures are
chiselled into the walls,
floors and ceilings.

**Carved figures at Dénézé-
sous-Doué**

La Fosse ⑦
This inhabited troglodyte
farmhouse is open
to visitors.

GENNES

⑥

D177

⑤

D213

⑦

D69

D177

D175

D960

Montfort

D162

④

Troglodyte houses at Rochemenier

Rochemenier ⑤
This former troglodyte
farming community has
been turned into a
museum displaying
underground
farmyards, barns,
houses and a simple
rock chapel.

Doué-la-Fontaine ④
The rue des Perrières was
excavated from a stratum of shell
marl *(faluns)*; its "cathedral"
vaults were dug vertically from
the top. The town also has an
amphitheatre cut from the rock
and an outstanding zoo in the
old quarries.

Château de Montsoreau ⑭

Road map C3. 🚉 *Saumur, then taxi.*
🚌 📞 *41 51 70 25.* 🕐 *Mar–Apr,
Oct–Nov: Wed–Mon, pm only;
May–Sep: Wed–Mon.* **Musée des
Goums Marocains** 🖼

Château de Montsoreau on the River Loire

AN IMPRESSIVE battlemented wall remains from a four-sided château completed by Jean de Chambes in 1455. This exterior, however, is much less forbidding when viewed from the château's former courtyard. A beautiful palm-vaulted staircase was added around 1520 and carries an amusing motif of monkeys labouring at work on its construction.

According to the Alexandre Dumas novel, *La Dame de Montsoreau*, the jealous Count Charles de Chambes forced his wife to lure her lover, the lecherous governor of Anjou, Bussy d'Amboise, to his death here. Although the story is based on historical fact, the murder actually took place at a château on the opposite bank of the river, long since vanished.

The **Musée des Goums Marocains** housed in the château covers the history of the Moroccan cavalry regiments from 1908–54.

KEY

▬▬ Tour route
══ Other roads

Souzay ①
East of Saumur, the little "château" at Souzay, like many local houses, projects from the cliff. Its back rooms are cut directly into the rock face

The "château" at Souzay

SAUMUR

D947

Tbouet

D93

Varrains

-tré

D205

D93

D405

D162

D162

Turquant ②
A chapel, a restaurant and extensive wine cellars lie behind the smartly-cut façades at La Grande Vignolle.

REUIL-
Y

St-Cyr-en-Bourg ③
The location of one of the few remaining active tufa quarries, this vast underground network of galleries is owned by the St-Cyr wine co-operative, which makes a full range of Saumur *appellations* in these caves.

TIPS FOR DRIVERS

Tour length: 52 km (32 miles) in one day, starting from Saumur.
Stopping-off points: Doué la Fontaine is a pleasant place to stop for lunch: Restaurant La France and Auberge le Bienvenue are excellent restaurants.

Abbaye de Fontevraud ⑯

Stained glass in church

FONTEVRAUD ABBEY, founded in 1101 by the hermit Robert d'Arbrissel for both women and men, is the largest and most extraordinary of its kind in France. It was run for nearly 700 years by aristocratic abbesses, almost half of them royal-born. They governed a monks' priory outside the main walls, and four distinct communities of nuns and lay sisters, ranging from rich widows to repentant prostitutes, as well as a leper colony and an infirmary. Ongoing restoration work is diligently removing traces of the ravages of the Revolution and the subsequent 150 years, when this "queen of abbeys" was used as a prison.

The grand refectory, with its Renaissance ribbed vaulting, is 60 m (200 ft) long.

Nursing sisters of the St Benoît order cared for invalids in this section of the abbey.

★ **Chapter House Paintings**
The paintings in the Chapter House date from the 16th century. However, some figures were added later.

★ **Plantagenet Effigies**
These four effigies (gisants), each a realistic portrait, are displayed in the nave of the abbey church.

Grand-Moûtier
The cloisters of the main convent are the largest, and possibly the finest, in France. They have Gothic and Renaissance vaulting and upper galleries built in the 19th century.

STAR FEATURES

★ **Plantagenet Effigies**

★ **Chapter House Paintings**

★ **Romanesque Kitchens**

THE RESTING PLACE OF THE PLANTAGENETS

The medieval painted effigy of Henry Plantagenet, count of Anjou and king of England (1133–1189), lies beside that of his wife, Eleanor of Aquitaine, who died here in 1204. With them are the effigies of their son, King Richard the Lionheart (1157–1199), and Isabelle, wife of his brother, King John. In all, 15 of the family are buried here.

Effigies of Eleanor of Aquitaine and Henry II

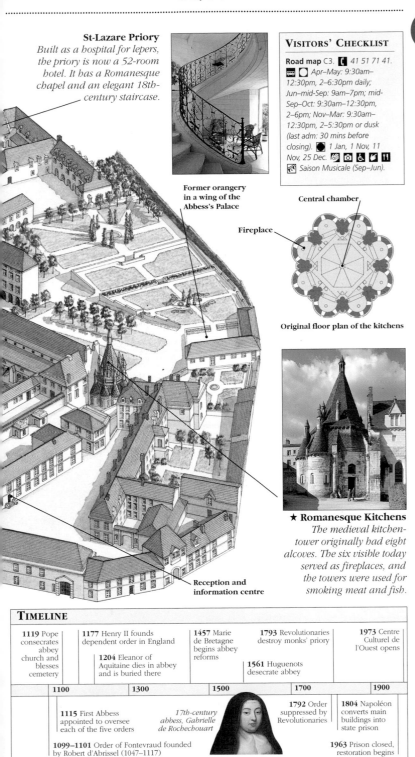

St-Lazare Priory
Built as a hospital for lepers, the priory is now a 52-room hotel. It has a Romanesque chapel and an elegant 18th-century staircase.

VISITORS' CHECKLIST

Road map C3. 🕿 41 51 71 41.
📠 ○ Apr–May: 9:30am–12:30pm, 2–6:30pm daily; Jun–mid-Sep: 9am–7pm; mid-Sep–Oct: 9:30am–12:30pm, 2–6pm; Nov–Mar: 9:30am–12:30pm, 2–5:30pm or dusk (last adm: 30 mins before closing). ● 1 Jan, 1 Nov, 11 Nov, 25 Dec. 🎟 ○ 🔊 📷 🍴
📅 Saison Musicale (Sep–Jun).

Former orangery in a wing of the Abbess's Palace

Central chamber

Fireplace

Original floor plan of the kitchens

★ Romanesque Kitchens
The medieval kitchen-tower originally had eight alcoves. The six visible today served as fireplaces, and the towers were used for smoking meat and fish.

Reception and information centre

TIMELINE

1119 Pope consecrates abbey church and blesses cemetery	**1177** Henry II founds dependent order in England	**1457** Marie de Bretagne begins abbey reforms	**1793** Revolutionaries destroy monks' priory	**1973** Centre Culturel de l'Ouest opens
	1204 Eleanor of Aquitaine dies in abbey and is buried there		**1561** Huguenots desecrate abbey	

1100	1300	1500	1700	1900

1115 First Abbess appointed to oversee each of the five orders	*17th-century abbess, Gabrielle de Rochechouart*		**1792** Order suppressed by Revolutionaries	**1804** Napoléon converts main buildings into state prison
1099–1101 Order of Fontevraud founded by Robert d'Abrissel (1047–1117)				**1963** Prison closed, restoration begins

TOURAINE

OURAINE IS KNOWN *chiefly for the magnificent white châteaux strung out along the broad Loire and its tributaries. Added to these are its rich history and fertile landscape, making it the archetypal Loire Valley region. The rolling terrain and lush forests that once attracted the kings and queens of France continue to work their charm over visitors from all around the world today.*

The feudal castles that still exist, at Loches and Chinon for example, remind visitors that this now tranquil region was once a battleground on which the warring counts of Blois and Anjou staged many an epic encounter. It was also here, at Chinon, that Joan of Arc managed to bully the future Charles VII into raising the army that she would lead to victory over the English.

François I brought the influence of the Italian Renaissance to France and set a fashion in architecture that produced the unforgettable châteaux of this region. The most magical – the delicate Azay-le-Rideau, the majestic Chenonceau, and Villandry with its extraordinary formal gardens – were built during this period. At the end of the 16th century, however, Touraine ceased to be a playground for the aristocracy, and its people then settled into the peaceful, unhurried routine that still prevails.

Tours, at the heart of the region, makes a natural base for visitors, who can enjoy its sensitively restored, medieval old town and marvel at the Cathédrale St-Gatien, a Gothic masterpiece.

The rolling terrain and gentle climate of Touraine encourage outdoor pursuits, including hiking, boating and fishing. The area is also famous for its *primeurs*, early fruit and vegetables, such as white asparagus, grown on its low-lying, fertile soils. Its many wines, including the well-known *appellations* of Bourgueil, Chinon and Vouvray, are the perfect accompaniment to the region's excellent cuisine.

A view of the Château de Chinon, on a cliff above the River Vienne

◁ The rooftops of Luynes, as seen from high on the hill on which the town is built

Exploring Touraine

CRISS-CROSSED BY RIVERS great and small, Touraine sits regally at the heart of the Loire Valley. Châteaux are distributed along the paths of the rivers: Langeais and Amboise by the Loire itself; Ussé, Azay-le-Rideau and Loches by the gentle Indre; and Chenonceau gracefully straddling the Cher. Tours, the main town in the region, is also on the Loire. The Gâtine Tourangelle to the north of the river was once a magnificent forest but was felled progressively from the 11th century by local people in search of wood and arable land. However, small pockets of woodland remain, delightful for walking and picnicking.

Candes-St-Martin, with its
12th- to 13th-century church

KEY

▬	Motorway
▬	Major road
▭	Minor road
▬	Scenic route
≈	River
☀	Viewpoint

GETTING AROUND

Tours is the natural hub of the region. The TGV from Paris takes an hour to St-Pierre-des-Corps, followed by a five-minute shuttle service to the centre of Tours. It is possible to rent a car either from Tours or St-Pierre-des-Corps. The A10 is the fastest route from Paris by car. The N152, running east– west along the north bank of the Loire, is the easiest way to get across the region. The smaller D751 along the south bank passes through attractive countryside. The prettiest drives, however, follow the banks of the Indre.

Le Mans

D959

D38

● CHATEAU-LA-VALLIERE

N138

D749

D959

Lac de Pincemaille

D34

D49

● CHAMPCHEVRIER

LUYN

CINQ-MARS-LA-PILE
②

LANGEAIS
①

④ VL

D7

⑤

BOURGUEIL

N152

AZAY-LE-RIDEAU **⑤**

Angers ←

D7

⑨

USSE

①

⑪

S.

VILLAIN
LES-ROC

⑧

CANDES-ST-MARTIN

D751

D57

⑦

LA DEVINIERE

⑥ CHINON

D760

D39

D759

Vienn

D749

⑫ RICHELIEU

Châtellerault

One of Touraine's renowned vineyards

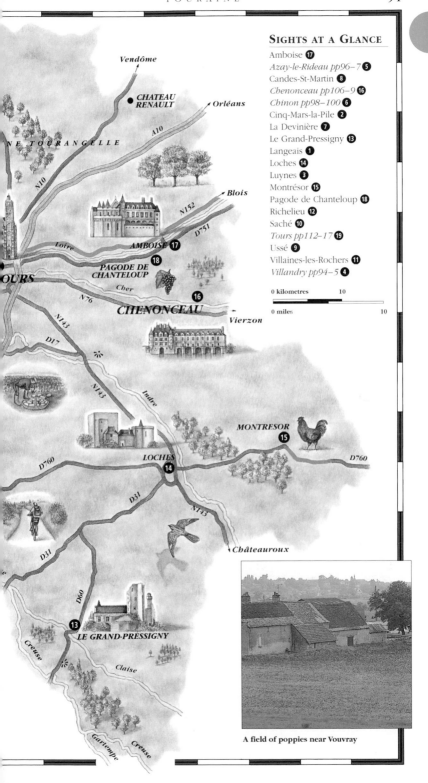

Vendôme

CHATEAU
RENAULT

Orléans

A10

NE TOURANGELLE

N10

Blois

N152

D751

Loire

AMBOISE 17

PAGODE DE
CHANTELOUP 18

OURS

Cher

16

N76

CHENONCEAU

N143

Vierzon

D17

Indre

MONTRESOR
15

D760

D760

LOCHES
14

D31

D31

N143

Châteauroux

D60

13
LE GRAND-PRESSIGNY

Creuse

Claise

Gartempe

Creuse

SIGHTS AT A GLANCE

Amboise **17**
Azay-le-Rideau pp96–7 **5**
Candes-St-Martin **8**
Chenonceau pp106–9 **16**
Chinon pp98–100 **6**
Cinq-Mars-la-Pile **2**
La Devinière **7**
Le Grand-Pressigny **13**
Langeais **1**
Loches **14**
Luynes **3**
Montrésor **15**
Pagode de Chanteloup **18**
Richelieu **12**
Saché **10**
Tours pp112–17 **19**
Ussé **9**
Villaines-les-Rochers **11**
Villandry pp94–5 **4**

| 0 kilometres | 10 |
| 0 miles | 10 |

A field of poppies near Vouvray

Chapel of the Château de Langeais, with its curved, wood ceiling

Château de Langeais ❶

Road map D3. 🚉 📞 47 96 72 60. ⭕ *daily.* ● *25 Dec.* ♿

THE FEUDAL Château de Langeais, looming up in the centre of this small town, was built for King Louis XI between 1465 and 1490 by his treasurer, Jean Bourré. It stands on the site of an earlier fortress built by the fearsome Foulques Nerra *(see p50),* of which only the rectangular keep remains.

Langeais' forbidding outer walls, towers, drawbridge and heavily machicolated sentry walk contrast strongly with its elegant interior courtyard. The whole has remained virtually unaltered over the centuries. Unlike many of the châteaux in the region, Langeais is largely furnished in keeping with its period, offering a fascinating picture of aristo-cratic life in the late Middle Ages and Renaissance. Its collection of 15th- and 16th-century furniture, paintings and tapestries was amassed in the late 19th century by its last private owner, the Alsace banker and philanthropist, Jacques Siegfried.

Among the treasures in the castle is the wedding chest brought by the 14-year-old Anne of Brittany when she married the tiny, hunchbacked Charles VIII here in the early hours of 6 December 1491. A waxwork tableau re-creates this clandestine event – both were already betrothed to others – and includes a copy of Anne's cloth-of-gold wedding gown, lined with 160 sable skins.

From the castle's parapets visitors can view the small town below, which has a good Sunday morning food market selling the delicious local melons in season.

The Gallo-Roman tower near Cinq-Mars-la-Pile

Château de Cinq-Mars-la-Pile ❷

Road map D3. 🚉 📞 47 96 40 49. ⭕ *daily.* ● *1–15 Feb; end-Oct–early Nov & Mon, except public hols.* ♿

THE MOST FAMOUS inhabitant of the feudal castle of Cinq-Mars was Henri Ruzé d'Effiat, Marquis de Cinq-Mars, and the eponymous hero of a popular novel by the Touraine writer Alfred de Vigny. The handsome marquis, a favourite of King Louis XIII, rashly became involved in a plot against Louis' minister, Cardinal Richelieu, and was beheaded in 1642, aged 22. Richelieu ordered the castle at Cinq-Mars to be truncated – it is said that even the trees had their crowns chopped off. A pair of towers remain, each with three vaulted chambers, surrounded by an extremely wide moat. The château's fragrant, romantic gardens are adorned with topiary.

The *Pile* in the town's name refers to a strange Gallo-Roman brick tower, more

Towers of the Château de Cinq-Mars-la-Pile

Luynes' imposing château, dominating the village below

than 30 m (98 ft) high, on a ridge just east of the village. The south side of the tower, whose purpose and precise date are a mystery, was decorated with 12 multi-coloured brick panels, laid out in a geometric design, four of which are still intact today.

Luynes ❸

Road map D3. 🏠 4,800. 🚌
ℹ️ bibliothèque, rue Paul-Louis-Courier (47 55 77 14). 🛒 Sat.

BROODING over this pretty little village is a château, originally called Maillé after the noble owners who rebuilt it in the early 13th century. Not open to the public, it is still inhabited by descendants of the first Duc de Luynes, who bought it in 1619. With its stout towers, the château looks much as it did in the Middle Ages. The old town developed to the south of the château, and its 15th-century wooden market hall remains.

The remaining 44 arches of a **Gallo-Roman aqueduct** can be seen 1.5 km (1 mile) northeast of Luynes. Standing in isolation amid fields, they are a striking sight.

The wealthy Maillé family also owned a feudal castle on the site of the **Château de Champchevrier**, 10 km (6 miles) northwest of Luynes. The present Renaissance manor house, with various 18th-century additions, is set in a lush forest. Its elegant rooms are beautifully furnished, with particularly fine family portraits and Beauvais tapestries. A pack of hounds is kept at the château, and demonstrations of their skills are regularly staged.

♠ Château de Champchevrier
Cléré-les-Pins. 📞 47 24 93 93.
🕐 Apr–mid-Jun: Sun & public hols; mid-Jun–mid-Sep: daily; mid-end-Sep: Sun. ⬤ mornings. 🖼️ 🔗 grd flr only.

The Chambre Royale in the Château de Champchevrier

LIFE IN A MEDIEVAL CHÂTEAU

During times of peace, life in a medieval château took on a pleasant routine. To fill the long winter days, nobles played board games, such as chess and draughts, or cards. Ladies, when they were not playing music or embroidering, had dwarves to entertain them, while the court jester kept banquet guests amused by making fun of everyone, even the king. Mystery plays (dramas based on the life of Christ) were very popular and cycles of these plays often lasted for several weeks. Outdoor pursuits enjoyed during the summer included bowling, archery and ball games, but it was the tournaments, with jousting and sword-play, that provoked the most excitement. Hunting was also favoured by kings and nobles and much practised in the woods and forests of the Loire Valley.

The illumination for August from *Les Très Riches Heures du Duc de Berry*

Château de Villandry ●

THE CHÂTEAU DE VILLANDRY, dating from the late Renaissance, has an under-stated, almost Classical elegance. But it is most famous for its superb gardens, which have been restored since the estate was bought in 1906 by the Spanish Carvallo family. Working from 16th-century designs, skilful gardeners mixed flowers and vegetables in strictly geometric patterns. The result is a fasci-nating insight into a typical Renaissance garden. The garden is on three levels: a water garden at the top, fringed by ancient lime trees; a flower garden level with the château; and, below it, the world's largest ornamental kitchen garden.

Jeune Infante **by Pantoja de la Cruz**

★ **Garden of Love**
Flower designs here sym-bolize four types of love: tragic, adulterous, tender and passionate.

A collection of Spanish paintings is housed in the château.

Herb garden

Gardeners
Eight full-time gardeners raise and plant out some 60,000 vegetables and 45,000 bedding plants a year to fill both the kitchen garden and the ornamental flower garden.

STAR FEATURES

★ **Garden of Love**

★ **Ornamental Kitchen Garden**

★ **Ornamental Kitchen Garden**
The current state of the garden can be studied in the plan pinned up near the moat. The plant and vegetable names for each square are listed and the colours shown.

CULTURE DE PRINTEMPS 1995

RENAISSANCE KITCHEN AND HERB GARDENS

A 16th-century French treatise on diet reveals that the melons, artichokes, asparagus and cauliflower that fill Villandry's kitchen gardens today all also commonly appeared on Renaissance dinner tables. Herbs were widely used both for their medicinal and culinary applications. They formed the borders in the kitchen gardens of monasteries, such as that at Solesmes *(see p162)*, which were the first to feature geometric planting. Villandry has a *jardin des simples* (herb garden) on its middle level.

Knautia dipsacifolia, from a 16th-century manual on plants

VISITORS' CHECKLIST

Road map D3. 47 50 02 09. Savonnières, then taxi. **Château** mid-Feb–May & mid-Sep–mid-Nov: 9am–5:30pm; Jun–mid-Sep: 9am–6:30pm daily. **Gardens** Jun–mid-Sep: 8:30am–8pm; mid-Sep–May: 9am–6pm daily.

Shaped Pear Trees
In Villandry's gardens, nature is completely controlled. The pear trees are carefully pruned to form neat oval shapes.

The elegant stone balustrades above the kitchen garden have been restored.

The pool for irrigating the gardens is shaped like a gilt-framed mirror.

The flower gardens, including the garden of love, level with the south façade of the château

Decorative Cabbage
Ornamental Japanese cabbages were introduced by the wife of the present owner to provide year-round colour in the kitchen garden.

Château d'Azay-le-Rideau ❺

MEMORABLY DESCRIBED by Honoré de Balzac as a "faceted diamond set in the Indre", Azay-le-Rideau is one of the most popular châteaux in the Loire. Its graceful silhouette and richly decorated façades are mirrored in the peaceful waters of its lake, once a medieval moat. Azay was built from about 1518 by Gilles Berthelot, only to be confiscated by François I in 1527. The unknown architect, influenced by Italian design and innovative in his use of a straight staircase, took the defensive elements of an earlier, more warlike age and transformed them into charming ornamental features. Although only partly furnished, the château has some notable Renaissance pieces and a famous portrait of Henri IV's mistress, Gabrielle d'Estrées.

Kitchen
The kitchen, situated in the west wing, has rib vaulting and a huge open fireplace.

Gabrielle d'Estrées
Henri IV's haughty mistress features in the château's finest painting, done in the style of François Clouet.

STAR FEATURES

★ **Central Staircase**

★ **South Façade**

AZAY'S CREATORS

Treasurer to François I and mayor of Tours, Gilles Berthelot acquired Azay-le-Rideau when his wife, Philippe Lesbahy, inherited the ruins of a medieval castle. He immediately began constructing a new pleasure palace, with his wife's guidance. The emblems of François I and Claude de France were engraved in stone above various doors in the château in an attempt to flatter the sovereigns. But flattery did not save Berthelot's career – about to be accused of embezzlement, he was forced to flee Azay before the building was completed.

François I's salamander emblem

The elegant turrets adorn the château's façade rather than protect it, as the sturdy towers of medieval fortresses had done in the past.

Entrance Façade

The entrance façade is dominated by the galleried stairwell topped by a tall gable. Its decoration, full of shells, medallions and candelabras, was influenced by Italian Renaissance artists.

Entrance

VISITORS' CHECKLIST

Road map D3. ☎ 47 45 42 04.
🚌 🔲 15 Mar–Jun & Sep –Oct:
9:30am– 6pm, daily; Jul–Aug:
9am–7pm; Nov–14 Mar: 9:30am
–12:30pm, 2–5:30pm (last adm
30 mins before closing).
⬤ public hols. 🖼 🎫
📅 Les Imaginaires d'Azay-le-
Rideau (daily, mid-May–Jul:
10:30pm–12:30am; Aug–Sep:
10pm–12:30am).

Red Room

The 17th-century bed in this room is covered with an original red silk bedspread, embroidered in gold thread. The walls are hung with portraits of, among others, François I, Henri II and Henri III.

★ Central Staircase

Azay's most significant design feature is its central staircase, consisting of three straight flights with landings, rather than the spiral staircase that was usual for the period.

Ballroom with Flemish tapestries

★ South Façade

Symmetry is the underlying motif of the exterior design, with its matching turrets and its stripe of decoration imitating machicolations.

Street-by-Street: Chinon ❻

THE CHATEAU DE CHINON stands on a golden-coloured cliff above the River Vienne. Below it, Chinon's old crooked streets resonate with history. The travel-weary Joan of Arc *(see p137)* arrived in the town on 6 March 1429, dismounting by a well in the Grand Carroi. It was here that she began her transformation from peasant girl to the warrior-saint shown sitting astride a charger in a statue in the marketplace. In the nearby Maison des Etats Généraux, now the Musée du Vieux-Chinon et de la Batellerie, Richard the Lionheart lay in state in 1199. His father, Henry II, had died a few years earlier in the château, from which he had ruled England as well as much of the Loire Valley.

Tour de l'Horloge
This 14th-century clock-tower, which now houses a small exhibition on the life of Joan of Arc, is the entrance to the château.

0 metres   50

0 yards   50

★ **Château**
The long walls enclose three separate citadels, some entirely ruined, with magnificent views over the river. Here, in the Great Hall, Joan of Arc recognized the dauphin (see p52), a scene beautifully represented in a fine 17th-century tapestry.

RUE HAUTE ST-MAURICE

RUE DEBEA

QUAI CHARLES VII

Eglise St-Maurice
Henry II rebuilt this church with Angevin vaults, retaining the Romanesque lower part of what is now the steeple.

Ramparts
The château's ramparts are an impressive sight from the opposite bank of the River Vienne.

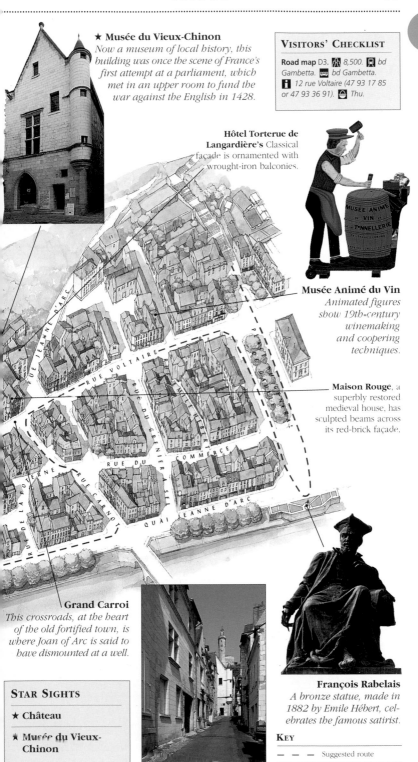

★ **Musée du Vieux-Chinon**
Now a museum of local history, this building was once the scene of France's first attempt at a parliament, which met in an upper room to fund the war against the English in 1428.

VISITORS' CHECKLIST

Road map D3. 👥 *8,500.* 🚉 *bd Gambetta.* 🚌 *bd Gambetta.*
🛈 *12 rue Voltaire (47 93 17 85 or 47 93 36 91).* 🛒 *Thu.*

Hôtel Torterue de Langardière's Classical façade is ornamented with wrought-iron balconies.

Musée Animé du Vin
Animated figures show 19th-century winemaking and coopering techniques.

Maison Rouge, a superbly restored medieval house, has sculpted beams across its red-brick façade.

Grand Carroi
This crossroads, at the heart of the old fortified town, is where Joan of Arc is said to have dismounted at a well.

STAR SIGHTS

★ **Château**

★ **Musée du Vieux-Chinon**

François Rabelais
A bronze statue, made in 1882 by Emile Hébert, cel-ebrates the famous satirist.

KEY

‒ ‒ ‒ Suggested route

Exploring Chinon

A WALK THROUGH the narrow streets to the east of the château shows how much Chinon has to offer. High above the place Jeanne d'Arc is the remarkable Chapelle de Ste-Radegonde, carved into the limestone cliff. Behind this 12th-century frescoed chapel are ancient hermit caves (now displaying traditional crafts) and dizzying steps to an underground well. Lower down the hill, the important Romanesque monastery of St-Mexme is Chinon's oldest building. Rue Jean-Jacques Rousseau, leading to the 15th-century church of St-Etienne, has medieval houses.

♣ Château de Chinon
▐ 47 93 13 45. ◯ daily.
● Dec–Jan: Wed. 🖼 ♿ courtyard & grd flr only.

The château, much of it now in ruins, was built largely by Henry II, count of Anjou, who became Plantagenet king of England in 1154. It consists of three castles – Fort St-Georges, Château du Milieu and Fort du Coudray – separated by moats. Passing the ruins of Henry's Fort St-Georges, visitors enter the middle castle via the Tour de l'Horloge, in which there is a display on the life of Joan of Arc. Further on, at the Logis Royaux, the west wall is all that remains of the Great Hall where, in the light of 50 smoking flares, Joan picked out the dauphin from among his courtiers. Wax figures re-create the scene in the Logis' restored rooms. The views of Chinon from these windows, and from the westerly ruins of the Fort du Coudray, are delightful.

Statue of Joan of Arc by Jules Roulleau

🏛 Musée du Vieux-Chinon et de la Batellerie
44 rue Haute St-Maurice. ▐ 47 93 18 12. ◯ Apr–mid-Oct: daily. 🖼

This intriguing museum of local history is housed in the 15th-century Maison des Etats Généraux, so called because the dauphin summoned representatives from his dwindling kingdom to a room here to help him gather sufficient funds to eject the English.

The earliest large Arab tapestry brought to France, the "Cope of St-Mexme", and a fine portrait of Rabelais by the French painter Eugène Delacroix (1798–1863) are among the treasures on display. Other attractions include a model collection of early Loire passenger steamboats (see p57), reassuringly called *Inexplosibles* as, unlike their predecessors, they were not in the habit of exploding on the river.

🏛 Musée Animé du Vin et de la Tonnellerie
12 rue Voltaire. ▐ 47 93 25 63. ◯ Apr–Sep: daily. 🖼

Here you can taste sharp, dry, strawberry-like Chinon red wine, while watching automated models demonstrate the various stages in wine- and barrel-making (both are important Chinon industries) using some of the museum's 19th-century implements. Around the corner in the Caves Painctes, the convivial Confrérie des Bons Entonneurs Rabelaisiens, a brotherhood of wine-growers, still hold regular banquets in a former troglodyte inn (not open to visitors). These caves are said to have inspired Rabelais' description of the Temple of the Divine Bottle.

The Tour de l'Horloge, leading to the middle castle

FRANÇOIS RABELAIS (1483–1553)

Priest, doctor, humanist and supreme *farceur* of French literature, François Rabelais is everywhere present in "Rabelaisie", as the area around La Devinière has become known. Rabelais enthusiasts will recognize in the old farmhouse the castle of Grandgousier, besieged by the hordes of King Picrochole, but saved by the arrival of giant Gargantua on his mare, who drowns most of them by creating a flood with her prodigious urination. Rabelais' thirst for knowledge imbued his *Gargantua* and *Pantagruel (see p22)* with a wealth of learning that sits surprisingly easily alongside a ribald *joie de vivre*.

The infant Gargantua

View of the Château d'Ussé from the bridge crossing the River Indre

Musée de la Devinière ➐

Road map D3. 🚊 *Chinon, then taxi.* ☎ *47 95 91 18.* ◯ *Feb–mid-Mar & Oct–Nov: Thu–Tue; mid-Mar–Sep: daily.* 🖼

THE RUMBUSTIOUS 16th-century writer François Rabelais was probably born in this pleasant, modest farmhouse, 2 km (1½ miles) southwest of Chinon. It now houses a small museum devoted to the man, his work, and that of his contemporaries. A dovecote, with its pigeonholes carved into the wall, and some troglodyte rooms add to the interest.

La Devinière farmhouse

Candes-St-Martin ➑

Road map C3. 🚶 *250.* 🚊 *Port Boulet, then taxi.* ℹ️ *Chinon (47 93 17 85, 47 93 36 91).* 🚲 *Wed.*

BEAUTIFULLY situated overlooking the shimmering waters where the Loire and Vienne rivers converge, picturesque Candes is famous as the place where St Martin died in 397. Stained glass in the 12th-century church depicts the saint's body being secretly rowed to Tours for burial. The porch of the church was fortified in the 15th century and is adorned with carved heads. Inside, the ceiling is a fine example of Angevin vaulting.

Château d'Ussé ➒

Road map D3. 🚊 *langeais, then taxi.* ☎ *47 95 54 05.* ◯ *late Feb–mid-Nov: daily.* 🖼 ♿ *park & grd flr only.*

WITH ITS COUNTLESS pointed turrets gleaming white against the sombre trees of the Forêt de Chinon, the Château d'Ussé is said to have inspired 17th-century French author Charles Perrault to write the fairy tale *The Sleeping Beauty*. The fortified château was begun in 1462 by Jean de Bueil on the foundations of a medieval castle. In 1485 it was sold to the Espinay family, chamberlains to both Louis XI and Charles VII, who softened the courtyard façades with Renaissance features that blend with its Gothic ancestry.

In the 17th century the north wing was demolished, opening up the main courtyard to views of the River Indre and the Loire Valley. Formal gardens were planted in terraces to the river and an orangery was added, completing the transformation from fortress to aristocratic country house *(see p17)*.

The château interior is also in a variety of styles. Some of the well-furnished rooms are populated with waxwork figures, including a tableau of *The Sleeping Beauty*.

On the edge of the forest is a lovely late-Gothic chapel, with some Renaissance decoration. Inside is a terracotta Virgin sculpted by Luca della Robbia (1400–82).

The late-Gothic exterior of Ussé's chapel

Mobile by Alexander Calder (1898–1976) in Saché

Saché ❿

Road map D3. 🏠 880. 🚆 Azay-le-Rideau, then taxi. 🚌 Azay-le-Rideau (47 45 44 40).

THE PRETTY VILLAGE of Saché is notable for having been second home to both a writer and an artist of world fame: the 19th-century novelist Honoré de Balzac and the 20th-century American sculptor Alexander Calder, one of whose mobiles adorns the main square.

Admirers of the work of Balzac make pilgrimages to the **Château de Saché**. The plain but comfortable manor house, built in the 16th and 18th centuries, was a quiet place to work and a source of inspiration for many of the writer's best-known novels. The house has been well restored – one of the reception rooms has even been redecorated with a copy of the

bright green wallpaper with a Pompeiian frieze that was there in Balzac's day.

It is full of busts, sketches and memorabilia of the great man, including the coffee pot that kept him going during his long stints of writing. The top floor displays manuscripts and letters, as well as portraits of the women in Balzac's life: his pretty, but casual, mother; his first love, Madame de Berny; and his loyal friend, Madame Hanska, whom he finally married shortly before his death in 1850.

🏠 Château de Saché
🕿 47 26 86 50. ⭘ Feb–Nov: daily. 🗺 ♿ park only.

Villaines-les-Rochers ⓫

Road map D3. 🏠 930. 🚆 Azay-le-Rideau, then taxi. 🚌 Azay-le-Rideau (47 45 44 40).

SINCE THE Middle Ages, willows from the local river valleys have been made into baskets in this peaceful town. Production has been on a more substantial scale since the mid-19th century, when the local priest organized the craftsmen into one of France's first cooperatives. Everything is still hand made by the many wickerworkers *(vanniers)* in the town. This explains the relatively high prices of the attractive furniture and baskets on sale in the **cooperative**'s shop. Craftsmen and women can be watched at work in

the adjoining studio. In the summer, you can also visit a small museum with displays on the subject of basket-making, the **Musée de l'Osier et de la Vannerie**.

🗝 Coopérative de Vannerie de Villaines
1 rue de la Cheneillère. 🕿 47 45 43 03. ⭘ Apr–Sep: daily; Oct–Mar: Mon–Sat, Sun: pm only. ● 1 Jan, 25 Dec.
🏛 Musée de l'Osier et de la Vannerie
22 rue des Caves-Fortes. 🕿 47 45 23 19. ⭘ May–mid-Sep: Tue–Sun, pm only. 🗺

A wickerworker in Villaines

Richelieu ⓬

Road map D4. 🏠 2,300. 🚆
🚌 6 Grande Rue (47 58 13 62).
🛒 Mon, Fri.

IT WOULD BE DIFFICULT to find a better example of 17th-century urban planning than the town of Richelieu, on the border between Touraine and Poitou. Its rigid design was the brainchild of Armand Jean du Plessis who, as Cardinal Richelieu and chief minister, was the most powerful man in the kingdom, not excepting his monarch, Louis XIII.

The Cardinal was determined to build a huge palace near his modest family estate of Richelieu. In 1625 he commissioned the architect Jacques Lemercier to draw up the plans and, in 1631, he received permission from the king to proceed, not only with the palace, but also with the creation of a new walled town. Lemercier had already

The Château de Saché, often visited by Honoré de Balzac

designed the Palais Royal and the Church of the Sorbonne in Paris, and would later be appointed chief royal architect. His brothers, Pierre and Nicolas, were put in charge of the building work, which kept nearly 2,000 labourers busy for more than a decade.

The resulting town is a huge rectangle, surrounded by walls and moats (mostly taken up with gardens today) and entered through three monumental gates. The Grande Rue, running from north to south through the centre of the town and linking two large squares, is lined with identical Classical mansions. In the south square, place du Marché, the buildings include the Classical **Eglise Notre-Dame**, the market building with its superb timber framework, and the former law courts, in which the **Hôtel de Ville** (town hall) and a small **history museum** are now housed. In the north square, the place des Religieuses, stands a convent and the Royal Academy, founded by Richelieu in 1640.

An old-fashioned steam train runs between the town and Chinon during the summer months.

Richelieu clearly intended that his palace should be incomparably luxurious. It was filled with priceless furniture and works of art, including paintings by

Richelieu's timber-framed market hall

Caravaggio and Andrea Mantegna. Michelangelo's *Dying Slaves*, statues that were originally designed for the tomb of Pope Julius II (now housed in the Louvre in Paris), adorned one of the courtyard façades.

Extremely fearful of competition, Richelieu ordered many of the châteaux in the area to be razed. While his town survived the ravages of the French Revolution intact, the palace, ironically, was confiscated, damaged and then dismantled. Today, only a few garden buildings remain intact, scattered around the 475-ha (1,174-acre) **Domaine du Parc de Richelieu**. In the Dôme, the only part of the château proper that is still standing, there is an exhibition on the architectural

Cardinal Richelieu (1585–1642)

history of what was once a magnificent building.

🏛 **Musée de l'Hôtel de Ville**
place du Marché. 【 47 58 10 13.
⭘ Sep–May: Mon, Wed–Fri; Jun–Aug: Wed–Mon. ⬤ public hols. 🖼

🍂 **Domaine du Parc de Richelieu**
5 pl du Cardinal. 【 47 58 10 09.
Dôme, cellars and orangerie
⭘ Apr–mid-Jun & mid-Sep–Oct: Sun & public hols; mid-Jun–mid-Sep: daily.
🖼 **Gardens** ⭘ Wed–Mon. ♿

ENVIRONS: Champigny-sur-Veude, 6 km (4 miles) to the north of Richelieu, was one of the châteaux demolished on Cardinal Richelieu's orders. All that can now be seen of this early 16th-century castle is the impressive Renaissance church of **Ste-Chapelle**, with its superb stained glass.

⛪ **Ste-Chapelle**
Champigny-sur-Veude. 【 47 95 73 48. ⭘ Apr–Oct: daily. 🖼

BALZAC AT SACHÉ

Honoré de Balzac's (1799–1850) regular stays at the Château de Saché between 1829 and 1837 coincided with the most productive period in his highly industrious career as a writer. Here, hidden well away from his creditors, he would work at least 12 hours a day. Despite starting in the early hours of the morning, he remained able to entertain his hosts, Monsieur and Madame de Margonne, and their guests in the evenings by reading aloud the latest chunk of text from his novels, acting out all the characters as he did so.

Two of Balzac's major novels, *Le Père Goriot (Father Goriot)* and *Le Lys dans la Vallée (The Lily of the Valley)*, were written at Saché. The latter is set in the Indre valley, which can be seen from the house and does indeed have something of that "intangibly mysterious quality" to which Balzac refers with typical eloquence.

Balzac's bedroom at Saché

Le Grand-Pressigny ⓭

Road map D4. 🏘 *1,100*.
🚉 *Châtellerault, then taxi.* 🚌
ℹ *La Mairie, pl des Halles (47 94 90 37)* 🗓 *Thu.*

PERCHED HIGH above the hilly streets of the town, the **Château du Grand-Pressigny** has lovely views over the peaceful Claise and Aigronne valleys.

The château itself is part medieval ruins (a section of the keep collapsed as recently as 1988), part 15th-century castle and part Renaissance residence. The rectangular, 12th-century ruined keep contrasts dramatically with the elegant 16th-century Italianate wing. The large gardens can also be visited.

Important prehistoric finds have been made in the area, and various excavations have revealed that the site was a key centre for the large-scale production of flint implements, such as blades, which were then exported as far afield as Switzerland and even Great Britain.

The château houses the **Musée de la Préhistoire**, whose collections, which were reorganized in 1992, are clearly displayed. Examples of tools and other objects from all the prehistoric eras are exhibited, along with rock flints, large blocks of obsidian and multi-coloured jasper. Particularly impressive are the yellowish flint blocks known familiarly as "pounds of butter". Interesting miniature reconstructions of villages show how prehistoric peoples lived, and a separate wing houses a collection of fossils, some of which date back 60 million years.

On summer afternoons you can visit the **Archéolab**, 6 km (4 miles) northwest at Abilly-sur-Claise, where a transparent dome covers a site inhabited by stone cutters between 2800 and 2400 BC.

⚜ **Château du Grand-Pressigny**
📞 *47 94 90 20* 🕐 *Feb–Nov: daily.*
🚫 ♿ *park and grd flr only.*
🏛 **Archéolab**
Abilly-sur-Claise. 📞 *47 59 80 82, 47 91 03 74* 🕐 *mid-Jun–mid-Sep: daily, pm only.* 🚫 ♿

Neolithic tool from the Musée de la Préhistoire

Loches ⓮

Road map D3. 🏘 *7,100.* 🚉 🚌
ℹ *pl de Wermelskirchen (47 59 07 98).* 🗓 *Wed, Sat.*

ITS MEDIEVAL STREETS lined with picturesque houses, the peaceful town of Loches lies beside the River Indre on the edge of the Forêt de Loches. Thanks to its strategic location, it became an important citadel in the Middle

Agnès Sorel as the Virgin, painted by Jehan Fouquet

Ages, with an 11th-century keep begun by Foulques Nerra (*see p50*). The **château** remained in the hands of the counts of Anjou until 1194, when John Lackland gave it to King Philippe Augustus. John's brother, Richard the Lionheart, recaptured Loches in a surprise attack in 1195. It took Philippe Augustus nearly ten years to retake the castle by force, and eventually it became a French royal residence. It was in the 15th-century **Logis Royal** (royal apartments) that Joan of Arc, fresh from her triumph in Orléans, persuaded the vacillating dauphin to travel to Rheims and be crowned king of France as Charles VII. This key event is commemorated in the tapestry-hung Salle Jeanne d'Arc.

Another woman of influence in Charles VII's life was his mistress, Agnès Sorel, whose Gothic marble tomb is in the château. The famous beauty is shown with lambs resting at her feet. In an adjacent room is the tiny, late Gothic private chapel of twice-queen Anne of Brittany, whose ermine tail emblem recurs in the decoration. Also on show in the château are a fine *Crucifixion* triptych by Tours painter Jehan Fouquet (c.1420–80) or one of his pupils, and a copy of his colourful *Virgin with Child*, which was modelled on Agnès Sorel.

The massive keep with its surrounding towers is famous for its torture chambers. Prisoners are said to have been locked for years into small wood-and-iron cages.

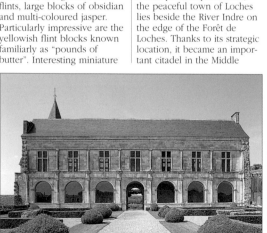

Renaissance façade of the Gallery, Château de Grand-Pressigny

Lodovico Sforza, the duke of Milan, died as a prisoner in the **Tour Martelet**, where the tempera wall paintings he made can still be seen.

Beside the château is the Collégiale St-Ours, a strange-looking church with four pyramid-like spires and a fine Romanesque portal. Near the Porte Royale lies the **Musée Lansyer**, which was the birthplace of the 19th-century painter Emmanuel Lansyer. Some of the artist's canvases are on display, along with his collection of Japanese armour and prints. It also houses a folklore museum, whose ex-hibits include a number of typical 19th-century interiors.

♣ Château de Loches
[**Logis Royal** 47 59 01 32; **Donjon** 47 59 07 86. ○ Feb–Nov: daily. 🗓 🎫 Spectacle d'été (Jul–Aug, Fri & Sat).

� Musée Lansyer
1 rue Lansyer. [47 59 05 45. ○ mid-Jan–mar & Nov–mid-Dec: Thu–Tue; Apr–Oct: daily. 🗓 🎫

Montrésor ⑮

Road map E3. 🗓 360. 🚉 Loches, then taxi. 🚌 Grande Rue (47 92 71 04). 🔄 Sat.

Tᴴᴱ ᴛᴜʀʀᴇᴛᴇᴅ **Château de Montrésor**, largely built in the 15th and 16th centuries, stands on the site of medieval fortifications built by Count Foulques Nerra (see p50). It was bought in the mid-19th century by Count Branicki, an émigré Polish financier closely linked to the future Napoleon III. Still owned by Branicki's descendants, the château's Second Empire decor remains virtually unaltered.

As well as a fine collection of early Italian paintings and some elegant portraits, there are many gold and silver pieces. The rooms, with their mounted stags' and wolves' heads and dark panelling, retain a somewhat Central European feel. The château terrace and pleasantly informal gardens offer fine views of the river.

An estate building, which used to house the château's wine press, has been converted into the Maison du Pays, an information centre and showcase for the Indrois Valley and its products.

The village's small Gothic and Renaissance church was built by Imbert de Bastarnay, lord of Montrésor, adviser to François I and grandfather of Diane de Poitiers (see p108). On the beautiful marble Bastarnay tomb lie gisants' (effigies) of the lord, his lady and their son, guarded by angels and with their feet resting on greyhounds. The tomb, believed to be the work of the Renaissance sculptor Jean Goujon (c.1510 – 68), is decorated with statues of the apostles. There are also some wonderful Flemish and Italian paintings in the church, and a 17th-century Annunciation by Philippe de Champaigne (1602–74), the Baroque painter who worked on the Luxembourg palace in Paris with Nicolas Poussin.

In a lovely forest setting, 4 km (2½ miles) west of the village of Montrésor, are the ruins of the **Chartreuse du Liget**, a Carthusian monastery founded by the Plantagenet

Farm buildings and poppy fields near the village of Montrésor

king Henry II of England in expiation for the murder of Archbishop Thomas à Becket. The nearby Chapel of **St-Jean-du-Liget** is decorated with 12th-century frescoes.

♣ Château de Montrésor
[47 92 60 04. ○ Apr–Oct: daily. 🗓 🦽 park and grd flr only.
⛪ Chartreuse du Ligct & Chapelle St-Jean-du-Liget
[47 92 60 02. ○ daily. 🗓 🦽

Château de Montrésor, built on medieval fortifications

Château de Chenonceau ⑯

CHENONCEAU, STRETCHING ROMANTICALLY across the River Cher, is considered by many the loveliest of the Loire châteaux. Surrounded by elegant formal gardens and wooded grounds, this pure Renaissance building was transformed over the centuries from a modest manor and water mill into a palace designed solely for pleasure. Visitors are allowed to wander freely through the beautifully furnished rooms. A small waxworks museum illustrates the château's history, and the site also includes a restaurant in the old stables and a miniature train ride down the lovely tree-lined drive. Wines from Chenonceau's own vineyards are on sale.

★ **Cabinet Vert**
The walls of Catherine de Médicis' study were originally covered with green velvet.

Chapelle
The chapel has a vaulted ceiling and pilasters sculpted with acanthus leaves and cockle shells. The stained glass, ruined by a bomb in 1944, was replaced in 1953.

Louise de Lorraine's room
was painted black and decorated with monograms, tears and knots in white after the death of her husband.

The Tour des Marques
survives from the 15th-century castle of the Marques family.

STAR FEATURES

★ Cabinet Vert

★ Grande Galerie

★ Formal Gardens

The Three Graces
Painted by Charles-André Van Loo (1705–65), The Three Graces *depicts the pretty Mailly-Nesle sisters, all royal mistresses.*

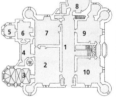

Tapestries

As was the practice in the 16th century, Chenonceau is hung with Flemish tapestries that both warm and decorate its well-furnished rooms.

VISITORS' CHECKLIST

Road map D3. ☎ *47 23 90 07.*
▣ *Chenonceaux-Chisseaux.*
◯ *Jan & mid-Nov–Dec: 9am–4:30pm daily; 1–15 Feb & 1–15 Nov: 9am–5pm; 16–28 Feb & 16–31 Oct: 9am–5:30pm; 1–15 Mar & 1–15 Oct: 9am–6pm; mid-Mar–mid-Sep: 9am–7pm; 16–30 Sep: 9am–6:30pm.* 🚫 ♿ *park and grd flr only.* 🅿 🍴 ♿ *Au Temps des Dames de Chenonceau (Jul–Aug. 10:15pm daily).*

CHÂTEAU GUIDE

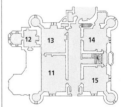

Ground floor

First floor

1 Vestibule
2 Salle des Gardes
3 Chapelle
4 Terrasse
5 Librairie de Catherine de' Médicis
6 Cabinet Vert
7 Chambre de Diane de Poitiers
8 Grande Galerie
9 Chambre de François I
10 Salon Louis XIV
11 Chambre des Cinq Reines
12 Cabinet des Estampes
13 Chambre de Catherine de Médicis
14 Chambre de Vendôme
15 Chambre de Gabrielle d'Estrées

★ **Grande Galerie**
Catherine de Médicis added this elegant gallery to the bridge designed by Philibert de l'Orme in 1556–9 for Diane de Poitiers.

Chenonceau's Florentine-style gallery, which stretches across the River Cher for 60 m (197 ft)

The Creation of Chenonceau

CHENONCEAU REFLECTS the combined influence of five women, who brought a feminine touch to this graceful building. First came Catherine Briçonnet, wife of the royal chamberlain, who supervised the construction of the château. Later, Diane de Poitiers, Henri II's mistress, created a formal garden and built a bridge over the Cher. After Henri's death, his widow, Catherine de Médicis, reclaimed the château and topped the bridge with a gallery. Chenonceau survived the 1789 Revolution – because of local respect for Louise Dupin, wife of a tax collector – to be restored by Madame Pelouze in the 19th century.

Sphinxes
Inscrutable stone sphinxes guarding the entrance to the gardens came from the Château de Chanteloup, which was destroyed in the 19th century (see p111).

Diane de Poitiers
Henri II's mistress, here painted by François Clouet, created a large, formal garden, as well as the bridge across the Cher.

★ **Formal Gardens**
The current designs of the formal gardens of Diane de Poitiers and Catherine de Médicis date from the 19th century.

TIMELINE

1512 Thomas Bohier acquires the medieval Chenonceau. His wife, Catherine Briçonnet, rebuilds it

1559 On Henri's death, Catherine forces Diane to leave

Henri II

1913 The château is bought by the Menier family, the *chocolatiers* who still own it today

1789 Chenonceau is spared in the French Revolution, thanks to Louise Dupin

1500	1600	1700	1800	1900

1575 Louise de Lorraine (1554–1601) marries Henri III, Catherine's son

1547 Henri II gives Chenonceau to Diane de Poitiers, his lifelong mistress

1533 Marriage of Catherine de Médicis (1519–89) to Henri II (1519–59). Chenonceau becomes a Loire royal palace

1730–99 Louise Dupin creates a salon for intellectuals at Chenonceau

1863 Madame Pelouze restores the château to its original state

1944 Chenonceau chapel is damaged in a bombing raid

Louise Dupin

A well-read beauty with huge brown eyes, Louise Dupin entertained all the literary lions of her day, including Montesquieu and Voltaire. One guest, Jean-Jacques Rousseau, stayed on to tutor her children and famously praised Chenonceau's cuisine, claiming he had become "as plump as a monk".

Catherine de Médicis

After ousting Diane de Poitiers, Catherine de Médicis made her own mark on Chenonceau's design. She built the Grande Galerie over the Cher and added a formal garden to rival Diane's.

Catherine de Médicis' emblem

Madame Pelouze bought Chenonceau in 1863 and restored it to Catherine Briçonnet's original design. Fortunately, she stopped short of taking down the Grande Galerie.

Court Festivities

Catherine de Médicis staged lavish balls and festivities at Chenonceau, some featuring plaster triumphal arches and statues designed by Francesco Primaticcio, others with living "nymphs" leaping out of the bushes chased by "satyrs".

Louise de Lorraine

Catherine de Médicis left Chenonceau to her daughter-in-law, Louise de Lorraine. Louise had her room redecorated in black upon the death of her husband, Henri III.

Catherine Briçonnet supervised the creation of an innovative château design, with rooms leading off a central vestibule on each floor.

The Château d'Amboise, high above the town and the River Loire

Amboise ⑰

Road map D3. 👥 *11,000.* 🚉
ℹ *quai du Général de Gaulle
(47 57 09 28).* 🚢 *Fri, Sun.*

THE BUSTLING little town of
Amboise is much visited
for its imposing royal château,
but this is not the town's only
attraction for visitors.

♣ Château d'Amboise
🎧 *47 57 00 98.* 🕐 *daily.* ⬤ *1 Jan,
25 Dec.* 📷 ♿ 🎭 *A la Cour du Roy
François (Jun–Aug, Wed & Sat).*
The château belongs to the
Comte de Paris, a direct
descendant of France's last
royal line. Much of it has been
destroyed, but it is still possible
to see the
splendour that
prevailed when
first Charles VIII and
then François I
brought the Italian
love of luxury
and elegance to
the French court.
    Amboise has
also played a
tragic part in
history. In 1560 a Protestant
plot to gain religious con-
cessions from the young King
François II was un-
covered, and 1,200
conspirators were
slaughtered, their
bodies strung up
from the castle and
town walls, from
trees, and even from
the balcony on the
Logis du Roi.
    This horrifying
episode was to spell
the end of Amboise's
glory, and over the
years that followed,
the château was
gradually disman-
tled. The enchanting,
late-Gothic **Chapelle
St-Hubert**, where
Leonardo da Vinci is
said to be buried,
has fortunately sur-
vived, perched on
the ramparts of the
château. Carvings on
the exterior lintel of

**Sculpted detail from the
Logis du Roi**

the chapel depict St Hubert
and St Christopher. Some of
the guard rooms and state
rooms in the part-Gothic, part-
Renaissance **Logis du Roi** are
open to visitors, along with
fascinating 19th-century
apartments once
occupied by King
Louis-Philippe.
Flanking the Logis
du Roi is the **Tour
des Minimes**, the
original entrance to
the château, with
its impressive spiral inner
ramp, up which horsemen
could ride.

🏛 Musée de la Poste
6 rue Joyeuse. 🎧 *47 57 00 11.*
🕐 *Feb–Dec: Tue–Sun.* 📷
A 16th-century mansion
houses the interesting postal
museum. The collection
concentrates mainly on the
mailcoach period and gives
an insight into the often
perilous journeys made by
the coachmen.

♣ Château du Clos-Lucé
2 rue du Clos-Lucé. 🎧 *47 57 62 88.*
🕐 *Feb–Dec: daily.* 📷 ♿
This graceful Renaissance
manor house in pinkish brick
and stone, on the outskirts of
Amboise, was the last home
of Leonardo da Vinci. In 1516
François I enticed Leonardo
to the royal court at Amboise
and the following year settled
him at Le Clos-Lucé (then called Cloux), where the genius
lived until his death in 1519.

The late-Gothic Chapelle St-Hubert, with its
highly ornate roof and spire

While staying at Le Clos-Lucé, Leonardo is widely believed to have conceived the plans for the Château de Chambord *(see pp132–5)*. He is known to have made various drawings of double staircases, similar to the one that was built there. His bedroom, reception room, study, kitchen and a small chapel built for Anne of Brittany by Charles VIII, are open to visitors. There are models made from Leonardo's technical drawings in the basement – among them a helicopter and a tank.

✿ Aquarium de Touraine
Lussault-sur-Loire. 🚌 ☎ 47 23 44 44. ◯ *daily.* 🔊 ♿
The Aquarium de Touraine at Lussault-sur-Loire, 6 km (4 miles) to the west of Amboise, has more than 10,000 freshwater fish on display in its 35 tanks. It is the largest such collection in Europe.

Leonardo da Vinci's bedroom at the Château du Clos-Lucé

Pagode de Chanteloup ⑱

Forêt d'Amboise. ☎ 47 57 20 97. ◯ *mid-Feb–mid-Nov: daily.* 🔊 ♿

IN THE FOREST of Amboise, southwest of Amboise itself, stands this curious Chinese-style pagoda, more than 44 m (140 ft) high and built in seven storeys, linked by steep spiral staircases. Each layer is smaller than the preceding one and contains an airy, octagonal room with a domed ceiling. Seven avenues lead into the forest from the

---

LEONARDO DA VINCI (1452–1519)

François I, who developed a love of Italian Renaissance art during his military campaigns there, persuaded Leonardo to join his court at Amboise, offering him an annual allowance and free use of the manor house at Clos-Lucé. The great Italian painter arrived in Amboise in 1516 with some precious items in his luggage – three major paintings, in leather bags tied to a mule. One of them was the *Mona Lisa*, which François was to buy and place in the royal collection (hence its presence today in the Louvre in Paris).

Engraving of Leonardo da Vinci

Leonardo spent the last three years of his life at Le Clos-Lucé as the *Premier Peintre, Architecte et Mécanicien du Roi* (first painter, architect and engineer to the king), mainly writing and drawing. As he was left-handed, the paralysis that affected his right hand was not a major handicap. Fascinated by hydrology, he produced plans to link the royal residences of the Loire Valley via waterways and even proposed rerouting the river. He also organized a series of elaborate court festivities, planning them down to the last detail with the same meticulous care he lavished on his scientific designs.

A model of Leonardo's prototype for a "car"

---

pagoda, which is reflected in a large, semicircular lake.

This is all that is left of a splendid château built by Louis XV's minister, the Duc de Choiseul (1719–85). In the 1770s, Choiseul fell out with the king's mistress, Madame du Barry – he had been a protégé of her predecessor Madame de Pompadour – and was exiled from Versailles. He retreated to the château he had bought at Chanteloup in 1761 and rebuilt it. He occupied his time entertaining on a large scale and dabbling in farming. After his death, the château was abandoned and then pulled down in 1823.

An exhibition in the pavilion explains the history of the once magnificent château and, for those visitors brave enough to make the climb, there are impressive views of the Loire Valley from the top of the tower.

The Pagode de Chanteloup, in the heart of the forest of Amboise

Street-by-Street: Tours ⑲

THE MEDIEVAL OLD TOWN, Le Vieux Tours, is full of narrow streets lined with beautiful half-timbered houses. Now sensitively restored, it is a lively area crammed with little cafés, bars and restaurants that attract locals as well as tourists. There are also numerous chic fashion boutiques and small shops devoted particularly to craft work and to stylish kitchen equipment. At its heart is the attractive place Plumereau, which in fine weather is filled with parasol-shaded café tables.

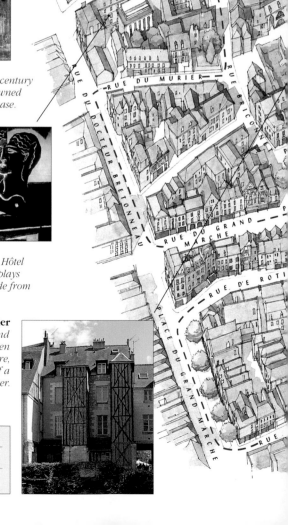

0 metres   50

0 yards   50

★ Maison de Tristan
The brick-and-stone 15th-century Maison de Tristan is renowned for its vaulted spiral staircase.

Musée du Gemmail
Inside the creeper-covered Hôtel Raimbault, a museum displays jewel-like works of art made from stained glass.

Place Pierre-le-Puellier
A Gallo-Roman and medieval cemetery has been excavated in this square, which once formed part of a Renaissance cloister.

STAR SIGHTS

★ Place Plumereau

★ Maison de Tristan

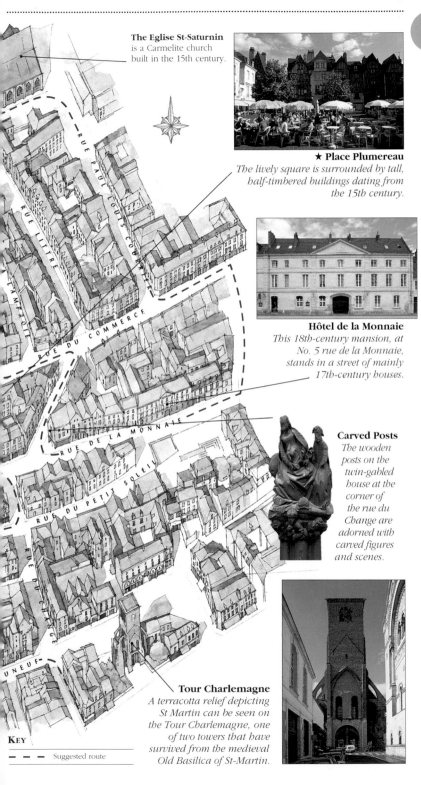

The Eglise St-Saturnin
is a Carmelite church
built in the 15th century.

★ **Place Plumereau**
*The lively square is surrounded by tall,
half-timbered buildings dating from
the 15th century.*

RUE PAUL LOUIS COURIER

RUE LITTRE

RUE DU COMMERCE

A LAMPROIE

Hôtel de la Monnaie
*This 18th-century mansion, at
No. 5 rue de la Monnaie,
stands in a street of mainly
17th-century houses.*

RUE DE LA MONNAIE

RUE DU PETIT SOLEIL

RUE DU CHANGE

Carved Posts
*The wooden
posts on the
twin-gabled
house at the
corner of
the rue du
Change are
adorned with
carved figures
and scenes.*

UNEUF

Tour Charlemagne
*A terracotta relief depicting
St Martin can be seen on
the Tour Charlemagne, one
of two towers that have
survived from the medieval
Old Basilica of St-Martin.*

KEY

- - - Suggested route

Exploring Tours

THE PLEASANT CATHEDRAL CITY of Tours, popular with foreign students eager to learn the country's purest French, is a perfect base for exploring Touraine's impressive châteaux. But Tours itself, its medieval heart imaginatively restored, repays exploration, too. Once a major Gallo-Roman centre and later filled with pilgrims flocking to St Martin's tomb, it has remained prosperous over the centuries. Yet despite the recent rapid expansion beyond the Loire and Cher rivers, it has kept its unhurried, provincial charm.

Tours' Pont Wilson, recently rebuilt, spanning the Loire

Tours Town Centre

The area of the town close to the magnificent **Cathédrale St-Gatien** *(see pp116–17)* was part of the original Roman settlement. In the 3rd century AD, it was enclosed by a wall, the shape of which can still be seen in the rue des Ursulines, circling the cathedral and the Musée des Beaux Arts. The rue du Général-Meunier, a curving cobbled street of elegant houses once occupied by the clergy, follows the line of a Roman amphitheatre.

On the west side of Tours, a religious community grew up around the sepulchre of St Martin *(see p49)*. The saint's tomb now lies in the crypt of the late 19th-century New Basilica, which was built on the site of the considerably larger, medieval Old Basilica. Two stone towers – the **Tour Charlemagne** and the **Tour de l'Horloge** – on either side of the rue des Halles, survive from the earlier building. Not far from the towers, the **place Plumereau**, with its charming medieval houses and tempting cafés, attracts locals, foreign students and tourists in large numbers.

The half-timbered house at No. 39 rue Colbert bears a wrought-iron sign dedicated to the *Pucelle Armée* (the armed maid), recalling that Joan of Arc *(see p137)* bought her suit of armour from a workshop here, before setting out to liberate Orléans in 1429. Nearby is the **place Foire-le-Roi**, a square where, thanks to a permit granted by the king in 1545, regular fairs were once held. The main merchandise was the silk that had been a key factor in the town's economy since the middle of the previous century. Of the smart gabled houses that line the square, the finest is the Renaissance Hôtel Babou de la Bourdaisière, named after the finance minister to François I, who lived there. Slightly to the west, the 13th-century **Eglise St-Julien** stands on the site of an abbey founded in the 6th century.

The central bridge crossing the Loire, the **Pont Wilson**, is known locally as the *pont de pierre* (stone bridge). It is an exact replica of the town's original 18th-century bridge, which collapsed suddenly in 1978, making national headlines. It was rebuilt following the original design after a referendum of local residents backed the idea.

🏛 Musée des Beaux-Arts

18 pl François-Sicard. 🄲 *47 05 68 73.* ⭕ *Wed–Mon.* ⬤ *1 Jan, 14 Jul, 1 & 11 Nov, 25 Dec.* 🔲

The Museum of Fine Arts, conveniently situated next to the Cathédrale St-Gatien, is shaded by a cedar of Lebanon nearly two centuries old and fronted by attractive formal gardens. Once the Archbishop's Palace, the building dates mainly from the 17th and 18th centuries.

Its collections of paintings range from the Middle Ages to contemporary artists and include two celebrated altarpiece panels by Andrea Mantegna, *The Resurrection* and *Christ in the Olive Grove*, which were painted between 1456 and 1460 for the church of San Zeno in Verona.

To the right of the entrance courtyard is an outbuilding housing a huge stuffed circus elephant that died in Tours in the early 20th century.

Christ in the Olive Grove (1456–1460) by Andrea Mantegna

The Hôtel Goüin's elaborate Renaissance façade

🏛 Hôtel Goüin & Musée Archéologique

25 rue du Commerce. 📞 47 66 22 32.
🕐 Feb–mid-Mar & Oct–Nov:
Sat–Thu; mid-Mar–Sep: daily. 🎫
This fine example of early Renaissance architecture, its highly ornamented façade beautifully re-created following World War II destruction, now houses the city's archaeological museum. The collection, which commences with the prehistoric era and continues to the 18th century, includes an interesting group of Celtic coins from the Chartres area,

whose different values are denoted not by numerals but by pictures of animals. The most famous exhibit in the museum, however, is a set of scientific instruments collected in 1743 by the owner of Chenonceau château.

🏛 Musée des Vins de Touraine

16 rue Nationale. 📞 47 61 07 93
🕐 Wed–Mon: daily. 🔴 1 Jan,
14 Jul, 1 & 11 Nov, 25 Dec. 🎫
The vaulted cellars and parts of the cloisters of the 13th-century **Eglise St-Julien** now form a wine museum, with a huge Renaissance wine press, displays on early viticultural

history and collections of winemaking tools dating from the Middle Ages to the 19th century. In an adjacent courtyard there is an original Gallo-Roman wine press, which was discovered near Azay-le-Rideau in 1946.

Exhibits in the Musée des Vins de Touraine

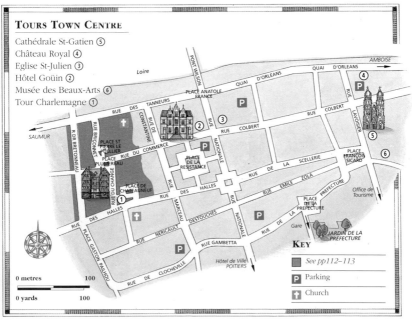

TOURS TOWN CENTRE

Cathédrale St-Gatien ⑤
Château Royal ④
Eglise St-Julien ③
Hôtel Goüin ②
Musée des Beaux-Arts ⑥
Tour Charlemagne ①

KEY

🟦 See pp112–113
🅿 Parking
✝ Church

0 metres 100
0 yards 100

Tours: Cathédrale St-Gatien

T HE FOUNDATION STONE of Tours' cathedral, named after St Gatien, a 3rd-century bishop, was laid in the early 13th century. Because building work continued until the mid-16th century, the cathedral provides an illustration of how the Gothic style developed over the centuries. The Early Gothic chancel was the first area to be completed, while the nave and transept represent the Middle or High Gothic period and the highly decorated west façade is Flamboyant (or Late) Gothic.

Cloître de la Psalette
The cloisters, which lead off the north aisle, are made up of three galleries dating from the mid-15th and early 16th centuries.

★ **West Façade**
The richly carved Flamboyant west façade has three portals surmounted by a fine rose window.

Inside the North Tower is an elegant 16th-century spiral staircase.

Colombe tomb

The narrow nave has a vaulted ceiling, dating from the late 15th century.

★ **Colombe Tomb** *(1499)*
The marble tomb of Charles VIII's and Anne of Brittany's infant sons features lifelike effigies by Michel Colombe or one of his pupils.

Fresco
This 14th-century fresco, discovered in 1993, shows St Martin giving half his cloak to a beggar.

Colombe Statue
This statue of Tours' famous sculptor, Michel Colombe, stands in a square near the cathedral.

In the chancel, the stained-glass windows, depicting Christ's Passion and the legends of St Martin and other saints, date from around 1265.

★ **Stained-Glass Windows**
The stained glass is notable for its rich, strong colours and for the paler stained panels, or grisailles, *which let in more light than ordinary stained glass.*

STAR FEATURES

★ **Colombe Tomb**

★ **Stained-Glass Windows**

★ **West Façade**

♣ **Château Royal de Tours**
25 quai d'Orléans. **Historial de Touraine** ☎ 47 61 02 95. ⭘ *Jan–mid-Mar & Nov–Dec: daily, pm only; mid-Mar–Oct: daily.* 🚫
Atelier Histoire de Tours *(entry from church square)* ☎ 47 61 07 93. ⭘ *mid-Mar–mid-Dec: Wed & Sun, pm only.* ● *public hols.* 🚫

Parts of the château, which served as a royal residence between the 13th and 15th centuries, have recently been restored. The Tour de Guise is named after the young Duc de Guise, who made a daring escape from imprisonment here following his father's assassination at the Château de Blois in 1588 *(see pp126–7)*.

The tower now houses the **Historial de Touraine**, a museum illustrating the region's history in waxworks. In the 18th-century Logis de Mars, the waxworks continue. One scene depicts the marriage in 1491 of Charles VIII and Anne of Brittany, while another shows Joan of Arc *(see p137)* trying on her suit of armour in a workshop in Tours. The Logis also has a tropical aquarium.

In the Renaissance Logis des Gouverneurs, the exhibitions of the **Atelier Histoire de Tours** explain the city's long urban history using models and plans.

🏛 **Musée du Compagnonnage**
8 rue Nationale. ☎ 47 61 07 93. ⭘ *Jan–mid-Jun & mid-Sep–Dec: Wed–Mon; mid-Jun–mid-Sep: daily.* ● *public hols.* 🚫 ♿

Housed in part of the abbey once attached to the medieval **Eglise St-Julien**, this unusual museum is devoted to crafts-manship. It has a fascinating collection of "master pieces" made by members of a guild of itinerant *compagnons* (journeymen) who applied to be awarded the prestigious title of Master Craftsman. Displays cover many trades, ranging from the work of stonemasons to that of clog makers, and even include some extraordinary spun-sugar creations.

A barrel on display in the Musée du Compagnonnage

GARLIC AND BASIL FAIR

On 26 July, the Feast of St Anne, the place du Grand-Marché in the Old Town, near the colourful covered market *(Les Halles)*, is the scene of the traditional Garlic and Basil Fair *(Foire à l'Ail et au Basilic)*. Pots of basil form a green carpet, and stalls are garlanded with strings of garlic heads, purple onions and grey or golden shallots.

Stalls laden with basil and garlic in the place du Grand-Marché

BLÉSOIS AND ORLÉANAIS

THESE TWO CLOSELY-LINKED *regions are excellent starting points for an exploration of the central Loire Valley. The area's forests and marshlands have attracted nature lovers for centuries. During the Renaissance, magnificent hunting lodges were built by kings and nobles throughout the area, including the great Chambord, the sumptuously furnished Cheverny and the charming Beauregard.*

Blésois and Orléanais remain richly forested, with abundant game, including rabbits and hares, deer and wild boar. The great forest of Orléans, still magnificent, contrasts with the heaths and marshy lakes of the Sologne, a secretive region of small, quiet villages and low, half-timbered brick farmhouses. Although a paradise for hunters and fishermen, other visitors rarely venture into the depths of this area.

The northern stretch of the Loire flows through towns whose names resound throughout the history of France. Bridges and castles at Gien, Orléans, Beaugency and Blois all assumed strategic significance during wars from the Middle Ages to the 20th century.

It was at Orléans in 1429 that Joan of Arc, lifting the English siege of the town, galvanized the spirit of the French army engaged in the Hundred Years' War. The modern city's proximity to Paris has led to its growth as a commercial centre, but careful reconstruction after the devastation of World War II has meant that a sense of the past survives in the old *quartier*.

During the Wars of Religion, the château at Blois was sunk in political intrigue. Now restored, its walls still echo with the events of 1588, when the Duc de Guise was assassinated on the orders of the king, Henri III.

To the west of the region, the River Loir, smaller than its majestic sound-alike, flows through the countryside of the Vendômois and also through Vendôme itself, one of the most attractive towns in the region. Vendôme's cathedral, La Trinité, is only one of the memorable churches in Blésois and Orléanais, many of them decorated with early frescoes and mosaics.

Anglers taking part in a competition on a local canal

◁ The nave of the Cathédrale Ste-Croix in Orléans

Exploring Blésois and Orléanais

ORLEANS, THE LARGEST CITY in Blésois and Orléanais, lies at the northernmost point of the River Loire. To the west is the Petite Beauce, fertile, wheat-growing land, while to the east is the great forest of Orléans, dense and teeming with wildlife. Blois, downstream from Orléans, is also surrounded by forests. To the south, the Sologne is a land of woods and marshes, scattered with small lakes, or *étangs*. The River Cher marks its southern border, as it flows through charming villages.

One of the region's stone farmhouses

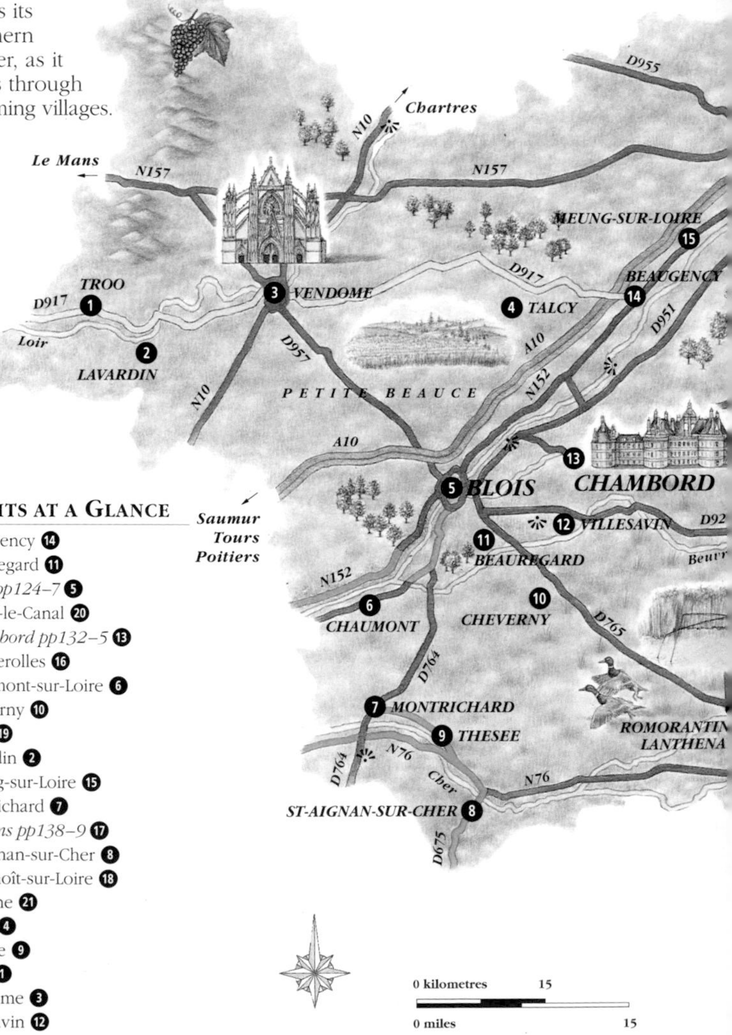

SIGHTS AT A GLANCE

Beaugency **14**
Beauregard **11**
Blois pp124–7 **5**
Briare-le-Canal **20**
Chambord pp132–5 **13**
Chamerolles **16**
Chaumont-sur-Loire **6**
Cheverny **10**
Gien **19**
Lavardin **2**
Meung-sur-Loire **15**
Montrichard **7**
Orléans pp138–9 **17**
St-Aignan-sur-Cher **8**
St-Benoît-sur-Loire **18**
Sologne **21**
Talcy **4**
Thésée **9**
Trôo **1**
Vendôme **3**
Villesavin **12**

GETTING AROUND

The fastest route by car from Paris is *L'Aquitaine* autoroute (A10), which passes through Orléans and Blois. Some Paris-to-Tours TGVs stop at Vendôme, only a 45-minute journey. The Corail express train from Paris takes one hour to Les Aubrais (a suburb of Orléans with a connecting train to the city centre) and 40 minutes to Blois via Beaugency and Meung-sur-Loire. Another Corail express (Tours to Nevers) follows the Cher, stopping at Montrichard, Thésée and St-Aignan. Bus services between towns are extremely limited, especially during the school holidays. The drive along the N76, which parallels the River Cher, is very scenic, and the roads through the cool, forested areas of the region are tranquil and pleasant.

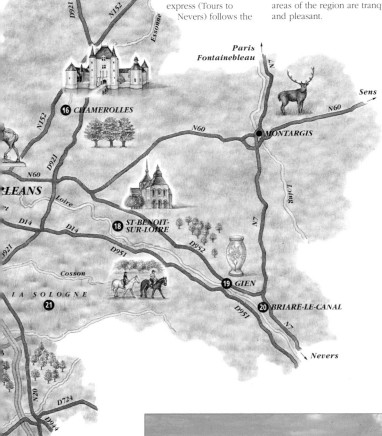

The town of Blois with its distinctive bridge spanning the Loire

KEY

▦▦▦	Motorway
▬▬	Major road
▬	Minor road
▬	Scenic route
≈	River
☆	Viewpoint

Trôo's "speaking well"

Trôo ❶

Road map D3. 🏘 *320.* 🚉 *Vendôme,
then taxi.* 🛈 *Montoire-sur-le-Loir
(54 85 00 29).*

O N A CLIFF above the Loir,
this village should be
entered from the top through
its ruined medieval gate. To
the left of the gate is a
covered "speaking well"; at
45 m (150 ft) deep, it produces a very clear echo.

During the Middle Ages, a
massive fortress stood here. It
was fought over at the end of
the 12th century by Richard
the Lionheart, who lost it to
the French king, Philippe
Augustus. In 1590, the
uncrowned Henri IV
ordered the fortress to
be dismantled. All that
remains today is a
mound, or *motte,* from
the top of which there
is a good view of the
valley below.

Parts of the **Eglise
St-Martin**, nearby,
date from the 11th
century, including the
nave walls. The win-
dows in the square
Angevin tower are
decorated with
ornamental columns.

Steep paths wind
down the hill towards
the attractive **Château
de la Voûte**, passing
on the way the pretty
flower gardens of a
group of troglodyte
dwellings, some of
which are open to
visitors. At the bottom
of the hill is the

Grotte Pétrifiante, a cave
full of stalactites that have
been developing for more
than 4,000 years.

Across the river, the little
church at **St-Jacques-des-
Guérets**, built in the 12th
century, is justly famous for
its 13 murals, painted in a distinctive Byzantine style. They
were rediscovered in 1890
during restoration work. The
Christ in Majesty in the apse
is particularly beautiful.

St-Gilles chapel in nearby
Montoire-sur-le-Loir is also
worth a visit. It has some
even finer 12th-century
murals, remarkable for the
range of colours used.

Lavardin ❷

Road map D3. 🏘 *250.* 🚉
Vendôme, then taxi. 🛈 *Montoire-
sur-le-Loir (54 85 00 29).*

T HE REMAINING fortifications
of Lavardin's ruined
château, towering above the
reconstructed medieval bridge
leading to the village, are an
impressive sight. Situated on
the boundary between the
Capetian and Angevin kingdoms, the fortress was for
centuries a key stronghold in
battles between the French
crown and the Plantagenet

dynasty. In 1590 it suffered a
similar fate to the castle at
Trôo when Henri IV ordered
it to be partly dismantled.

Memorable buildings in the
town include the 11th-century
town hall and the old stone
houses in the route de
Villavard. Lavardin's chief
treasure is the Romanesque
Eglise St-Genest with its
fragile, charmingly naïve
murals dating from the 12th–
16th centuries. Scenes from
the life of Christ are alongside
astrological symbols. Among
the oldest of the frescoes is
the *Baptism of Christ*, which
is found at the entrance to the
left chapel.

⛪ **Château de Lavardin**
📞 *54 85 07 74 (Mairie).* ⬜ *Jun–
Sep: daily.* ⬛ *Oct–May.* 🈺

Vendôme ❸

Road map D3. 🏘 *18,000.* 🚉 🚌
🛈 *Hôtel du Bellay "Le Saillant"
(54 77 05 07).* 🛒 *Fri & Sun.*

O NE OF FRANCE'S most scenic
towns, Vendôme is built
over a group of islands in the
Loir, its bridges, water gates
and old stone buildings
forming a delightful tableau.
Now that it is just 45 minutes
from Paris by rail, it has
become a popular
weekend retreat for
many Parisians.

Situated on the
border between the
French and English
feudal territories, the
town changed hands
many times. During
the Hundred Years'
War, it passed to the
Bourbons in 1371,
eventually becoming a
duchy in 1515.

Later, held by the
Holy League during
the Wars of Religion, it
was recaptured by
Henri IV in 1589; the
skulls of his leading
Catholic opponents are
by far the most grisly
exhibit in the **Musée
de Vendôme**. Set in
an old abbey's cloisters,
the museum also has a
harp said to have been
played by the ill-fated

Delicate murals in Lavardin's Eglise St-Genest

Ornate façade of Abbaye de la Trinité in Vendôme

Marie-Antoinette, and some frescoes in the adjoining chapter house.

Vendôme's jewel is the abbey church of **La Trinité**, founded in 1034 by Geoffroy Martel, son of Foulques Nerra. It stands beside a 12th-century Romanesque bell-tower, with a spire reaching more than 80 m (260 ft). The church's bold, ornate façade was created by Jean de Beauce, who also designed the Old Bell-tower of Notre-Dame de Chartres. Its flame-like tracery is a virtuoso statement of the Flamboyant Gothic style.

Inside, beyond the transept, which dates from the 11th century, are choir stalls carved with amusing figures. To the left of the altar, a pretty latticework base with teardrop motifs once held a cabinet displaying a famous relic, which was said to be the tear shed by Jesus on the grave of Lazarus.

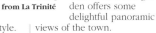

Wooden carving from La Trinité

Shopping is centred around the place St-Martin, with its 15th-century clock-tower and carillon, and a statue of the count of Rochambeau, who commanded the French forces during the American Revolution. There is also a graceful, *fin-de-siècle* covered market just off rue Saulnerie.

The best views of the town's old fortifications are from the square Belot. Also visible from here is the Porte d'Eau, a water gate built during the 13th and 14th centuries, which once controlled the water for the town's mills and tanneries.

In the centre of town is the Parc Ronsard, with its 15th-century wash house, the Lavoir des Cordeliers, and the Old Oratorians College, which dates from the 17th and 18th centuries. Vendôme's ruined château stands on a bluff above the town, with the 12th-century Tour de Poitiers at one corner. The garden offers some delightful panoramic views of the town.

Musée de Vendôme

Cloître de la Trinité. *54 77 26 13.* *Wed–Mon.* *1 Jan, 1 May, 25 Dec.*

The Lavoir des Cordeliers in Vendôme's Parc Ronsard

Talcy's 300-year-old wine press, still in working order

Château de Talcy ❹

Road map E3. *Mer, then taxi.* *54 81 03 01.* *Apr–Sep: daily; Oct–Mar: Wed–Mon.* *1 Jan, 1 May, 1 & 11 Nov, 25 Dec.*

After the grander châteaux of the Loire Valley, Talcy comes as a delightful surprise: a fascinating, human-scale home, hiding behind a stern façade. The original building, a donjon, dates from the 15th century. It was transformed by Bernardo Salviati, a Florentine banker and cousin of Catherine de' Médicis, who bought it in 1517 and added to the building significantly.

In 1545, the poet Pierre de Ronsard *(see p22)* fell in love with Salviati's 15-year-old daughter, Cassandre. Over the following decade, his love for her inspired the sonnets of his famous collection, known as *Amours de Cassandre*.

Bernardo Salviati gave Talcy its feudal look, adding the crenellated sentry walk and fake machicolations to the gatehouse. In the first courtyard, with its arcaded gallery, is an elegant domed well. A 3,000-bird dovecote in the second courtyard, dating from the 16th century, is the best-preserved in the Loire.

A gigantic, 300-year-old wooden wine press, still in working order, is also worth a look. The château's vineyards are no longer productive, so the press is not in use. The grounds also contain some old flower gardens.

Inside the château, the charming rooms have retained their original 17th- and 18th-century furnishings and decorative touches.

Street-by-Street: Blois ❺

A POWERFUL FEUDAL stronghold in the 12th century, Blois rose to glory under Louis XII, who established his court here in 1498. The town remained at the centre of French royal and political life for much of the next century. Now an important commercial centre for the agricultural districts of the Beauce and Sologne, Blois, with its harmonious combination of white walls, slate roofs and red brick chimneys, is the quintessential Loire town. The hilly, partly pedestrianized old quarter, bordered by the river, the château and the cathedral, is full of architectural interest.

Hôtel d'Alluye
Blois' outstanding Renaissance mansion was built in 1508 by Florimond Robertet, treasurer to three kings.

0 metres

0 yards   10

Façade des Loges, the château's most theatrical side, has Renaissance window bays rising in tiers to a gallery.

★ **Château de Blois**
The rich history of the Château de Blois is reflected in its varied architectural styles.

Blois as seen from the Loire, with the three spires of the Eglise St-Nicolas in the centre

★ **Eglise St-Nicolas**
This striking, three-spired church once belonged to a 12th-century Benedictine abbey. Its high, narrow Gothic nave leads to an apse of magical beauty, sheltered by elegant Corinthian columns and lit through lovely blue glass.

KEY

– – –   Suggested route

Escalier Denis-Papin
Named after the native son (1647–1714) who invented the pressure cooker, these stairs provide a remarkable view over the town and the river.

VISITORS' CHECKLIST

Road map E3. 🏠 *50,000*.
🚉 ☐☐☐ *pl de la Gare*. 🛈 *3 av Jean-Laigret (54 74 06 49)*.
🛒 *Wed, Sat, Sun*. 🎭 *Le Soleil a Rendez-vous avec la Lune (street festival, Jul–Aug).*
Musée d'Histoire Naturelle
Couvent des Jacobins. ☎ *54 74 13 89*. ☐ *Jun–Aug: Tue–Sun; Sep–May: pm only*. ● *public hols*. ♿
Musée Diocésain des Arts Religieux Couvent des Jacobins. ☎ *54 78 17 14*. ☐ *Tue–Sat, pm only*. ● *public hols*. ♿

Cathédrale St-Louis
Most of the original building was destroyed by a hurricane in 1678. The present cathedral was erected during the reign of Louis XIV.

Maison des Acrobates, in the place St-Louis, has carvings of medieval characters on its posts.

Couvent des Jacobins
now houses museums of religious art and natural history.

★ Quartier Vieux Blois
This well-preserved area of Blois has some marvellous 16th-century buildings. This galleried town house is at the top of rue Pierre de Blois.

STAR SIGHTS

★ **Château de Blois**

★ **Eglise St-Nicolas**

★ **Quartier Vieux Blois**

Château de Blois ❺

Porcupine emblem of the House of Orléans

H OME TO KINGS Louis XII, François I and Henri III, no other Loire château has such a sensational history of skulduggery at court. It culminated with the stabbing, on the order of Henri III, of the ambitious Duc de Guise, leader of the Catholic Holy League *(see pp54–5)*. This macabre event, which took place in the king's own bedroom, marked the end of the château's political importance. The building itself juxtaposes four distinct architectural styles dating from the 13th century, through the Gothic and Renaissance periods, to the Classical. The château is now emerging from major restorations begun in 1989.

Gaston d'Orléans Wing
The simplicity of the Classical design of this wing, as shown in the ceiling of the entrance hall, marked a departure from the rich decor of the Renaissance.

King Louis XII
A statue of Louis XII (1462–1515) is the centrepiece of the entrance archway. Known as "Father of the People", he was popular for his benevolent domestic policies.

The Tour du Foix remains from the ramparts that surrounded the 13th-century feudal fortress.

STAR FEATURES

★ **François I's Staircase**

★ **Cabinet de Catherine de Médicis**

★ **Salle des Etats Généraux**

TIMELINE

1200	1300	1400	1500	1600	1700	1800	1900

1200 Counts of Blois rebuild feudal fortress dating from 9th century

1391 Fortress passes to Louis d'Orléans, brother of Charles VI

1498 Louis XII adds three new wings and rebuilds the St-Calais chapel

1515 François I rebuilds north wing

1576 Etats Généraux meets in feudal hall

1588 Etats Généraux meets again. Henri III has Duc de Guise assassinated

1635 Gaston d'Orléans replaces west wing with Classical building

1788 The decaying château is turned into barracks

1810 Napoléon makes city of Blois responsible for the château

1843 Félix Duban begins restoration of the château

Architect Félix Duban

1989 Major restoration programme begins

★ **Cabinet de Catherine de Médicis**
The queen's room has 237 carved panels, four with secret cupboards for her state papers, jewels or, some believed, poisons.

Pl du Château. ☎ 54 78 06 62.
◯ mid-Mar–mid-Jun & Sep–mid-Oct: 9am–6:30pm daily; mid-Jun–Aug: 9am–8pm; mid Oct–mid-Mar: 9am–12:30pm, 2–5:30pm. (Last adm: 45 mins before closing.) ● 25 Dec, 1 Jan. 🎭 🎞 ✍ 🛒 *Ainsi Blois vous est conté (see p42).*

The nave of the St-Calais chapel was pulled down during the 17th century to make way for Gaston d'Orléans' wing, leaving only the chancel standing today.

The Salle d'Honneur, previously partitioned, has a sumptuous west fireplace bearing the salamander and ermine emblems of François I and his mother, Louise.

Statue of Louis XII

The Gothic Louis XII wing has intricate, decorative brickwork.

★ **François I's Staircase**
Enclosed in an octagonal well, the staircase, with its highly ornate carving, is a Renaissance tour de force. From its open balconies, the royal family could watch events in the courtyard.

★ **Salle des Etats Généraux**
Used for royal receptions and Etats Généraux meetings (see pp54–5), the 13th-century room survives from the original fortress.

Château de Chaumont, towering above the town

Château de Chaumont **6**

Chaumont-sur-Loire. **Road map** D3. 🚉 Onzain, then taxi. 🗐 54 20 98 03. ⭘ daily. ⬤ public hols. 🈹

SEEN FROM ACROSS the Loire, Chaumont, set on a wooded hill above the river, appears like a fantasy of a feudal castle. Its tall, white donjon and round towers, built between 1466 and 1510, were never tested in battle and have thus remained in immaculate condition.

The main entrance, with its double drawbridge and elaborate machicolated parapets, is particularly beautiful. There are emblems carved on the towers including the crossed Cs of Charles II d'Amboise, whose family had owned a previous 12th-century fortress on the site.

When Charles inherited Chaumont in 1481, he undertook several major alterations. These were early examples of the Renaissance architectural style in France and included the east wing, with its elaborate frieze, and the south wing, with its entrance towers.

At one end of the south wing, the projecting octagonal tower, enclosing the main spiral staircase, predates those at Blois and Chambord (see pp126–7 and pp132–5).

Catherine de Médicis, wife of Henri II, acquired the château in 1560. Legend has it that Catherine's astrologer, Ruggieri, used the tower connected to her room as an observatory. Here he is said to have shown the queen the fate of her three royal sons in a magic mirror. Catherine's chamber also has a balcony adjoining the attractive chapel, which was restored towards the end of the 19th century. In 1562 Catherine gave Chaumont to Diane de Poitiers, mistress of the late Henri II, after forcing her out of Chenonceau (see pp108–9). Diane's entwined Ds and hunting motifs are carved on the machicolations of the entrance façade and on the east wing.

Subsequent owners either neglected the château or altered it, sometimes radically, to their own purposes. One 18th-century owner, abandoning the fortress design, demolished the north wing so that the whole courtyard was opened up to the river views.

Sweeping improvements began in 1875 when Prince Amédée de Broglie came to live in the château with his

Stained glass from the dining room at Chaumont

wife Marie, a sugar heiress. Their lavish lifestyle can be sensed in the handsome stables, which once housed an elephant, given to them on a visit to the Maharajah of Kapurtala in India.

The council room is hung with Flemish tapestries by Martin Reymbouts and has majolica floor tiles, brought from a 17th-century Palermo palace, while the library contains medallions made in the château by JB Nini in the 18th century.

The château's extensive park was landscaped in 1884 by Achille Duchêne and follows the lines of an English country garden.

Montrichard **7**

Road map D3. 🏠 3,800. 🚉 🚌 🛈 rue du Pont (54 32 05 10). 🗓 Mon pm, Fri am.

THIS SMALL VILLAGE built of tufa rock is dominated by the ruins of its **château**. The 11th-century drawbridge, archers' tower and the

Montrichard, seen from across the River Cher

remains of its Renaissance apartments are still standing, and the keep houses the small **Musée Tivoli** on local archaeology and life.

The adjoining **Eglise Ste-Croix** has a Romanesque arched entrance. Here, in 1476, the future Louis XII reluctantly wed Jeanne, the deformed daughter of Louis XI. The marriage was later annulled so Louis could marry Anne of Brittany.

On summer afternoons, the château's eagles take part in breathtaking falconry displays above Montrichard.

♠ Château de Montrichard & Musée Tivoli

[54 32 01 16.] *Palm Sun–Sep: daily.* 🖾 *Eagle flights: Palm Sun–Sep: daily, pm only.*

White tiger from Beauval Zoological Park

St-Aignan-sur-Cher ⑧

Road map E3. 👥 *3,700.*
🚂 *St-Aignan-Noyers-sur-Cher.* 🚌
🛈 *54 75 13 31 (Jul–Aug: Ile Plage 54 75 22 85).* 🗷 *Sat.*

ONCE A RIVER PORT, St-Aignan is now an engaging summer resort for boating, swimming and fishing. The town is dominated by the Renaissance château of the dukes of Beauvillier and the collegiate church of St-Aignan, an underrated marvel of Romanesque art.

The château interior is not open to the public, but visitors can climb 19th-century stairs to look at its two elegant wings and enjoy the views from its courtyard terrace. Ruined towers and

walls remain from a feudal fortress built by the counts of Blois. In rue Constant-Ragot, leading to the château and church, there is a fine half-timbered Renaissance house at No. 27.

The **Eglise de St-Aignan**, with its two impressive bell-towers, was begun around 1080. Its majestic chancel and sanctuary are built over an earlier Romanesque church, which now forms the crypt. Once used as a cowshed, the crypt still retains its Romanesque feel. Among the important frescoes to survive here are a portrayal of the miracles of St Gilles in the southern chapel and a rare 11th-century *Christ in Majesty* on the chancel vault.

Some of the 250 sculpted capitals in the main church are carved with scenes from the Old and New Testaments as well as allegories of sin and punishment. Others are worked with decorative motifs. In the Chapel of Our Lady of Miracles, the 15th-century ceiling paintings are equally fascinating.

The **Beauval Zoological Park**, 2 km (1¼ miles) south of the village, is among France's best. It contains 300

St-Aignan's Chapel of Our Lady of Miracles

species of bird, a superb jungle house and otter pool, and landscaped enclosures for big cats, including several magnificent white tigers.

🦌 Beauval Zoological Park

[54 75 05 56.] *daily.* 🖾 🚻

Thésée ⑨

Road map E3. 👥 *1,100.* 🚂
🛈 *Rue Nationale (54 71 42 22).*
🗷 *Thu.*

JUST OUTSIDE the little wine village of Thésée is the most important Gallo-Roman site in the Loire-et-Cher *département*, Les Maselles.

Impressive ruined walls with brick courses testify to the skills of stonemasons who, in the 2nd century AD, built Tasciaca. This settlement was a major staging post and ceramic-making centre on the road between Bourges and Tours. Thésée's town hall, set in an attractive park, houses the **Musée Archéologique** displaying jewels, coins, statuettes, pottery and other artifacts from the site.

🏛 Musée Archéologique

Hôtel de Ville. [54 71 40 20.] *Easter–mid-Jun: Sat & Sun, public hols, pm only; mid-Jun–mid-Sep: Wed–Mon; mid-Sep–mid-Oct: Sat & Sun, public hols, pm only. Mid-Oct–Easter: groups by appt.* 🖾

Fresco of *Christ in Majesty*, from the Eglise de St-Aignan

Classical façade of the Château de Cheverny

Château de Cheverny ⑩

Road map E3. 🚌 **📞** 54 79 96 29.
⭕ daily. 🎦 ♿ grd floor & park only.
🎭 Le Cours du Temps: Jul–Aug,
10:30pm (54 79 95 63).

THE ELEGANCE of Cheverny's white tufa façade, with its pure Louis XIII lines, was achieved in a single phase of construction between 1620 and 1634, with all the finishing touches completed by 1648 (see pp16–17). Initiating a new architectural style for the châteaux and stately homes of the Loire Valley, Cheverny has no defensive elements, such as large turreted towers or formidable entrances.

Arms and armour on display in Cheverny's Salle des Armes

Instead, its Classical façade is striking in its simplicity. The château stands on the site of a previous castle, owned by the Hurault family. Henri Hurault, with his wife, Marguerite (who is thought to have been an influence on the feminine elegance of the château), directed the reconstruction of Cheverny, and the family has retained ownership of the château ever since.

The painter Jean Mosnier worked on the interior for ten years, decorating the major rooms richly with gilded beams, panels and ceilings. His finest work is in the dining room, with its scenes from Don Quixote's travels, and in the king's bedroom, where the combined effect of wall-hangings, painted ceilings and a bed canopied in Persian silk is stunning. The largest room in the château, the huge Salle des Armes, displays a collection of arms and armour and is adorned with Mosnier's paintings and a large Gobelins tapestry, the *Abduction of Helen.*

Paintings in the château include a portrait of Cosimo de' Médici by Titian and Pierre Mignard's striking portrait of the Countess of Cheverny above the fireplace in the Grand Salon. There are fine portraits by Jean Clouet and Hyacinthe Rigaud in

the adjoining gallery. The Tapestry Room, with work designed by David Teniers, also features a remarkable lacquered commode and a balance-wheel clock showing phases of the moon, both in the Louis XV style.

The Cheverny hunt, which rides twice a week in winter to the call of ornate spiral horns, is famous throughout the Sologne. A visit to the kennels is a highlight of the château, especially at 5pm when 70 hounds politely wait their turn to eat. The Trophy Room is an eerie sight, with 2,000 pairs of antlers mounted on the walls and ceiling.

The Trophy Room at Cheverny

Château de Beauregard ⑪

Cellettes. **Road map** E3. 🚉 Blois, then taxi. **📞** 54 70 40 05.
⭕ mid-Feb–Mar & Oct–Dec: Thu–Tue; Apr–Sep: daily. ● mid-Jan–mid-Feb. 🎦 ♿

BEAUREGARD STANDS in a well-tended park on the edge of the Russy forest. Originally built at the beginning of the 16th century as a hunting lodge for François I, it was transformed into a graceful private manor house more than a century later by Jean du Thier, scholarly secretary of state to Henri II. It was du Thier who commissioned the king's Italian cabinet-maker, Scibec de Carpi, to make him an exquisite study panelled in gilded oak, the Cabinet des Grelots. This little room is

Detail from Beauregard's portrait gallery

Château de Villesavin ⓬

Villesavin. **Road map** E3. 🚉 *Blois, then taxi.* 📞 *54 46 42 88.* 🗓 *Mar–Sep: daily; Oct–mid-Dec: pm only.* ⬤ *mid-Dec–Feb.* 🅿 ♿ *grd & 1st flrs only.*

VILLESAVIN, built between 1527 and 1537 by Jean Breton, was his home while he supervised works at Chambord *(see pp132–5)* nearby. Stone carvers from the royal château ornamented Villesavin and presented Breton with the beautiful Florentine basin made of Carrara marble that stands proudly in the entrance courtyard.

Now in need of restoration, this is one of the least altered of the many late-Renaissance châteaux in the Loire Valley. Villesavin, with its low walls and unusually high roofs, was built around three very spacious courtyards. The elegant southern façade ends with a large dovecote, which has 1,500 pigeonholes and a revolving ladder.

The château's essentially domestic spirit is also evident in the service court, overlooked by a spacious kitchen with a working spit. The interesting collection of old carriages on display here includes an 18-m (59-ft) long *voiture de chasse* with four rows of seats, from which ladies could watch the hunt.

ENVIRONS: Situated on the southern banks of the Beuvron river, Bracieux is worth a visit for its grand covered market, which was built during the reign of the Renaissance king François I (1515–47). At that time, the town acted as an important staging post on the routes between the towns of Tours, Chartres and Bourges.

The market is built of brick, stone and wood, with an upper tithe barn. Its original oak posts were strengthened during the 19th century. There are also attractive 17th- and 18th-century houses.

decorated with the bells, or *grelots*, found on du Thier's crest, and has some charming paintings from the studio of Niccolo dell'Abate.

The portrait gallery, the château's most spectacular feature, was added in the 17th century by Henry IV's former treasurer, Paul Ardier. A complete catalogue of famous European faces from 1328 to 1643 – kings, queens, saints, explorers – is arranged in three rows around the gallery. Adding to the impact of these 327 portraits are beautiful beams and panels painted by Jean Mosnier and the largest delft-tiled floor in Europe, which depicts an army on the move in Louis XIII costume.

Other delights include the southern gallery, with its rich Brussels tapestry and carved furniture, and the kitchen, with its flagstone floors and a table built around the central column. Above the ratchet-operated spit, a motto on the chimney breast advises that those who keep promises have no enemies.

One of Villesavin's antique carriages

Garden façade of the Château de Villesavin

Château de Chambord ⑬

Statue of Diana in the Salle de Diane

H ENRY JAMES once said: "Chambord is truly royal – royal in its great scale, its grand air, and its indifference to common considerations." The brainchild of the extravagant François I, the château began as a hunting lodge in the Forêt de Boulogne. In 1519 the original building was razed and Chambord begun, to a design probably initiated by Leonardo da Vinci. By 1537 the keep, with its towers and terraces, had been completed by 1,800 men and two master masons. The following year, François I began building a private royal pavilion on the northeast corner, with a connecting two-storey gallery. His son Henri II added the west wing, and Louis XIV completed the 440-roomed edifice in 1685.

The Château de Chambord with the Closson, a tributary of the Loire, in the foreground

The roof terraces include miniature spires, stair turrets, sculpted gables and cupolas.

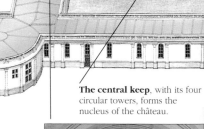

The central keep, with its four circular towers, forms the nucleus of the château.

★ **Skyline**

Chambord's skyline is its most astonishing feature – a bizarre jumble of different forms, likened to an overcrowded chess board.

Salamander

François I's emblem appears more than 700 times in the château. It symbolizes patronage of the good and destruction of the bad.

Chapel

Begun by François I shortly before his death in 1547, the chapel was given a second storey by Henri II. Later, Louis XIV embellished the roof.

STAR FEATURES

★ **Skyline**

★ **Grand Staircase**

François I Staircase
The external spiral staircase located in the northeastern courtyard was added at the same time as the galleries, starting in 1538.

The lantern tower, 32 m (105 ft) high, is supported by arched buttresses.

The guardrooms, which were once the setting for royal balls and plays, have ornate, vaulted ceilings.

François I's bedchamber in the east wing was first decorated in 1547.

Cabinet de François I
The king's barrel-vaulted study (cabinet) in the outer north tower was turned into an oratory in the 18th century by Queen Catherine Opalinska, wife of Stanislas Leszczynski (Louis XV's father-in-law and the deposed king of Poland).

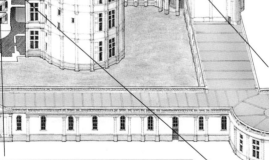

★ Grand Staircase
Seen here from the guardrooms, this innovative double staircase was supposedly designed by Leonardo da Vinci. Two flights of stairs spiral around each other.

Louis XIV's Bedchamber
The Sun King's state apartments are the grandest in the château.

The History of Chambord

CHAMBORD, the largest château in the Loire, was a *folie de grandeur* of the young François I, whose ruling passions were hunting and flirting. "He is forever chasing, now stags, now women," the Venetian ambassador once said of him. The king personally supervised the enclosure of the game park surrounding Chambord with the most extensive wall in France – nearly 32 km (20 miles) long and 2.5 m (8 ft) high. At one point, he even suggested diverting the Loire to flow in front of his château, but instead settled for redirecting the nearer Closson to fill his moat.

Louis XIV portrayed as Jupiter, conquering La Fronde

François I as a young man, with various symbols of his kingship

After François I

On his father's death, Henri II took charge of François I's ambitious project. Subsequent owners – Louis XIII, who had no great love of hunting, and his brother Gaston d'Orléans – continued to modify the château. By the 17th century, Chambord comprised 440 rooms and had 365 chimneys, 14 main staircases and 70 smaller stairways.

Louis XIV, whose chief youthful amusement was hunting, took Chambord very seriously. His full court retinue visited the château numerous times. With balls, plays by Molière and operatic ballets, he re-created the glittering lifestyle of François I.

Louis XV also hawked at Chambord, but by 1725 he was ready to relinquish the château to his father-in-law, Stanislas Leszczynski. The exiled King of Poland is reported to have disliked the winter draughts. Certainly, he filled in the moats to prevent malarial fevers.

The last owner to enjoy Chambord's theatricality was the Maréchal de Saxe, victor over the English troops at the Battle of Fontenoy in 1745.

As well as lodging his actress mistress here, Saxe also kept two cavalry regiments whose mock battles he watched from the roof terraces.

During the second half of the 18th century, Chambord fell into neglect. Stripped during the French Revolution, the château was hardly used by the Bourbon pretender, Henri, Duc de Bordeaux, to whom it was given by public subscription in 1821. It was sequestered by the state in 1915, which bought it in 1930. A restoration programme was begun in the 1970s.

A view of Chambord (detail) by PD Martin (1663–1742)

TIMELINE

1547–59 Henri II adds the west wing and second storey of the chapel	**1560–74** Charles IX continues tradition of royal hunting at Chambord and writes *Traité de la Chasse Royale*	*Maréchal de Saxe*	**1840** Chambord declared a *Monument Historique*	
1500	**1600**	**1700**	**1800**	**1900**
1670 Molière's *Le Bourgeois Gentilhomme* staged at Chambord		**1748** Acquired by the Maréchal de Saxe. On his death the château falls into decline		
1519–47 The Count of Blois' hunting lodge is demolished by François I and the château created	**1685** Louis XIV completes the building	**1725–33** Inhabited by exiled king of Poland	**1970s** Under Giscard d'Estaing, Chambord is restored and refurnished and the moats redug

Royal Hunting at Chambord

UNDER THE INFLUENCE of François I and his heirs, hunting and hawking were the foremost pastimes of the court during the 16th century. A Tuscan nobleman complained that the king only stayed in a place "as long as the herons last". They were quick prey for the 500 falcons that travelled with the rest of the royal retinue.

St Hubert, patron saint of hunting

Within his vast oak forests, the king rode out at dawn to a prepared picnicking spot, there to feast and await the selection of a red deer tracked by his beaters. The quarry flushed, he would ride at full tilt in pursuit, sometimes for hours. For ladies of the court, Chambord's roof terraces offered matchless views of these exertions.

François' son Henri II and grandson Charles IX were also keen and practised hunters, sometimes pursuing quarry on foot. Louis XIV favoured the English sport of following packs of hounds, but falconry was preferred by Louis XV.

Hunting was regarded as an art by the court, and its tools – weapons, horns and costumes – were carefully designed and crafted. For centuries, it was also a favourite subject for painters and tapestry designers, whose works were used to decorate palaces and hunting lodges.

Matchlock

Engraved barrel

Arquebus, an early form of musket, dating from the 16th century

Wild boar was a favourite beast of the chase because of its strength and ferocity. Its head was considered a delicacy.

The crossbow was a popular hunting weapon thanks to its versatility and rapid rate of fire.

Greyhounds, prized for their speed and keen eyesight, were used as hunting dogs.

The Boar Hunt *comes from the* Traités de Fauconnerie et de Vénerie *(1459), one of many treatises on falconry and hunting to hounds. In the foreground, beaters and dogs chase their quarry. Behind them, animals and men witness the end of the hunt.*

Beaugency ⑭

Road map E3. 🏛 *7,000*.
🚉 🚌 ℹ *3 pl de l'Hôtel de Ville
(38 44 54 42).* 🛒 *Sat.* 🎭 *Festival de
Beaugency (end Jun–Jul).*

WITH THE LOIRE racing beneath its famous 23-arch bridge, the medieval town of Beaugency makes a delightful base for exploring the Orléanais area. The town is surprisingly well preserved, although its bridge, the best on the Loire between Orléans and Blois, has attracted the attentions of a number of armies over the centuries. Restored in the 16th century, the bridge was damaged again in 1940 when the Allied army blew up its southern end to prevent the Nazis from crossing the river.

On the place Dunois at the top of rue de l'Abbaye stands a massive 11th-century keep. Opposite is the Romanesque abbey church of **Notre-Dame**, where Eleanor of Aquitaine's marriage to Louis VII was annulled in 1152, leaving her free to marry the future Henry II of England.

Higher up is the 16th-century Tour St-Firmin, near an equestrian statue of Joan of Arc. Next to the keep, her companion-in-arms, Jean Dunois, Bastard of Orléans and Lord of Beaugency, built the **Château Dunois**, now a folk museum. Nearby, in rue des Trois Marchands, is a

Beaugency's 11th-century clock-tower, once gateway to the town

medieval clock-tower and the Renaissance façade of the Hôtel de Ville. A flower-lined stream runs through the old mill district.

♣ **Château Dunois (Musée Régional de l'Orléanais)**
Pl Dunois. 📞 *38 44 55 23.*
🕐 *Wed–Mon.* ⚫ *1 Jan, 1 May,
25 Dec.* 🄳

Meung-sur-Loire ⑮

Road map E3. 🏛 *6,000*. 🚉 🚌
ℹ *42 rue Jehan-de-Meung
(38 44 32 28).* 🛒 *Sun am, Thu pm.*

THIS PRETTY little village, sloping down to the Loire, was the birthplace of Jean de Meung *(see p22)*, one of the

authors of the 13th-century masterpiece *Le Roman de la Rose.* There has been a town on this site since Gallo-Roman times, when it was known as Magdunum.

Beside the impressive Romanesque church of **St-Liphard**, built from the 11th to the 13th century, rise the feudal towers of the **Château de Meung**. Frequently altered from the 12th century to the 18th century, the château was built in a variety of styles. The 18th-century wing has an interesting collection of furniture, paintings and tapestries put together by the current owner.

More intriguing are the spooky rooms, underground passages and dungeons of the older castle, dating from the 12th to 13th centuries and used for 500 years by the bishops of Orléans as a prison. In 1461, the poet François Villon *(see p22)*, renowned for his life of disrepute as well as his fine writing, spent five months fighting with the other condemned criminals for scraps of bread on a ledge above a cesspool in the château's claustrophobic oubliette. Thanks to a royal pardon from Louis XI, he was the only prisoner ever to emerge alive from there.

♣ **Château de Meung**
📞 *38 44 36 47.* 🕐 *Easter–Oct:
daily; Nov–Easter: Sun pm only.
Groups by appt.* 🄳 ♿ *grd flr only.*

Beaugency's medieval bridge, the Tour St-Firmin and the keep rising above the trees

The entrance to the Château de Chamerolles

Château de Chamerolles ⑯

Chilleurs-aux-Bois. **Road map** E2.
🚉 Orléans, then taxi. 📞 38 39 84 66. ⬜ Feb–Dec: Sat–Thu.
⬛ 25 Dec. 🈺

O N THE EDGE of the huge forest of Orléans, this Renaissance château was built between 1500 and 1530 by Lancelot du Lac, Governor of Orléans (who was named after the legendary Arthurian knight).

Although it was constructed in the form of a fortress, with a drawbridge crossing a moat and a courtyard enclosed by turreted wings, Chamerolles was designed as a pleasant personal residence.

Baccarat perfume bottle Chamerolles' museum

Pretty Renaissance gardens, accurately reconstructed with trellised walks, extend to a gazebo offering views back to the château across a "mirror" lake. There is an area of rare aromatic plants, many of which were used during the 16th century for making medicines and perfumes.

A museum in the château traces the development of perfumery through the centuries, covering the variety of uses for perfumes as well as the refinement of the science of making them. This includes the laboratories of perfumers and naturalists and glittering displays of bottles, as well as a gift shop.

JOAN OF ARC

Joan of Arc is the supreme national heroine, a virgin-warrior, patriot and martyr whose shining self-belief turned the tide of the Hundred Years' War against the English. Nowhere is she more honoured than in the Loire Valley, scene of her greatest triumphs.

Responding to heavenly voices telling her to "drive the English out of France", Joan left her home soon after her 17th birthday in 1429 and travelled via Gien to Chinon to see the dauphin, the as yet uncrowned Charles VII. He

Joan of Arc, pictured in a medieval tapestry

faced an Anglo-Burgundian alliance on the verge of capturing Orléans. Joan convinced him she could save the city, armed herself in Tours, had her standard blessed in Blois and entered Orléans with a small force on 29 April. Galvanized by her leadership, the French drove the English off on 7 May. The people of Orléans have celebrated 8 May as a day of thanksgiving almost ever since. Joan returned to Gien to urge Charles forward to Reims for his coronation in July. In 1430 she was captured and accused of witchcraft. Handed over to the English, she was burned at the stake at the age of 19. Joan's piety, patriotism and tragic martyrdom led to her canonization almost 500 years later, in 1920.

Stained-glass portrait of Charles VII from Loches

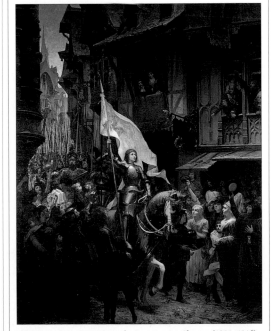

***Joan of Arc Entering Orléans** by Jean-Jacques Sherrer (1855–1916)*

Orléans

ORLÉANS WAS THE CAPITAL of medieval France and a royal duchy until the 18th-century French Revolution, when it became staunchly Republican. Its historical fame might, at first glance, seem submerged by its 20th-century role as a rail junction, food processing and business centre, especially as the old quarter of the city was badly damaged during World War II. However, an area of the old town near the river, now reconstructed, is full of interest for the visitor, and there are many beautiful gardens in this "city of roses".

Heroic Joan of Arc

Exploring Orléans

A sense of grandeur lingers in Vieil Orléans, the old quarter bounded by the cathedral, the River Loire and the **place du Martroi**. Dominating this square is Denis Foyatier's statue of the city's heroine, Joan of Arc, whose festival on 8 May is a highlight of the year. The plinth of the statue, which was erected in 1855, is beautifully sculpted with the events of her life. Two splendid Classical buildings, the Chancellery and the Chamber of Commerce, are also found in the square.

A few medieval buildings have survived in the narrower streets around rue de Bourgogne, a partly pedestrianized shopping street with an astonishing range of ethnic restaurants. Other delightful and often inexpensive restaurants can also be found close to the **Nouvelles Halles**, the city's covered market. The most sophisticated shopping street is the rue Royale, which leads to the 18th-century bridge, the Pont George V.

🏛 Maison de Jeanne d'Arc

3 pl de Gaulle. 📞 38 52 99 89.
🕐 May–Oct: Tue–Sun; Nov–Apr: pm only. ● 1 Jan, 1 May, 1 Nov, 25 Dec. 🎫

A reconstruction of the half-timbered house that lodged the warrior-saint for ten days in 1429, the Maison de Jeanne d'Arc presents scenes from her life as well as mementos, costumes and banners.

The evocative audiovisual dioramas include one that shows Joan's assault on the English-held Tourelles fort.

Orléans' Renaissance Hôtel Groslot, once a private residence

🏨 Hôtel Groslot

Pl de l'Etape. 📞 38 79 22 22.
🕐 daily (except Sat am).

The most handsome of the many Renaissance buildings in the city, the Hôtel Groslot, built between 1549 and 1555, served until recently as the town hall.

Built out of red brick crossed with black, this was a grand residence, with scrolled staircase pillars, caryatids and an ornately tooled interior. It was once considered fine enough to lodge the kings of France. Here, in 1560, the sickly, young François II died after attending a meeting of the Etats Généraux with his child bride, Mary, later Queen of Scots. The beautiful statue

of Joan of Arc guarding the steps was sculpted by Princess Marie d'Orléans in 1840. Walk through the building to visit a charming little park, backed by the re-erected façade of the 15th-century Flamboyant Gothic chapel of St-Jacques.

🔒 Cathédrale Ste-Croix

Pl Ste-Croix. 📞 38 53 47 23.
🕐 daily.

The cathedral, set on a spacious esplanade, was begun in the 13th century. The original building was completely destroyed by Huguenots in the 16th century and then restored in a supposedly Gothic style between the 17th and 19th centuries. Behind the ornate façade, the towering nave is lit by the radiating spokes of the rose window dedicated to the "Sun King", Louis XIV. The chapel of Joan of Arc, whose martyrdom is portrayed in stained glass, features a kneeling sculpture of Cardinal Touchet, who fought for her canonization. In the crypt, ecclesiastical treasures in gold and enamel are on display, as well as the masterly painting *Christ Bearing the Cross,* by the Spanish religious painter, Francisco de Zurbarán (1598–1664).

The nave of the Cathédrale Ste-Croix

The peaceful Parc Floral in Orléans-la-Source

🏛 Musée des Beaux-Arts

Pl Ste-Croix. 📞 38 53 39 22.
⭕ Wed–Mon. ● 1 Jan, 1 & 8 May,
1 Nov, 25 Dec. 🔲 ♿

The high standard of the
collection, which includes a
self-portrait by Jean-Baptiste-
Siméon Chardin (1699–1779)
and *St Thomas* by the young
Diego Velázquez (1599–1660),
represents the strength of
European painting from the
14th to the early 20th century.
There is a charming collection
of miniature enamelled
statuettes on the second floor,
a contrast to the richness of
the 19th-century paintings.

🏛 Musée Historique et Archéologique

Pl de l'Abbé Desnoyers 📞 38 53 39
22. ⭕ Wed–Mon. ● 1 Jan, 1 & 8
May, 1 Nov, 25 Dec. 🔲

The chief treasures of this
museum, housed in the
Renaissance Hôtel Cabu, are
the Celtic statues discovered
at Neuvy-en-Sullias in 1861,
which include a wonderful
2nd-century AD horse *(see
p49)*. Mementos of Joan of
Arc include a beautiful
painted stone head. The
museum also has collections
of arts and crafts from the
Middle Ages onwards.

VISITORS' CHECKLIST

Road map E2. 🏠 100,000.
🚉 rue Copernic. 🚌 rue Marcel
Proust. ❶ pl Albert Ier (38 53
05 95). 🏪 daily. 🎉 Fête Jeanne
d'Arc: Apr 29–May 5.

ENVIRONS: The suburbs of
Orléans can be pleasant
places to relax after a day
spent sightseeing in the city
centre. In Olivet, for example,
it is possible to go boating on
the River Loiret. This river
also provides opportunities
for many pretty walks. A
tributary of the Loire, the
Loiret flows underground
from near the town of St-
Benoît-sur-Loire *(see p140)*
and rises in the grand **Parc
Floral** of Orléans-la-Source.
A 100-ha (245-acre) nature
reserve, the park is a mass of
blooms from April onwards.
Adjoining the park is the 17th-
century Château de la Source
and the buildings of the University of Orléans.

🌸 Parc Floral

Orléans-la-Source. 📞 38 49 30 00.
⭕ Apr–mid-Nov: daily; mid-Nov–
Mar: pm only. 🔲 ♿

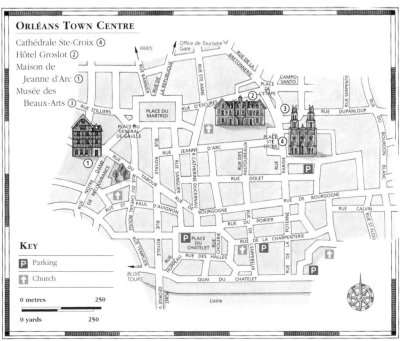

ORLÉANS TOWN CENTRE

Cathédrale Ste-Croix ④
Hôtel Groslot ②
Maison de
   Jeanne d'Arc ①
Musée des
   Beaux-Arts ③

KEY

🅿 Parking
✝ Church

0 metres   250
0 yards   250

The Romanesque façade of the abbey church of St-Benoît

St-Benoît-sur-Loire ⑱

Road map F3. 🏛 *2,000.* 🚌
ℹ *44 rue Orléanaise (38 35 79 00).*

T HIS QUIET TOWN can boast one of the finest Romanesque abbey churches in France, constructed between 1067 and 1108. Perhaps the most appealing feature of an otherwise sober façade is the belfry porch, probably built early in the 11th century by Abbot Gauzlin, son of the first Capetian king, Hugh. On the capitals of its 50 golden pillars are carved figures, including beasts and goblins.

Inside, thickset columns separate the side aisles from the rib-vaulted Gothic nave. The chancel, dating from the earlier Romanesque period, has blind arcades and a mosaic floor brought from Rome. The bas-relief head of a Norman raider is carved on the wall of the north transept. Its cheeks are pierced to expel its pagan spirit.

In the crypt, a lamplit casket contains the relics of St Benedict, the 6th-century father of Western monasticism. They were spirited here in 672 from Benedict's own monastery of Monte Cassino in Italy. By the 11th century, when the present building was begun, the Benedictine order was rich and St-Benoît-sur-Loire was renowned for its scholarship as well as its purloined relics. St-Benoît is a living monastery, and one of the best ways to experience the spirit of the place is to attend evening vespers or recitals of Gregorian chant.

The 9th-century church of **St Germigny-des-Prés** lies 5 km (3 miles) along the D60 from St-Benoît-sur-Loire. The small cupola of the east apse has an enchanting mosaic of angels bending over the Ark of the Covenant – a composition made up of 130,000 coloured-glass cubes probably assembled during the 6th century.

Gien ⑲

Road map F3. 🏛 *16,500.* 🚉 🚌
ℹ *pl Jean-Jaurès (38 67 25 28).*
🗓 *Wed, Sat.*

S ENSITIVELY RESTORED after being devastated during World War II, Gien is considered one of the Loire's prettiest towns. From its handsome quays and 16th-century bridge, houses of brick, slate and pale stone rise steeply to a château. It was built for Anne de Beaujeu, who acted as regent for her brother Charles XIII at the end of the 15th century.

Only the steeple tower of the **Eglise Ste-Jeanne d'Arc**, next to the château, survived the

Max Ingrand's stained glass

destruction of the war, but a remarkable church replaced it in the 1950s. Warm facings, composed of bricks made in Gien's famous pottery kilns, blend with the patterned red and black brickwork of the château. The interior glows with stained glass by Max Ingrand and the faïence that is a speciality of the area. A museum of fine china and earthenware is open daily at the factory, which was founded in 1821 *(see p221)*.

The **château** of Anne de Beaujeu, built between 1484 and 1500 on the site of one of the Loire's oldest castles, sheltered the young Louis XIV and the Queen Mother during the Fronde civil war (1648–53). Its grand beamed halls and galleries now house a superb museum of hunting, tracing the sport's development since prehistoric times. The collection covers the weaponry, costumery, techniques and related artistry of almost every associated activity, from falconry to the royal chase. The memorable entrance hall of the château features a 17th-century painting of St Hubert, the patron saint of hunting, depicting his conversion by the vision of a resurrected stag carrying a

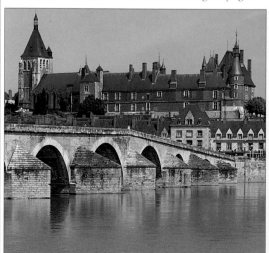

Gien's château and its 16th-century bridge across the Loire

crucifix between its horns. An Italian crossbow and a powder horn decorated with images of the mythical Diana and Actaeon are beautiful examples of 17th-century carving. Other prominent artists on display here include the 20th-century sculptor Florentin Brigaud, the Flemish etcher, Stradanus, and François Desportes, whose fine paintings dominate the spectacular trophy hall.

Château et Musée International de la Chasse
38 67 69 69. Mar–Dec: Tue–Sun. Jan–Feb, 25 Dec. grd flr only.

A pleasure boat crossing Briare's elegant bridge-canal

Briare-le-Canal ⓴

Road map F3. *6,000. pl Charles-de-Gaulle (38 31 24 51). Fri.*

THIS SMALL TOWN, with its attractive marina, is the setting for a sophisticated engineering masterpiece – the longest bridge-canal in Europe *(see pp56–7)*. With stonework and wrought-iron flourishes designed by Gustave Eiffel (1832–1923), the structure crosses the Loire, linking the Briare-Loing canal with the Canal Latéral. These waterways in turn join the Seine and the Rhône rivers respectively. Visitors can stroll its length, lined in the style of a Parisian boulevard with elegant lampposts, or sail across the 662-m (2,170-ft) bridge in a *bateau-mouche*.

Fishing on one of the peaceful *étangs* of the Sologne

The Sologne ㉑

Road map E3. *Romorantin-Lanthenay. Maison des Etangs, St Viâtre (54 88 93 20).*

BETWEEN GIEN and Blois, the Loire forms the northern boundary of the Sologne, a vast area of flat heathland, marshes and forests covering nearly 500,000 ha (1,235,000 acres). The area is dotted with *étangs*, broad lakes teeming with fish, which are magnets for migratory birds and waterfowl. The forests are as attractive to hunters and nature lovers now as they were during the Renaissance, when royalty chose to build their grand hunting lodges here. Much of the land is privately owned, although there are public paths.

Romorantin-Lanthenay is the "capital" of the Sologne. With its 17th- to 19th-century buildings and its medieval quarter, it is pleasant to visit. The town is also home to the **Musée de Sologne**, whose exhibits explain the economy and wildlife of the area.

St-Viâtre, just north of Romorantin-Lanthenay, is a centre for bird-watching on the *étangs* of Brosses, Grande Corbois, Favelle, Marcilly and Marguilliärs. The **Maison des Etangs** at St-Viâtre gives guidance on ornithology.

For game, there are four observation hides within the park of Chambord *(see pp134–5)*, where deer can often be seen – and heard in the autumn rutting season. Another large nature reserve open to the public is the **Domaine du Ciran**, 25 km (15 miles) south of Orléans, near Ménestreau-en-Villette.

Musée de Sologne
54 95 33 66. daily. Tue; Sun & public hols: am.

Maison des Etangs
54 88 93 20. Jun: Sat–Sun & public hols; 1 Jul–15 Sep: daily.

Domaine du Ciran
Ménestreau-en-Villette. *La Ferté-St-Aubin, then taxi. Ménestreau-en-Villette (38 76 90 93).*

A typical, half-timbered building of La Sologne

BERRY

BERRY LIES IN THE VERY CENTRE OF FRANCE, *south of the Paris Basin and just north of the Massif Central. It is a varied land of wheat fields, pastures and vineyards, ancient forests, rolling hills and lakes, peaceful villages and elegant manor houses. Mainly off the beaten tourist track, the region gives visitors an opportunity to experience the rural heart of France.*

Bourges, the principal town of Berry, was one of the capitals of Aquitaine in the Gallo-Roman period. It then enjoyed another moment of glory in the 14th century, with the administration of Jean, Duc de Berry. This warmongering patron of the arts built a splendid palace in the city (now destroyed) and collected paintings, tapestries, jewellery and illuminated manuscripts.

In the 1420s, when Charles VII was fighting for the French crown *(see pp52–3)*, Bourges was his campaign base. Afterwards, his treasurer Jacques Cœur did much to make the kingdom financially secure. The Palais Jacques-Cœur in Bourges competes with the city's magnificent cathedral in drawing crowds of admiring visitors.

Berry is ideal for those who love the outdoors, whether walking in the many well-tended forests, fishing or bird-watching in La Brenne, or sailing and canoeing on its rivers and lakes. Among the region's literary associations are George Sand's novels *(see p22)* and Alain-Fournier's evocative tale *Le Grand Meaulnes* (1913), which combines his childhood memories of the Sologne in the north and the rolling country of the south.

The culinary highlights of Berry include dishes made from local game and wild mushrooms. To the northeast, the renowned Sancerre wine district *(see p155)* is also known for its excellent goats' cheeses, such as the famous Crottin de Chavignol.

A river view by the village of Nohant

◁ **The vineyards of Sancerre**

Exploring Berry

BOURGES IS THE NATURAL starting point for exploring the heart of France. From here it is only a short drive to the edge of the Sologne *(see p141)* in the north or La Brenne in the southeast, both havens for wildlife. Below Bourges is the Champagne Berrichonne, a vast agricultural region producing wheat, barley and oil-rich crops such as rape and sunflowers. The River Loire forms the ancient border between Berry and Burgundy to the east as it flows through the vineyards of the Sancerrois hills.

The Palais Jacques-Cœur in Bourges

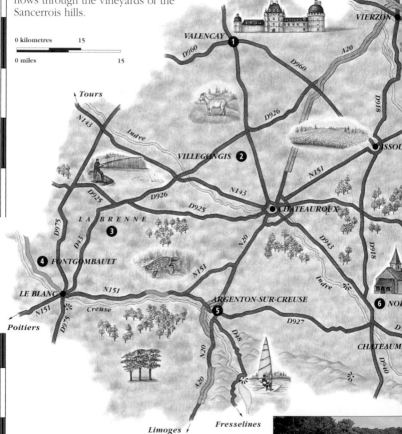

0 kilometres 15

0 miles 15

Orléans

VIERZON

VALENCAY ①

D960

D960

A20

Tours

N143

Indre

D926

D918

VILLEGONGIS ②

ISSOU

N151

D925

D926

N143

N151

CHATEAUROUX

L A B R E N N E

③

D975

D43

N20

D943

D918

④ FONTGOMBAULT

N151

LE BLANC

N151

Creuse

N151

ARGENTON-SUR-CREUSE

⑤

⑥ NO

Poitiers

D975

D927

D

CHATEAUM

D68

N20

CHATEAUM

A20

D940

Limoges

Fresselines

A riverside scene, typical of the Ber region's gentle landscape

GETTING AROUND

The A71 autoroute from Paris passes through Vierzon, Bourges and St-Amand-Montrond and is an excellent way of travelling from north to south. The TGV does not stop in the region, but Corail trains from Gare d'Austerlitz in Paris take just over two hours to either Bourges (not direct) or Châteauroux. There are also frequent trains between Bourges and Tours. Public transport to the more isolated sights is limited and a car is a great advantage, especially when touring the Sancerre wine estates or La Brenne nature reserves.

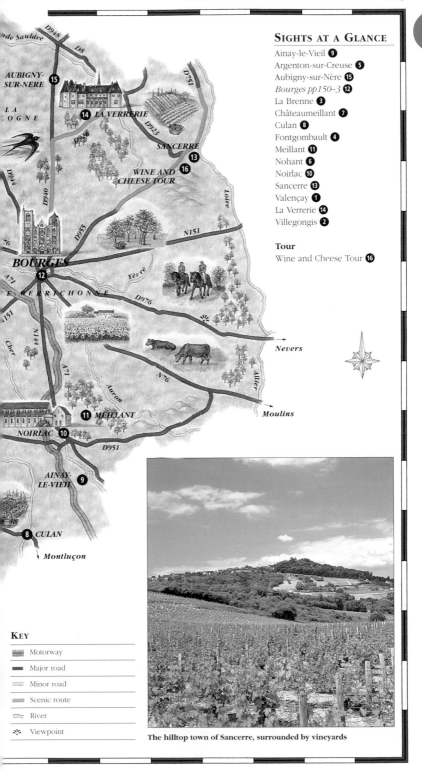

KEY

▬ Motorway

▬ Major road

▬ Minor road

▬ Scenic route

➤ River

☀ Viewpoint

The hilltop town of Sancerre, surrounded by vineyards

A resident peacock in front of the Château de Valençay

Château de Valençay ❶

Road map E4. 🚉 *Valençay*. 🕿 *54 00 10 66*. **Château & Musée de l'Auto** ☐ *Mar–Nov: daily.* **Park** ☐ *Mar–Oct: daily; Nov–Feb: pm only.* 📷 ♿ *park and grd flr only.*

FROM ITS TREE-LINED approach, the Château de Valençay is a fine sight. Started in 1510, it took more than 300 years to complete, but its Renaissance and Classical elements are convincingly blended. In 1803, it was bought by Bonaparte's foreign minister, Charles-Maurice de Talleyrand-Périgord, and the statesman died here in 1838. His descendants owned and lived in the château until 1980.

Valençay's rooms are very richly furnished, mostly in the Empire style, and they display many *objets d'art* connected with Talleyrand. The grounds are full of peacocks, swans, deer and some more exotic creatures, such as llamas and kangaroos. They also contain the **Musée de l'Auto**, a collection of vintage cars and motoring memorabilia.

Château de Villegongis ❷

Road map E4. 🚉 *Châteauroux, then taxi.* 🕿 *54 36 60 51.* ☐ *Apr–Sep: by appt.* 📷

ELEGANT AND MOATED, the Château de Villegongis was almost certainly built by Pierre Nepveu, one of the master masons for Chambord

(see pp132–5). Since the 15th century, ownership has stayed in the same family. During that time it has hardly been modified, and it remains one of the purest examples of the French Renaissance style.

The château's most striking features are its richly decorated chimneys, which suggest the link with Chambord, and its cylindrical towers at either end of the main building.

The interior is exceptionally well furnished, with some fine 17th- and 18th-century pieces. There is also a remarkable carved stone staircase.

La Brenne ❸

Road map E4. 🚌 *Mézières-en-Brenne, Le Blanc.* 🛈 *Maison du Parc, Rosnay (54 28 12 13).*

THE PARC NATUREL Régional de la Brenne, covering 165,000 ha (407,700 acres), is better known as the *Pays des*

Mille Etangs (The Land of a Thousand Meres). A beautiful region of lakes and wooded hills, La Brenne is a paradise for nature lovers. It has been estimated that 250 of the 450 bird species known in Europe can be observed here, including some of the rarest.

Several specialist reserves are open to visitors, such as the **Réserve Naturelle de Chérine**, good for spotting European pond tortoises, and the **Parc Animalier de la Haute-Touche**, home to endangered species of deer. The town of Mézières-en-Brenne houses the **Maison de la Pisciculture**, whose aquaria display local fish species.

In the northwest of La Brenne is **Azay-le-Ferron**, a largely Renaissance château with a formal garden and richly furnished rooms.

⚜ Réserve Naturelle de Chérine
St-Michel-en-Brenne. 🕿 *54 38 12 24.* **Observatory** ☐ *daily.* ● *1 Jan, 25 Dec.* 🖼 *Bird-watching tours: Apr–Jun: Tue, Thu, Sat 4–6pm; Jul–Aug: Tue 6–8pm, Sat, Sun 8–10pm.* 📷

⚜ Parc Animalier de la Haute-Touche
Obterre. 🕿 *54 39 20 82.* ☐ *Easter–Oct: daily.* 📷 ♿

⚜ Maison de la Pisciculture
Mézières-en-Brenne. 🕿 *54 38 12 99.* ☐ *Wed–Mon, pm only.* ● *1 Jan, 25 Dec.* 📷 ♿ *grd flr only.*

♠ Château d'Azay-le-Ferron
Azay-le-Ferron. 🕿 *54 39 20 06, 47 05 68 73.* ☐ *Feb–Mar & Oct–Dec: Wed, Sat & Sun; Apr–Sep: Wed–Mon.* ● *1 Jan, 1 & 11 Nov, 25 Dec.* 📷

One of the many idyllic lakes in La Brenne

Abbaye de Notre-Dame de Fontgombault ❹

Road map E4. ☎ *54 37 12 03.*
◯ *daily.* ✝ *Mon–Sat: 10am & 6pm; Sun: 10am & 5pm.* ♿

THE BEAUTIFUL Benedictine **Abbaye de Notre-Dame de Fontgombault**, famous for its Gregorian chant, was founded in 1091 but, by 1741, when the number of monks had dwindled to just five, it was abandoned. Restored by a local priest in the 19th century, it now houses monks from Solesmes *(see p162)*.

The church, with its five radiating chapels, has a richly decorated doorway, carved capitals and a much-venerated 12th-century statue known as Notre-Dame du Bien-Mourir, believed to bring comfort to the dying. Gregorian chant is still sung during services and is more prominent in the morning service. The monks run a pottery workshop, whose products can be bought from the exhibition centre located beside the church.

The radiating chapels of the Abbaye de Notre-Dame de Fontgombault

Old houses overhanging the river in Argenton-sur-Creuse

Argenton-sur-Creuse ❺

Road map E4. 👥 *5,200.* 🚉 🚌
ℹ *pl de la République (54 24 05 30).*
🛒 *Sat.* 🎭 *Leurica International Folklore Festival, (Jul); Jazz Festival (Aug).*

ARGENTON-SUR-CREUSE is one of the prettiest towns along the river, which winds from Fresselines to Argenton, passing through deep gorges. Streets of picturesque houses climb the hillside to Argenton's chapel of Notre-Dame-des-Bancs, dominated by its 6-m (20-ft) gilded statue of the Virgin Mary. There are fine views from here and from the Vieux Pont, a medieval bridge.

In the 19th century, the town became an important centre for the clothing industry.

This feature of the town's heritage is honoured by the informative collections of the **Musée de la Chemiserie et de l'Elégance Masculine**.

🏛 **Musée de la Chemiserie et de l'Elégance Masculine**
Argenton-sur-Creuse. ☎ *54 24 34 69.*
◯ *mid-Feb–Dec: Tue–Sun.* 🖼 ♿

Château de Nohant ❻

Road map E4. ☎ *54 31 06 04.*
🚉 🚌 *Châteauroux.* ◯ *daily.*
⬤ *public hols.* 🖼 🎭 *Fêtes Romantiques de Nohant (Jun); Chopin chez George Sand (Jul).*

GEORGE SAND, the *nom de plume* of the celebrated novelist, Baroness Aurore Dudevant (1804–76), was largely brought up in this charming manor house beside a tiny Romanesque church. She frequently returned here during her eventful and unconventional life, to enjoy the calm and beauty of her beloved Berry countryside.

Many of George Sand's novels, including *La Mare au Diable (The Devil's Pool)* and *La Petite Fadette (The Little Fairy)*, are set in the area *(see p22)*. Sand's admirers can view the boudoir where she first wrote, at a desk built inside a cupboard; the stage on which she and her guests acted out her plays; the puppets made by her son, Maurice; the bedroom used by her lover, the composer Frédéric Chopin; and the room in which she died in 1876.

MONET AT FRESSELINES

In 1889 the Impressionist painter Claude Monet travelled to the village of Fresselines, perched high above the Creuse. He visited a local beauty spot, with views plunging down into the river gorge, was captivated, and painted a series of canvases showing the scene in different lights. In February, bad weather forced him to stop painting and wait for spring. He then found that new growth had changed the view and had to pay the owner of an oak featured in five of his paintings to strip the tree of its new leaves.

Valley of the Petite Creuse by Claude Monet

Châteaumeillant ⓻

Road map F4. 🏘 2,000. 🚌
ⓘ Jun–Sep: rue de la Victoire (48 61 39 89); Oct–May: La Mairie (48 61 39 89). 🛒 Fri.

THE CHIEF GLORY of this town is the Romanesque **Eglise St-Genès**, built between 1125 and 1150, with its elegant pink and grey west façade. The interior is exceptionally airy, due not only to its great height, but also to its very wide chancel with six apsidal chapels and side passages that are separated by graceful double bays to create a cloisters effect.

Châteaumeillant was once an important Gallo-Roman centre and has a museum of Roman artifacts. Based in a 15th-century manor house, the **Musée Emile-Chenon** also exhibits local medieval finds.

🏛 Musée Emile-Chenon
Rue de la Victoire. ⓒ 48 61 39 89.
🕐 Jun–Sep: daily. 🎫 🅰 grd flr only.

Château de Culan ⓼

Road map F4. 🚌 ⓒ 48 56 64 18.
🕐 Apr–Oct: daily. 🎫

STRATEGICALLY positioned on a rocky escarpment high above the River Arnon, this medieval fortress dates from the 13th and 14th centuries. Its three imposing conical towers are topped by wooden siege hoardings, which have been well preserved. Inside, a series of furnished rooms relate the castle's long history,

The interior courtyard of the Château d'Ainay-le-Vieil

recalling famous visitors who have stayed there, including the Admiral of Culan, who was a comrade-in-arms of Joan of Arc (who also stayed there in 1430), and the writers George Sand *(see p22)* and Madame de Sévigné, and telling of an attack during the 17th-century Fronde uprising.

Lovely views over Culan's newly replanted gardens and the pastoral Arnon Valley can be enjoyed from the terrace of the château.

Château d'Ainay-le-Vieil ⓽

Road map F4. 🚉 St-Amand-Montrond, then taxi. ⓒ 48 63 50 03.
🕐 Feb: Wed–Mon pm only; Mar & Nov: Wed–Mon; Apr–Oct: daily. 🎫
🅰 grd flr only.

FROM THE OUTSIDE, Ainay-le-Vieil has the appearance of a severe fortress, with its thick, formidable walls and its nine massive towers, lit only by

thin arrow slits. The octagonal enclosure, surrounded by a flowing moat, is entered through a huge, 13th-century postern gate. Inside, however, hides a graceful Renaissance château designed for an elegant lifestyle, with its richly decorated façade enlivened by sunny loggias.

The castle changed hands many times during its early history. In the 15th century, it belonged briefly to Charles VII's treasurer Jacques Cœur *(see p151)*, but in 1467 it was bought by the Seigneurs de Bigny whose descendants still live here today.

The Grand Salon was decorated in honour of a visit by Louis XII and Anne of Brittany around 1500. It has a painted ceiling and a monumental fireplace, which is said to be one of the most attractive in the Loire Valley. On display is a portrait of Louis XIV's chief minister Jean-Baptiste Colbert and portraits of other family members, as well as an amber pendant that belonged to Queen Marie-Antoinette and several *objets de vertu*, friendship gifts given by Napoleon to General Auguste Colbert.

The tiny Renaissance chapel has some beautiful, late 16th-century wall paintings, which were discovered under 19th-century decoration. Its stained-glass windows were made by an artist who also worked on the Cathédrale St-Etienne in Bourges *(see pp152–3)*.

In the park is a delightful and fragrant rose garden. Some of the varieties of roses which are grown here date back to the 15th century.

The Château de Culan, set high above the River Arnon

Abbaye de Noirlac ❿

Road map F4. 🚉 *St-Amand-Montrond, then taxi.* 📞 *48 96 23 64.* 🕐 *Feb–Sep: daily; Oct–Jan: Wed–Mon.* ⬤ *1 Jan; 25 Dec.* ♿ *grd flr only.* 🎭 *L'Été de Noirlac (Jul–Aug).*

THE CISTERCIAN Abbaye de Noirlac, founded in 1136, is a fine example of medieval monastic architecture. The Cistercian Order's austerity is reflected in the pure lines of the partly 12th-century church and visually echoed in its sober, modern stained glass.

The chapter house, where the monks' daily assemblies were held, and the *cellier*, where the lay brothers were in charge of the food, wine and grain stores, were also built in this plain but elegant style. The cloisters, with their graceful arches and decorated capitals, date from the 13th and 14th centuries, which was a less severe period.

At **Bruère-Allichamps**, 4 km (2½ miles) northwest of the abbey, a Gallo-Roman milestone marks the alleged exact centre point of France.

The austere lines of the Abbaye de Noirlac

Château de Meillant ⓫

Road map F4. 🚉 *St-Amand-Montrond, then taxi.* 📞 *48 63 30 58, 48 63 32 05.* 🕐 *Feb–mid-Dec: daily.* ♿ *grd flr only.*

SUMPTUOUSLY furnished rooms and the elaborate carved ceilings of this well-preserved Berry château complement its rather exuberantly decorated courtyard façade. Built for Charles d'Amboise in 1510 by skilful Italian craftsmen, the château represents a fine combination of late Gothic and early Renaissance architecture. It is dominated by the Tour de Lion (Lion's Tower), an octagonal three-storey staircase tower. The plainer west façade, mirrored in a moat, dates from the early 14th century.

A small grotesque carving in Meillant

Other highlights of a visit include the château's graceful chapel and its surrounding grounds in which peacocks strut. The grounds also feature **La Mini'stoire**, an interesting miniature park, where models of buildings depict the ways in which architectural styles have varied over the centuries.

🏛 **La Mini'stoire** 🕐 *Feb–mid-Dec: daily.* ♿

LIFE IN A CISTERCIAN ABBEY

The Rules of the Cistercian Order were based on the principles of austerity and simplicity. Abbeys were divided into two communities, which did not mix. Lay brothers, not bound by holy vows, ensured the self-sufficiency of the abbey by managing the barns, tilling the fields, milling corn and welcoming guests. The full, or choir, monks were the only ones allowed into the cloister, at the heart of the

A Cistercian monk labouring in the fields

complex, and could not leave the abbey without the permission of the abbot.

The monks' days started at 2am and ended at 7pm and were regularly punctuated by religious devotions, which included prayers, confession, meditation and mass. The strict rule of silence was broken only to read from the Bible or from the Rules of the Order. Many monks were literate, and monasteries played a leading role in copying manuscripts.

Bourges ⓬

THE HEART OF MODERN BOURGES, once the Roman city of Avaricum, is the network of ancient streets around its magnificent cathedral. Despite a dramatic fire in 1487, the city was an important religious and arts centre in the Middle Ages and, by the late 19th century, it was a prosperous industrial town. Today, Bourges has a quiet atmosphere that complements its excellent museums, housed in superb old buildings. It comes to life in the spring during the *Printemps de Bourges*, a rock festival attracting a large, predominantly young audience.

The 16th-century *Concert Champêtre*, displayed in the Hôtel Lallemant

🏛 Hôtel des Echevins & Musée Estève

12 rue Edouard Branly. 📞 *48 24 75 38.* ☐ *Mon, Wed–Sat; Sun (pm only).* ● *public hols.* 📷 ♿

The Hôtel des Echevins (the house of the aldermen), which is remarkable for its intricately carved octagonal tower, was built in 1489 and served as the seat of the city council that governed Bourges for more than three centuries.

The building was classified an historic monument in 1886. In 1985 work to renovate the building began, and in 1987, it became the Musée Estève, displaying paintings by the self-taught artist Maurice Estève, who was born in the town of Culan in the south of Berry *(see p148)*. The collection is for the most part made up of Estève's powerful, brightly coloured canvases. However, this permanent display is augmented by temporary exhibitions of his watercolours, collages and line drawings. The collection is arranged in chronological order on three levels, connected by elegant stone spiral staircases. This modern work as a whole seems surprisingly at home in the spacious Gothic rooms.

Samsâra by Maurice Estève (1977)

🏛 Hôtel Lallemant & Musée des Arts Décoratifs

6 rue Bourbonnoux. 📞 *48 57 81 17.* ☐ *Tue–Sat; Sun (pm only).* ● *public hols.* 📷

This Renaissance mansion, built for a rich merchant family originally from Germany, houses the city's decorative arts museum. It still has the little chapel used by the Lallemant family, its coffered ceiling carved with alchemical symbols, and an elegant, restored courtyard. On display is a fine collection of tapestries, clocks, ceramics, glass, paintings and furniture, including a beautiful 17th-century ebony inlaid cabinet. In another part of the mansion, there is a collection of toys dating from the 17th century to the present.

🏛 Musée du Berry

4–6 rue des Arènes. 📞 *48 70 41 92.* ☐ *Mon, Wed–Sat; Sun (pm only).* ● *public hols.* 📷 ♿ *grd flr only.*

The Musée du Berry, housed in the Renaissance Hôtel Cujas, concentrates on local history. The collections include a large display of Gallo-Roman artifacts, many of which were unearthed in the area. There is also some wonderful Gothic sculpture, especially Jean de Cambrai's weeping figures from the base of the marble tomb of Jean, Duc de Berry, the upper section of which can be seen in the crypt of the Cathédrale St-Etienne *(see pp152-3)*.

On the upper floor of the museum is a permanent exhibition of Berry's rural arts, crafts and everyday objects, including the distinctive stoneware made in La Borne near Sancerre.

Jehan Fouquet's Angel Ceiling in the Palais Jaques-Cœur

JACQUES CŒUR

The son of a Bourges furrier, Jacques Cœur (c.1400–56) became one of the richest and most powerful men in medieval France. With his merchant fleet he sailed to the eastern Mediterranean and Far East, bringing back luxury goods such as silks, spices and precious metals, until Charles VII appointed him head of the Paris Mint, then treasurer of the Royal Household.
In 1451 he was accused of fraud and falsely implicated in the death of the king's mistress, Agnès Sorel. He was arrested, tortured and imprisoned, but escaped to Rome. There he took part in the pope's naval expedition against the Turks and died on the Greek island of Chios.

The merchant Jacques Cœur

VISITORS' CHECKLIST

Road map F4. 🚶 76,000. 🚉 pl du Général Leclerc. 🚌 rue du Pré Doulet. 🛈 21 rue Victor Hugo (48 24 75 33). 🕿 Thu, Sat & Sun. 🎭 Printemps de Bourges (Apr); Balades à Bourges (street festival, Jul–Aug).

The fireplace in the south gallery of the Palais Jacques-Cœur

🏛 Palais Jacques-Cœur

Rue Jacques-Cœur. 🕿 48 24 06 87. ⭘ daily. ● public hols. 🎟

This splendidly decorated palace, built onto the remains of the city's ancient Gallo-Roman walls, is among the finest secular Gothic buildings in Europe. It was constructed at great expense between 1443 and 1451 for Jacques Cœur, one of the most fascinating men in medieval France.

The palace has a number of innovations remarkable for their period. Rooms open off corridors instead of leading into each other, as they did in most buildings at the time, and a stone lavatory shows that sanitation was a consideration. Appealingly, each room is "labelled" over the doorway with carved scenes that illustrate its function.

From trompe l'oeil figures peeping out from the turreted entrance façade to the mysterious, possibly alchemical, symbols carved everywhere, the palace offers a feast of interesting details. Hearts are a common motif – the newly ennobled owner naturally had hearts, cœurs in French, on his coat of arms.

Other notable features are a large courtyard, superb wooden vaulting in the galleries, and the beautiful ceiling in the chapel, painted by Tours artist Jehan Fouquet (see p23).

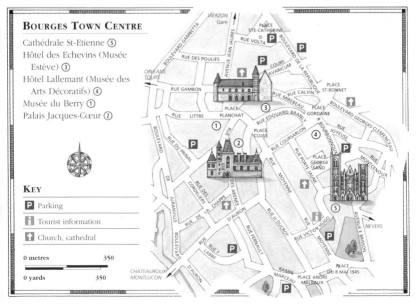

BOURGES TOWN CENTRE

Cathédrale St-Etienne ⑤
Hôtel des Echevins (Musée Estève) ③
Hôtel Lallemant (Musée des Arts Décoratifs) ④
Musée du Berry ①
Palais Jacques-Cœur ②

KEY

🅿 Parking
🛈 Tourist information
✝ Church, cathedral

0 metres   350
0 yards   350

Bourges: Cathédrale St-Etienne

Stained-glass window detail

ST-ETIENNE, ONE OF FRANCE'S finest Gothic cathedrals, was built mainly between 1195 and 1260. The unknown architect designed St-Etienne without transepts, which, combined with the interior's unusual height and width, makes it seem much lighter than most Gothic cathedrals. This effect is beautifully enhanced by the brilliant hues of the medieval stained glass. Also unusual are the asymmetrical west front; the double row of flying buttresses rising in pyramid-shaped tiers; and a "crypt", a lower, window-lit church, created because the ground is 6 m (20 ft) lower at the east end.

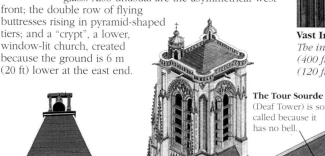

Vast Interior
The interior is 124 m (400 ft) long and 37 m (120 ft) high.

The Tour Sourde
(Deaf Tower) is so called because it has no bell.

★ **Astrological Clock**
Dating from the 1420s, this fascinating clock was designed by Canon Jean Fusoris, a mathematician.

Entrance

THE LAST JUDGMENT

The tympanum on the central portal of the west façade depicts Archangel Michael weighing souls. Those found wanting are hustled by devils into the mouth of Hell, while the elect are gathered into the bosom of Abraham. The youthful, naked dead lift up their tombstones in a dramatic Resurrection scene.

The Last Judgment portal of the Cathédrale St-Etienne

The Grand Housteau is a striking rose window, donated by the renowned patron of the arts Jean, Duc de Berry.

The five portals of the west front are surrounded by carved scenes. The doorways vary in size and shape, adding to the asymmetry of the façade.

★ Stained-Glass Windows
The medieval stained glass in the choir was sponsored by local guilds, whose members are depicted practising their crafts at the bottom of each window.

VISITORS' CHECKLIST

Pl Etienne Dolet. ☎ 48 24 75 33.
⭘ daily: 8am–6pm (except during services). ☒ Apr–Oct. ⬆ Sat: 6:30pm; Sun: 9am & 11am.
Crypt ⭘ *Mon–Sat: 9–11am, 2–4:30pm (Easter–Sep: until 5:30pm), Sun; pm only. ☒ ⊡

The Chapelle Jacques-Cœur has a glorious Annunciation window.

Praying Figures
In the crypt are statues of the Duc and Duchesse de Berry. During the Revolution the statues were decapitated and the existing heads are copies.

The crypt, or lower church, was built in the earlier Gallo-Roman moat.

The Romanesque portal on the cathedral's south side is decorated with a *Christ in Majesty* and the 12 apostles.

★ St Sépulcre
This dramatic sculpture of the Entombment of Christ *was placed at the far end of the lower church in 1540.*

STAR FEATURES

★ Astrological Clock

★ Stained-Glass Windows

★ St Sépulcre

Jean, Duc de Berry
The recumbent marble effigy of Jean, Duc de Berry, his feet resting on a bear, was originally part of his tomb.

A Sancerre vineyard

Sancerre ⑬

Road map F3. 🏛 *2,100.* 🚌
ℹ️ *Hôtel de Ville (48 54 00 26).*
🗓 *Tue, Sat.* 🎪 *Foire aux Crottins
(goat's cheese fair, early May); Foire aux
Vins (wine fair, Whitsun); Foire aux Vins
de France (French wine fair, late Aug).*

THE ANCIENT Berry town of
Sancerre is perched on a
domed hill, a rare sight in the
generally flat landscape of the
Loire Valley. Its narrow streets
boast some interesting 15th-
and 16th-century houses. All
that remains of the medieval
castle that once dominated the
town is the **Tour des Fiefs**.
From the top of this tower is a
superb view of the broad River
Loire, before it turns to flow
westwards. The town and surrounding area are famous for
their dry white wines.

Located in a lovely pastoral
setting, 10 km (6 miles) to the
west of Sancerre, the **Château
de Boucard** is part medieval
in origin, but has an elegant
Renaissance courtyard.

🏛 **Tour des Fiefs**
⭕ *Summer: Sat, Sun & public hols
pm only.*
🏛 **Château de Boucard**
Le Noyer. 📞 *48 58 72 81.*
⭕ *Fri–Wed.* ⚫ *Jan.* 🈺

Château de la Verrerie ⑭

Road map F3. 🚉 *Gien, then taxi.*
📞 *48 58 06 91.* ⭕ *Easter–Oct: daily.*
🈺 🔧 *See Where to Stay, p205.*

THIS FINE, early Renaissance
château is on the edge of
the Forêt d'Ivoy. The land
was given to the Scot Sir John

Stewart of Darnley by Charles
VII, in thanks for defeating the
English at the battle of Baugé
in 1421. John's son, Béraud
Stewart, began to build the
château several decades later.
It was completed by Béraud's
nephew, Robert.

La Verrerie reverted to the
French crown in 1670. Three
years later Louis XIV gave the
château to Louise de Kéroualle.
She lived here until her death
in 1734 at the age of 85.

La Verrerie has a lovely
Renaissance gallery with 16th-
century frescoes. The chapel
also has fine frescoes, which
date from the same period. In
the 19th-century wing are four
beautiful alabaster statuettes
from the tomb of the Duc de
Berry (see pp152–3).

The grounds have a good
restaurant and some of the
château's rooms are available
for visitors to stay overnight.

**Alabaster statuettes in the Château
de la Verrerie's 19th-century wing**

Aubigny-sur-Nère ⑮

Road map F3. 🏛 *6,000.* 🚌 ℹ️
*Hôtel de Ville (48 81 50 00). May–Oct:
rue des Dames (48 58 40 20).* 🗓 *Sat.*
🎪 *Fête Franco-Ecossaise (mid-Jul).*

ATTRACTIVE AUBIGNY, with its
half-timbered houses, is
proud of its association
with the Scottish
Stewart clan. In 1423
the town was given
by Charles VII to Sir
John Stewart of
Darnley, along with
nearby La Verrerie.
After a major fire in
1512, the Stewarts
rebuilt Aubigny in the
Renaissance style and
also constructed a
new château.

In 1673 Louis XIV
gave the duchy of
Aubigny to Louise de
Kéroualle. Although

she spent most of her time at
La Verrerie, Louise had a large
garden created at the Château
d'Aubigny. The Aubusson
tapestries presented to her by
the king are displayed in the
château, which now serves as
the town hall and also houses
two museums. The unusual
**Musée de la Vieille Alliance
Franco-Ecossaise** is devoted
to the Auld Alliance, the
town's long ties with Scotland:
Jacobite refugees settled here
during the 18th century.

The 13th-century **Eglise St-
Martin**, in transitional Gothic
style, was largely rebuilt by
the Stewarts. It has a beautiful
wooden Pietà and a moving
16th-century Entombment.

Berry has a reputation for
sorcery, a tradition well illustrated in Concressault's lively
Musée de la Sorcellerie, 10
km (6 miles) east of Aubigny.
Here waxworks bring to life
the history of herbalism, heal-
ing and magic, and portray
the gruesome fate of those
accused of witchcraft during
the Inquisition.

🏛 **Musée de la Vieille
Alliance Franco-Ecossaise
& Musée Marguerite-
Audoux**
Château d'Aubigny. 📞 *48 81 50 00.*
⭕ *Easter–Jun & Oct–Nov: Sat, Sun &
public hols; Jul–mid-Sep: daily; Dec–
Easter: Sun & public hols (pm only).* 🈺
🔧 *Musée de la Vieille Alliance only.*
🏛 **Musée de la Sorcellerie**
La Jonchère, Concressault. 📞 *48 73
86 11.* ⭕ *Easter–Oct: daily.* 🈺 🔧

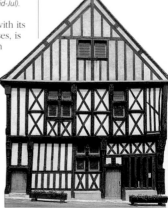

**The Maison de François I, one of the many
old houses in Aubigny-sur-Nère**

Wine and Cheese Tour 🟢

The sancerrois in eastern Berry is renowned for its wines and goats' cheese. Gourmets can visit the top-class Sancerre caves and taste the fresh and fragrant white wines made from the Sauvignon grape, or charming light reds and rosés made from the Pinot Noir. The flavours combine beautifully

Sancerre wine

with the sharp little goats' cheeses called Crottins de Chavignol, which are also produced locally. This rural route passes by gently hilly vineyards and fields of grazing red goats. It takes in the locales of many of the major producers, as well as a few local museums that explain the long history of both wine and cheese.

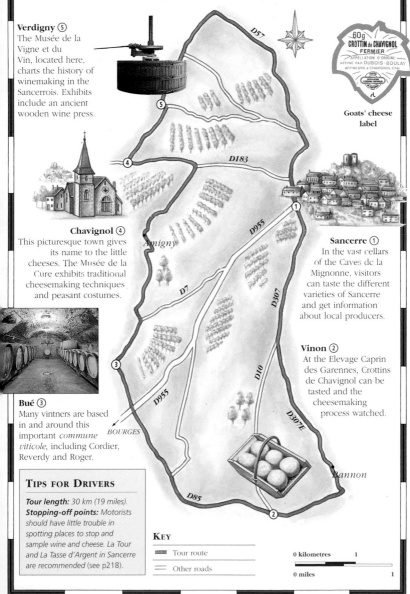

Verdigny ⑤
The Musée de la Vigne et du Vin, located here, charts the history of winemaking in the Sancerrois. Exhibits include an ancient wooden wine press.

Goats' cheese label

60 g
CROTTIN de CHAVIGNOL
FERMIER
APPELLATION D'ORIGINE
AFFINÉ PAR DUBOIS · BOULAY
AFFINEURS à CHAVIGNOL Cher

Chavignol ④
This picturesque town gives its name to the little cheeses. The Musée de la Cure exhibits traditional cheesemaking techniques and peasant costumes.

Sancerre ①
In the vast cellars of the Caves de la Mignonne, visitors can taste the different varieties of Sancerre and get information about local producers.

Vinon ②
At the Elevage Caprin des Garennes, Crottins de Chavignol can be tasted and the cheesemaking process watched.

Bué ③
Many vintners are based in and around this important *commune viticole*, including Cordier, Reverdy and Roger.

D57 · *D183* · *D955* · *D307* · *D7* · *D10* · *D307E* · *D955* · *D85*

Amigny · *BOURGES* · *Bannon*

TIPS FOR DRIVERS

Tour length: 30 km (19 miles).
Stopping-off points: Motorists should have little trouble in spotting places to stop and sample wine and cheese. La Tour and La Tasse d'Argent in Sancerre are recommended (see p218).

KEY

▬▬ Tour route
═══ Other roads

0 kilometres   1
0 miles   1

NORTH OF THE LOIRE

HE PEACEFUL MAYENNE *and Sarthe regions seem worlds away from the tourist-frequented château country of the central Loire Valley. A grouping of districts with little common history, the area north of the Loire has very different attractions from the former royal domains to the south. The rivers, hills, forests and plains abound with opportunities for fishing, boating and country walks.*

River boats cruise along the quiet Sarthe, through pretty wooded scenery and meadowlands, to Sablé-sur-Sarthe, near the Abbaye de Solesmes, famous for its tradition of superb Gregorian chant.

The more dramatic scenery of the Mayenne valley, from Laval southwards, with steep cliffs and villages perched on wooded hills, makes a pleasant spot for a restful break from château-visiting. The river, studded with locks, runs into the Maine and then into the Loire, a pattern also followed by the Loir (Le Loir, which is not to be confused with La Loire).

The valley of the Loir is also very pretty, the slow-moving river flowing through peaceful villages. It is a perfect place for relaxing and enjoying the countryside. The valley also offers a few spectacular sights of its own, including the château at Le Lude, where one of France's most elaborate son et lumière shows is staged, and the château of Châteaudun, which was once a stronghold of the counts of Blois. Le Mans, world famous for its 24 hour car race, also has an attractive old town, Le Vieux Mans. East of the town, gentle scenery gives way first to the wooded hills of the Perche and then to the vast wheat-fields on the plain of the Beauce, which is dominated by the magnificent cathedral at Chartres. Two lovely châteaux, Anet and Maintenon, were homes to royal mistresses: Diane de Poitiers *(see p55)*, mistress of Henri II, retreated to Anet, and Madame de Maintenon was the mistress of Louis XIV. Like Chartres Cathedral, these great houses stand on the edge of the Ile de France, the region around Paris, so they attract many day visitors from the country's capital.

Clog-making at the woodwork centre in Jupilles in the Forêt de Bercé

◁ **The River Sarthe near the village of St-Céneri-le-Gérei**

Exploring the North of the Loire

CONSISTING OF THE *départements* of Mayenne, Sarthe and Eure-et-Loire, the region north of the Loire borders Brittany, Normandy and the Ile de France. It combines characteristics of all these regions with those of the central Loire Valley. In the north, the hills of the Alpes Mancelles have more in common with the landscapes of Normandy than they do with the rolling fields further south. The rivers traversing the region – the Loir, Sarthe and Mayenne – are smaller and gentler than the mighty Loire but still very scenic. The largest towns in the region are Chartres, Le Mans and Laval, all of them worth a visit.

One of Chartres' wind
cobbled str

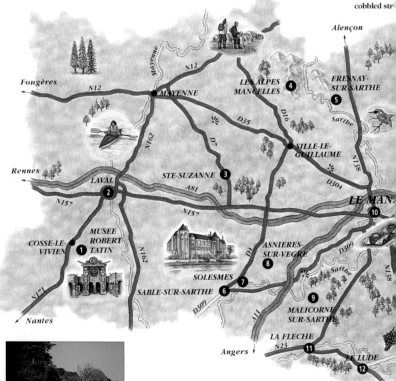

Cruising on the River Sarthe,
upstream from Sablé

GETTING AROUND

Chartres and Le Mans are both reached from Paris by the A11 autoroute (*L'Océane*), which continues to Angers. The A81 crosses the region from Le Mans to Laval. Trains from Paris are frequent, with the TGV taking 55 minutes to reach Le Mans and Corail express trains taking one hour to Chartres. The train journey between Chartres and Le Mans also takes an hour. Bus services link most of the main towns in the region but are less regular during school holidays. Boating is one of the best ways of seeing the countryside.

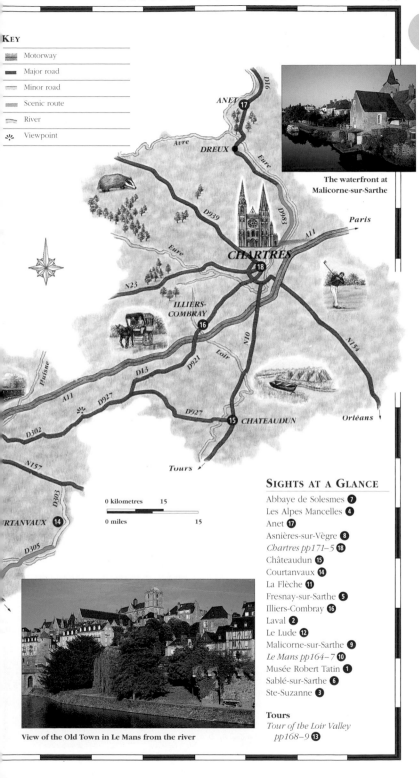

KEY

▰▰	Motorway
▰	Major road
▭	Minor road
▭	Scenic route
⌐	River
✻	Viewpoint

The waterfront at
Malicorne-sur-Sarthe

ANET **17**

Avre

DREUX ●

D16

Eure

D939

D983

Paris

CHARTRES

18

A11

N23

Eure

**ILLIERS-
COMBRAY**

16

D921

N10

Loir

N154

Puisne

A11

D13

D927

D927

15 **CHATEAUDUN**

Orléans →

D302

N157

D303

RTANVAUX **14**

D305

Tours →

0 kilometres   15

0 miles   15

View of the Old Town in Le Mans from the river

SIGHTS AT A GLANCE

Abbaye de Solesmes **7**
Les Alpes Mancelles **4**
Anet **17**
Asnières-sur-Vègre **8**
Chartres pp171–5 **18**
Châteaudun **15**
Courtanvaux **14**
La Flèche **11**
Fresnay-sur-Sarthe **5**
Illiers-Combray **16**
Laval **2**
Le Lude **12**
Malicorne-sur-Sarthe **9**
Le Mans pp164–7 **10**
Musée Robert Tatin **1**
Sablé-sur-Sarthe **6**
Ste-Suzanne **3**

Tours
*Tour of the Loir Valley
  pp168–9* **13**

Musée Robert Tatin ❶

Road map B2. La Frénouse. 🚗
Laval. 🚌 *Cossé-le-Vivien.* 📞 *43 98
80 89.* 🕐 *Wed–Mon.* 📷 ♿
courtyard & grd flr only.

T HE MULTI-TALENTED artist,
Robert Tatin (1902–83),
devised an extraordinary
museum, which is
located in the little
village of La Frénouse,
near Cossé-le-Vivien. The
museum building is
approached via the Allée
des Géants (Giants'
Avenue): lining the path
are huge, strange
concrete figures,
depicting people who
impressed Tatin,
including Pablo
Picasso, Toulouse-
Lautrec, Joan of
Arc and the Gallic
warrior,
Vercingetorix.
Beyond them, a statue of a
huge dragon with enormous
jaws stands guard.
In the museum are some
400 examples of Tatin's work:
paintings, sculpture, frescoes,
mosaics and ceramics. Tatin
was also a cabinet-maker and
much else besides. He was
influenced by the megalithic
monuments in Brittany and
the traditional costumes worn
by Breton men and women,
as well as by Aztec art – he
lived and travelled in South
America for five years.

**Tatin's statue of Picasso
at the Musée Robert Tatin**

Laval ❷

Road map C2. 🏛 *54,000.* 🚗 🚌
🛈 *1 allée du Vieux St-Louis (43 49
46 46).* 🚌 *Tue, Sat.*

L AVAL STRADDLES the River
Mayenne, which can be
crossed via the humpbacked
Gothic Vieux Pont (Old
Bridge). Beside it on the west
bank, in the heart of the old
town, is the **Vieux Château**.
This imposing castle dates
from the early 11th century,
when the region was under
the sway of Foulques Nerra,
Count of Anjou – it formed
one link in his chain of
fortresses designed to keep
out the invading Bretons and
Normans. Although it has
been heavily rebuilt and
added to over the centuries,
the original medieval round
keep has survived. The
flower-filled courtyard, with a
terrace offering good river
views, has an attractive
Renaissance façade.
The château has a collection
of the equipment used
by Laval native,
Ambroise Paré (1510–
c.1592), known as "the
father of modern surgery".
It is best known, however,
for its **Musée d'Art Naïf**
(Museum of Naïve Art)
which was inspired in
part by the work of
the painter Henri
Rousseau *(see p23)*,
born in Laval. He
was known as *Le
Douanier*, his
nickname deriving
from the period
when, as a young
artist in Paris, he
worked as a customs officer.
His Paris studio, complete

with piano, has been neatly
reconstructed here. Although
the museum has only two of
Rousseau's paintings, there
are many gems in its 450-
strong collection, including a
bright-red painting of the
ocean liner *Normandie* by
Jules Lefranc (1887–1972).
Laval's old town boasts some
attractive houses as well as
the **Cathédrale de la Ste-
Trinité**, with its Aubusson
tapestries. Laval also has one
of France's few surviving
bateaux-lavoirs, **Bateau-Lavoir
St-Julien**, now a museum.
Such floating laundries first
appeared in the mid-19th
century on the banks of rivers
in the western Loire Valley.

🏛 **Château & Musée du
Vieux Château**
Pl de la Trémoille. 📞 *43 53 39 89.*
🕐 *Tue–Sun.* ⬤ *public hols.* 📷
♿ *grd flr only.*
🏛 **Bateau-Lavoir St-Julien**
Quai Paul-Boudet. 📞 *43 53 39 89.*
🕐 *Jul–Aug: Tue–Sun, pm only.*
⬤ *public hols.*

Le Lancement du Normandie **by Jules Lefranc, at the Musée d'Art Naïf**

Ste-Suzanne ❸

Road map C2. 👥 950. 🚉 Evron, then taxi. 🛈 pl Amboise-de-Loré (43 01 43 60).

THIS VILLAGE, perched high up on a hill, is still partly surrounded by the fortifications originally designed as a defence against marauding Normans in the 10th century – it was sturdy enough to withstand an attack by William the Conqueror, whose former encampment site can be seen just 3 km (2 miles) outside the town. Although much of the original castle was pulled down by the English in the early 15th century, a 10th-century keep still stands.

The present castle, the **Château des Fouquet de la Varenne**, constructed of white tufa and grey slate, dates from the early 17th century.

The village has a small museum, the **Musée de l'Auditoire**, covering more than 1,000 years of local history, with reconstructions of major events and vignettes of daily life in the region.

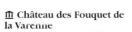
Church doorway, St-Léonard-des-Bois

🏛 **Château des Fouquet de la Varenne**
Promenade de la Poterne. 📞 43 01 40 77. 🕐 mid-Apr–mid-Jun & mid-Sep–early Nov: daily, pm only; mid-Jun–mid-Sep: daily. 📷 ♿ grd flr only.

🏛 **Musée de l'Auditoire**
7 Grande Rue. 📞 43 01 42 65, 43 01 42 16. 🕐 Apr–Sep: daily, pm only. 📷 ♿ grd flr only.

Les Alpes Mancelles ❹

Road map C2. 🚉 🚌 Fresnay-sur-Sarthe. 🛈 19 av du Dr Riant, Fresnay-sur-Sarthe (43 33 28 04).

THE NAME of this region of wooded hills and green meadows, stretching between Fresnay-sur-Sarthe and Alençon, means "Alps of Le Mans". This is certainly an exaggeration, although there is something faintly alpine in the pleasant landscape, with its streams winding through

St-Céneri-le-Gérei's Romanesque church, perched on a hill

gorges, grazing sheep, fruit trees and heather-clad hillsides.

The prettiest villages are **St-Céneri-le-Gérei**, which has a Romanesque church containing 12th- and 14th-century frescoes, and **St-Léonard-des-Bois**, also with a Romanesque church. There are beautiful walks through the countryside and along the River Sarthe, and the area is also very popular for canoeing, angling and other sports (see pp224–7).

Fresnay-sur-Sarthe ❺

Road map C2. 👥 2,500. 🚉 Sillé-le-Guillaume, La Hutte. 🚌 🛈 19 av du Dr Riant (43 33 28 04). 🚆 Sat.

ALTHOUGH INDUSTRIAL on its outskirts, the rest of Fresnay still retains a somewhat medieval feel. There were originally three rings of walls surrounding the town and fragments of them are still visible from the river.

The castle, which is strategically located on a rocky spur above the Sarthe, was besieged by William the Conqueror in 1073. During the Hundred Years' War (see pp52–3), this was the last fortress in the region to be surrendered by the English. The remains of the castle now stand amid acres of pleasant parkland.

From the 16th to the 19th century, Fresnay-sur-Sarthe was an important centre for cloth-weaving, and its involvement in the clothing industry is documented in the interesting **Musée des Coiffes** (Headdress Museum) which is now housed in the remains of the castle.

The town also has a long tradition of encouraging local craftspeople, some of whose work is displayed in the **Maison du Tourisme et de l'Artisanat**.

Situated at the end of the avenue du Dr Riant, the **Eglise Notre-Dame**, with both Romanesque and Gothic elements, has an unusual tower with an octagonal base and a beautifully carved, old oak door.

🏛 **Musée des Coiffes**
Pl de Bassum. 📞 43 97 22 20. 🕐 Easter–Jun & Sep: Sun & public hols; Jul–Aug: daily. 📷

🏛 **Maison du Tourisme et de l'Artisanat**
Pl de Bassum. 📞 43 33 75 98. 🕐 Apr–May & Oct–Nov: Sat, Sun & public hols; Jun–Sep & Dec: daily. ♿ grd flr only.

The River Sarthe from the town of Fresnay-sur-Sarthe

Sablé-sur-Sarthe ❻

Road map C2. 🏘 *14,000*. 🚉 🚌
ℹ️ *pl Raphaël-Elizé (43 95 00 60)*. 🛒
Mon, Fri. 🎭 *Carnaval (Mar); Festival
et Académie de Danses et Musiques
Anciennes (Aug).*

A GOOD BASE from which to
take river cruises along
the Sarthe, Sablé is pleasant,
although fairly industrial. It is
an enjoyable town to explore
on foot. There is some surprising modern sculpture in this
traditional setting: in the cobbled place Raphaël Elizé in
the town centre stands a contemporary sculpture entitled
Hymne à l'Amour, by local
sculptor Louis Derbré, and
around the square are several
piles of "cannon balls", a
rather curious modern instal-
lation that was inspired by an
18th-century fashion.

Sablé has some attractive
shops in the pedestrian rue de
l'Ile and in the square, where
the Maison du Sablé sells the
famous shortbread-like biscuits to which the town has
given its name.

The town's sombre château,
which was built in the early
18th century by a nephew of
Louis XIV's chief minister, Jean-
Baptiste Colbert, now houses
workshops for restorers of old
books and manuscripts of the
Bibliothèque Nationale, the

The Tomb of Our Lord, part of the "saints of Solesmes" group of stone
carvings in the church of the Abbaye de Solesmes

national library of France.
Although the château cannot
be visited, the pleasant park
that surrounds it is open to
the public.

On the route de Solesmes,
opposite the summer swim-
ming pool, is the Jardin Public,
from which there are views of
the Abbaye de Solesmes.

Abbaye de Solesmes ❼

Road map C2. 🚉 *Sablé-sur-Sarthe,
then taxi.* 📞 *43 95 03 08.* **Abbey
Church** 🕐 *daily.* ♿

S ERVICES AT THE Benedictine
Abbaye de St-Pierre, part of
the Abbaye de Solesmes, attract
visitors who come from far and
wide to listen to the monks'

Gregorian chant. For over a
century, the abbey has been
working to preserve and
promote this ancient form of
prayer. Some of the many
books and recordings pro-
duced by the monks are sold,
outside church service times,
in the shop near the entrance
to the abbey.

Originally founded in 1010
as a priory, the abbey was
substantially rebuilt in the late
19th century in a somewhat
forbidding, fortress-like style.

The interior of the **abbey
church** has an austere beauty.
Its nave and transept are both
Romanesque, while the 19th-
century choir imitates the
medieval style. Both arms of
the transept are adorned by
groups of stone carvings made
in the 15th and 16th centuries
and known collectively as the
"saints of Solesmes". The
chapel to the left of the high
altar contains *The Tomb of
Our Lord*, with the haunting
figure of Mary Magdalene
kneeling at Christ's
feet, deep in prayer. In
*The Dormition of the
Virgin*, which can be
seen in the chapel on
the right, the lower
scenes illustrate the
Virgin Mary's death
and burial, while the
scenes above depict
her Assumption and
heavenly Coronation.

The little **parish
church**, which is locat-
ed beside the entrance
to the abbey, is worth
visiting for its interesting modern stained-
glass windows.

The imposing Abbaye de Solesmes, reflected in the River Sarthe

Asnières-sur-Vègre ❽

Road map C2. 🏠 *340.* 🚉 *Sablé-sur-Sarthe, then taxi.* ℹ️ *Sablé-sur-Sarthe (43 95 00 60).*

THIS PRETTY VILLAGE of old houses and water mills, with a 12th-century humpbacked bridge, is largely built in pinkish-yellow stone. Its tiny church has lively wall paintings, dating from the 12th and 15th centuries. In warm ochre and terracotta tones, they depict scenes from medieval life and moral warnings in the shape of the damned being herded into hell by huge, slavering hounds. The 13th-century **Cour d'Asnières** is an impressive Gothic building, built as a meeting place for the canons of the Cathédrale St Julien in Le Mans.

Nearby **Juigné** is situated on the old road from Le Mans to Sablé-sur-Sarthe. Its château was rebuilt in the early 17th century. Although private, its park and terraces, with their panoramic views of the river, are open to the public. It is possible to hire boats from Juigné's tiny harbour, from which there are good views of the church perched on the cliff above.

The 12th-century humpbacked bridge in Asnières-sur-Vègre

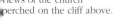

Detail from the frescoes in Asnières' church

🏛 **Cour d'Asnières**
Rue du Lavoir. ☎️ *43 92 40 47.*
🕐 *Mon, Tue, Thu, Fri: pm only; Wed & Sat: am only.* 📷 ♿ *grd flr only.*

Malicorne-sur-Sarthe ❾

Road map C3. 🏠 *1,700.* 🚉 *Noyen-sur-Sarthe or La Suze-sur-Sarthe, then taxi.* ℹ️ *pl Bertrand Duguesclin (43 94 74 45).* 🛒 *Fri.* 🎭 *Fête de la Pôterie (late Sep).*

THE CHIEF CLAIM to fame of this little town on the Sarthe is its faïence (decorated porcelain), which has been made here for nearly 250 years. Jean Loiseau, a potter from Nevers, first set up his business here in 1747. At the **Faïenceries Artistiques du Bourg Joly** visitors can buy the open-work ware known as *Faïence de Malicorne*, as well as copies of the traditional French forms and patterns. The **Faïenceries d'Art de Malicorne**, (pottery) just outside the village, also has a factory shop and a small museum, which is open to visitors.

Malicorne's small harbour, attractively framed by former water mills, is a popular spot for boaters, and both cruises and the hire of small motor-boats are possible. The village also boasts the pretty, riverside **Château de Malicorne**, dating from the 18th century, as well as a Romanesque church.

🏺 **Faïenceries Artistiques du Bourg-Joly**
16 rue Carnot. ☎️ *43 94 80 10.*
🕐 *Mon–Sat; Sun & public hols pm only.*

🏺 **Faïenceries d'Art de Malicorne**
18 rue Bernard Palissy. ☎️ *43 94 81 18.* 🕐 *Easter–Sep: Tue–Sat; Sun & public hols pm only.* 🔵 *Whit Sunday & 3rd Sun in Sep.* ♿ 📷

⚜ **Château de Malicorne**
☎️ *43 94 86 03.* 🕐 *Jul–mid-Sep: Mon, Thu, Fri, Sun pm only.* 📷 ♿

The harbour at Malicorne, surrounded by former water mills

Street-by-Street: Le Mans ⑩

THE HILLY, PICTURESQUE Old Town (Le Vieux Mans) can only be explored on foot. Its narrow, cobbled streets are lined by 15th- and 16th-century half-timbered houses interspersed with Renaissance mansions. Several of the finest buildings served as temporary residences for France's kings and queens, although the one

Carving on house in rue des Chanoines named after Richard the Lionheart's queen Bérengère, or Berengaria, was built two and a half centuries after her death. The quarter is bounded to the northwest by the old Roman walls, which run beside the River Sarthe.

Maison d'Adam et Eve
The carvings on this doctor's house illustrate the importance of astrology in 16th-century medicine.

Hôtel d'Argouges
Louis XI is said to have stayed in this 15th-century turreted mansion in 1467.

The Roman walls are among the best-preserved in Europe.

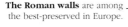

| 0 metres | 50 |
| 0 yards | 50 |

Hôtel Aubert de Clairaulnay
The sundial on the side of this late 16th-century mansion was placed there in 1789 by Claude Chappe, the inventor of semaphore.

RUE DE VAU
RUE DE LA VERRERIE
GRANDE RU
RUE ST-FLACEA
RUE DES FOSS
RUE ST-BENOIT
RUE DE LA VIEILLE PORTE

KEY
‒ ‒ ‒ Suggested route

Le Grabatoire is a 16th-century mansion, built on the site of an infirmary for sick canons.

VISITORS' CHECKLIST

Road map C2. 👥 *146,000.*
🚉 *bd de la Gare.* 🚌 *av du Général Leclerc.* 🛈 *rue de l'Etoile (43 28 17 22).* 🛒 *Wed, Fri, Sun.* 🎷 *Europa Jazz Festival (Apr); Les Cénomanies (street festival, Jul).*

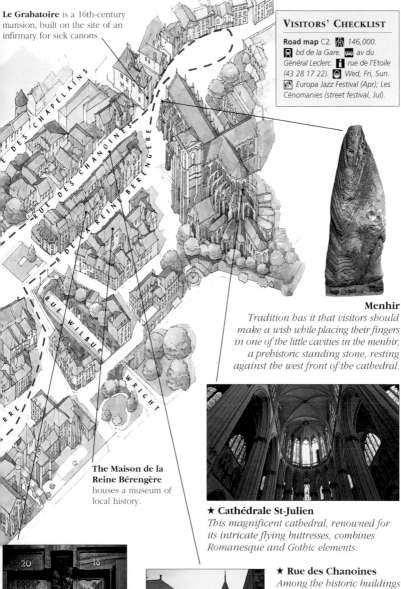

Menhir
Tradition has it that visitors should make a wish while placing their fingers in one of the little cavities in the menhir, a prehistoric standing stone, resting against the west front of the cathedral.

The Maison de la Reine Bérengère houses a museum of local history.

★ Cathédrale St-Julien
This magnificent cathedral, renowned for its intricate flying buttresses, combines Romanesque and Gothic elements.

★ Rue des Chanoines
Among the historic buildings in this attractive street is the 12th-century St Martin's Priory at No. 11.

★ Maison des Deux Amis
This building is named for its carving of two friends holding a coat of arms.

STAR SIGHTS

★ **Rue des Chanoines**

★ **Maison des Deux Amis**

★ **Cathédrale St-Julien**

Exploring Le Mans

ALTHOUGH BEST KNOWN for its gruelling 24-hour motor race, Le Mans has many other attractions, not least of which is the magnificent Cathédrale St-Julien. The city's history stretches back to Roman times. The walls surrounding the Old Town, once the Roman city of Vindunum, date from the late 3rd and early 4th centuries. They originally stretched for some 1,300 m (1,400 yards). Eleven towers are still standing, all but one on the river side, and their massive walls are decorated with geometric patterns created by using courses of brick alternating with undressed stone in various colours. Outside the city walls, Le Mans has developed into a bustling, modern city with several memorable museums and a number of attractive churches.

The Plantagenet Enamel (1150) displayed in the Musée de Tessé

⛪ Cathédrale St-Julien

Pl du Cardinal Grente. **[** 43 28 28 98. **○** daily. **[**
The best view of Cathédrale St-Julien's highly dramatic flying buttresses, unlike those of any other cathedral in their complex arrangement, is from the place des Jacobins. The cathedral is something of a hybrid: the 12th-century nave is essentially Romanesque, and the transepts were built a century later than the pure Gothic choir, one of the tallest in France, which dates from the 13th century. From the entrance via the Romanesque south portal, the view of the detailed 16th-century tapestries that hang against the pillars in the choir and are suspended over the choir stalls is striking. The splash of colour they provide is echoed in the beautiful medieval stained glass.

🏛 Musée de la Reine Bérengère

Rue de la Reine Bérengère. **[** 43 47 38 51. **○** daily. **●** public hols. **[**
This museum enjoys the attractive setting of three half-timbered houses in the Old Town, their wooden façades lively with carved figures. Its collections of art and local history include a display of faïence and pottery from many periods, with some interesting examples of Malicorne ware (*see p163*). The museum also shows some furniture made in the region. On the second floor, the 19th-century paintings by local artists show how relatively little the town

The Curate's Meal (1786), from the Musée de la Reine Bérengère

of Le Mans has changed over the years. Also of note is Jean Sorieul's dramatic canvas, *The Battle of Le Mans of 13 December, 1793*.

🏛 Musée de Tessé

2 av de Paderborn. **[** 43 47 38 51. **○** daily. **●** public hols. **[** **[**
The former bishop's palace, with its well-kept garden, was converted in 1927 into Le Mans' art museum, devoted to the fine and decorative arts as well as archaeology. The permanent collections of paintings on the ground floor range from the late Middle Ages to the 19th century, and the archaeology section is mainly Egyptian and Greco-Roman. The Tessé's most famous exhibit is the vivid Plantagenet Enamel, a medieval enamelled panel depicting Geoffroy V, known as Le Bel (The Handsome). Geoffroy's son, King Henry II of England, was born in Le Mans in 1133.

🏛 Musée de l'Automobile de la Sarthe

Circuit des 24-Heures. **[** 43 72 72 24. **○** Jan–mid-Feb: Sat & Sun; mid-Feb–Dec: daily. **[** **[**
Near Le Mans' famous race track is this museum, which displays a dazzling range of vintage, classic and modern racing cars and motorbikes. It includes some of the early designs of Amédée Bollée, an industrialist whose first pioneering car design dated from 1873. Bollée's family made the city famous for car design decades before the first 24-hour race (*see p57*).

16th-century tapestry hanging in the Cathédrale St-Julien

La Flèche ⓫

Road map C3. 🏠 *16,500.* 🚌
ℹ️ *espace Pierre-Mendès-France
(43 94 02 53).* 🛒 *Wed, Sat & Sun.*
🎪 *Festival des Affranchis (2nd
weekend Jul).*

L A FLÈCHE'S CHIEF glory is the
Prytanée Militaire, the
French military academy.
Founded as a Jesuit college in
1604 by Henri IV, it was
assigned its present function
by Napoléon in 1808.

The entrance to the academy
is through a monumental,
Baroque doorway, the Porte
d'Honneur, which leads into
the Cour d'Austerlitz, the first
of three courtyards. The
Chapelle St-Louis is in the
central courtyard. Its interior
is richly decorated, and urns
containing the ashes of the
hearts of Henri IV and Marie
de Médicis are displayed.

The château's gardens, with
spectacular views over the
river, are open to the public.
On the opposite bank of the
river is Port Luneau: it was
from here that Jérôme le Royer
de la Dauversière and his
companions, the founders of
Montreal, set off for the New
World. Nearby, the bustling
place Henri IV, with a statue
of the king, is lined with cafés.

At the heart of the town, the
15th-century **Château des
Carmes**, the former town hall
(now an art gallery), is reflected in the River Loir.

🏛 **Prytanée Militaire**
Rue du Collège. 📞 *43 94 03 96.*
🕐 *Jul–Aug: daily.* 🎫

Place Henri IV in La Flèche, with the statue of the king in the centre

Le Lude ⓬

Road map C3. 🏠 *4,500.* 🚌 ℹ️ *pl
F-de-Nicolay (43 94 62 20).* 🛒 *Thu.*
🎪 *Foire du Raillon (Sep).*

T HE OLDEST SECTION of this
market town is the area
surrounding the **Château du
Lude**, where houses dating
from the 15th to 17th centuries line the narrow streets.
Although the site has been
fortified for more than 1,000
years, the present château
dates from the 15th century.
Over the next 300 years the
building's originally square
layout and four corner towers
were transformed as its function changed to that of a
country house.

The interior is beautifully
furnished, largely in the 19th-
century style, although there
are some pieces from the 17th
and 18th centuries, including
both French and Flemish
tapestries. The Oratory is
decorated with 16th-century
frescoes, which depict scenes
from the Old Testament.

The château's formal gardens,
on two levels, lead down to
the River Loir. During the
season they are brought to
life in a remarkable son et
lumière show *(see p42–3).*

⚓ **Château du Lude**
📞 *43 94 60 09.* 🕐 **Château**
Apr–Sep: daily, pm only; **Park** *daily.*
🎫 ♿

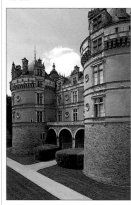
**The imposing towers of the
Château du Lude**

LES 24 HEURES DU MANS

The name of Le Mans is known throughout
the world, thanks to its famous 24-hour car
race. Since it began on 26 May 1923, the
event has attracted huge crowds every June,
both from France and abroad – these days,
more than 250,000 spectators and 1,800
journalists watch the race. The circuit is to
the south of the city and is 13.6-km (8½-
miles) long, including some stretches on
ordinary roads. Nowadays, drivers can cover
some 5,000 km (3,100 miles) within the time
limit. Within the course is the Hunaudières
track where, in 1908, Wilbur Wright staged
the first aeroplane flight in France.

One of the early races in Le Mans

Tour of the Loir Valley **⑬**

BETWEEN PONCÉ-SUR-LE-LOIR and La Flèche, the River
Loir passes through peaceful, unspoiled countryside and picturesque villages. An unhurried tour of
the valley takes two days and allows time to try some
of the numerous riverside and forest walks. Families
may enjoy the sailing, riding, angling and cycling
facilities available in the area, while art lovers can
seek out little-known churches adorned with delicately
coloured Romanesque frescoes. Wine buffs will be
interested in trying some of the area's wines, which
can be sipped from locally blown glass – the Loir
Valley also has an excellent reputation for its crafts.

**The banks of the tranquil Loir
river, ideal for fishing and walking**

La Flèche ①
The home of the Prytanée
Militaire (military academy,
see p167), La Flèche is a
charming town with
wonderful views across
the River Loir.

**Entrance to the
Prytanée Militaire**

N23

D306

Vaas ④
The Moulin de Rotrou, on the edge of
this pretty village, is a working flour mill
and museum of breadmaking. In Vaas,
the Eglise St-Georges has fine
17th-century paintings.

D307

D305

D141

③

D307

D306

SAUMUR

Zoo de la Flèche ②
Just outside the town, this zoo
is one of the largest in France,
with nearly 900 inhabitants.

TIPS FOR DRIVERS

Tour length: 103 km (64 miles).
Stopping-off points: The forests
and riverbanks along the Loir are
ideal for picnicking, and shops in
the region sell delicacies to make
a cold meal very special. This will
be a doubly satisfying experience
if you buy local produce from a
market, such as that in Le Lude,
first. If you prefer to eat in a
restaurant, La Fesse d'Ange in La
Flèche has local dishes on the
menu (see p218). For those
wishing to stay overnight, Le
Relais Cicéro in La Flèche is
recommended (see p206).

Le Lude ③
This market town is known mainly for its
château (see p167), which forms the
backdrop to a spectacular son et lumière
pageant (see pp42–43).

The entrance to the Château du Lude

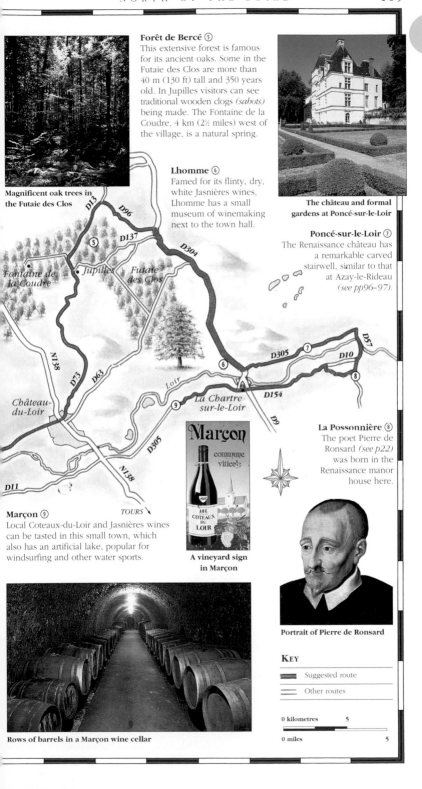

Forêt de Bercé ⑤
This extensive forest is famous for its ancient oaks. Some in the Futaie des Clos are more than 40 m (130 ft) tall and 350 years old. In Jupilles visitors can see traditional wooden clogs *(sabots)* being made. The Fontaine de la Coudre, 4 km (2½ miles) west of the village, is a natural spring.

Magnificent oak trees in the Futaie des Clos

Lhomme ⑥
Famed for its flinty, dry, white Jasnières wines, Lhomme has a small museum of winemaking next to the town hall.

The château and formal gardens at Poncé-sur-le-Loir

Poncé-sur-le-Loir ⑦
The Renaissance château has a remarkable carved stairwell, similar to that at Azay-le-Rideau *(see pp96–97).*

La Possonnière ⑧
The poet Pierre de Ronsard *(see p22)* was born in the Renaissance manor house here.

Marçon ⑨
Local Coteaux-du-Loir and Jasnières wines can be tasted in this small town, which also has an artificial lake, popular for windsurfing and other water sports.

A vineyard sign in Marçon

Portrait of Pierre de Ronsard

Rows of barrels in a Marçon wine cellar

KEY

▬▬▬	Suggested route
═══	Other routes

0 kilometres   5

0 miles   5

The Château de Courtanvaux with its towering walls

Château de Courtanvaux ⓮

Road map D3. 🚉 *Bessé-sur-Braye, then taxi.* ⬛ *43 35 34 43.*
⭕ *Easter–Oct: Thu–Tue (often closed for receptions).* 🈲

ALTHOUGH DIFFICULT to find and rather unpromisingly approached through an ugly industrial estate, this large Gothic and Renaissance private château is a romantic sight as it looms up at the end of a tree-lined drive. Turrets surmount the towering walls and the impressive gateway, and willows weep gracefully over the moat.

From the 15th century until 1978, when its Renaissance gateway was officially classed an historical monument, the château was never sold – its ownership was transferred either through inheritance or through marriage. Although it is not furnished, it has formal gardens and 63 ha (156 acres) of parkland, with woods and an ornamental pool, which visitors can explore.

Châteaudun ⓯

Road map E2. 🏘 *15,300.* 🚊
ℹ *1 rue de Luynes (37 45 22 46).*
📅 *Thu, Sat.* 🎉 *Fête de la Rosière (crowning of the rose queen, late Jul).*

DOMINATED BY ITS fierce-looking **château**, the town of Châteaudun is situated above the River Loir where the Beauce plain meets the Perche district. Châteaudun was owned at one time by the aristocratic poet Charles d'Orléans *(see p22)*, who then handed it on to his half-brother Jean Dunois, known as the bastard of Orléans and one of Joan of Arc's loyal companions-in-arms *(see p137)*. It was Jean who began the château's south wing in 1460, and built the beautiful late Gothic chapel, adorned with murals and life-size statues. The other wing, Renaissance in its decoration, was built half a century later.

Both wings are hung with wonderful tapestries, which date from the 16th and 17th centuries. Visitors can tour the château's living rooms, kitchens and prison, and walk around its sentry path.

Châteaudun's Old Town has a number of picturesque buildings, as well as several interesting churches: the Romanesque **Eglise de la Madeleine**, built in stages and now restored after damage sustained in 1940, and **St-Valérien**, with its tall square belfry. Situated on the far bank of the River Loir, the **Eglise St-Jean-de-la-Chaine** is also Romanesque in its origin.

Remembrance of Things Past by Proust

🏰 **Château**
⬛ *37 45 22 70.* ⭕ *daily.* ⬤ *public hols.* 🈲 🈵 *courtyard and chapel only.*

Illiers-Combray ⓰

Road map E2. 🏘 *3,400.* 🚊
ℹ *5 rue Henri Germond (37 24 21 79).* 📅 *Fri.* 🎉 *Journée des Aubépines (Proustian May Day, May).*

THE LITTLE MARKET TOWN of Illiers has added the word "Combray" to its name in honour of Marcel Proust's magnificent novel, *Remembrance of Things Past*, in which it is depicted as Combray *(see p23)*. As a child, Proust spent many happy summer holidays in the town, walking by the banks of the River Loir, which he later portrayed in his work, as the "Vivonne". With its quiet church square, it seems surprisingly unspoilt to the author's admirers, who make pilgrimages to the places described in the novel. They can also visit the house once owned by Proust's uncle Jules Amiot, **La Maison de Tante Léonie**. The house is now a small and touching museum, with displays about the famous writer's life, complete with the kitchen where the "Françoise" of the novel (who was actually Ernestine, the family cook) reigned supreme.

🏛 **La Maison de Tante Léonie**
4 rue du Dr Proust. ⬛ *37 24 30 97.*
⭕ *Tue–Sun pm.* ⬤ *1 & 11 Nov, mid-Dec–mid-Jan.* 🈲

A view of Châteaudun's castle from across the River Loir

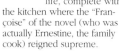

Carved hounds and stag on the gateway of the Château d'Anet

Château d'Anet ⑰

Road map E1. 🚉 *Dreux, then taxi.* 📞 *37 41 90 07* 🕐 *Sun & public hols; Apr–Oct: Mon, Wed–Sat, pm only; Nov–Mar: Sat pm.* 📷 ♿ *grd flr only.*

W HEN THE MISTRESS of Henri II, Diane de Poitiers, was banished from Chenonceau after the king's accidental death in 1559, she retired to Anet, which she had inherited from her husband, and remained here until her death in 1566. It had been rebuilt for her by Philibert de l'Orme, who also designed the bridge over the Cher at Chenonceau *(see pp106–7)*. The château was superbly decorated and furnished, as befitted the woman who reigned over a king's heart for nearly 30 years.

The château was sold after the Revolution and, in 1804, the new owner pulled down the central apartments and the right wing. However, you can still admire the magnificent entrance gate (although the bronze relief of a recumbent Diane by Benvenuto Cellini is a copy), the chapel, which is decorated with bas-reliefs by the Renaissance sculptor Jean Goujon (c.1510–68), and the richly furnished west wing. Just beside the château stands the mausoleum where Diane de Poitiers is buried.

Chartres ⑱

Road map E2. 🏠 *42,000.* 🚉 🚌 🛈 *pl de la Cathédrale (37 21 50 00).* 🗓 *Sat.* 🎵 *Festival d'Orgue (organ music; Jul–Aug).*

S URROUNDED BY the wheat fields of the Beauce plain, Chartres was for many years a major market town. Visitors who come to see the magnificent Gothic cathedral *(see pp172–3)* should not miss the opportunity to explore the town's picturesque old streets, particularly the rue Chantault, the rue des Ecuyers, the rue aux Herbes and, on the other side of the Eure, the rue de la Tannerie (which took its name from the tanneries that once lined the river).

The **Musée des Beaux-Arts**, occupying the elegant 18th-century building that was once the bishop's palace, is to the north of the cathedral. It has some fine Renaissance enamel plaques, a striking portrait of Erasmus in old age by Hans Holbein, and many 17th- and 18th-century paintings, mainly by French and Flemish artists. There is also a good collection of 17th- and 18th-century harpsichords and spinets.

Beautiful stained glass is not restricted to the cathedral: the Gothic **Eglise St-Pierre** beside

Half-timbered houses in the rue Chantault in Chartres

the river has lovely windows dating from the 14th century, those in **St-Aignan** date from the 17th century.

The **Centre International du Vitrail**, an international stained glass centre, is housed in the converted attics of the Cellier de Loëns, which was originally part of the cathedral's chapter house. Visitors can enjoy temporary exhibitions of old and new stained glass, as well as two informative permanent exhibitions that explain the techniques used in making stained glass and describe the glass in the cathedral's windows.

🏛 **Musée des Beaux-Arts**
29 cloître Notre–Dame. 📞 *37 36 41 39.* 🕐 *Wed–Mon.* ⬤ *public hols.* 📷
🏛 **Centre International du Vitrail**
5 rue du Cardinal Pie. 📞 *37 21 65 72.* 🕐 *daily.* 📷 ♿
🏛 **Conservatoire de l'Agriculture**
1 rue de la République. 📞 *37 36 11 30.* 🕐 *Tue–Sat.* ⬤ *public hols.* ♿

IN THE FOOTSTEPS OF PROUST

No visit to Illiers-Combray is complete without retracing the hallowed walks of Marcel Proust's childhood holidays. When he stayed with his Aunt and Uncle Amiot, he would join in the family walks that became, in *Remembrance of Things Past*, "Swann's Way" and "Guermantes Way".

The first takes the walkers towards the village of Méréglise, crossing the Loire and passing through a park that was once Uncle Jules' Pré Catelan and appears in the novel as "Tansonville Park". The "Guermantes" walk covers a few kilometres towards St-Eman, following the river to its source, now trapped unromantically in a wash house in the village. The walks are signposted and guides are available at the local tourist office.

Illiers-Combray's "Tansonville Park"

Chartres: Cathédrale Notre-Dame

ACCORDING TO ART HISTORIAN Emile Male, "Chartres is the mind of the Middle Ages manifest". The Romanesque cathedral, begun in 1020, was destroyed by fire in 1194; only the south tower, west front and crypt remained. Inside, the sacred Veil of the Virgin relic was the sole treasure to survive. In a wave of enthusiasm, peasant and lord alike helped to rebuild the church in just 25 years. There were few alterations after 1250 and, unlike other cathedrals, Chartres was unscathed by the Wars of Religion and the French Revolution. The result is a Gothic cathedral with a true "Bible in stone" reputation.

Part of the Vendôme Window

Elongated Statues
These statues on the Royal Portal represent Old Testament figures.

The taller of the two spires dates from the start of the 16th century. Flamboyant Gothic in style, it contrasts sharply with the solemnity of its Romanesque counterpart.

STAR FEATURES

★ **Royal Portal**

★ **South Porch**

★ **Stained-Glass Windows**

Gothic Nave
As wide as the Romanesque crypt below it, the nave reaches a record height of 37 m (121 ft).

★ **Royal Portal**
The central tympanum of the Royal Portal (1145–55) shows Christ in Majesty.

The lower half of the west front is a survivor of the earlier Romanesque church, dating from the 11th century.

Labyrin

THE LABYRINTH

The 13th-century labyrinth, inlaid in the floor of the nave, was a feature of most medieval cathedrals. As a penance, pilgrims used to follow the tortuous route on their knees, echoing the Way of the Cross. The journey of 262 m (860 ft), around 11 bands of broken concentric circles, took at least an hour to complete.

VISITORS' CHECKLIST

Pl de la Cathédrale. 37 21 56 33. Apr–Sep: 7:30am–7:30pm (Oct–Mar: until 7pm) daily. Mon–Sat: 8am & 6pm; Sun: 9:15am & 11am. in English: 12 noon & 2:45pm; in French: 10:30am & 3pm.

St-Piat Chapel
Built between 1324 and 1353, the chapel houses the cathedral treasures, including the Veil of the Virgin relic and fragments of the fragile 13th-century rood screen dismantled in 1763.

Vaulted Ceiling
A network of ribs supports the vaulted ceiling.

★ **Stained Glass Windows**
The windows cover a surface area of over 3,000 sq m (32,300 sq ft).

★ **South Porch**
Sculpture on the South Porch (1197–1209) reflects New Testament teaching.

Crypt
This is the largest crypt in France, most of it dating from the early 11th century. It comprises two parallel galleries, a series of chapels and the 9th-century St Lubin's vault.

The Stained Glass of Chartres

DONATED BY THE GUILDS between 1210 and 1240, this glorious collection of stained glass is world-renowned. Over 150 windows illustrate biblical stories and daily life in the 13th century (bring binoculars if you can). During both World Wars the windows were dismantled piece by piece and removed for safety. Some windows were restored and releaded in the 1970s, but much more remains to be done.

Stained glass above the apse

Redemption Window
Six scenes illustrate Christ's Passion *and death on the Cross (c.1210).*

★ Tree of Jesse
This 12th-century stained glass shows Christ's genealogy. The tree rises up from Jesse, father of David, at the bottom, to Christ enthroned at the top.

★ West Rose Window
This window (1215), with Christ seated in the centre, shows the Last Judgment.

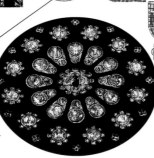

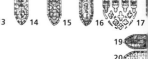

KEY

1 Tree of Jesse	**12** Noah	**22** St Anthony and St Paul	**33** St Theodore and St Vincent
2 Incarnation	**13** St John the Evangelist	**23** Blue Virgin	**34** St Stephen
3 Passion and Resurrection	**14** Mary Magdalene	**24** Life of the Virgin	**35** St Cheron
4 North Rose Window	**15** Good Samaritan and Adam and Eve	**25** Zodiac Window	**36** St Thomas
5 West Rose Window	**16** Assumption	**26** St Martin	**37** Peace Window
6 South Rose Window	**17** Vendôme Chapel Windows	**27** St Thomas à Becket	**38** Modern Window
7 Redemption Window	**18** Miracles of Mary	**28** St Margaret and St Catherine	**39** Prodigal Son
8 St Nicholas	**19** St Apollinaris	**29** St Nicholas	**40** Ezekiel and David
9 Joseph	**20** Modern Window	**30** St Remy	**41** Aaron
10 St Eustache	**21** St Fulbert	**31** St James the Greater	**42** Virgin and Child
11 St Lubin		**32** Charlemagne	**43** Isaiah and Moses
			44 Daniel and Jeremiah

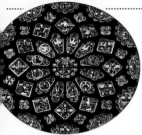

North Rose Window
This depicts the Glorification of the Virgin, *surrounded by the kings of Judah and the prophets (c.1230).*

GUIDE TO READING THE WINDOWS

Each window is divided into panels, which are usually read from left to right, bottom to top (earth to heaven). The number of figures or abstract shapes used is symbolic: three stands for the Church; squares and the number four symbolize the material world or the four elements; circles eternal life.

Mary and Child in the sacred mandorla (c.1150)

Two angels doing homage before the celestial throne

Christ's triumphal entry into Jerusalem

Upper panels of the Incarnation Window

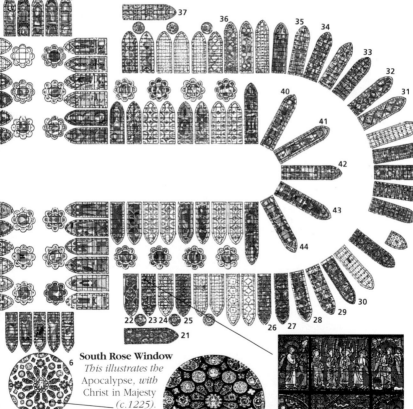

South Rose Window
This illustrates the Apocalypse, *with* Christ in Majesty *(c.1225).*

STAR WINDOWS

★ West Rose Window

★ Tree of Jesse

★ Blue Virgin Window

★ Blue Virgin Window
Scenes of The Marriage at Cana *show Christ changing water into wine at the request of the Virgin Mary.*

LOIRE-ATLANTIQUE AND THE VENDÉE

T HE REGION STRETCHING *from Guérande in the north to the Marais Poitevin in the south turns away from the Vallée des Rois, the land of châteaux, to face the sea. Pale limestone gives way to darker granite and, beyond the hilly, wooded areas to the east, plains stretch into marshlands and estuaries inhabited by clouds of birds.*

Here, people have for centuries won their living either from the land or from the sea. Local communities were until quite recently isolated, conservative, religious and fiercely independent. Their loyalties were the basis of the Vendée Uprising *(see p187)* which, at the end of the 18th century threatened the new French Republic and ended in the devastation of an entire region south of the Loire. Until the 1790s, Nantes, the capital of the Loire-Atlantique, and its environs were part of Brittany, one of the last French duchies to be brought under the crown.

Nantes itself grew prosperous on the wealth generated by its maritime trade to become the seventh largest city of France in the 18th and 19th centuries. With its fine museums and elegant 18th-century *quartiers*, it remains a fascinating and likeable city.

The coast and islands of the Loire-Atlantique to the north, and the Vendée – as the region to the south is known – now draw thousands of summer visitors. Part of their charm is that most of the holiday-makers are French, since the rest of the world has barely begun to discover the beauty of the rocky headlands of Le Croisic or the beaches of golden sand that stretch from La Baule to Les Sables d'Olonne. In the south, dry summers and warm winters on the Ile de Noirmoutier have given it an almost Mediterranean look, with its whitewashed houses and Roman tiles.

In contrast, the Marais Poitevin, at the southern tip of the Vendée, is one of France's most fascinating natural environments. This land has been won back from rivers and the sea through the construction of dykes, canals and dams over hundreds of years.

An oyster gatherer in the Bay of Aiguillon

◁ Roman capitals in the nave of the Collégiale St-Aubin in Guérande

Exploring Loire-Atlantique and the Vendée

THE MIGHTY RIVER LOIRE finally reaches the sea at St-Nazaire, in the west of the Loire-Atlantique *département*. To the northwest lies the Guérandaise Peninsula, where long expanses of sandy, south-facing beaches give way to the dramatic, rocky Atlantic coastlines. The best Atlantic beaches stretch along the Vendée coastline, from the Ile de Noirmoutier to the Marais Poitevin in the south. The Marais Poitevin, 80,000 hectares (198,000 acres) of marshland, is networked with canals. To the east lie the Vendée Hills, where the roads wind gently through towns and along the hillsides, giving lovely views of the surrounding area.

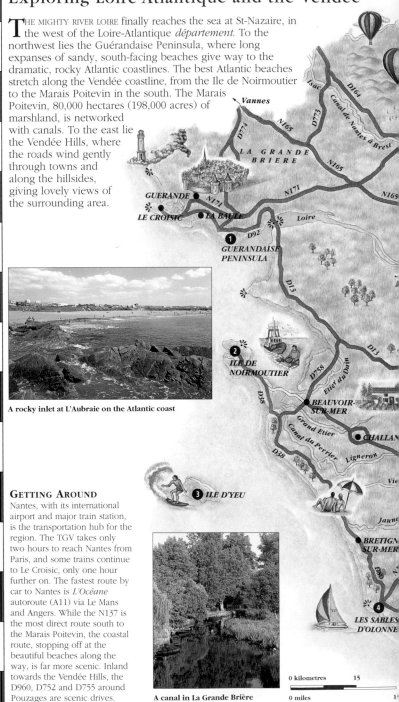

Vannes

LA GRANDE BRIERE

Loire

GUERANDE

LE CROISIC   **LA BAULE**

1 **GUERANDAISE PENINSULA**

2 **ILE DE NOIRMOUTIER**

BEAUVOIR-SUR-MER

CHALLAN

3 **ILE D'YEU**

BRETIGN SUR-MER

4 **LES SABLES D'OLONNE**

A rocky inlet at L'Aubraie on the Atlantic coast

GETTING AROUND

Nantes, with its international airport and major train station, is the transportation hub for the region. The TGV takes only two hours to reach Nantes from Paris, and some trains continue to Le Croisic, only one hour further on. The fastest route by car to Nantes is *L'Océane* autoroute (A11) via Le Mans and Angers. While the N137 is the most direct route south to the Marais Poitevin, the coastal route, stopping off at the beautiful beaches along the way, is far more scenic. Inland towards the Vendée Hills, the D960, D752 and D755 around Pouzages are scenic drives.

A canal in La Grande Brière

0 kilometres   15

0 miles   1

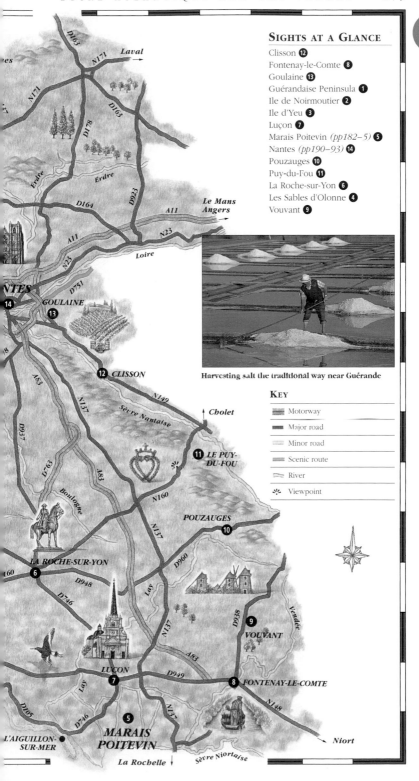

SIGHTS AT A GLANCE

Clisson ⑫
Fontenay-le-Comte ⑧
Goulaine ⑬
Guérandaise Peninsula ①
Ile de Noirmoutier ②
Ile d'Yeu ③
Luçon ⑦
Marais Poitevin *(pp182–5)* ⑤
Nantes *(pp190–93)* ⑭
Pouzauges ⑩
Puy-du-Fou ⑪
La Roche-sur-Yon ⑥
Les Sables d'Olonne ④
Vouvant ⑨

Harvesting salt the traditional way near Guérande

KEY

▬▬	Motorway
▬▬	Major road
▭▭	Minor road
▬▬	Scenic route
⇀	River
☀	Viewpoint

Guérandaise Peninsula ●

Road map A3. 🚊 *Le Croisic, La Baule*. 🚌 *Le Croisic, La Baule, Brière, Guérande*. ℹ️ *Le Croisic (40 23 00 70), La Baule (40 24 34 44), Guérande (40 24 96 71).*

LA BAULE, ONE OF the grandest seaside resorts of the late 19th century, has a superb 8-km (5-mile) sweep of golden sand, now dominated by apartment blocks built since the 1930s. However, in the pines behind the modern buildings, there is a fascinating assortment of eccentric turn-of-the-century villas. The resort of Pornichet, which adjoins La Baule, also retains some older villas beyond a modern marina crammed with yachts.

Le Croisic, reaching into the Atlantic on the west, has a wilder charm. Beyond the lively main port are miles of salty headlands with small beaches, pounding surf and wind-sculpted pines. The **Océarium** near the port is one of France's largest, privately-owned aquaria.

The medieval walled town of Guérande grew rich on its *fleur de sel* – gourmet Breton salt "farmed" on extensive marshlands between here and Le Croisic. Exhibitions and a video in the **Musée des Marais Salants** at Batz-sur-Mer give an excellent idea of the painstaking techniques used to maintain its quality.

Guérande is protected by its ramparts, which are entered through four fine, 15th-century gateways. The main gatehouse, St-Michel, houses a regional museum. In the centre of the town is the **Collégiale St-Aubin**, a church first built in the 12th century and later renovated. It has stained glass from the 14th and 16th centuries and Roman capitals depicting scenes from the lives of the martyrs, mythology, arts and entertainment.

Just 10 km (6 miles) to the east

A traditional thatched house in La Grande Brière

of Guérande is **La Grande Brière**, a regional park of 40,000 hectares (100,000 acres) of marshlands. Guided tours by flat-bottomed boat or on foot, bicycle or horseback are available from the tourist office in what was once a clog-maker's house in La Chapelle-des-Marais. Kerhinet, a village of 18 restored cottages, has displays on regional life.

✕ Océarium
Av de St-Goustan, Le Croisic.
📞 *40 23 02 44.* ○ *Feb–Dec: daily.*
🅿️ ♿

🏛 Musée des Marais Salants
Batz-sur-Mer. 📞 *40 23 82 79.*
○ *Jun–Sep & school hols: daily; Oct–May: Sat & Sun, pm only.* 🅿️
♿ *grd flr only.*

✕ La Grande Brière
Road map A3. 🚊 *Pontchâteau, St Nazaire.* 🚌 ℹ️ *La Chapelle-des-Marais. (40 66 85 01).*

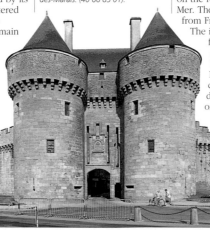
Porte St-Michel gatehouse, one of the entrances to Guérande

Ile de Noirmoutier ●

Road map A4. 🚌 *Noirmoutier-en-l'Ile.* ℹ️ *Noirmoutier-en-l'Ile (51 39 80 71).*

WHITEWASHED Midi-style beach villas on a long, low island of fertile polders (land reclaimed from the sea) give Noirmoutier a unique character. The adventurous visitor arrives along a bumpy causeway nearly 5 km (3 miles) long, which is above the sea for only three hours at low tide. Cockle-collecting locals park their cars in the mud, but those who flirt with the tides sometimes have to climb to safety on platforms *(balises)* along the causeway. Crossing periods are posted on the road at Beauvoir-sur-Mer. There is also a tollbridge from Fromentine.

The island's mild climate, fishing industry and salt marshes were the basis of its wealth. Now summer tourists come to visit its long dunes, pretty beaches on the northeast and the neat main village of Noirmoutier-en-l'Ile. The dry-moated **Château de Noirmoutier** dates from the 12th century. It has displays on aspects of local history, including the bullet-riddled chair in which the Duc d'Elbée was executed during the Vendée Uprising *(see p187)*. There is also an **aquarium** and the **Musée de la Construction Navale**, with exhibitions of both boat-making and salt-panning techniques. **Parc Océanîle**, a water park that opened in 1994, includes water chutes and slides, pools with artificial waves, torrents and hot geysers.

♣ **Château de Noirmoutier**
Pl d'Armes. ☎ 51 39 10 42.
◯ Feb–mid-Jun: Wed–Mon; mid-Jun–Sep: daily; Oct–mid-Nov: Wed–Mon. 🖼 .
🐟 **Aquarium-Sealand**
Rue de l'Ecluse. ☎ 51 39 08 11.
◯ daily. 🖼 ♿
🏛 **Musée de la Construction Navale**
Rue de l'Ecluse. ☎ 51 39 24 00.
◯ Apr–mid-Jun: Tue–Sun; mid-Jun–Sep: daily; Oct–mid-Nov: Tue–Sun. 🖼 ♿
🐟 **Parc Océanîle**
Site des Oudinières, route de Noirmoutier. ☎ 51 35 91 35. ◯ mid-Apr–mid-Sep: daily. 🖼 ♿ 🍴

Polyprion americanas, one of the fish in Noirmoutier's aquarium

Ile d'Yeu ❺

Road map A4. ⛴ *from Fromentine to Port-Joinville.* ℹ *Port-Joinville (51 58 32 58).*

THE SANDY coves and rocky coastline of this sun-drenched island, only 10 by 4 km (6 by 2½ miles), attract summer visitors who enjoy walking or cycling. Near the old fishing harbour of Port-de-la-Meule are a ruined 11th-century **castle** and the **Pierre Tremblante**, a giant Neolithic stone said to move when pressed at a critical spot.

The fishing village of La Chaume, near Les Sables d'Olonne

Les Sables d'Olonne ❹

Road map A4. 👥 *16,000.* 🚉 🚌 ℹ *rue du Maréchal Leclerc (51 32 03 28).* 🛒 *daily.*

THE JUSTIFIABLE popularity of the fine, curving sands has helped to preserve the most elegant beach promenade in western France. Behind the 18th-century esplanade, hilly streets lead to a lively port on the sea channel. Opposite, the fishing village of La Chaume has a chic marina.

In Les Sables itself, apart from the surf, attractions include the morning market that takes place every day at Les Halles, near the church of

Notre-Dame-de-Bon-Port. Running between Les Halles and the rue de la Patrie lies France's narrowest street, rue de l'Enfer, which is only 53 cm (21 in) wide at the entrance on rue de la Patrie.

Masterly views of Les Sables in the 1920s by the artist Albert Marquet can be seen in the **Musée de l'Abbaye Ste-Croix**. Built as a convent in the 17th century, this museum houses a collection of mainly modern paintings, Surrealist multimedia works and maritime exhibits.

🏛 **Musée de l'Abbaye Ste-Croix**
Rue de Verdun. ☎ 51 32 01 16.
◯ mid-Jun–Sep: Tue–Sun; Oct–mid-Jun: pm only. ◯ public hols. 🖼 except Wed.

THE BEST ATLANTIC COAST BEACHES

Les Sables d'Olonne hosted both the European surfing championship in 1987 and the world windsurfing championship in 1988. It also offers family bathing at the Grande Plage. Surfers enjoy the bigger waves at Le Tanchet (Le Château d'Olonne) and L'Aubraie (La Chaume). Other good surfing beaches are Sauveterre and Les Granges (Olonne-sur-Mer) and, further north, La Sauzaie at Brétignolles-sur-Mer. Apart from Les Sables, major esplanades and beaches with fine sands and good facilities include the Grande Plage at La Baule and Les Demoiselles at St-Jean-de-Monts.

The wide, sandy beach of L'Aubraie at La Chaume

Marais Poitevin ❺

Kingfisher

THE VAST REGIONAL PARK of the Marais Poitevin stretches 80,000 ha (198,000 acres) across the south of the Vendée. In Roman times, most of it was under water. One thousand years of dyke-building and drainage, first started by medieval monks, have produced the agricultural plains of the western Marais Desséché (dry marsh), which are protected from river floods inland by a complex network of canals. The enchanting aquatic mosaic of the Marais Mouillé (wet marsh), also known as the Venise Verte (Green Venice), lies to the east. Here, summer visitors punt or paddle along quiet, jade-coloured waterways under a canopy of willow, alder, ash and poplar.

White Charolais Cattle
Prized for their meat, these cows are often transported by boat.

The Réserve Naturelle Michel Brosselin is a flourishing 200-ha (500-acre) nature reserve.

Flat-bottomed Barque
This typical Marais Mouillé boat has a broad prow and a chisel-shaped stern. Skilled oarsmen paddle or pole the boat along the canals.

STAR SIGHTS

★ Eglise St-Nicolas, Maillezais

★ Coulon

★ Arçais

Mussel Farms
Mussels are farmed on the coast around L'Aiguillon-sur-Mer. The larvae are placed on ropes strung between posts embedded in the silt, exposed to the tide's ebb and flow.

KEY

	Mud flats
	Marais Desséché
	Marais Mouillé
﹉	Viewpoint
🧍	Hiking route
U	Horse riding
ℹ	Tourist information
⛵	Boating
🚲	Bicycles for hire

Map labels: Lucon, Canal de la Ce, N137, St-Denis-du-Payré, Chai les-M, Lay, D25, D747, D60, D50, Canal de Lucon, Canal de Champlié, Canal de Vienne, D25, D746, St-Michel-en-l'Herm, Cheral Vieux, D10a, Canal du Clain, Canal des Cinq Abbés, L'Aiguillon-sur-Mer, D60, La Dive, Mar, D105, Pointe de l'Aguillon, D105, Esnandes

★ Eglise St-Nicolas, Maillezais

The 12th-century Eglise St-Nicolas is in the town of Maillezais, which is situated at the heart of the Marais Poitevin. The church has a Romanesque façade and an unusually spacious interior. To the left of the choir is a beautiful stone statue of the Virgin and Child, *dating from the 14th century. The town also has an attractive, ruined 10th-century abbey.*

VISITORS' CHECKLIST

Road map B5. 🚉 *Niort.*
ℹ️ *Maillezais (51 87 23 01); Coulon (49 35 99 29). Good embarkation points for boating: Coulon, Maillezais, Arçais, Sansais, La Garette, St-Hilaire-la-Palud, Damvix; Motor launches: Maillé (51 87 07 52). Tourist train: Coulon (49 35 02 29). Facilities for hiking tours, hiring bicycles, caravans and horses.*

0 kilometres   5

0 miles   5

Le Poiré-sur-Velluire is a small village where the annual opening of the common grazing rights is celebrated at the end of April.

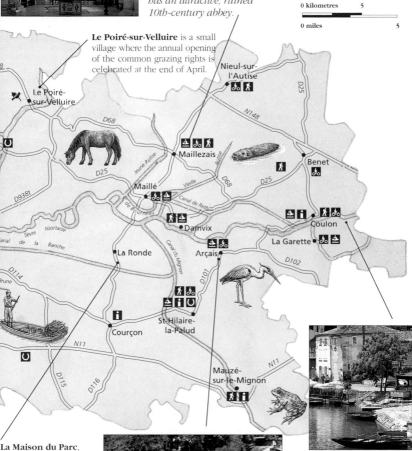

La Maison du Parc, at La Ronde, gives information on the complex hydraulic system of the entire Marais Poitevin.

★ Arçais

This village in the Venise Verte has a small, stylish port and a 19th-century château.

★ Coulon

Coulon is the largest village in the Marais Poitevin. Its port is always crowded with the narrow, flat-bottomed boats that are traditional in this area.

Exploring the Marais Poitevin

Sign advertising trips in a *barque*

EARLY DYKES, built to hold back the tide, did nothing to solve the problem of the rivers' annual flooding of the marshlands. So large canals were dug in the 12th and 13th centuries, under the supervision of monks who had acquired land rights to marshy areas. The Marais Mouillé (wet marsh) and the Marais Desséché (dry marsh) are still separated by one of these canals: the 13th-century Canal des Cinq Abbés, south of Chaillé-les-Marais, which was a joint effort by five abbeys. Peasants labouring for the monks were rewarded with common grazing rights, some of which are still in force. During the 17th century, Henri IV brought in Dutch engineers to improve the canals, hence the "Dutch Belt" (*La Ceinture des Hollandais*) southeast of Luçon. Current measures to control flooding on lands below high-tide level range from pressure-operated dam gates to bung holes that let water into the plains of the *marais* in summer.

The newly-restored quay on the Sèvre Niortaise river is lively in summer with punt tours and unguided crews armed with maps starting off for the tangle of canals. The fish that hide under the duck-weed can be seen at the **Aquarium de la Venise Verte**. Exhibits explaining local ways of life and the history of reclamation are displayed at the **Maison des Marais Mouillés**.

🦢 Aquarium de la Venise Verte
8 pl de l'Eglise. **📞** 49 35 90 31. **🕐** mid-Mar–Oct: daily; Nov–mid-Mar: groups by appt. 🈂️ &

🏛 Maison des Marais Mouillés
Pl de la Coutume. **📞** 49 35 81 04. **🕐** Feb–Jun: Tue–Sun; Jul–Aug: daily; Sep–mid-Nov: Tue–Sun. 🈂️

Eastern Marais

The best way to see this area is by boat. Guided tours are available from a number of towns in the region, and braver souls can hire their own boats from Arçais, Coulon, Damvix, La Garette or Maillezais.

Coulon

Road map B5. **🏘** 1,900. 🚌 **ℹ** pl de l'Eglise (49 35 99 29). 🛒 Fri, Sun.
With its narrow streets of old whitewashed houses and imposing 12th-century church, Coulon is the main entry point to the Marais Mouillé.

Maillezais

Road map B5. **🏘** 900. 🚉 Fontenay-le-Comte, then taxi. **ℹ** rue du Dr-Daroux (51 87 23 01).
Maillezais was one of the most important inhabited islands in the former Gulf of Poitou. Whether from a canal boat or from a viewpoint within the

---

WILDLIFE OF THE MARAIS POITEVIN

An area of diverse natural habitats, including flood-plains, copses, reclaimed agricultural land and estuaries, the Marais Poitevin supports a rich array of wildlife. It is a paradise for bird-watchers, featuring 130 different species of nesting bird and more than 120 species of migrating and wintering birds. It also supports 44 species of mammal, 22 species of snake, 32 species of fish and hundreds of insect species. The stands of elms, alders, willows and haw-thorns supply herons with nest sites. Birds of prey such as the European kestrel and the common buzzard are present all year round, as well as breeding pairs of black kites, hobbys and, less commonly, honey buzzards in spring and summer. At night, long-eared and tawny owls scour the marshes for small rodents.
For bird-watchers, the real interest of the area lies in migratory waders and wildfowl. These can be seen on the huge, marshy plains of the Marais Mouillé, on the drier expanses of the Marais Desséché and on the wide mud flats of the Bay of Aiguillon where the Sèvre Niortaise river reaches the sea. Birds to be seen here in autumn and winter include the common redshank, black-tailed godwit and whimbrel, and rare species such as the spotted crake. The Marais Desséché is also an ideal winter refuge for frogs, toads and grass snakes, and its wide canals, bordered by thick vegetation, are home to two rare species of warbler: the great reed warbler and savi's warbler. Small numbers of another rare species, Montagu's harrier, hunt field voles in the area's reclaimed agricultural land.

Reed warbler

The kestrel, one of the Marais' birds of prey

The ruins of the 10th-century Abbaye St-Pierre at Maillezais

town, the great ruined **Abbaye St-Pierre**, founded in the 10th century, is a dramatic sight. Much of the monastery was destroyed in 1587 by the Protestant armies. The church retains decorated capitals in the 11th-century narthex, the north wall of the nave and the Renaissance transept.

The abbey refectory is still standing, as is the kitchen, now a museum with stone carvings and ecclesiastical treasures. To the right of the entrance is a small château, built in 1872 on the ruins of the bishop's palace.

🔒 Abbaye St-Pierre
📞 51 00 70 11. ⬜ Mar–mid-Nov: daily; mid-Nov–Feb: Fri–Wed. 🏷 ♿

Chaillé-les-Marais
Road map B5. 🏠 1,200. 🚆
ℹ Luçon (51 56 36 52). 🚌 Thu.
This little village, beside cliffs once washed by the tide, was a centre for the reclamation works that established the fields of dark soil in the Marais Desséché. The techniques are explained at the **Maison du Petit Poitou**. This museum, one of six in the area that cover different aspects of the Marais Poitevin, also introduces visitors to the shaggy donkey, a rare Poitou breed.

Long-haired Poitou donkey

🏛 Maison du Petit Poitou
📞 51 56 77 30. ⬜ mid–late Feb & Oct–Nov: daily, pm only; Mar–Sep: daily. ⬤ Mar–May: Sun am. 🏷 ♿

Western Marais
Much of the early drainage work in the *marais* was led by the monks of **St-Michel-en-l'Herm**. The Benedictine abbey on this former island was originally founded in 682, but has been destroyed and rebuilt several times since then. Its 17th-century chapter house and refectory are the most important remnants.

A short drive to the south, on the River Lay estuary, are the ancient fishing port of **L'Aiguillon-sur-Mer** and the Pointe d'Aiguillon, with its 19th-century Dutch-built dyke. From here, there are marvellous views across the bay to the Ile de Ré and La Rochelle.

Shellfish farming, especially mussels and oysters, is a leading industry along this part of the coast as well as in the estuaries of the western *marais*. Mussels are grown on a forest of posts, which are visible at low tide, or on ropes hung from rafts in the Bay of Aiguillon.

Male garganey duck

A nesting purple heron

HABITATS
The Marais Mouillé's extensive network of canals provides an ideal refuge for otters, while its many trees provide an ample choice of nest sites for the purple heron. Migrating birds, such as garganey ducks, and waders, such as the lapwing, thrive in the Marais Desséché.

Otter

A lapwing wintering in the Marais Poitevin

Statue of Napoléon in the main square in La Roche-sur-Yon

La Roche-sur-Yon ❻

Road map B4. 🏚 49,000. 🚊 🚌
🛈 rue Georges Clemenceau (51 47 48 49). 🛒 Tue, Thu, Sat. 🎭 La Roche aux Contes (Mar); Fête de la Musique (Jun); Café de l'Eté (Jul).

IN 1804, La-Roche-sur-Yon was plucked from obscurity by Napoleon, who made it the administrative and military capital of the rebellious Vendée region.

The town's rectangular grid layout was centred on a very large parade ground, which is now called **place Napoléon**. In the middle of the square is a statue of the emperor seated astride his horse. As if to deflate these imperial pretensions, a fountain made of squashed oil cans stands playfully outside the Classical theatre building on the place du Théâtre. The 19th-century **Eglise St-Louis** is the largest church in the area.

Restored buildings of the old village are grouped around the place de la Vieille-Horloge. In one of these, **La Maison des Métiers**, is a permanent exhibition of local products, including weaving, pottery and leather work.

🏛 **La Maison des Métiers**
Pl de la Vieille-Horloge. 📞 51 62 51 33. 🕐 Tue–Sat.

Luçon ❼

Road map B4. 🏚 10,000. 🚊 🚌
🛈 square Edouard Herriot (51 56 36 52). 🛒 Wed & Sat.

LUÇON, ONCE a marshland port, was described by its most famous inhabitant, Cardinal Richelieu (see p56), then known as Armand Jean du Plessis, as the muddiest bishopric in France. Sent there as a 23-year-old bishop in 1608, he went on to reorganize first the town and then the kingdom. Richelieu's statue stands in the square south of the **Cathédrale Notre-Dame**.

The cathedral has an impressive Gothic nave with Renaissance side chapels. One of these contains a pulpit and two canvases painted by Richelieu's gifted successor as bishop, Pierre Nivelle, a naturalist painter. The beautiful cloisters date from the 16th century.

Painted pulpit in Luçon cathedral

Fontenay-le-Comte ❽

Road map C4. 🏚 15,000. 🚊 🚌
🛈 quai Poëy d'Avant (51 69 44 99). 🛒 Sat. 🎭 L'Eté Sportif et Culturel (Jul–Aug); Festival du Rock (Oct).

FONTENAY, sloping down to the River Vendée, was the proud capital of Bas-Poitou until the French Revolution. Napoléon downgraded it in favour of a more centrally-placed administrative centre, La Roche-sur-Yon, from which he could easily control the Royalist Vendée.

Although the city's castle and fortifications were destroyed in 1621, following repeated conflicts in the Wars of Religion, much of its Renaissance quarter survived, and a prosperous postwar town has sprung up around it.

The **Eglise Notre-Dame**, with its commanding spire, is a good place to begin threading through the old streets that lead down from the place Viète. The building with the corner turret at No. 9 rue du Pont-aux-Chèvres was once the palace of the bishops of Maillezais. Many Renaissance luminaries, including the poet Nicolas Rapin and François Rabelais (see p100), lived in rue Guillemet, rue des Jacobins and the arcaded place Belliard. Rabelais was later to satirize soirées he attended here during his five years as an unruly young priest in the Franciscan friary (1519–24).

Fontenay's motto "A fountainhead of fine spirits" is incised on the **Quatre-Tias** fountain in the rue de la Fontaine, which was built in the 16th century and embellished in 1899 by Octave de Roche-brune, a local artist and intellectual.

In the **Musée Vendéen**, displays range from Gallo-Roman archaeology to an excellent scale model of Fontenay during the Renaissance. Several 19th-century portraits convey the suffering of the Vendée in the wake of the 1793 insurrection. There are also displays on daily life in the bocage, the wooded region bordering the city.

Once a manor house, the **Château de Terre-Neuve** on the rue de Jarnigande, was converted into something

The high Gothic nave of the Cathédrale Notre-Dame in Luçon

The medieval walls surrounding Vouvant, reflected in the River Mère

more imposing for Nicolas Rapin, poet and grand provost, at the beginning of the 17th century. Two hundred years later, Octave de Rochebrune added decorative flourishes, including statues of the Muses.

The interior of the château has beautiful ceilings and two wonderful fireplaces together with a collection of fine art, furniture, panelling and a door brought from the royal study in the Château de Chambord.

🏛 **Musée Vendéen**
Pl du 137e Régiment d'Infanterie.
📞 51 69 31 31. ◯ mid-Jun–mid-
Sep: Tue–Sun; mid-Sep–mid-Jun:
Wed–Sun, pm only. 🖼 ♿

♦ **Château de Terre-Neuve**
Rue de Jarnigande. 📞 51 69 99 41,
51 69 17 75. ◯ May: daily, pm only;
Jun–Sep: daily; Oct–Apr: groups by
appt. 🖼

Vouvant ❾

Road map B4. 🏃 *900.* 🚌
Fontenay-le-Comte, then taxi. ℹ️
pl du Bail (51 00 86 80). 🚆 *alternate
Thu.* 🎭 *Fête Folklorique (mid-Aug).*

THE ROMANESQUE **Eglise Notre-Dame** in the medieval village of Vouvant has a fantastically carved twin-portal doorway, from which rows of sculptures look down on an arch decorated with a typical Romanesque bestiary. On the tympanum, Samson wrestles a lion as Delilah advances with her infamous shears.

Vouvant is a starting point for tours of the popular Mervant-Vouvant forest with its signposted walks, boating lakes, grottoes and folklore surrounding the serpent-fairy

Mélusine: she tried to lead a life as a woman, but once a week her lower half would turn into a serpent's tail. The **Tour Mélusine** has splendid views of the River Mère.

The twin portals of Vouvant's
Eglise Notre-Dame

Portrait of Cathelineau (1824)
by Anne-Louis Girodet-Trioson

THE VENDÉE UPRISING

Although it may at times seem a footnote to the French Revolution, the Vendée Uprising has never been forgotten in this region. The Revolution outraged the conservative, Royalist people here. Rising taxes, the persecution of Catholic priests and the execution of Louis XVI in January 1793 were then followed by attempts to conscript locals for the Republican army. This triggered a massacre of Republican sympathizers in the village of Machecoul on 11 March by a peasant mob. As the riots flared, peasant leaders, such as the wagoner Cathelineau and the gamekeeper Stofflet, took charge. They were joined by nobles including Charette, Bonchamps and La Roche-jaquelain under the emblem of the sacred heart.

Using guerilla tactics, the Grand Royal and Catholic Army (Whites) took nearly all the Vendée plus Saumur and Angers by June 1793. They won several battles against Republican armies (Blues) but lost at Cholet on 17 October. Nearly 90,000 Whites fled, vainly hoping for reinforcements to join them. The Blues laid waste to the Vendée in 1794, massacring the populace. More than 250,000 people from the Vendée died.

Detail from the frieze in the church in Pouzauges

Pouzauges ❿

Road map C4. 🚶 *5,500.* 🚉 🚌
ℹ️ *rue Georges Clemenceau (51 91 82 46).* ♘ *Thu.*

THIS SMALL TOWN's ruined
12th-century castle was
one of several in the Vendée
owned by Gilles de Rais in
the 15th century. Once
Marshal of France, de Rais'
distinguished military career
ended in charges of abduction
and murder, and he later
came to be associated with
the story of Bluebeard.

The little **Eglise Notre-Dame du Vieux-Pouzauges**,
with its 13th-century frescoes
uncovered in 1948, is one of
the treasures of the Vendée.
In soft colours, the frescoes
depict charming scenes from
the life of the Virgin Mary and
her family. A short audio-visual programme describes
the paintings. On the left,

4 m (12 ft) from the ground, a
bestiary frieze, also discovered
in 1948, illustrates the months
of the year.

Château du Puy-du-Fou ⓫

Road map B4. 🚌 ℹ️ *30 rue Georges Clemenceau, Les Epesses.*
☏ *51 64 60 60.* ◐ *Feb–Dec: daily.*
♿

THE BRICK-AND-GRANITE
Renaissance château of
Puy-du-Fou is 2 km (1 mile)
from the little village of Les
Epesses. Partly restored after
its destruction in the Vendée
Uprising, it now houses a
museum and an ambitious
theme park, and is the back-drop to the **Cinéscénie**, a
thrilling son et lumière
spectacle *(see pp58–9).*

In the **Ecomusée de la Vendée**, the Vendée Uprising
is imaginatively explained by
an illuminated model accom-panied by slides, together
with a display of paintings
and portraits. Prehistoric,
Gallo-Roman and medieval
exhibits illustrate the history,
character and architecture of
the region.

The large theme park, **Le Grand Parcours**, offers
plenty of entertainment. It has
two reconstructed villages,
one medieval and one 18th-century, with costumed
"villagers" and artisans. Other
features include wooded
walks, lakes, aquatic organ
pipes, a wolf's lair and lively

displays of juggling, jousting,
stunt-riding and especially
falconry, during which falcons,
eagles and vultures skim over
the heads of seated spectators.

🎥 **Cinéscénie**
☏ *51 64 11 11.* ◐ *mid-Jun–Aug: Fri, Sat. Spectacle begins: Jun–Jul: 10:30pm; Aug: 10pm; arrive one hour earlier; reservations required.* ♨ ♿
🏛 **Ecomusée de la Vendée**
◐ *Feb–Dec: daily.* ♨ ♿
🎡 **Le Grand Parcours**
◐ *May: Sun, public hols; Jun–mid-Sep: daily.* ● *mid-Sep–Apr.* ♨ ♿

Château de Clisson, a feudal fortress now in ruins

Clisson ⓬

Road map B4. 🚶 *5,500.* 🚉 🚌 ℹ️
pl de la Trinité (40 54 02 95). ♘ *Tue, Wed, Fri.* 🎵 *Festival de Musique (Jul).*

CLISSON, PERCHED on two
hills straddling the Sèvre
Nantaise river, is notable for
its Italianate beauty. After
much of the town was
destroyed in 1794 by punitive
Republican forces following
the collapse of the Vendée
Uprising, Clisson was largely
rebuilt by two wealthy
brothers, Pierre and François
Cacault, working with the
sculptor Frédéric Lemot.
Lemot's country home is now
the romantic **Parc de la Garenne Lemot**, which
extravagantly celebrates the
style of ancient Rome with
grottoes, columns and tombs,
including Lemot's own, the
Temple de l'Amitié.

The evolution of defensive
strategies can be followed in
the massive, ruined **Château de Clisson**, dating from the

"Villagers" at work in Puy-du-Fou's Grand Parcours

12th century and gradually strengthened in stages up to the 16th century. This was a key feudal fortress for the dukes of Brittany.

Visitors can peer into the dungeons, and into a well with a grisly story behind it: in the vengeful aftermath of the Vendée's defeat, Republican troops butchered and flung into it 18 people who were trying to make bread in the ruins. Next to the château is a fine Renaissance covered market, which survived the destruction because it was used as Republican barracks.

Parc de la Garenne Lemot & Maison du Jardinier

40 54 75 85. Apr–Sep: daily; Oct–Mar: Thu–Sat.

Château de Clisson

Pl du Minage. 40 54 02 22. Wed–Mon.

The machicolated entrance tower at the Château de Goulaine

Château de Goulaine ⓭

Road map B3. *Nantes, then taxi. 40 54 91 42. Easter–Oct: Sat, Sun, public hols, pm only; mid-Jun–mid-Sep: Wed–Mon pm only. Groups by appt. butterfly park only.*

ONLY A SHORT distance southeast of Nantes, this is the most westerly of all the limestone-and-slate Loire châteaux. Although the same family has lived and made wine on this spot for 1,000 years, the building dates from the 15th century with 17th-century wings. One machicolated tower survives from the 14th century. Elegant towers rise on each side of the central building: on one, there is a sculpture of brave Yolande de Goulaine, who is said to have spurred on her soldiers to repulse the besieging English by threatening to stab herself.

The château survived the Revolution because the family sold it to a Dutchman, only to recover it 70 years later. The present marquis, Robert de Goulaine, has restored the château and also opened a butterfly park where exotic species flutter about a large glasshouse. Butterflies also embellish the label of one of his *sur lie* Muscadets. The multicoloured fireplace in the grand salon is typical of the château's rich decorations.

CINÉSCÉNIE

Puy-du-Fou's late-night show is on a grand scale, with 800 performers and 12,000 seated spectators. It was conceived as a theatre of Vendée history using the full resources of contemporary open-air multimedia techniques. Laser lighting, music, water-jets and fireworks are all carefully orchestrated by computer.

Against the backdrop of the ruined château and its lake, hundreds of locally-recruited actors form living tableaux to dance or grieve, joust or slaughter each other. Horses thunder about, fountains and fireworks soar, bells ring and the château bursts into "flames".

Although the spectacle can be enjoyed for itself, translations of the commentary are available in English, German, Italian or Japanese to 150 of the seats on the huge stand. Warm clothing and advanced booking are advised.

A fire-eater in the Cinéscénie at Puy-du-Fou

Nantes ⓮

THE ANCIENT PORT of Nantes was the ducal capital of Brittany for 600 years, but is now considered to be part of the Pays de la Loire. Many of its fine 18th- and 19th-century buildings and houses were built on profits from maritime trade, especially in slaves, sugar, cotton and ship's supplies. The port has been extended downstream towards St-Nazaire, where a modern bridge, the longest in France, crosses the estuary *(see p34)*. This has become an industrial zone attracting trade and breathing new life into the area. Nantes itself remains a vigorous modern city, with good museums, wide open spaces and chic restaurants, bars and shops.

The Neo-Classical theatre in the place Graslin

Exploring Nantes

The most fashionable area of town is the **quartier Graslin**. Constructed between 1780 and 1900, the district's centrepiece is the place Graslin, with its Neo-Classical theatre approached by a steep flight of monumental steps. The architect, Mathurin Crucy, designed the place Graslin as a rectangle within a semicircle with eight streets radiating from it. The theatre is fronted by eight Corinthian columns, and statues of eight Muses look down on the square. The wall behind the columns is made of glass, allowing light to stream into the foyer during the day.

Crucy's elegant architecture is seen again in the nearby cours Cambronne, a pedestrianized avenue with fine matching houses built in the early 1800s, and in the place Royale with its splendid fountain celebrating ocean and river spirits.

On the **Ile Feydeau**, the former island where Jules Verne *(see p193)* was born, 18th-century town planning combined with middle-class trading wealth helped to produce beautiful Neo-Classical façades along streets such as allée Turenne, allée Duguay-Trouin and especially rue Kervégan where 18th-century architect Pierre Rousseau occupied No. 30. Wrought-iron balconies rise in pyramidal sequence supported by luxuriant carvings.

Just north of the Ile Feydeau is the place du Commerce and the ancient Bourse, an elegant 18th-century building, now the tourist office.

🚇 La Cigale

4 pl Graslin. 📞 40 69 76 41.
◐ daily. See **Restaurants** p219.

Facing the theatre, and in dazzling counterpoint to it, stands the famous brasserie-restaurant La Cigale, opened on 1 April 1895. This *fin-de-siècle* fantasy was conceived and largely executed by Emile Libaudière. The building is crammed with Art Nouveau motifs including the cicada from which it takes its name. The rich blues of its Italian tiling, its sinuous wrought-iron, bevelled windows and mirrors, sculptures and painted panels and ceilings have made this restaurant a favourite venue for aesthetes and food-lovers for a century.

🚇 Passage Pommeraye
◐ daily.

To the east of place Graslin, rue Crébillon is the most elegant shopping street in Nantes. It is linked with the rue de la Fosse by a remarkable covered shopping arcade, the passage Pommeraye.

The dining room of Nantes' Art Nouveau brasserie, La Cigale

The interior of the elegant passage Pommeraye

Named after the lawyer who financed its construction, it opened in 1843 and must have astonished the bourgeoisie visiting its 66 shops.

The arcade's three galleries are on different levels, each linked by a handsome wooden staircase, lined with statues and lamps. The decoration is highly ornate. Charming sculpted children look down on the galleries, lined with shops and rich with busts, bas-reliefs and other details in stone and metal, all beneath the original glass roof.

🏛 Musée Dobrée

Pl Jean V. 📞 40 71 03 50.
🔲 Tue–Sun. ⬤ public hols.
🎟 except Sun. ♿ grd flr only.
Thomas Dobrée (1810–95), son of a rich shipowner and industrialist, spent most of his life building this collection of paintings, drawings, sculpture, tapestries, furniture, porcelain, armour, religious works of art, stamps, books, letters and manuscripts. The palatial museum he built for them is based on a plan by the Gothic Revival architect Eugène-Emmanuel Viollet-le-Duc.

Part of the carved alabaster altarpiece in the Musée Dobrée

One of the reliquaries stands out – it is a gold casket, surmounted by a crown, which contains the heart of Anne of Brittany, who asked for it to be buried in her parents' tomb

in Nantes cathedral (see p55). A complete 15th-century altarpiece carved in alabaster statues from Nottingham, England, is another treasure.

In a second part of the complex, the Manoir de la Touche, there are exhibits dealing with the Vendée Uprising. These include the death mask of François de Charette, a charismatic Vendéen Royalist leader who was captured and shot in Nantes in March 1796. An adjoining modern museum houses an archaeological collection, with Egyptian, Greek and some locally found Gallo-Roman artifacts.

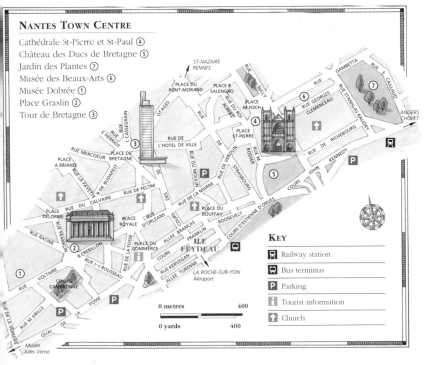

NANTES TOWN CENTRE

Cathédrale St-Pierre et St-Paul ④
Château des Ducs de Bretagne ⑤
Jardin des Plantes ⑦
Musée des Beaux-Arts ⑥
Musée Dobrée ①
Place Graslin ②
Tour de Bretagne ③

KEY

🚉 Railway station
🚌 Bus terminus
P Parking
ℹ Tourist information
✝ Church

0 metres 400
0 yards 400

Around the Château

THE TOUR DE BRETAGNE, the skyscraper built in 1976 that towers above Nantes, is a landmark dividing the city centre around place du Commerce and place Graslin to the west from the older district around the château and cathedral to the east. There are sensational views from the top. It can be entered (free of charge) from the cours des Cinquante Otages, which sweeps through the centre where the Erdre canal once flowed. This busy avenue has a memorial at the top, in place du Pont Morand, to the 50 hostages after which it is named. Their execution by the Nazis in reprisal for the assassination of the city's military commandant in 1941 turned many Nantais against the Vichy government.

The façade of the Cathédrale St-Pierre et St-Paul

♣ Château des Ducs de Bretagne

4 pl Marc Elder. **[** 40 41 56 56. **○** Wed–Mon. **🖾** **&**

The château, now surrounded by a landscaped moat, has strong curtain walls and round bastions in the style of the Château d'Angers *(see pp74–5)*. This was the birthplace of Anne of Brittany, who became duchess at 11 and then was coerced into marrying Charles VIII of France in 1491 at the age of 14. Charles died at Amboise in 1498 and, the following year, Anne married his successor, Louis XII, in the château chapel.

Anne's influence can be seen most clearly in the dormer windows and loggias of the **Grand Logis** to the right of the entrance, a graceful blend of Flamboyant and Renaissance styles. It was begun by her father, Duc François II, who built most of the château to replace the one in which Anne was born.

A smaller royal lodging lies to the west of it. It was here, in Brittany's Catholic bastion, that Henri IV signed the 1598 Edict of Nantes, which granted all Protestants permission to worship. A temporary museum in the château houses displays of Breton culture and Nantes' maritime history.

♠ Cathédrale St-Pierre et St-Paul

Place St-Pierre. **○** daily.

Nantes has the most accident-prone cathedral on the Loire. The story of its construction and destruction over centuries is vividly told in the crypt. Most recently, on 28 January 1972, a workman's match caused an explosion that blew off the roof. Following the resulting fire, a major restoration programme was undertaken, now completed. The cathedral has been left with an unusual lightness and unity.

A notable feature of this spacious Flamboyant Gothic building is the splendid black-and-white marble tomb of François II, father of Anne of Brittany, and his two wives, sculpted by Michel Colombe *(see pp116–17)*. Situated in the southern transept, it was created between 1500 and 1507 and is among the earliest examples of the Renaissance style in France.

🏛 Musée des Beaux-Arts

10 rue Georges Clemenceau. **[** 40 41 65 65. **○** Wed–Mon. **●** public hols. **🖾** except Sun. **&**

The grandeur of this museum and its collections is a good measure of Nantes' civic pride and wealth in the early 19th century. The galleries are on two levels and surround a huge, arched patio, whose clean lines are an appropriate setting for contemporary exhibitions. Although the museum has some sculptures, it is known mainly for its large collection of paintings,

Gustave Courbet's *The Corn Sifters* (1854) in the Musée des Beaux-Arts

Nantes' lovely botanical garden, the Jardin des Plantes

especially those representing
key movements from the 15th
to the 20th centuries.

Notable Italian works from
the 14th century include a
Madonna and Saints (c.1340)
by Bernardo Daddi. This came
from the collection of the
Cacault brothers who restored
Clisson *(see p189)*. So did an
elegant altarpiece section by
Perugino, *Saints Sebastian
and Anthony* (c.1475).

Tranquil Dutch and Flemish
landscapes and still lifes are
offset by a typically robust
Rubens, *The Triumph of Judas
Maccabaeus* (1635). The
master of light, Georges de
la Tour, dominates a section
of fine, French 17th-century
paintings with some of his
best work – *The Hurdy-Gurdy
Player, The Dream of St Joseph*
and *The Denial of St Peter*, all
dating from the 1620s.

Other highlights of the
museum are in the 19th- and
early 20th-century sections,
beginning with a luxuriant
portrait by Jean-Auguste-
Dominique Ingres, *Madame
de Senonnes* (1814). Talented
local painters, including James
Tissot of Nantes and Paul
Baudry of La Roche-sur-Yon,
are represented, as well as
the great innovators Eugène
Delacroix, Gustave Courbet,
Claude Monet and Vasili Kandinsky. Perhaps the most
famous picture in the museum
is Courbet's memorable scene,
The Corn Sifters (1854).

🏛 Musée Jules Verne

3 rue de l'Hermitage. **☏** *40 69 72
52.* ☐ *Wed–Sat, Sun pm–Mon.*
● *public hols.* 🖼 *except Sun.*
A remarkably comprehensive
display representing the life,
work and world of Jules
Verne (1828–1905) starts with
a room of furnishings from
the house in Amiens in which
he wrote most of his books.
The museum is packed with
mementos, splendidly bound
books, cartoons, maps, magic
lanterns and models.

🌿 Jardin des Plantes

Bd Stalingrad. ☐ *daily.*
Covering 7 ha (17 acres), the
plants that make up this extensive botanical garden began

as an 18th-century collection
of medicinal and exotic plants.
The original specimens were
brought to Nantes by home-
coming ships when a royal
decree obliged sea captains to
bring exotic plants and seeds
back from their travels.

In the mid-19th century, the
director, Dr Ecorchard, made
changes to the gardens after
an inspirational visit to Kew
Gardens in London. He
introduced the English style of
landscaping, with ponds and
winding paths, transforming
the entire area into a delightful
park. Here visitors can see
Europe's oldest magnolia tree
as well as several outstanding
displays of camellias.

THE WORLD OF JULES VERNE

Just past the Pont Anne de Bretagne is a disused section of
cobbled quay which, in 1839, was lined with boats.
It was here that the 11-year-old Jules Verne
slipped aboard a ship to see the world. He
got as far as Paimbœuf, a short trip down
river, before his father caught up with
him. Later, while studying law, Verne
started to publish plays and librettos. His
science-fiction novels, including *A
Journey to the Centre of the Earth*
(1864), *Twenty Thousand
Leagues Under the Sea* (1870)
and *Around the World in
Eighty Days* (1873), have been
hugely successful, and he is
among the most widely read and
translated authors in the world.

Bust of Jules Verne (1906) by Albert Roze

TRAVELLERS' NEEDS

WHERE TO STAY

LOIRE VALLEY HOTELS are as charming as their surroundings. Family-style inns predominate, with dining rooms that are also popular among locals and comfortable, usually old-fashioned, bedrooms. The region also boasts some prestigious *Relais et Châteaux* establishments, often mansions or châteaux converted into luxury hotels with elegant rooms, superb cuisine – and prices to match. A fascinating alternative is staying in a private château or manor house *(see pp200–201)*, which allows you access to privately-owned, often historic buildings as a (paying) guest of the owners. The hotel listings on pages 202–7 give details of establishments throughout the region, in every price category and style. *Gîtes*, the self-catering accommodation for which France is rightly famous, are also widely available in the Loire Valley, allowing you to take advantage of the marvellous range of fresh ingredients on offer in the local markets.

A hotel doorman

THE CITY HOTEL

THE MAIN TOWNS and cities along the banks of the Loire have at least one long-established *grand hôtel* in the centre. These large hotels typically have spacious entrance halls and public rooms, but some of the once large bedrooms may well have been carved up to allow for en suite bathrooms. Rooms are liable to vary considerably in quality, so it is advisable to ask to see the room offered if you have not made a booking in advance. When you make a reservation, be sure to specify a room away from a main road or busy square (most of these city hotels have some much quieter rooms, which overlook a courtyard). Bars are likely to be frequented by members of the local business community, who also entertain clients in the hotel restaurant, where you can expect classic French cuisine rather than regional dishes.

THE CHÂTEAU HOTEL

A NUMBER OF CHATEAUX and manor houses in the Loire Valley have been converted into expensive hotels. Often set in well-kept grounds and offering outstanding cuisine, they range from Renaissance manor houses to huge, turreted 19th-century piles. The **Relais et Châteaux** association, of which many are members, publishes an annual brochure.

Rooms are usually spacious and elegant, with some suites available. Some château hotels also offer more modest accommodation, in outbuildings or even in bungalows in the grounds, enabling you to acquire a taste for *la vie de château* and enjoy the restaurant's cuisine without breaking the bank. If you prefer to be in the main building, specify this when booking – advance reservations are essential.

THE CLASSIC FAMILY HOTEL

THESE TYPICALLY French small hotels, generally run by the same family for several generations, are to be found throughout the Loire Valley. The bar and dining room are likely to be widely used by locals, especially for Sunday lunch in country districts. The atmosphere is usually friendly, with helpful staff able to provide leaflets and other information about local sightseeing and shopping.

Most of these hotels have only a small number of rooms, often reasonably spacious and pleasantly furnished with well-worn antiques and flowery wallpaper. Plumbing may be erratic, although many hotels of this type have made efforts to spruce up their bathrooms. Few family hotels in the rural

The elegant Domaine des Hauts-de-Loire hotel in Onzain *(see p205)*

The grand staircase of the Hôtel de l'Univers in Tours *(see p203)*

areas have single rooms, but these are more common in the region's towns.

Many family hotels belong to the **Logis de France** association, which publishes an annual booklet listing more than 4,000 family-run hotels in France. *Logis* hotels are proud of their restaurants, which tend to specialize in regional cuisine. Most are basic roadside inns, with only a few listed in the main towns, but off the beaten track you can find charming farmhouses and inexpensive hotels.

Many family-run hotels are shut in the afternoon and do not like visitors to arrive then, although hotel guests have keys. Their restaurants are also shut at least one day a week (except possibly in the tourist season).

Logo of the Logis de France association

THE MODERN CHAIN HOTEL

FRANCE HAS an increasing number of modern chain hotels, on the edges of towns or close to motorways.

The cheapest are the one-star, very basic **Formule 1** motels. Two-star chains, which are widely used by French families on a low budget, include **Ibis/Arcade**, **Campanile**, **Climat de France** and **Interhôtel**. More comfortable, but lacking in regional charm or atmosphere, are the **Novotel** and **Mercure/Altéa** three-star chains. All the chain hotels offer some family rooms, and

in some children can sleep in their parents' room without charge. Most have restaurants where the food is adequate.

THE RESTAURANT-WITH-ROOMS

A FEW OF THE well-known and expensive restaurants in the Loire Valley region also have rooms available for overnight guests. The rooms may be as chic as the restaurant. However, they might be modest bedrooms left over from the days before the restaurant was a gourmet's magnet and will therefore allow you to spend an inexpensive night to make up for a budget-busting meal.

In rural areas, it may be practical to spend the night at the restaurant, rather than return to a remote hotel. Check in the listings on pages 214–19 for restaurants-with-rooms.

MEALS AND FACILITIES

B ECAUSE MOST VISITORS to the Loire Valley choose to tour around, few hotels offer full-board rates to those who settle in for holidays. However, for more than three nights in one place, it may be possible to obtain *pension* (full-board) or *demi-pension* (half-board). But half-board may apply only to lunch, which makes sightseeing difficult, and the meals for full-board guests are likely to be less interesting than the fixed-price menus. Always

check whether the room rate includes breakfast. If not, you may prefer to have your breakfast in a nearby café.

Traditionally, family hotel rooms offer double beds, but twin beds are more likely to be found in city and chain hotels. Prices are usually fixed per room, but single travellers may be allowed a small reduction. Bathrooms with a shower rather than a bath make the room less expensive. Those with only a *cabinet de toilette* (an alcove containing basin and bidet) are the cheapest.

It is perfectly acceptable to ask to view the room before making a decision.

GRADINGS AND PRICES

FRENCH HOTELS are officially graded into one, two, three and four stars, plus four-star deluxe. These categories take account of facilities such as telephones, televisions and en suite bathrooms, but do not necessarily indicate the quality of the decor or service. A few very modest hotels do not rate a star ranking.

Prices rise as the number of stars increases. Rooms may vary in quality within an establishment, so it is not easy to classify hotels solely by price. Rates for a double room start at around F140 per night without breakfast, although they may start at F1,000 in château hotels. Check whether a local tax *(taxe de séjour)* will be added to your bill, but service will already be included. It is usual to leave a small tip for the chambermaid.

Le Manoir du Colombier in Châteauroux *(see p206)*

The Domaine des Hautes Roches at Rochecorbon *(see p203)*

BOOKING

RESERVE WELL IN ADVANCE for hotels in popular tourist areas during July and August. If booking by telephone it may be necessary to send a fax confirmation, giving a credit card number. You may need to speak French to make a telephone booking for some hotels, but letters in English are normally acceptable. Local tourist offices can supply listings of hotels and provide a reservation service (for up to a week in advance).

BED AND BREAKFAST

FRENCH bed-and-breakfast accommodation, called *chambres d'hôte*, can vary widely from modest rooms above a hayloft to an elegant room in a manor house. Local tourist offices keep lists of those families willing to take in guests. Some hosts will cook dinner if given advance warning. A large number of such rooms are registered and inspected by the **Gîtes de France** organization – look out for the green and yellow signboards in rural areas. Another bed-and-breakfast organization, **Café-Couette** (*couette* being French for duvet), has a pool of rural and urban accommodation that can be reserved through a central clearing house by those who pay a modest annual membership fee.

SELF-CATERING

THE BEST-KNOWN organization monitoring and booking self-catering accommodation is the **Gîtes de France**. First known as *Gîtes Ruraux*, it still offers predominantly rural accommodation in the Loire Valley, ranging from cottages to an entire wing of a château. Booking is essential and can be made using the company's main brochure, available from international offices, or direct. *Gîtes* are also listed in a series of booklets covering each *département*. Don't expect luxury from the lower-priced *gîtes*, as they have only very basic facilities, but a holiday in a *gîte* is a great way to experience Loire Valley life.

DIRECTORY

HOTELS

Campanile
📞 *0181-569 6969 in UK.*
📞 *64 62 46 46 in France.*

Climat de France
📞 *0171-287 3181 in UK.*
📞 *64 46 01 23 in France.*

Interhôtel
📞 *0171-287 3181 in UK.*
📞 *42 06 46 46 in France.*

Formule 1
📞 *0181-741 1001 in UK for brochure.*
📞 *60 78 29 90 in France for brochure.*

Ibis/Arcade, Novotel, Mercure/Altéa
📞 *0171-724 1000 in UK.*
📞 *60 77 27 27 in France.*

Relais et Châteaux
📞 *0171-287 0987 in UK for brochure.*

Logis de France
83 av d'Italie, 75013 Paris.
📞 *45 84 70 00.*

BED AND BREAKFAST

Café-Couette
8 rue d'Isly, 75008 Paris.
📞 *42 94 92 00.*
FAX *42 94 93 12.*

SELF-CATERING

Gîtes de France
178 Piccadilly, London W1V 9DB.
📞 *0171-493 3480.*
FAX *0171-495 6417.*

Gîtes de France/ Cléconfort
ARART, B.P. 139, 38 rue A-Fresnel, 37171 Chambray-les-Tours.
📞 *47 48 37 13.*
FAX *47 48 13 39.*

CAMPING

Castels et Camping Caravaning
BP301, 56008 Vannes.
📞 *97 42 55 83.*
FAX *97 47 50 72.*

UK CAMPING CARNETS

Car Club
📞 *(01794) 515444.*

Cyclists Touring Club
📞 *(01483) 417217.*

Gîtes de France Camping and Caravanning Club
📞 *(0203) 422024.*

HOSTELS

CROUS
39 av. G-Bernanos, 75231 Paris.
📞 *40 51 36 00.*

Fédération Unie des Auberges de Jeunesse
27 rue Pajol, 75018 Paris.
📞 *44 89 87 27.*

YHA (Youth Hostel Association)
8 St Stephens Hill, St Albans, Herts Al1 2DY.
📞 *(01727) 855215.*

DISABLED TRAVELLERS

Association des Paralysés de France
17 bd Auguste Blanqui 75013 Paris.
📞 *40 78 69 00.*

CNFLRH
38 bd Raspail, 75007 Paris.
📞 *45 48 90 13.*

RADAR (Royal Association for Disability and Rehabilitation)
12 City Forum, 250 City Rd, London EC1V 8AF.
📞 *0171-250 3222.*

TOURIST OFFICES

French Government Tourist Office
178 Piccadilly, London W1V 0AL.
📞 *0891-244 123.*
FAX *0171-493 6594.*

CAMPING

CAMPING IS A CHEAP and fun way of seeing the Loire Valley. Information on camp sites can be obtained from departmental tourist offices. Some of these do not accept visitors without a special camping *carnet* (available from the AA and RAC and from the addresses listed in the Directory). French camp sites are graded into four starred categories, but even one-star sites have lavatories, public telephones and running water (although this may be only cold). The top-ranked sites are remarkably well equipped. Always book ahead where possible.

The **Gîtes de France** organization has a guide to unpretentious sites on farm land (ask for *camping à la ferme*), and *camping sauvage* (camping outside official sites) is occasionally possible if you come to an agreement with the landowner. **Castels et Camping Caravaning** is an up-market association of sites within the grounds of châteaux and manor houses.

HOSTELS

HOSTELS PROVIDE budget accommodation, but for two or more people sharing a room, an inexpensive hotel will probably cost the same. To stay in a youth hostel, you need to purchase a membership card from the **Youth Hostel Association** in your own country, or buy an "Ajiste" card from French hostels. See the Directory for the address of the *auberges de jeunesse* (youth hostel) organization. **CROUS**, the Centre Régional des Oeuvres Universitaires, can provide details of university rooms available during the summer vacation. **Gîtes de France** is once again a valuable source of information: ask for the *Gîtes d'étape* guide to dormitory accommodation in farmhouses for those on walking, riding or cycling holidays.

Gîtes de France logo

DISABLED TRAVELLERS

A GUIDE PUBLISHED by **RADAR** (Royal Association for Disability and Rehabilitation), *Holidays and Travel Abroad*, details wheelchair access to hotels, youth hostels and self-catering accommodation, and *Gîtes accessibles à tous* lists officially classified *gîtes* suitable for the disabled. Information on hotel access is also available from **CNFLHR** (Comité National Français de Liaison pour la Réadaptation des Handicapés). The **Association des Paralysés de France** also publishes a guide to accessible accommodation.

SOURCES OF INFORMATION

THE INVALUABLE *Traveller in France Reference Guide*, listing hotel chains, booking agencies and tour operators specializing in travel to and in France, is published by the **French Government Tourist Office**. The tourist office is also able to supply brochures and booklets for **Logis de France** hotels, **Café-Couette** and other bed-and-breakfast establishments, **Gîtes de France** and many other types of accommodation. **Regional Tourist Committees** will send lists of hotels, hostels, camp sites and private self-catering accommodation. The regional **Loisirs Accueil** centre and Departmental Tourist Committees are also useful sources of information. When you are in the Loire Valley, contact local tourist offices *(see p231)* for hotel lists and details of local families taking in bed-and-breakfast guests.

USING THE LISTINGS

The hotels on pages 202–7 are listed according to area and price category. The symbols summarize the facilities at each hotel.

🛁 all rooms with bath or shower
24 24-hour room service
📺 TV in all rooms
❄ rooms with good views
🗄 air-conditioning in all rooms
♨ hotel swimming pool or beach
🧒 children's facilities
♿ wheelchair access
🛗 lift
P hotel parking available
🌳 grounds or terrace
🍴 restaurant in hotel
★ highly recommended
💳 credit cards accepted
AE American Express
MC Mastercard
DC Diners Club
V Visa

Price categories for a standard double room (not per person) with bath or shower for one night, including tax and service, but not breakfast.

Ⓕ Under F200
ⒻⒻ F200–400
ⒻⒻⒻ F400–600
ⒻⒻⒻⒻ F600–1,000
ⒻⒻⒻⒻⒻ Over F1,000.

Camping in a forest in the Loire Valley

Staying in a Château

THE HOTELS FEATURED HERE have been selected from our lists of recommended places to stay on pages 202–7. They offer a unique opportunity to experience the style of life in a private Loire Valley château, spending a night within walls steeped in history, but often with all the comforts of a modern hotel. You will be greeted like a house guest, and efforts are made to make you feel part of the owner's family, who may have lived in the château for many generations. They may also create the atmosphere of a private party at dinner, which can be booked and paid for in advance.

Château de Blanville
Close to Chartres and surrounded by beautiful formal gardens, the Château de Blanville, owned by the same family for more than 250 years, has a swimming pool as well as a gym. (See p206.)

Château des Briottières
This 18th-century château, furnished in period and lived in by the same family for six generations, has attractive grounds and a heated pool. (See p202.)

0 kilometres   50

0 miles   50

Château de la Millière
Close to Les Sables d'Olonne, this 19th-century château is set in extensive grounds, complete with an open-air pool. (See p207.)

Château des Réaux
The owners of this pretty 15th-century château, with red and white brickwork, offer a warm welcome and attractive rooms. (See p202.)

The countryside surrounding the Château du Plessis-Beauregard in the region close to Orléans offers visitors a scene of pastoral tranquillity.

Château de la Verrerie
The "Stuarts' château" (see p154), magically reflected in a lake and surrounded by dense woodland, has spacious, comfortable rooms and an attractive cottage-style restaurant in the grounds. (See p205.)

Château du Plessis-Beauregard
This turreted château has a lived-in feel, with light, pretty bedrooms. (See p204.)

Château de Jallanges
An energetic couple have turned this brick and stone Renaissance dwelling, with a period garden and pretty chapel, into a charming home. (See p204.)

Château de la Bourdaisière
A princely greeting (from one of the Princes de Broglie) awaits you in this beautifully modernized château, the birthplace of Gabrielle d'Estrées. (See p203.)

Château de la Commanderie
Owned by the same family for four generations, this 12th-century manor house was once the Commandery of the Knights Templar. A château was added in the 19th century. (See p206.)

ANJOU

ANGERS

Hôtel Continental

Road map C3. 12 rue Louis de Romain, 49000. 【 41 86 94 94. FAX 41 86 96 60. **Rooms:** 25. ▦ TV ⌨ ♨ ⎙ AE, DC, V. Ⓕ Ⓕ

Modernized in bright Kandinsky colours, this hotel is in a quiet side street only minutes from the best shopping areas. The rooms are all soundproofed, and the balconies are decorated with flowers and plants. Parking is available in the place du Ralliement nearby.

Hôtel du Mail

Road map C3. 8 rue Ursules, 49000. 【 41 88 56 22. FAX 41 86 91 20. **Rooms:** 27. TV P ⎙ AE, MC, DC, V. Ⓕ Ⓕ

This old-fashioned hotel was built in 1643 as part of a convent, and the first floor rooms have particularly high ceilings. Despite being centrally located, it is quiet and has parking. Self-service breakfasts are included.

BRIOLLAY

Château de Noirieux

Road map C3. 26 rte du Moulin, 49125. 【 41 42 50 05. FAX 41 37 91 00. **Rooms:** 19. ▦ TV ♨ ≋ ♻ P ◉ ⊪ ⎙ AE, MC, DC, V. Ⓕ Ⓕ Ⓕ Ⓕ

Overlooking the Loire and Sarthe valleys, this hotel combines a 15th-century manor house and a chapel. Each bedroom is decorated in a different style, ranging from the 17th to the 20th centuries. The restaurant offers new versions of classic dishes and a seven-course gastronomic menu.

CHÂTEAUNEUF-SUR-SARTHE

Château des Briottières

Road map C3. Champigné 49330. 【 41 42 00 02. FAX 41 42 01 55. **Rooms:** 10. ▦ ♨ ♻ P ◉ ★ ⎙ AE, MC, DC, V. Ⓕ Ⓕ Ⓕ Ⓕ

This 18th-century château hotel, midway between Angers and the Abbaye de Solesmes, has extensive grounds with on-site cycling, fishing and swimming. Visitors can join their hosts for a candlelit dinner. Booking is essential.

FONTEVRAUD-L'ABBAYE

Hôtellerie Prieuré St-Lazare

Road map C3. Abbaye de Fontevraud, 49590. 【 41 51 73 16. FAX 41 51 75 50. **Rooms:** 52. ▦ TV ♨ ≋ ♻ P ◉ ⊪ ⎙ AE, MC, V. Ⓕ Ⓕ

Located in the abbey complex (*see pp86–7*), this hotel is in the former St-Lazare priory. Now modernized, it is a very comfortable hotel. The bedrooms are in a 19th-century wing, and the restaurant in the *salle capitulaire* spreads out into the cloisters in the summer.

GENNES

Hôtel le Prieuré

Road map C3. Chênehutte-les-Tuffeaux, 49350. 【 41 67 90 14. FAX 41 67 92 24. **Rooms:** 34. ▦ TV ♨ ≋ ♻ P ◉ ⊪ ⎙ AE, MC, DC, V. Ⓕ Ⓕ Ⓕ Ⓕ

This Renaissance manor house, a *Relais et Châteaux* member, has rooms decorated in the Louis XIII style, some with views of the Loire. It is set in a 15-ha (37-acre) park, with a swimming pool and tennis courts. The restaurant extends onto the terrace in fine weather.

MONTREUIL-BELLAY

Splendid Hôtel

Road map C4. 139 rue Docteur-Gaudrez, 49260. 【 41 53 10 00. FAX 41 52 45 17. **Rooms:** 60. ▦ TV ♨ ≋ ♻ P ◉ ⊪ ⎙ MC, DC, V. Ⓕ Ⓕ

Part of this hotel is located in a renovated house in the centre of town. It also has a 17th-century annexe, Le Relais du Bellay, to which 22 new rooms have been added. The restaurant serves excellent regional food.

SAUMUR

Hôtel St-Pierre

Road map C3. Rue Haute St-Pierre, 49400. 【 41 50 33 00. FAX 41 50 38 68. **Rooms:** 14. TV ♨ ⌨ P ⎙ AE, DC, MC, V. Ⓕ Ⓕ

Located in a small street just off the place St-Pierre, this elegant hotel is generally quiet, apart from the occasional sound of organ practice taking place in the nearby church. The bedrooms have been renovated with great style. There are two *salons*, one with a 17th-century open fireplace.

TOURAINE

AMBOISE

Le Lion d'Or

Road map D3. 17 quai Charles-Guinot, 37400. 【 47 57 00 23. FAX 47 23 22 49. **Rooms:** 22. ★ P ⊪ ⎙ MC, V. Ⓕ Ⓕ

Well situated beside the Loire, this typically French, traditional hotel is welcoming and efficiently run. It has comfortable rooms as well as a restaurant.

AZAY-LE-RIDEAU

Hôtel de Biencourt

Road map D3. 7 rue Balzac, 37190. 【 47 45 20 75. **Rooms:** 18. ▦ ★ ♻ P ⎙ AE, MC, V. Ⓕ Ⓕ

Only a few paces away from the entrance to one of the loveliest Loire Valley châteaux, this small hotel is in an 18th-century town house. The rooms are quiet and pretty, some of them overlooking a garden, and there are several restaurants nearby.

Le Grand Monarque

Road map D3. 3 pl de la République, 37190. 【 47 45 40 08. FAX 47 45 46 25. **Rooms:** 26. ▦ ★ P ◉ ⊪ ⎙ AE, MC, DC, V. Ⓕ Ⓕ

Run by the same family for generations, this hotel offers comfortable well-furnished rooms and friendly service. In summer, the courtyard garden, shaded by tall trees, provides a delightful setting for the restaurant's regional cuisine.

BOURGUEIL

Château des Réaux

Road map C3. Le Port Boulet, 37140. 【 47 95 14 40. FAX 47 95 18 34. **Rooms:** 12. ▦ ♨ ★ ♻ P ◉ ★ ⎙ AE, MC, DC, V. Ⓕ Ⓕ Ⓕ

This Renaissance château has been home for the Goupil de Bouillé family for more than a century. They welcome guests in their attractive rooms and suites, four of them in a cottage in the gardens. *Table d'hôte* meals are available.

CHENONCEAUX

Hôtel du Bon Laboureur et du Château

Road map D3. 6 rue du Docteur-Bretonneau, 37150. **(** *47 23 90 02.* **FAX** *47 23 82 01.* **Rooms:** *33.* 🚗 📺 🏊 ☰ 🏇 ♿ P 🐕 🍴 ☲ *AE, MC, DC, V.* **Ⓕ Ⓕ**

This family-run hotel, a short walk from the château, looks like a cosy inn. However, its many sophisticated delights include a heated outdoor pool with its own cocktail bar, and a restaurant with a good reputation.

CHINON

La Boule d'Or

Road map D3. 66 quai Jeanne-d'Arc, 37500. **(** *47 93 03 13.* **FAX** *47 93 24 25.* **Rooms:** *15.* 🚗 ☰ 🏇 🐕 🍴 ☲ *AE, MC, DC, V.* **Ⓕ Ⓕ**

This friendly hotel, set in an ancient coaching inn beside the Vienne, has pretty rooms, some overlooking a courtyard. Its restaurant serves outdoor meals in fine weather.

Château de Marçay

Road map D3. Marçay, 37500. **(** *47 93 03 47.* **FAX** *47 93 45 33.* **Rooms:** *38.* 🚗 ☰ 🏊 🏇 ♿ 🏊 P 🐕 🍴 ★ ☲ *AE, MC, DC, V.* **Ⓕ Ⓕ Ⓕ Ⓕ**

This turreted medieval château, 9 km (5 miles) south of Chinon, is built of traditional white tufa. There are tennis courts, a swimming pool and even a heliport in the grounds. The restaurant and its excellent wine cellar are renowned.

LANGEAIS

Hôtel l'Hosten

Road map D3. 2 rue Gambetta, 37130. **(** *47 96 82 12.* **FAX** *47 96 56 72.* **Rooms:** *11.* 🚗 📺 🏇 ♿ P 🍴 🐕 ☲ *AE, MC, DC, V.* **Ⓕ Ⓕ**

This traditional hotel close to the castle has been run by the same family for decades. Some of the rooms look onto a pretty terrace. It also has an excellent restaurant serving classical cuisine.

LOCHES

Le George Sand

Road map D4. 39 rue Quintefol, 37600. **(** *47 59 39 74.* **FAX** *47 91 55 75.* **Rooms:** *20.* 🚗 📺 🏇 🐕 🍴 ☲ *MC, V.* **Ⓕ Ⓕ**

This *Logis de France* is set in an old coaching inn below the château ramparts. Some of the rooms are reached by a stone staircase from a medieval watchtower. The restaurant serves regional dishes.

LUYNES

Domaine de Beauvois

Road map D3. Le Pont Clouet, 37230. **(** *47 55 50 11.* **FAX** *47 55 59 62.* **Rooms:** *40.* 🚗 📺 ☰ 🏊 🏇 🐾 P 🐕 🍴 ★ ☲ *AE, MC, DC, V.* **Ⓕ Ⓕ Ⓕ Ⓕ**

A 15th- and 16th-century manor house, with an outdoor pool and tennis courts, this elegant *Relais et Châteaux* hotel is 4 km (2 miles) northwest of Luynes.

MONTBAZON

Château d'Artigny

Road map D3. Rte de Monts, 37250. **(** *47 26 24 24.* **FAX** *47 65 92 79.* **Rooms:** *55.* 🚗 📺 ☰ 🏊 🏇 P 🐕 🍴 ★ ☲ *AE, MC, DC, V.* **Ⓕ Ⓕ Ⓕ**

The *parfumier* François Coty built this château between 1912 and 1928 in 18th-century style. Now it is a deluxe *Relais et Châteaux* member. There are tennis courts and a pool, and musical weekends in winter.

MONTLOUIS-SUR-LOIRE

Château de la Bourdaisière

Road map D3. 25 rue de la Bourdaisière, 37270. **(** *47 45 16 31.* **FAX** *47 45 09 11.* **Rooms:** *12.* 🚗 ☰ 🏊 🏇 🐾 P 🐕 🍴 ★ ☲ *MC, V.* **Ⓕ Ⓕ Ⓕ Ⓕ**

In 1565, Gabrielle d'Estrées, Henri IV's mistress, was born in this château. It has been refurbished as luxury accommodation, and offers a pool, tennis courts and horse riding.

TOURS

Central Hôtel

Road map D3. 21 rue Berthelot, 37000. **(** *47 05 46 44.* **FAX** *47 66 10 26.* **Rooms:** *41.* 🚗 📺 🏇 ♿ 🐾 P 🐕 ☲ *AE, MC, DC, V.* **Ⓕ Ⓕ**

As central as the name suggests, this pleasant hotel has comfortable rooms and a little garden as well as parking, a real benefit in Tours.

Hôtel Colbert

Road map D3. 78 rue Colbert, 37000. **(** *47 66 61 56.* **FAX** *47 66 01 55.* **Rooms:** *18.* 🏨 📺 🏇 ♿ 🐕 ☲ *AE, MC, DC, V.* **Ⓕ Ⓕ**

This friendly hotel near the cathedral has been renovated, but retains its classic style. Many good-value restaurants are nearby. In summer, breakfast is served in the tiny courtyard garden.

Domaine des Hautes Roches

Road map D3. 86 quai de la Loire, Rochecorbon, 37210. **(** *47 52 88 88.* **FAX** *47 52 81 30.* **Rooms:** *11.* 🚗 📺 ☰ 🏇 ♿ 🐾 P 🐕 🍴 ★ ☲ *AE, MC, V.* **Ⓕ Ⓕ Ⓕ Ⓕ**

This unique hotel combines an 18th-century building with troglodyte bedrooms carved out of the tufa cliffside, which are as comfortable as they are unusual. Tours is only 5 km (3 miles) away.

Hôtel de l'Univers

Road map D3. 5 bd Heurteloup, 37000. **(** *47 05 37 12.* **FAX** *47 61 51 80.* **Rooms:** *85.* 🚗 🏨 📺 🏇 ♿ 🐾 P 🐕 🍴 ☲ *AE, MC, DC, V.* **Ⓕ Ⓕ Ⓕ Ⓕ**

Tours' "grand hotel", recently done up, is now a deluxe establishment. The *trompe l'oeil* paintings in the lobby depict some well known past guests, including Winston Churchill and Sarah Bernhardt. The rooms are elegant and air-conditioned.

VEIGNÉ

Le Moulin Fleuri

Road map D3. Rte de Ripault, 37250. **(** *47 26 01 12.* **FAX** *47 34 04 71.* **Rooms:** *12.* 🏇 P 🐕 🍴 ☲ *AE, V.* **Ⓕ Ⓕ**

An old watermill beside the Indre has been turned into this charming hotel. Its modest yet large bedrooms are above a riverside restaurant.

VILLANDRY

Le Cheval Rouge

Road map D3. 9 rue Principale, 37510. **(** *47 50 02 07.* **FAX** *47 50 08 77.* **Rooms:** *20.* 🚗 🏇 🏇 P 🐕 🍴 ☲ *MC, V.* **Ⓕ Ⓕ**

Just a few minutes' walk from the gardens of Château de Villandry, this hotel offers good-value, modern bedrooms. It also makes a handy base for visiting Azay-le-Rideau, Langeais and Ussé.

For key to symbols see p199

VOUVRAY

Château de Jallanges

Road map D3. Vernou-sur-Brenne, 37210. **C** *47 52 01 71.* **FAX** *47 52 11 18.* **Rooms:** *6.* 🛏 🌂 🏃 **P** 🔊 ★ 🈂 *AE, MC, DC, V.* Ⓕ Ⓕ Ⓕ Ⓕ

An energetic family offer private accommodation in this 15th-century château. The rooms overlook the peaceful grounds, where guests can go horse riding, travel in carriages or hot-air balloons, or stroll in the Renaissance garden before dining with the owners.

YZEURES-SUR-CREUSE

Hôtel de la Promenade

Road map D4. 1 pl du 11 Novembre, 37290. **C** *47 94 55 21.* **FAX** *47 94 46 12.* **Rooms:** *17.* 🛏 TV 🌂 🏃 **P** 🍴 🈂 *MC, V.* Ⓕ Ⓕ

This former coaching inn in Touraine is near the archaeological sites of Le Grand-Pressigny and Preuilly-sur-Claise and is also convenient for the nature reserve of La Brenne. It has cosy rooms and a beamed dining room.

BLESOIS AND ORLEANAIS

BEAUGENCY

La Sologne

Road map E3. 6 pl St-Firmin, 45190. **C** *38 44 50 27.* **FAX** *38 44 90 19.* **Rooms:** *16.* TV 🏃 **P** 🈂 *MC, V.* Ⓕ Ⓕ

This attractive little hotel, housed in a stone building in the old town, makes a pleasant stopover. Its small but pretty and well-equipped rooms overlook a garden, where breakfast is served. It is advisable to book ahead.

BLOIS

Hôtel Anne de Bretagne

Road map E3. 31 av Jean-Laigret, 41000. **C** *54 78 05 38.* **FAX** *54 74 37 79.* **Rooms:** *29.* 🛏 TV 🌂 🏃 **P** 🔊 🈂 *AE, MC, DC, V.* Ⓕ Ⓕ

This modest inn – a *Logis de France* but, unusually, with no restaurant – is popular with both French and foreign tourists for its good-value, brightly decorated rooms and its

friendly atmosphere. It is situated close to the château, but away from the summer crowds, on a small square.

Le Médicis

Road map E3. 2 allée François-1er, 41000. **C** *54 43 94 04.* **FAX** *54 42 04 05.* **Rooms:** *12.* 🛏 **P** 🅿 TV 📺 🈂 *AE, MC, DC, V.* Ⓕ Ⓕ Ⓕ

This stylish 19th-century building is conveniently near the train station and only 15 minutes' walk from the château. Le Médicis has elegant, air-conditioned rooms, each of which has been attractively decorated in a different style. The restaurant is popular for its classic cuisine and wide range of fixed-price meals.

CHAMBORD

Le Grand St-Michel

Road map E3. Le Village, 41250. **C** *54 20 31 31.* **FAX** *54 20 36 40.* **Rooms:** *40.* TV 🌂 🏃 🅿 **P** 🔊 🍴 🈂 *MC, V.* Ⓕ Ⓕ

Opposite the magnificent château, this traditional hotel is peaceful retreat at the end of the day. Some of the comfortable bedrooms have spectacular château views. The hotel's tennis courts are good for an early-evening workout, before adjourning to one of restaurant's terrace tables, which are, not surprisingly, in great demand.

CHÂTEAUNEUF-SUR-LOIRE

Château du Plessis-Beauregard

Road map E2. Vitry-aux-Loges, 45530. **C** *38 59 47 24.* **FAX** *38 59 47 48.* **Rooms:** *3.* 🛏 🌂 🈐 **P** 🔊 ★ Ⓕ Ⓕ Ⓕ

Set in the Forêt d'Orléans, 6 km (4 miles) from Châteauneuf-sur-Loire, this turreted, brick château has light, airy rooms and a swimming pool. A set dinner is available if ordered well in advance.

CHEVERNY

Château de Breuil

Road map E3. Rte de Fougère-sur-Brièvre, 41700. **C** *54 44 20 20.* **FAX** *54 44 30 40.* **Rooms:** *18.* 🛏 TV 📺 🏃 **P** 🔊 🍴 🈂 *AE, MC, V.* Ⓕ Ⓕ Ⓕ

This grand 18th-century château is set in extensive grounds, and all the bedrooms, suites and public rooms are furnished with antiques. A surviving 15th-century tower has also been converted into a unique bedroom and sitting area. The dining room is luxurious.

COUR-CHEVERNY

Le St-Hubert

Road map E3. Rue Nationale, 41700. **C** *54 79 96 60.* **FAX** *54 79 21 17.* **Rooms:** *20.* 🛏 📺 🏃 **P** 🔊 🍴 🈂 *MC, V.* Ⓕ Ⓕ

Named after the patron saint of hunting, this family-style hotel is very popular during the shooting season. In the summer it offers angling. Each room is decorated in modern style. The restaurant has special meals for children.

GIEN

Le Rivage

Road map F3. 1 quai de Nice, 45500. **C** *38 37 79 00.* **FAX** *38 38 10 21.* **Rooms:** *19.* 🛏 TV 📺 目 🏃 **P** 🍴 ★ 🈂 *AE, MC, DC, V.* Ⓕ Ⓕ

All the rooms in this elegant hotel are furnished with antiques, and some have views across the gardens to the river. The air-conditioned restaurant successfully blends classic and *nouvelle* cuisine.

MONTRICHARD

La Tête Noire

Road map D3. 24 rue de Tours. **C** *54 32 05 55.* **FAX** *54 32 78 37.* **Rooms:** *38.* 🏃 **P** 🔊 🍴 🈂 *MC, V.* Ⓕ Ⓕ

This traditional, reliable hotel has pleasant rooms, some of them in an annexe. The buildings are set in a garden beside the River Cher.

NOUAN-LE-FUZELIER

Moulin de Villiers

Road map E3. Rte de Chaon, 41600. **C** *54 88 72 27.* **FAX** *54 88 78 87.* **Rooms:** *19.* 📺 🏃 **P** 🔊 🍴 🈂 *MC, V.* Ⓕ Ⓕ

This converted mill gives a real sense of the Sologne. Surrounded by woods, it has a lake that is certain to delight both anglers and bird-watchers. The rooms are basic but charming, and the restaurant is also good value.

OLIVET

Les Quatre-Saisons

Road map E2. 351 rue de la Reine-Blanche, 45160. 🚗 38 66 14 30. **FAX** 38 66 78 59. **Rooms:** 10. 🛏️ 📺 🔆 🏃 🅿️ 🈺 🍴 🍽️ AE, MC, V. Ⓕ Ⓕ

The bedrooms of this comfortable hotel are bright and furnished with antiques. Many rooms have views of the River Loiret, as does the delightful dining room.

ONZAIN

Domaine des Hauts-de-Loire

Road map D3. Rte d'Herbault, 41150. 🚗 54 20 72 57. **FAX** 54 20 77 32. **Rooms:** 35. 🛏️ 📺 🔆 🈺 🅿️ 🈺 🍴 🍽️ ★ 🈺 AE, MC, DC, V. Ⓕ Ⓕ Ⓕ Ⓕ
See also **Restaurants**, p216.

Once a hunting lodge, this *Relais et Châteaux* member is now an elegant hotel. Guests can swim, play tennis or even ride in a hot-air balloon or a helicopter in the grounds. The restaurant has two Michelin stars.

ORLÉANS

Hôtel Jackotel

Road map E2. 18 Cluître St-Aignan, 45000. 🚗 38 54 48 48. **FAX** 38 77 17 59. **Rooms:** 42. 🛏️ 📺 🔆 🏃 🔆 🈺 🅿️ 🈺 AE, MC, DC, V. Ⓕ Ⓕ

This unpretentious hotel, near the rue de Bourgogne with its many restaurants, is housed in a former cloister. Corner rooms have views of the typical slate roofs of the city and of the cathedral towers.

ROMORANTIN-LANTHENAY

Grand Hôtel du Lion d'Or

Road map E3. 69 rue Georges-Clemenceau, 41200. 🚗 54 76 00 28. **FAX** 54 88 24 87. **Rooms:** 16. 🛏️ 📺 🈺 🔆 🈺 🅿️ 🈺 🍴 ★ 🈺 AE, MC, DC, V. Ⓕ Ⓕ Ⓕ Ⓕ

This Renaissance mansion has been a hotel since 1774. A *Relais et Châteaux* member, it has attractive rooms, a courtyard modelled on a medieval herb garden and an excellent restaurant.

SALBRIS

Le Parc

Road map E3. 8 av d'Orléans, 41300. 🚗 54 97 18 53. **FAX** 54 97 24 34. **Rooms:** 27. 🔆 🈺 🏃 🅿️ 🈺 🍴 🈺 AE, MC, DC, V. Ⓕ Ⓕ

This hotel in the heart of the Sologne is surrounded by park-land, and the elegant rooms (some with a terrace) are always filled with flowers. The good restaurant boasts a large stone fireplace.

VENDÔME

Hôtel Vendôme

Road map D3. 15 faubourg Chartran, 41100. 🚗 54 77 02 88. **FAX** 54 73 90 71. **Rooms:** 35. 🛏️ 📺 🈺 🔆 🅿️ 🈺 🍴 🈺 MC, V. Ⓕ Ⓕ

This attractive hotel near the old centre is typical of a French provincial establishment. Rooms are well planned and stylish, as is the restaurant. The hotel was built on the site of a medieval *auberge*, once a pilgrims' rest on the road to Santiago de Compostela.

BERRY

ARGENT-SUR-SAULDRE

Relais de la Poste

Road map F3. 3 rue Nationale, 18410. 🚗 48 73 60 25. **FAX** 48 73 30 62. **Rooms:** 10. 🛏️ 📺 🔆 🈺 🈺 🅿️ 🈺 🍴 🈺 MC, V. Ⓕ Ⓕ

Exposed beams and floral upholstery give a cottagey feel to this typical Sologne inn. The restaurant offers delicious game and wild mushrooms in season.

ARGENTON-SUR-CREUSE

Le Manoir de Boisvillers

Road map E4. 11 rue du Moulin-de-Bord, 36200. 🚗 54 24 13 88. **FAX** 54 24 27 83. **Rooms:** 14. 🔆 📺 🈺 🏃 🅿️ 🈺 🍴 🈺 AE, MC, V. Ⓕ Ⓕ

A surprising find in the heart of the town, this is a peaceful 18th-century manor house. Its pretty garden, reached through wrought-iron gates, centres on an open-air swimming pool. The rooms are spacious and comfortable.

AUBIGNY-SUR-NÈRE

Auberge de la Fontaine

Road map F3. 2 av du Général Leclerc, 18700. 🚗 48 58 34 41. **FAX** 48 58 36 80. **Rooms:** 16. 🛏️ 📺 🔆 🏃 🔆 🅿️ 🈺 🍴 🈺 AE, MC, DC, V. Ⓕ Ⓕ

This friendly modern hotel is only a short walk from the château and its museums. The front bedrooms look onto a pleasant park, while the back bedrooms have views of the pretty garden. The restaurant offers special children's meals.

Château de la Verrerie

Road map F3. Oizon, 18700. 🚗 48 58 06 91. **FAX** 48 58 21 25. **Rooms:** 12. 🛏️ 🔆 🏃 🅿️ 🈺 🍴 ★ 🈺 AE, MC, V. Ⓕ Ⓕ Ⓕ Ⓕ

Scots Stewart connections abound in this early Renaissance château, romantically mirrored in a lake. La Verrerie is owned by the Comte and Comtesse de Vogüé, who are unfailingly charming and helpful. They offer private dining for those staying in their spacious and beautifully furnished rooms and also run a cottagey restaurant in the grounds.

LE BLANC

Domaine de l'Etape

Road map D4. Rte de Bélâbre, 36300. 🚗 54 37 18 02. **FAX** 54 37 75 59. **Rooms:** 35. 🛏️ 📺 🔆 🏃 🅿️ 🈺 🍴 🈺 AE, MC, DC, V. Ⓕ Ⓕ

An ideal base for holidays in the open air, this peaceful hotel, set in extensive gardens, offers a good mixture of modern facilities and antique furnishings. It has its own lake for angling and canoeing, and stables from which it offers pony treks through the surrounding countryside. It is also well placed for exploring the nature reserves of La Brenne.

BOURGES

Hôtel de Bourbon

Road map F4. Bd de la République, 18000. 🚗 48 70 70 00. **FAX** 48 70 21 22. **Rooms:** 59. 🛏️ 📺 🈺 🔆 🅿️ 🈺 🍴 🈺 AE, MC, DC, V. Ⓕ Ⓕ Ⓕ See also **Restaurants**, p217.

Set in a renovated Renaissance abbey, this hotel offers modern, soundproofed bedrooms and elegant public areas. Its restaurant is in the superb setting of the former chapel.

Hôtel d'Angleterre

Road map F4. 1 pl des Quatre Piliers, 18000. **[** 48 24 68 51. **FAX** 48 65 21 41. **Rooms:** 31. 🛏 🔢 📺 🌡 🧍 ♿ 🔾 **P** 🍽 🎫 AE, MC, DC, V. ⒻⒻⒻ

This established hotel is in the heart of Bourges, very close to the Palais Jacques-Cœur. Although it has been modernized, it has nonetheless retained its traditional, courteous ambiance.

BRINON-SUR-SAULDRE

La Solognote

Road map F3. Le Village, 18410. **[** 48 58 50 29. **FAX** 48 58 56 00. **Rooms:** 13. 🛏 📺 **P** 🖊 🍽 ★ 🎫 MC, V. ⒻⒻ

This charming *Logis de France* is a typical Sologne inn, furnished with antiques. The rooms overlook a quiet courtyard garden. Popular in the shooting season, the hotel also has an excellent restaurant.

CHÂTEAUROUX

Le Manoir du Colombier

Road map E4. 232 rue du Châtellerault, 36000. **[** 54 29 30 01. **FAX** 54 27 70 90. **Rooms:** 11. 🛏 📺 **P** 🖊 🍽 🎫 AE, MC, DC, V. ⒻⒻⒻ

The River Indre flows through the park that surrounds this hotel, which is set in a late 18th-century manor. Some rooms, which are contemporary in style, have river views. The pleasant restaurant serves local specialities.

LA CHÂTRE

Château de la Vallée Bleue

Road map E4. Rte de Verneuil, 36400. **[** 54 31 01 91. **FAX** 54 31 04 48. **Rooms:** 13. 🛏 📺 🌡 📋 ♨ 🧍 **P** 🖊 🍽 🎫 MC, V. ⒻⒻ

This elegant 19th-century château was once the home of George Sand's doctor, who used to walk over to Nohant to visit his illustrious patient. It is now a hotel set in large grounds with an open air swimming pool and a practice course for golfers. There are two very good golf courses within 18 km (11 miles) of the hotel, one at Pouligny-Notre-Dame and the other at Issoudun.

ST-AMAND-MONTROND

Hôtel de la Poste

Road map F4. 9 rue du Docteur-Vallet, 18200. **[** 48 96 27 14. **FAX** 48 96 97 74. **Rooms:** 20. 🧍 **P** 🖊 🍽 🎫 AE, MC, V. Ⓕ

This friendly hotel, built around an inner courtyard, started life in 1584 as a pilgrims' inn. Rooms on the second floor have sloping ceilings. It is a cosy base for visiting Abbaye de Noirlac and the châteaux of Ainay-le-Vieil, Culan and Meillant. There is also a popular restaurant.

Château de la Commanderie

Road map F4. Farges-Allichamps, 18200. **[** 48 61 04 19. **FAX** 48 61 01 84. **Rooms:** 7. 🛏 🌡 🧍 **P** 🖊 ★ 🎫 AE, MC, V. ⒻⒻⒻⒻ

This charming 12th-century manor house, once part of the Knights Templars' Commandery, has been owned by the same family since the 17th century. The Comte and Comtesse de Jouffroy-Gonsans offer elegant accommodation both here and in a 19th-century château, as well as candle-lit dinners.

SANCERRE

Hôtel Panoramic

Road map F3. Rempart des Augustins, 18300. **[** 48 54 22 44. **FAX** 48 54 39 55. **Rooms:** 57. 🛏 📺 🌡 ♨ 🧍 ♿ 🔾 **P** 🖊 🍽 🎫 AE, MC, V. ⒻⒻ

Many of the rooms in this modern hotel have views over the Sancerre vineyards. The hotel has its own car park, which is useful in this town of narrow, winding streets, as well as a garden, an outdoor pool and a pleasant restaurant.

VALENÇAY

Hôtel d'Espagne

Road map: E4. 9 rue du Château, 36600. **[** 54 00 00 02. **FAX** 54 00 12 63. **Rooms:** 16. 🛏 📺 🌡 🧍 🔾 **P** 🖊 🍽 ★ 🎫 AE, MC, DC, V. ⒻⒻⒻ

Quiet and elegant, this *Relais et Châteaux* member has been run by the same family since 1875. It is known for courteous service, comfortable bedrooms and classic cuisine, served in a delightful courtyard in the summer.

NORTH OF THE LOIRE

CHARTRES

Hôtel de la Poste

Road map E2. 9 rue du Docteur Vallet, 28000. **[** 37 21 04 27. **FAX** 37 36 42 17. **Rooms:** 58. 🛏 📺 🧍 ♿ 🔾 **P** 🍽 🎫 AE, MC, DC, V. ⒻⒻ

This attractive hotel is close to the cathedral. One room is furnished with Breton antiques, while the others are decorated in a contemporary style. Two rooms have views of the cathedral. The restaurant serves special low-priced children's meals.

Le Grand Monarque

Road map E2. 22 pl des Epars, 28000. **[** 37 21 00 72. **FAX** 37 36 34 18. **Rooms:** 54. 🛏 📺 🧍 🔾 **P** 🍽 🎫 AE, MC, DC, V. ⒻⒻⒻⒻ
See also **Restaurants**, *p218*.

Established as a coaching inn in the 18th century, this hotel has long been popular with visitors to Chartres. Now modernized, it is efficiently managed. Some of the comfortable rooms overlook a little garden, and it also has an elegant restaurant.

COURVILLE-SUR-EURE

Château de Blanville

Road map E2. St-Luperce, 28190. **[** 37 26 77 36. **FAX** 37 26 78 02. **Rooms:** 5. 🛏 🌡 ♨ 🧍 **P** 🖊 ★ 🎫 AE, MC, V. ⒻⒻⒻⒻ

The Cossé-Brissac family has owned this elegant château, 15 km (10 miles) southwest of Chartres, for 250 years. Guests can enjoy candlelit dinners after a day spent angling, swimming and cycling in the grounds, wandering through formal gardens or walking in the nearby forest.

LA FLÈCHE

Le Relais Cicéro

Road map C3. 18 bd d'Alger, 72200. **[** 43 94 14 14. **FAX** 43 45 98 96. **Rooms:** 21. 🛏 📺 🌡 🧍 **P** 🔾 🎫 AE, MC, DC, V. ⒻⒻⒻ

This quiet hotel, located near the Prytanée Militaire, is housed in a rather grand 17th-century mansion. The rooms are stylishly furnished with antiques, but unfortunately there is no restaurant.

FRESNAY-SUR-SARTHE

Hôtel Ronsin

Road map C2. 5 av Charles-de-Gaulle, 72130. **【** 43 97 20 10. **FAX** 43 33 50 47. **Rooms:** 12. 🚗 📺 ♿ 🅿 🍴 *AE, MC, DC, V.* Ⓕ Ⓕ

This is a traditional French hotel, with plain, but well-planned rooms. Its restaurant offers a wide range of fixed-priced meals.

LAVAL

Hôtel des Blés d'Or

Road map B2. 83 rue Victor-Boissel, 53000 **【** 43 53 14 10. **FAX** 43 49 02 84. **Rooms:** 8. 🚗 📺 ♿ 🍴 🏧 *AE, MC, V.* Ⓕ Ⓕ

This friendly inn is situated on the old corn market square, not far from the River Mayenne. It has an excellent restaurant with cheerful, cottagey decor.

LE MANS

Hôtel Chantecler

Road map C2. 50 rue de la Pelouse, 72000. **【** 43 24 58 53. **FAX** 43 77 16 28. **Rooms:** 35. 🚗 🏧 📺 🔁 🅿 🍴 🏧 *AE, MC, V.* Ⓕ Ⓕ

This modern hotel, within walking distance of the Old Town, has comfortable bedrooms and attractive bar and lounge areas.

ST-LÉONARD-DES-BOIS

Touring Hôtel

Road map C2. Le Village, 72590. **【** 43 97 28 03. **FAX** 43 97 07 72. **Rooms:** 35. 🚗 📺 📺 ♿ ♿ 🔁 🅿 🍴 🏧 *AE, MC, DC, V.* Ⓕ Ⓕ

This modern hotel makes a pleasant base for exploring the Alpes Mancelles. The rooms have either hill or garden views. There is an indoor pool and a good restaurant.

SOLESMES

Grand Hôtel de Solesmes

Road map C2. 16 pl Dom-Guéranger, 72300. **【** 43 95 45 10. **FAX** 43 95 22 26. **Rooms:** 34. 🚗 📺 📺 ♿ 🔁 🅿 🍴 🏧 *AE, MC, DC, V.* Ⓕ Ⓕ Ⓕ *See also* **Restaurants,** *p219.*

Opposite the abbey and 3 km (2 miles) from Sablé, this hotel has large rooms, a fitness centre, an art gallery and an excellent restaurant overlooking a garden.

LOIRE-ATLANTIQUE AND THE VENDEE

ILE D'YEU

Flux Hôtel

Road map A4. 27 rue Pierre-Henry, Port-Joinville, 85350. **【** 51 58 36 25. **FAX** 51 59 44 57. **Rooms:** 16. 🚗 📺 📺 ♿ 🅿 🍴 🏧 *MC, V.* Ⓕ Ⓕ *See also* **Restaurants**, *p219.*

Ask for a room in the annexe of this modern hotel if you would like a balcony. If you bring your freshly caught fish or shellfish back in the afternoon, the chef will serve them to you for dinner.

NANTES

Hôtel de la Duchesse Anne

Road map B3. 3–4 pl de la Duchesse Anne, 44000. **【** 40 74 30 29. **FAX** 40 74 60 20. **Rooms:** 70. 🚗 📺 🅿 🍴 🏧 *AE, MC, DC, V.* Ⓕ Ⓕ

Located in a 19th-century building, the hotel offers renovated rooms, or less modern ones for a reduced price. Some of the older rooms are charming, and many of both types have cathedral and château views.

Hôtel La Pérouse

Road map B3. 3 allée Duquesne, 44000. **【** 40 89 75 00. **FAX** 40 89 76 00. **Rooms:** 66. 🚗 📺 📺 🅿 🏧 *AE, MC, DC, V.* Ⓕ Ⓕ

Built in a minimalist style, this hotel has won architectural awards. Centrally placed at the cours des Cinquante Otages, it is still quiet for a city hotel. There is free parking nearby at the Tour de Bretagne.

NOIRMOUTIER-EN-L'ISLE

Hôtel du Général d'Elbée

Road map A4. Pl d'Armes, 85330. **【** 51 39 10 29. **FAX** 51 39 08 23. **Rooms:** 29. 🚗 📺 🏧 *AE, MC, DC, V.* Ⓕ Ⓕ Ⓕ

Named after the Vendéen general who died in the square, the hotel occupies an historic building beside a canal. It also has a walled garden with swimming pool.

LA ROCHE-SUR-YON

Logis de la Couperie

Road map B4. D80, La Roche-sur-Yon, 85000. **【** 51 37 21 19. **FAX** 51 47 71 08. **Rooms:** 7. 🚗 📺 📺 ♿ 🅿 🏧 *AE, MC, DC, V.* Ⓕ Ⓕ

A ducal residence from the 14th century until 1789, La Couperie is still surrounded by parkland with a lake. Five minutes' drive from the town centre, its rooms are furnished with antiques, and the main *salon* has a log fire.

LES SABLES D'OLONNE

Les Roches Noires

Road map A4. 12 promenade Georges-Clemenceau, 85100. **【** 51 32 01 71. **FAX** 51 21 61 00. **Rooms:** 37. 🚗 📺 📺 ♿ ♿ 🅿 🏧 *AE, MC, DC, ♿ V.* Ⓕ Ⓕ

This hotel is reasonably inexpensive considering its beachfront location, but it is a bracing walk to the town centre. Some of the rooms have sea views.

Château de la Millière

Road map A4. St-Mathurin, 85100. **【** 51 36 13 08. **FAX** 51 22 73 29. **Rooms:** 5. 🚗 📺 📺 🔁 🅿 ♿ ★ 🏧 *V.* Ⓕ Ⓕ Ⓕ

Situated 8 km (5 miles) from the town, this 19th-century château has 18 ha (44 acres) of parkland. Visitors can enjoy some lovely walks or take advantage of the on-site fishing or swimming pool. Dinner in the château must be ordered before midday.

ST-LYPHARD

Auberge de Kerhinet

Road map A3. Kerhinet, 44410. **【** 40 61 91 46. **FAX** 40 61 97 57. **Rooms:** 7. 🚗 ♿ ♿ 🅿 🍴 🍴 🏧 *AE, MC, DC, V.* Ⓕ Ⓕ *See also* **Restaurants**, *p219.*

A pretty cottage in creamy local stone with a thatched roof, the *auberge* is in the salt marshes of La Grande Brière *(see p180).* It is simply decorated in rustic style, with a fine collection of old photographs on the walls. Its restaurant specializes in local fish dishes.

For key to symbols *see p199*

RESTAURANTS, CAFÉS AND BARS

IN THIS GENERALLY prosperous region, with its excellent local produce, eating out is popular, and interest in cuisine is high even by the standards of this food-loving country. Lunch remains the main meal of the day: even in larger towns such as Tours, Orléans or Nantes, most office workers return home during their two-hour lunch break. Restaurants serve lunch from about noon, and it can be hard to find one willing to serve a meal if you arrive after 1pm, although cafés and brasseries in the towns are more flexible. Dinner is served from about 8pm onwards (sometimes earlier in the main tourist areas). Beware of last orders, which may be as early as 9pm, especially in country districts. The restaurants on pages 214–19 have been carefully selected for their excellence of food, decor and ambience, and cover all price ranges.

A café sign in Berry

An outdoor café in the historic heart of Richelieu

TYPES OF RESTAURANT

IN COUNTRY DISTRICTS and small towns, the most pleasant restaurants are often to be found in hotels, especially if they belong to the **Logis de France** association, which puts particular emphasis on good (and good value for money) regional cooking. Larger towns offer a broad range of places to eat, from basic pizzerias and crêperies to chic, gourmet establishments via cafés and brasseries. Cafés are handy for a snack, coffee or aperitif, or as places from which to watch the world go by, and brasseries are good for quick meals. Unlike restaurants, brasseries and cafés generally serve a limited range of dishes outside regular mealtimes.

The Loire also has an ever-widening choice of restaurants specializing in foreign cuisines (most commonly Vietnamese and North African).

VEGETARIAN FOOD

TRUE VEGETARIANS do not fare well in France. It can be more convenient to head for a Vietnamese restaurant or a pizzeria, although in some of the university towns, the occasional vegetarian restaurant may be found. A few large cafés or brasseries in the tourist districts of major towns sometimes offer a small number of vegetarian dishes, and omelettes and other egg-based dishes are usually available. Alternatively, ask the chef for the meat or fish to be left out of a salad. In full-scale restaurants, it is essential to enquire in advance whether it is possible to have a vegetarian dish specially prepared. Non-meat-eaters need have no fears: Loire Valley restaurants serve excellent fish dishes, and cafés and brasseries usually offer at least one fish dish on the menu.

READING THE MENU

THE VAST MAJORITY of Loire Valley restaurants offer at least one *menu*, or fixed-price menu. You will often find a range of *menus*, culminating in an expensive *menu gastronomique* (gourmet meal), which may be available only if all members of your party choose it. Look out for a *menu régional* or *menu du terroir*, which will feature a selection of regional specialities.

The less expensive menus often feature starters such as local *charcuterie* (pork specialities), a salad or *crudités* (raw vegetables), whereas gourmet menus offer more complex dishes. Vegetables are often served separately.

Cheese is considered a separate course, served between the main course and dessert – local goats' cheeses are likely to predominate.

A typical Loire Valley restaurant terrace

Many restaurants, especially in country districts, do not have a *carte* from which individual dishes may be selected. If they do, eating *à la carte* almost always works out to be more expensive than choosing from a fixed-price menu, since it is not considered acceptable to skip the starter and order only a main dish (skipping dessert is more acceptable).

Cafés and brasseries offer a *plat du jour* (dish of the day), often with a regional flavour, along with standard French fare such as steak or fish with fried potatoes, complemented by a range of salads or vegetables.

The rustic Auberge de la Petite Fadette in Nohant *(see p217)*

Auberge du Moulin de Chaméron at Bannegon in Berry *(see p217)*

MAKING RESERVATIONS

IT IS ALWAYS advisable to book tables in advance at restaurants near the well-known châteaux, especially during the main tourist season (Easter to late September). If you enjoy eating alongside the residents at local restaurants in towns, which rarely take reservations over the telephone, make sure you arrive early. Restaurants in country districts are often closed on Sunday evenings as well as for at least one whole day during the week.

DRESS CODE

MOST FRENCH people take considerable trouble with their appearance but, with the exception of a few very chic and expensive places, formal dress is not required, and ties are rarely a necessity even in the top restaurants, providing you are neatly turned out.

HOW MUCH TO PAY

IT IS DIFFICULT to classify restaurants by price, as most offer a range of fixed-price meals. Prices can be as low as F65 or as high as F500, but good, copious meals can be had everywhere for between F150 and F200.

A service charge of 12.5–15 per cent is usually included in the prices on menus, which in all but the most expensive places are posted up outside for you to study before venturing in. It is usual to leave a few extra francs as an additional tip. In the more expensive restaurants, cloakroom attendants are given about F5 and lavatory attendants about F2.

Visa credit cards are widely accepted. Check first with the restaurant to find out whether Eurocheques and American Express, MasterCard or Diners Club cards can be used.

CHILDREN AND PETS

CHILDREN ARE well received everywhere in the region, but they should be discouraged from leaving their seats and wandering about during the meal. High chairs are rarely available. Some restaurants offer special low-priced children's menus, called *repas d'enfant*. Well-behaved dogs are usually accepted in restaurants (but are often banned from food shops).

WHEELCHAIR ACCESS

BECAUSE FEW restaurants make special provision for wheelchairs, it is wise when booking to mention that you or one of your party need

space for a *fauteuil roulant*. A list on page 198 gives names and addresses of various organizations that offer advice to disabled travellers to the Loire Valley region.

SMOKING

FRENCH LEGISLATION requires restaurateurs to offer the choice of smoking or non-smoking areas, but the latter is often no more than a table or two in an alcove with a "No Smoking" sign pinned to the wall. Bars and cafés are likely to be smoke-filled.

USING THE LISTINGS

Key to the symbols in the listings on pages 214–19.

🕐 opening times
🍴 fixed-price menu(s)
🚼 children's portions
Ⓥ vegetarian or vegetarian options
⛱ outdoor eating
♿ wheelchair access
👔 jacket and tie required
🚭 non-smoking section
🍷 excellent wine list
★ highly recommended
💳 credit cards accepted
AE American Express
MC Mastercard
DC Diners Club
V Visa

Price categories for a three-course evening meal for one, including a half-bottle of house wine, cover charge, tax and service:
Ⓕ Under F150
ⒻⒻ F150–250
ⒻⒻⒻ F250–350
ⒻⒻⒻⒻ F350–500
ⒻⒻⒻⒻⒻ Over F500.

What to Eat in the Loire Valley

OIRE VALLEY CUISINE is made up of straightforward dishes carefully cooked from wonderfully fresh ingredients. Shad, pike-perch, pike and salmon, all straight from the rivers, are served with a subtle *beurre blanc* or sorrel sauce while, at the mouth of the Loire, fresh prawns and oysters glisten on seafood platters. The mild climate and fertile soil produce

Fresh seasonal strawberries

succulent early fruit and vegetables. The sandy soil beside the Loire is perfect for growing asparagus, and in autumn the trees are laden with apples and pears. Berry's forests offer plump game, served with wild mushrooms or the button variety *(champignons de Paris)* grown in the tufa caves near Saumur.

Rillons de Tours, *largish chunks of pork cooked slowly in their own fat until crisp, are found in every* charcuterie *in the Touraine region.*

Noisettes de porc au pruneaux, *a speciality of Tours, is pork loin gently stewed in Vouvray wine, served with prunes steeped in Vouvray and a smooth sauce made with redcurrant jelly and cream.*

Caneton de Nantes aux navets *is roast duckling from Nantes, traditionally served with young turnips.*

Rillettes du Mans, *a tasty, traditional first course, is made from shredded and potted pork, or sometimes goose or rabbit.*

Poulet en barbouille, *a speciality of the Berry region, is made with a plump chicken, braised with carrots and onions in brandy and wine, and served with a sauce that is traditionally made from the chicken's own blood.*

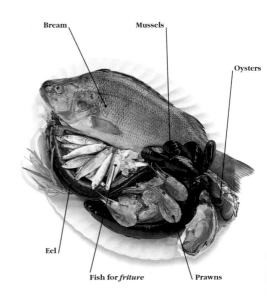

Bream   Mussels   Oysters   Eel   Fish for *friture*   Prawns

FISH AND SEAFOOD

Local fish and seafood is served throughout the region. Fish is usually simply prepared, served with a complementary sauce that allows its fresh flavour to come through.

Alose à l'oseille *is grilled shad, a round fish not unlike herring, served with a creamy sorrel sauce.*

Chapon du Mans à la broche, *generally spit-roasted, is a fine capon from the Le Mans region.*

Friture de la Loire, *a dish often found in restaurants near rivers, offers a mound of tiny, freshwater fish, quickly fried and served with a lemon wedge.*

Sandre au beurre blanc *is pike-perch (also known as zander) accompanied by the Loire speciality of a melted butter sauce flavoured with shallots and wine vinegar.*

Matelote d'anguilles *is chunks of eel stewed in Chinon red wine with button mushrooms and tiny onions.*

Pithiviers *is a puff-pastry almond cake, named after a town near Orléans.*

Crémets d'Anjou *is a delicious dessert made from whipped double cream and egg whites.*

Tarte Tatin, *perhaps the most famous dessert of the Loire, is a caramelized upside-down apple tart invented by the Tatin sisters in their Sologne inn.*

Valençay

Crottins de Chavignol

Sainte-Maure de Touraine

Selles-sur-Cher

Poirat, *a Berry speciality, is a pear pie flavoured with pure fruit spirit and often served with a glass of rosé wine.*

CHEESES

The Loire Valley's finest cheeses are made with goats' milk: the round Crottins de Chavignol from Sancerre; Sainte-Maure de Touraine with a straw through the middle and often coated with ashes (*cendré*); and Valençay, like a truncated pyramid. But Olivet is a cows' milk cheese not unlike Camembert.

What to Drink in the Loire

THE LOIRE VALLEY is a wine region *(see pp30–31)*, so naturally the traditional tipple in cafés and bars is *un petit coup de rouge* or *un petit coup de blanc* (a small glass of red or white wine). The light rosés, such as Rosé d'Anjou or Rosé de Touraine, are drunk chilled, either in the afternoon with a slice of cake or as an apéritif. In November, bars and cafés serve *bernache*, the greenish, fermented juice left after the grapes have been pressed for winemaking. There is also a wide variety of other alcoholic drinks, including *eaux de vie* made with local fruits and light, lager-style beers, as well as non-alcoholic drinks such as coffees, teas and juices.

A waiter in a Loire Valley bar

White Sancerre

Red Bourgueil

Sparkling wine

WINE

WINE USUALLY accompanies meals in the Loire, as it does throughout France. Local wine is often served in carafes. Ordering a *demi* (50 cl, approximately ½ pint) or *quart* (25 cl) is an inexpensive way to try out a wide variety of the wines of the region before buying any to take home *(see pp30–31)*.

French law divides domestic wines into four classes, in ascending order of quality:

Vin de Table, Vin de Pays, Vin Délimité de Qualité Supérieure (VDQS) and finally *Appellation d'Origine Contrôlée* (AOC). The blended *Vin de Table* wines are rarely found in good restaurants. If in doubt, order the house wine *(la réserve)*. Very few restaurants will risk their reputation on an inferior house wine, and they often provide value for money.

APÉRITIFS AND DIGESTIFS

A GLASS of locally-produced sparkling wine can be an excellent apéritif or a pleasant accompaniment to the dessert course. Slightly sparkling Vouvray *pétillant* is popular, and further west in Anjou you will find Saumur *champenoise*, made by the méthode *champenoise*. Keep an eye open, too, for Crémant de Loire, another local sparkling wine.

A *kir* – white wine with a touch of *crème de cassis*, a blackcurrant liqueur – is a

---

HOW TO READ A WINE LABEL
Even the simplest label will provide a key to the wine's flavour and quality. It will bear the name of the wine and its producer, its vintage if there is one, and whether it comes from a strictly defined area *(appellation contrôlée* or VDQS) or is a more general *vin de pays* or *vin de table*. It may also have a regional grading. The shape and colour of the bottle is also a guide. Most good-quality wine is bottled in green glass, which helps to protect it from light. The label's design may be appealing, but does not indicate quality.

The property or producer

Estate-bottled, rather than a blend from a merchant or growers' co-operative

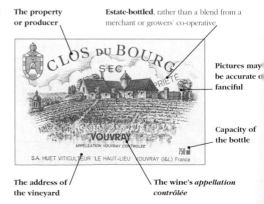

Pictures may be accurate or fanciful

Capacity of the bottle

The address of the vineyard

The wine's *appellation contrôlée*

popular Burgundian apéritif, and an appealing variation, often served as the house apéritif, combines sparkling wine with raspberry or peach liqueur. Bars, cafés and restaurants also stock the usual range of French apéritifs as well as international gins, sherries, ports and whiskies.

After dinner, a little glass of clear fruit brandy made from local raspberries, pears or plums *(eaux de vie de framboise, de poire, de prune)* is a delicious aid to digestion. Other traditional French *digestifs*, such as cognac or calvados, are also drunk after meals in the region.

BEER

THE LOCALS DRINK mostly lager-style draught beer in cafés – ask for *un demi*. A range of bottled beers can also be found, both French (which is considerably cheaper) and imported.

Café crème, often served at breakfast with a fresh croissant

COFFEE AND TEA

CAFES, STILL THE MAIN focus of community life, serve good strong *exprès* (a tiny cup of black coffee). White coffees are prepared with hot milk and come in two sizes: small *(petit crème)* and large *(grand crème)*. Together with fresh croissants, they make a good breakfast.

Tea served in cafés is often of the teabag variety (with a slice of lemon, it is *un thé citron)*. Tearooms in towns, however, are more likely to use tea leaves. Many cafés also offer a range of exotic fruit and herb teas, which are caffeine-free. In restaurants an infusion of limeflower leaves *(tilleul)*, mint *(menthe)* or camomile *(camomille)* is often drunk after dinner as an aid to digestion.

OTHER DRINKS

CHILDREN ENJOY the colourful drinks served in tall glasses known as *menthe à l'eau* (green, minty syrup with tap water) and *grenadine* (a red fruit syrup), but these may be too sweet for adult tastes. Served with Vittel mineral water, for example, they become *Vittel menthe, Vittel grenadine*, and so on. *Vittel citron amer* (with bottled, still bitter lemon) is more refreshing than *Vittel citron* (with lemon syrup). Best of all for quenching the thirst – but also more expensive – is a *citron pressé* : freshly-squeezed lemon juice served with a carafe of water and packets of sugar to mix to taste. *Orange pressée* is orange juice served in the same way. Bottled fruit juices *(jus de fruits)* are also available everywhere.

Tap water is safe to drink, but many people prefer mineral water *(eau minérale)*, either sparkling *(gazeuse)* or still *(non-gazeuse)*.

WHERE TO DRINK

CAFES ARE THE traditional place to pop in for a coffee or beer, to meet a friend or watch the world go by. City centres have bustling cafés on every corner, and many squares are crowded with outdoor tables when the weather is fine. However, the traditional café, with its long bar counter lined by regulars, is gradually being superseded, at least in towns, by more elaborate places.

Bars and *bars à vin* (old-style wine bars) are often the haunts of more hardened drinkers and of late-night revellers, although hotel bars can attract a more eclectic clientele. In larger towns,

A wood-panelled hotel bar in Touraine

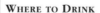

Locally-made apple juice

many new-style wine bars, often with high-tech decor, serve wine by the glass, with light meals, plates of *charcuterie* or cheeses with crusty bread. Traditional *salons de thé* (tearooms), which serve coffee, tea and hot chocolate, are mainly frequented by women. They also serve *pâtisseries* and chocolates, which can be bought to take away. The newer version offers light lunches and less sophisticated sweets, cakes and tarts to a younger, mixed clientele.

People enjoying a break in a stylish café in Orléans

ANJOU

ANGERS

La Salamandre

Road map C3. 1 bd Maréchal-Foch.
🛈 41 88 24 82. ☐ noon–2pm,
7:30–10pm Mon–Sat. 🍴 V 💺
🍷 🅮 AE, MC, DC, V. Ⓕ Ⓕ

The restaurant in the Hôtel d'Anjou
is decorated in the Renaissance
style. But the reasonably-priced
cuisine is far from over-elaborate,
and the wine list is excellent. Try
the ravioli stuffed with lobster,
steaks, fish soups and cheeses.

Le Toussaint

Road map C3. 7 pl Kennedy.
🛈 41 87 46 20. ☐ noon–2pm
Tue–Sun, 7:30–9:30pm Tue–Sat. 🍴
🏃 V 💺 🍷 🅮 AE, MC, V. Ⓕ Ⓕ

The upstairs dining room of this
restaurant offers fine views of the
château, and the downstairs is less
formal and also pleasant. It offers
regional dishes, with a *nouvelle*
twist, and an excellent list of
Anjou wines. Book in advance.

CHOLET

La Touchetière

Road map B4. 41 bd du Docteur-Roux.
🛈 41 62 55 03. ☐ noon–2pm Sun–
Fri, 7:30–9:30pm Mon–Fri (closed 3
weeks Aug, 1 week Feb). 🍴 🏃 V
💺 🍷 🅮 MC, V. Ⓕ

An old farmhouse, with its original
fireplace, has been converted into
a restaurant serving a menu that
emphasizes fish dishes. Everything
is beautifully fresh. Book ahead
for Sunday lunch.

FONTEVRAUD
L'ABBAYE

La Licorne

Road map C3. Allée Ste-Catherine.
🛈 41 51 72 49. ☐ 12:15–1:30pm
Tue–Sun, 7:15–8:45pm Tue–Sat
(summer: daily). 🍴 🏃 V 💺 🍷
🅮 AE, MC, DC, V. Ⓕ Ⓕ

This delightful restaurant is very
near St-Michel, the church built by
Henry II of England. The cuisine
served in the elegant 18th-century
building, with a little garden, is
refined, and the lowest-priced
lunch menu (not available on
Sunday) is great value. Advance
booking is recommended.

GENNES

L'Aubergade

Road map C3. 7 av des Cadets.
🛈 41 51 81 07. ☐ noon–2pm,
7:15–9pm Thu–Mon (summer: daily).
🍴 🏃 V 💺 🍷 MC, V. Ⓕ Ⓕ

A traditional Anjou building houses
this reliable restaurant with a menu
strong on dishes from the regional
repertoire. Wines from Touraine
and Anjou make the perfect accom-
paniments to meals here.

LE LION-D'ANGERS

La Table du Meunier

Road map C3. Le Moulin, Chenillé-
Changé. 🛈 41 95 10 83 or 41 95
10 98. ☐ noon–2:30pm Thu–Mon,
6–11pm Thu–Sun (summer: daily).
🍴 🏃 💺 🍷 MC, V. Ⓕ Ⓕ

This old mill, 10 km (6 miles) from
Le Lion-d'Angers, once produced
the walnut oil that gives French
country cooking its special flavour.
The menu has some sophisticated
touches but is largely traditional.
Among the specialities are *terrine
d'anguilles maison* (an eel terrine)
and *crème d'oignons gratinée* (a
type of onion soufflé).

MONTSOREAU

Diane de Méridor

Road map C3. 9 quai Philippe de
Commynes. 🛈 41 51 70 18.
☐ noon–2pm, 7–10pm Wed–Mon.
🍴 🏃 💺 🍷 MC, V. Ⓕ

From the rustic dining room there
are fine views of the Loire and of
Montsoreau château. The menu
offers many freshwater fish dishes,
including *sandre* (freshwater pike-
perch) and *brochet* (pike).

LES ROSIERS-SUR-
LOIRE

Auberge Jeanne de
Laval

Road map C3. 54 rue Nationale.
🛈 41 51 80 17. ☐ 12:30–2pm,
5:30–9:30pm daily. 🍴 🏃 V 🏠
💺 🍷 🅮 AE, MC, V. Ⓕ Ⓕ

This family-run restaurant (with a
hotel called Les Ducs d'Anjou)
serves mainly classic cuisine, but
the son of the previous chef has
introduced some interesting new
dishes, including popular home-
made terrines.

ST-GEORGES-SUR-
LOIRE

Relais d'Anjou

Road map B3. 29 rue Nationale.
🛈 41 39 13 38. ☐ noon–1:30pm
Tue–Sun, 7:30–9pm Wed–Sat. 🍴
🏃 V 💺 🍷 🅮 AE, MC, V. Ⓕ

This inn is close to the Château de
Serrant. The cuisine is satisfying
and good value, drawn from the
classic French repertoire. Many of
the dishes are served with sauces
prepared using Anjou wines.

SAUMUR

Les Caves de Marson

Road map C3. Rou-Marson.
🛈 41 50 50 05. ☐ mid-Jun–mid-Sep:
8pm Tue–Sat, 12:30pm Sun; mid-Sep–
mid-Jun: 8pm Fri–Sat, 12:30pm Sun.
🍴 🏃 💺 🍷 MC, V. Ⓕ

Booking is a must at this troglodyte restaurant. Set sittings of the
three-course menu include fresh
bread rolls filled with specialities
such as goats' cheese and *rillettes*
(see p210), and home-made fruit
tarts for dessert.

Les Chandelles

Road map C3. 71 rue St-Nicolas.
🛈 41 67 20 40. ☐ noon–2:30pm
Fri–Mon, 7–9:30pm Thu–Mon. 🍴
🏃 V 💺 🍷 🅮 AE, MC, DC, V. Ⓕ

This restaurant still resembles the
shop it once was. Saumur wine
features in some dishes, such as the
anguille de Loire au vin rouge
(Loire eel in a red wine sauce).

Les Ménestrels

Road map C3. 11 rue Raspail. 🛈 41
67 71 10. ☐ 12:15–1:30pm Tue–Sun,
7:15–9:30pm Tue–Sat. 🍴 🏃 V
🏠 💺 🍷 🅮 AE, MC, DC, V. Ⓕ Ⓕ

In this oak-beamed extension to
the Hôtel Anne d'Anjou, classic
cuisine with a regional touch is
served. Views of the château add
to the ambiance.

TOURAINE

AMBOISE

Le Choiseul

Road map D3. 36 quai Charles-Guinot.
🛈 47 30 45 45. ☐ noon–2pm,
7–9pm daily. 🍴 🏃 V 💺 🍷
★ 🅮 AE, MC, DC, V. Ⓕ Ⓕ Ⓕ

The River Loire flows past this elegant restaurant, whose menu centres on fish with sauces based on regional wines. A stroll up to the nearby "Caesar's grainstores", caves hollowed out of the tufa cliff, rounds off the evening.

Le Manoir St Thomas

Road map D3. Pl Richelieu. 【 47 57 22 52. ◯ 12:30–2pm Tue–Sun, 7:30–9:30pm Tue–Sat. ¶❶ ⚑ ▉ 🍴 AE, MC, DC, V. ⒻⒻⒻⒻ

The Baroque decor, the fine chef, and a sensational wine cellar, make this place irresistible. The *canard laqué médiéval* (honey-glazed roast duck with cinnamon and ginger) is typical – traditional cuisine with a modern touch.

AZAY-LE-RIDEAU

L'Aigle d'Or

Road map C3. 10 rue Adelaïde-Riché. 【 47 45 24 58. ◯ noon–2pm Tue–Tue, 7:30pm–9pm Mon–Tue & Thu–Sat. ¶❶ ⚑ Ⓥ ⬥ ⚑ ★ 🍴 MC, V. ⒻⒻ

This excellent restaurant near the château offers local produce such as freshwater pike-perch *(sandre)* or rabbit with a sauce based on Chinon wine. The lunchtime menu is great value.

BLÉRÉ

Le Cheval Blanc

Road map D3. Pl C Bidault. 【 47 30 30 14. ◯ 12:30–2:30pm Tue–Sun, 7:30–10:30pm Tue–Sat. ¶❶ ⚑ Ⓥ ⬥ ★ 🍴 AE, MC, DC, V. ⒻⒻⒻ

Tucked away in a market town near Chenonceau is one of Touraine's best restaurants. The chef-owner won his first Michelin star in 1995. The delicious *escalope de sandre* (pike-perch escalope) served with a crab and *beurre blanc* sauce is typical of his style. The prices are very reasonable for the quality, and the atmosphere is friendly.

CHENONCEAUX

Au Gâteau Breton

Road map D3. 16 rue du Docteur-Bretonneau. 【 47 23 90 14. ◯ noon–3pm daily, 7–10pm Thu–Tue. ¶❶ ⚑ Ⓥ ⬥ ⚑ ⚑ 🍴 MC, V. Ⓕ

This cheerful place, a short walk from the château, is no tourist trap. The cooking is traditionally French, and its good-value meals are served in the garden in the summer.

CHINON

Hostellerie Gargantua

Road map D3. 73 rue Haute-St-Maurice. 【 47 93 04 71. ◯ 12:15–2:30pm Fri–Tue, 7:15–10pm Thu–Tue. ¶❶ ⚑ Ⓥ ⬥ ▉ 🍴 MC, V. ⒻⒻ

Chinon's visitors have long flocked to this medieval-style restaurant in a 15th-century mansion in the heart of the Old Town. At weekends, waiting staff dress in period costume. The portions are as generous as Gargantua, Rabelais' giant hero, would have expected.

Au Plaisir Gourmand

Road map C3. 2 rue Parmentier. 【 47 93 20 48. ◯ noon–1:30pm Tue–Sun, 7:30–9:15pm Tue–Sat. ¶❶ ⚑ Ⓥ ⬥ ▉ ★ 🍴 AE, MC, V. ⒻⒻⒻ

Chinon's top restaurant is housed in a 16th- and 17th-century building of local white tufa stone. The food is superb, with a special menu of regional dishes that will give you a taste for Touraine's gastronomic delights. The wine list, featuring local wines, is top class. Book ahead in the summer for a table in the quayside garden.

CORMERY

L'Auberge du Mail

Road map D3. 2 pl du Mail. 【 47 43 40 32. ◯ noon–1.45pm, 7:30–9pm Sun–Wed, noon–1:45pm Thu–Fri, 7:30–9pm Sat. ¶❶ ⚑ Ⓥ ⬥ ▉ 🍴 MC, V. Ⓕ

This delightful restaurant is situated in a quiet village in the Indre Valley, famous for its biscuits *(see p222)*. The wholesome cooking and friendly atmosphere never fail to please. Whimsically, the fixed-price menus are all named after composers. The restaurant is halfway between Tours and Loches.

LE PETIT-PRESSIGNY

La Promenade

Road map D4. Le Village. 【 47 94 93 52. ◯ noon–2pm Tue–Sun, 7:30–9:30pm Tue–Sat. ¶❶ Ⓥ ⬥ ★ 🍴 MC, V. ⒻⒻⒻ

Once a modest inn, this restaurant is now owned by Jacques Dallais, a former pupil of top Paris chef Joël Robuchon. If you have a sweet tooth, sample the *feuilleté de cacao au chocolat épicé* (fine-layered pastry with spicy chocolate), served with a topping of vanilla ice cream.

SACHÉ

Auberge du XIIe Siècle

Road map D3. Rue Principale. 【 47 26 88 77. ◯ noon–2pm Thu–Tue, 7:30–9pm Thu–Mon. ¶❶ ⚑ Ⓥ ⬥ 🍴 AE, MC, V. ⒻⒻ

This picturesque, half-timbered inn is situated opposite the manor house where Balzac wrote some of his best-loved novels *(see p103)*. It has a large dining room with old beams and a superb fireplace, and a smaller one that is more cosy. A range of fixed-price meals include some local specialities, such as the flavoursome breed of chicken known as *géline*.

TOURS

Le Charolais

Road map D3. 123 rue Colbert. 【 47 20 80 20. ◯ noon–2pm Tue–Sat, 7:30–10pm Mon–Sat. ¶❶ ⚑ Ⓥ ⬥ ⚑ ▉ 🍴 MC, V. ⒻⒻ

Also known as "Chez Jean-Michel", this lively *restaurant à vin* (wine restaurant) is popular with the locals for its cheerful atmosphere. Jean-Michel, previously a top wine waiter, has designed the short menu of traditional French dishes to complement the restaurant's excellent range of wines, which are available by the glass.

La Ruche

Road map D3. 105 rue Colbert. 【 47 66 69 83. ◯ noon–1:30pm Tue–Sun, 7–9pm Tue–Sat. ¶❶ Ⓥ ▉ ⚑ 🍴 MC, V. ⒻⒻ

This small restaurant, in the attractive rue Colbert, is well run by a husband-and-wife team. It has a loyal local clientele who appreciate the preparation and presentation, using elegant tableware, of the mainly regional dishes. Prices are very reasonable.

Jean Bardet

Road map D3. 57 rue Groison. 【 47 41 41 11. ◯ noon–2pm Tue–Sun, 7:30–10pm Tue–Sat. ¶❶ ⚑ Ⓥ ⬥ ▉ ⚑ ★ 🍴 AE, MC, DC, V. ⒻⒻⒻⒻⒻ

One of France's top chefs, Jean Bardet, and his wife, Sophie, have converted a 19th-century mansion into a light, spacious restaurant and an elegant hotel. After feasting on exquisite dishes prepared from the finest ingredients, you can wander through the grounds, admiring the herb and vegetable gardens whose produce has added a distinctive flavour to your meal.

For key to symbols *see p209*

VILLANDRY

Domaine de la Giraudière

Road map D3. Rte de Druye.
[47 50 08 60. ○ noon–3pm, 7:30–9pm daily. ⓘ Ⓥ & ⚡ Ⓕ

A working farm, which visitors are welcome to explore, is ideal for a rustic lunch, including pâtés, quiches and omelettes. Most of the ingredients are produced on the farm or in the vicinity.

VOUVRAY

Au Virage Gastronomique

Road map D3. 25 av Brûlé.
[47 52 70 02. ○ noon–2:30pm, 7–9:45pm Thu–Tue. ⓘ ⚘ Ⓥ & ⏀ ⚡ Ⓔ AE, MC, V. Ⓕ

After a Vouvray wine-tasting and a visit to Hardouin for the region's finest *charcuterie*, you'll find a meal in this typical French provincial restaurant satisfying. Portions are generous, the service courteous and the menus are good value.

BLESOIS AND ORLEANAIS

LES BÉZARDS

Auberge des Templiers

Road map F3. Boismorand. [38 31 80 01. ○ noon–2:30pm, 7:30–9:30pm. ⓘ ⚘ Ⓥ ⏀ & ⚡ ★ Ⓔ AE, MC, DC, V. Ⓕ Ⓕ Ⓕ Ⓕ

Once a country inn, this creeper-covered building is now a *Relais et Châteaux* hotel-restaurant. The oak-beamed dining room looks onto a garden where meals are served in fine weather. The cuisine is a blend of classic and modern, with Sologne game in season.

BLOIS

La Péniche

Road map E3. Promenade du Mail.
[54 74 37 23. ○ noon–2:30pm, 7:30–10pm Mon–Sat. ⓘ ⚘ Ⓥ ⚡ Ⓔ AE, MC, DC, V. Ⓕ Ⓕ

Dining on a barge on the Loire is certainly an experience. This barge is a superior, air-conditioned model and serves, appropriately enough, mainly straightforward fish dishes.

Au Rendez-Vous des Pêcheurs

Road map E3. 27 rue du Foix.
[54 74 67 48. ○ noon–2pm Tue–Sat, 7:30–10pm Mon–Sat. ⓘ ⚘ Ⓥ ★ Ⓔ AE, MC, V. Ⓕ Ⓕ

This lively bistro, in what was once a café-cum-grocer's, offers some of the best cuisine in town. Booking is essential.

BRACIEUX

Bernard Robin

Road map E3. 1 av de Chambord.
[54 46 41 22. ○ 12:15–1:30pm Thu–Tue, 7:30–9pm Thu–Mon. ⓘ ⚘ Ⓥ & ⏀ ★ Ⓔ AE, MC, V. Ⓕ Ⓕ Ⓕ

In a half-timbered inn between Chambord and Cheverny, Bernard Robin, one of France's finest chefs, produces superb regional cuisine. Game features highly on the menu: look out for the *lièvre à la Royale* (hare served with a *foie gras* sauce). Booking is essential.

CHAUMONT-SUR-THARONNE

La Croix Blanche

Road map E3. Pl de l'Eglise.
[54 88 55 12. ○ noon–1:45pm, 7:30–9:30pm daily. ⓘ ⚘ Ⓥ & ⚡ Ⓔ AE, MC, DC, V. Ⓕ Ⓕ Ⓕ

This former abbey has been an inn since the 15th century. Since 1779 its chef-owner has been a woman, with an all-female staff. You pass through her kitchen on the way to the panelled dining room. The cuisine is a mixture of Sologne and southwestern dishes.

· COMBREUX

L'Auberge de Combreux

Road map F2. 34 rue du Gâtinais.
[38 59 47 63. ○ 12:15–2pm daily, 7:15–9:30pm Sun–Thu, 7:15–10pm Fri–Sat. ⓘ ⚘ Ⓥ ⏀ ⚡ Ⓔ MC, V. Ⓕ Ⓕ

This creeper-covered inn in the Forêt d'Orléans, with gabled windows and antique furniture, is full of charm. The food is traditional, emphasizing wholesome *cuisine bourgeoise*. In the summer, meals are served outside on the terrace, and in the winter you dine inside by a log fire, accompanied by gentle piano music.

GIEN

Côté Jardin

Road map F3. 14 rte de Bourges.
[38 38 24 67. ○ noon–2pm daily, 7:30–10pm Tue–Sun. ⓘ ⚘ Ⓥ ⏀ Ⓔ MC, DC, V. Ⓕ Ⓕ

The name (meaning "on the garden side") is apt, as there is an open, airy feel to this cheery little place across the river from the château. The good-value menu, with many seafood and fish dishes, changes every two months to take advantage of seasonal produce.

MONTOIRE-SUR-LE-LOIR

Le Cheval Rouge

Road map D3. Pl Foch. [54 85 07 05. ○ noon–2pm Thu–Tue, 7:30–9pm Thu–Mon. ⓘ ⚘ Ⓥ & ⚡ Ⓔ AE, MC, V. Ⓕ Ⓕ

Close to Trôo and Lavardin, this restaurant serves classic cuisine in a lighter, contemporary style, so it is never too rich. A range of fixed-price menus is on offer, and the inn also has 15 modest rooms.

OLIVET

Le Rivage

Road map E2. 635 rue de la Reine-Blanche. [38 66 02 93. ○ noon–2pm, 7:15–9:30pm daily. ⓘ ⚘ Ⓥ ⏀ ⏀ ⚡ Ⓔ AE, MC, DC, V. Ⓕ Ⓕ

The best tables for summer dining in this hotel-restaurant are on the terrace beside the River Loiret. But in winter, the airy dining room will still make you feel like you're on the river as you enjoy some of the finest cuisine in the area.

ONZAIN

Domaine des Hauts-de-Loire

Road map D3. Route de Herbault.
[54 20 72 57. ○ noon–2pm, 7:30–9:30pm daily. ⓘ ⚘ & Ⓔ AE, MC, DC, V. Ⓕ Ⓕ Ⓕ Ⓕ *See also* **Where to Stay**, *p203.*

The restaurant of this *Relais et Châteaux* hotel has two Michelin stars. The menu includes delights such as *filet de boeuf poché au vin de Montlouis* (poached fillet of beef cooked in white Montlouis – one of the best Loire Valley wines).

ORLÉANS

Les Antiquaires

Road map E2. 2–4 rue au Lin.
🍴 38 53 52 35. ⏰ noon–2pm,
7:30–10pm Tue–Sat. 🍴 🏃 Ⓥ
🍽 AE, MC, DC, V. Ⓕ Ⓕ

This restaurant is popular with
locals for its inventive cuisine.
Sologne game is served when in
season, including wild duck, boar,
hare and the house speciality of
noisettes de biche sauce poivrade
(marinaded venison fillet in a
peppery garlic and herb sauce).

La Chancellerie

Road map E2. Pl Martroi. 🍴 38 53
57 54. ⏰ noon–3pm, 7–midnight
Mon–Sat. 🍴 Ⓥ 🕊 🍽 Ⓨ
🍽 AE, MC, V. Ⓕ Ⓕ

In an 18th-century building on a
busy square near the cathedral,
this lively brasserie and wine bar
offers adventurous dishes to complement their excellent wines. In
season, *faisan aux champignons*
(pheasant with wild mushrooms)
and *lièvre aux airelles* (hare with
bilberries) are popular.

SOUVIGNY-EN-
SOLOGNE

La Perdrix Rouge

Road map E3. 22 rue du Gâtinais.
🍴 54 88 41 05. ⏰ noon–1:30pm
Wed–Mon, 7–9pm Wed–Sun. 🍴
🕊 🍽 🍽 AE, MC, V. Ⓕ Ⓕ

This typical Sologne inn, with half-
timbering and a garden, is popular
in the shooting season when it
serves excellent game, including
the partridge that gives it its name.
Other local produce is made good
use of during the rest of the year.

SULLY-SUR-LOIRE

Hostellerie Le Grand
Sully

Road map F3. 10 bd du Champ-de-
Foire. 🍴 38 36 27 56. ⏰ noon–2pm
daily, 7:30–9pm Mon–Sat. 🍴 🕊
Ⓥ 🕊 Ⓨ 🍽 AE, MC, DC, V. Ⓕ Ⓕ

This is a sophisticated restaurant,
ideally located for visiting the
abbey at St-Benoît-sur-Loire. The
chef-owner's attention to detail is
admirable whether you choose
classic or more inventive dishes.
The wine list includes various local
vintages – delicious Ménetou-Salon
is recommended to accompany the
fish specialities.

BERRY

ARGENTON-SUR-
CREUSE

Moulin des Eaux-Vives

Road map E4. Tendu. 🍴 54 24
12 25. ⏰ 12:15–1:30pm Mon,
7:30–9pm Wed–Sun. 🍴 🕊 Ⓥ 🍽
🍽 AE, MC, V. Ⓕ

Once an 18th-century water mill,
this restaurant is 8 km (5 miles)
north of Argenton-sur-Creuse. The
menu changes seasonally and may
have *côtes de sanglier au vinaigre
de framboises* (boar in raspberry
vinegar sauce) and *coupe de vignes*
(grape sorbets). The food is good
value, but wine is expensive.

AUBIGNY-SUR-NÈRE

Le Bien-Aller

Road map F3. Les Naudins.
🍴 48 58 03 92. ⏰ noon–2:30pm
Thu–Tue, 7–10pm Thu–Mon. 🍴
🕊 Ⓥ 🍽 🍽 AE, MC, V. Ⓕ

This inn lies only 1 km (just over
half a mile) from the Château de
la Verrerie. The menu includes
many original recipes, such as the
crème brûlée au thym (a crème
caramel with fresh thyme).

BANNEGON

Auberge du Moulin de
Chaméron

Road map F4. Le Village. 🍴 48 61
83 80. ⏰ 12:15–1:45pm, 7:30–9pm
Wed–Mon (closed 15 Nov–1 Mar).
🍴 🕊 🍽 🍽 AE, MC, V. Ⓕ Ⓕ

A welcoming hotel-restaurant has
been created from a picturesque
18th-century water mill, its machin-
ery still in place. The dining room,
complete with old beams and a
fine fireplace, serves good cuisine
with many regional touches.

BOURGES

Le d'Antan Sancerrois

Road map F4. 50 rue Bourbonnoux.
🍴 48 65 96 26. ⏰ noon–2pm
Wed–Sun, 7–10:30pm Tue–Sun. 🕊
Ⓥ 🍽 Ⓨ 🍽 AE, MC, V. Ⓕ Ⓕ

The locals flock to this restaurant
set in a medieval building with
exposed beams. The hearty cuisine
is prepared with finesse, and the
wine list is excellent.

Le Jardin Gourmand

Road map F4. 15 bis av Ernest Renan.
🍴 48 21 35 91. ⏰ noon–2pm Tue–
Sun, 7:30–9:30pm Tue–Sat. 🍴 🕊
🍽 🍽 AE, MC, DC, V. Ⓕ Ⓕ

Specialities of this elegant, gourmet
restaurant include seafood and fish,
lamb in a curry sauce and poultry.
Game dishes are served in season.

Abbaye St-Ambroix

Road map F4. Bd de la République.
🍴 48 70 00 00. ⏰ noon–2pm
Sun–Fri, 7–10pm daily. 🍴 🕊
Ⓨ 🍽 AE, MC, DC, V. Ⓕ Ⓕ Ⓕ Ⓕ
See also **Where to Stay,** *p205.*

The Hôtel de Bourbon's restaurant
is set in the abbey's former chapel.
The sophisticated cuisine uses the
best of French produce. All desserts
are made to order. The fixed-price
menus are good value.

BRUÈRE-ALLICHAMPS

Auberge de l'Abbaye
de Noirlac

Road map F4. Le Village. 🍴 48 96
22 58. ⏰ noon–2:30pm, 7–9:30pm
Thu–Tue. 🍴 🕊 Ⓥ 🕊 🍽
🍽 MC, V. Ⓕ Ⓕ

This inn, surrounded by meadows,
is just a few minutes' walk from
the beautiful Abbaye de Noirlac.
The decor is rustic and the cuisine
satisfying. Light meals are also
available for those in a hurry.

CHÂTEAUMEILLANT

Le Piet-à-Terre

Road map F4. Rue du Château. 🍴 48
61 41 74. ⏰ noon–1:30pm Tue–Sun,
7:30–9pm Tue–Sat (summer: daily).
🍴 🕊 Ⓥ 🕊 🍽 MC, V. Ⓕ Ⓕ

This is a serious restaurant offering
interesting cooking. Its specialities
include *poulette braisée farcie*, a
braised young chicken stuffed with
foie gras. The weekday lunch
menu is particularly good value.

NOHANT

Auberge de la Petite
Fadette

Road map E4. Le Village. 🍴 54 31
01 48. ⏰ noon–2pm, 7–9:30pm.
🍴 🕊 Ⓥ 🕊 🍽 MC, V. Ⓕ Ⓕ

Named after one of George Sand's
novels, this inn is cosy in winter yet
airy in summer. Try the Berry dish,
poulet en barbouille (see p210).

For key to symbols *see p209*

ST-AMAND-MONTROND

La Croix d'Or

Road map F4. 28 rue du 14 juillet.
📞 48 96 09 41. ⏰ noon–2pm, 7–9:30pm. 🍴 🔥 Ⓥ ♿ 🎵 🚭 AE, MC, V. Ⓕ

Charolais beef, best accompanied by a good Sancerre, is a speciality of this restaurant. The dining room, with its curved ceiling and forest of plants, is spacious.

SANCERRE

La Tour

Road map F3. 31 pl de la Halle.
📞 48 54 00 81. ⏰ noon–2pm, 7:30–10pm daily. 🍴 🔥 Ⓥ ♿ 🎵 🚭 AE, MC, V. ⒻⒻ

With views of the tower that gives it its name, this restaurant has two dining rooms. Downstairs has exposed beams and a welcoming fire; upstairs is more modern. In both, the food is excellent. *Sandre* (pike-perch) with a red Sancerre sauce is one of many local dishes.

VIERZON

Le Prieuré

Road map E3. 2 rte de St-Laurent, Vignoux-sur-Barangeon. 📞 48 51 58 80. ⏰ noon–1:30pm Thu–Tue, 7:30–9pm Thu–Mon. 🍴 🔥 ♿ 🅣 🚭 AE, MC, DC, V. ⒻⒻ

As the name suggests, this restaurant is housed in a former priory. *Pigeon du Berry à la truffe* (pigeon with truffles) is typical of the inventive menu. For dessert, try the *terrine de crêpes*, a gateau of pancakes with orange sauce.

NORTH OF THE LOIRE

ARNAGE

Auberge des Matfeux

Road map C2. 289 av Nationale.
📞 43 21 10 71. ⏰ noon–2pm Tue–Sun, 7–9pm Tue–Sat. 🍴 🔥 Ⓥ ♿ 🅣 🚭 AE, MC, DC, V. ⒻⒻⒻ

This old inn, 9 km (6 miles) south of Le Mans, serves light cuisine making use of the vegetables and herbs grown in the garden. The dining room has a conservatory.

CHARTRES

Le Buisson Ardent

Road map E2. 10 rue au Lait.
📞 37 34 04 66. ⏰ noon–2pm daily, 7:30–9:30pm Mon–Sat. 🍴 🔥 Ⓥ 🅣 🚭 MC, V. ⒻⒻ

This popular restaurant, close to the cathedral, is good for a speedy, satisfying lunch during sightseeing, or for a more leisurely dinner. The classic cuisine is good value, and children's meals are available.

Le Grand Monarque

Road map E2. 22 pl des Epars.
📞 37 21 00 72. ⏰ noon–2:30pm, 7:30–10pm daily. 🍴 🚭 🅣 AE, MC, DC, V. ⒻⒻⒻ See also Where to Stay, *p206.*

The restaurant of this hotel serves both traditional French food and local delicacies, including *pâté de Chartres* (*foie gras* inside duck liver pâté). The wine cellar offers one of the widest selections of Loire Valley wines in France.

CHÂTEAUDUN

L'Arnaudière

Road map E2. 4 rue St-Lubin.
📞 37 45 98 98. ⏰ noon–2pm daily, 7:30–9:30pm Tue–Sun. 🍴 🔥 Ⓥ 🖨 ♿ 🚭 AE, MC, V. ⒻⒻ

In a Renaissance building in the Old Town, this restaurant has a courtyard garden for summer meals. The cuisine is tasty, and the fixed-price menus are good value. Some wines are served by the glass.

LA FLÈCHE

La Fesse d'Ange

Road map C3. Pl du 8 mai 1945.
📞 43 94 73 60. ⏰ noon–1:30pm Tue–Sun, 7:15–9:30pm Tue–Sat. 🍴 🔥 Ⓥ ♿ 🅣 🚭 MC, V. ⒻⒻ

Based on seasonal produce, the cooking is much appreciated by its mainly local clientele. The famous plump chickens and ducks from Loué are often on the menu and should certainly be tried.

LAVAL

Bistro de Paris

Road map B2. 67 rue du Val-de-Mayenne. 📞 43 56 98 29. ⏰ noon–2pm Mon–Fri, 7–10pm Mon–Sat. 🍴 🔥 Ⓥ ♿ 🚭 ★ MC, V. ⒻⒻ

Beside the River Mayenne and close to the château, this bistro serves beautifully cooked, tasty meals that are remarkable value for their quality. The wines are also well priced. Be sure to book in advance.

MALICORNE-SUR-SARTHE

La Petite Auberge

Road map C3. Au Pont. 📞 43 94 80 52. ⏰ Jun–Sep: noon–2pm, 7–9pm daily; Mar–May & Oct–Nov: noon–2pm Tue–Sun, 7–9pm Wed–Sat; Dec–Feb: noon–2pm Tue–Sun, 7–9pm Fri–Sun. 🍴 🔥 Ⓥ 🚭 AE, MC, V. Ⓕ

This small restaurant, beside the town's marina and close to the famous faïence workshops, is a good spot for lunch during a tour of the Sarthe valley.

LE MANS

Le Grenier à Sel

Road map C2. 26 pl de l'Eperon.
📞 43 23 26 30. ⏰ noon–2:15pm Tue–Sun, 7–10pm Tue–Sat. 🍴 🔥 Ⓥ ♿ 🅣 🚭 AE, MC, V. ⒻⒻ

Well situated for exploring the Old Town, this restaurant is housed in a picturesque building where the salt-tax collectors once stored their proceeds. The chef specializes in fish recipes served with subtle, often herb-flavoured sauces.

La Vie en Rose

Road map C2. 55 Grande Rue. 📞 43 23 27 37. ⏰ 11:30am–2pm, 7–10pm (summer: 11pm) Mon–Sat. 🍴 🔥 ♿ 🚭 AE, MC, DC, V. ⒻⒻ

Once the oldest theatre in Le Mans, this building is now a restaurant, where the cuisine is essentially *nouvelle*. Portions of seafood are beautifully presented, particularly the *feuilleté de la mer Vie en Rose* (halibut fillet in filo pastry, with a mushroom and shallot sauce).

ST-DENIS-D'ANJOU

Auberge du Roi-René

Road map C3. 4 Grande-Rue.
📞 43 70 52 30. ⏰ noon–2pm, 7–10pm. 🍴 🔥 Ⓥ 🖨 ♿ 🚭 AE, MC, DC, V. Ⓕ

The dining room is set in a medieval building. The cuisine is light, with some dishes, like the *nougat de foie de canard aux figues* (duck liver terrine with figs), combining sweet and savoury flavours.

SOLESMES

Grand Hôtel de Solesmes

Road map C2. 16 pl Dom-Guéranger.
▯ 43 95 45 10. **◯** noon–2pm daily,
7:30–9:30pm Mon–Sat (closed Nov–
Mar). **▯◉▯ ▯ ▯ ▯ ▯** AE, MC,
DC, V. **Ⓕ Ⓕ Ⓕ** See also **Where to
Stay**, p207.

This hotel has an excellent restaurant overlooking a garden. The traditional cuisine features local fish specialities, including *sandre à la mousse d'oseille* (pike-perch with sorrel mousse).

LOIRE-ATLANTIQUE AND THE VENDEE

ARÇAIS

L'Auberge de la Venise Verte

Road map B4. Route de Damvix.
▯ 49 35 37 15. **◯** noon–2pm Fri–
Wed, 7:30–9:30pm Fri–Tue. **▯◉▯ ▯**
▯ ▯ ▯ MC, V. **Ⓕ**

If you are touring the canals of the Marais Poitevin by road or water, this restaurant makes a cheap and cheerful stop for lunch. The menu emphasizes local fish and eels.

CLISSON

Bonne Auberge

Road map B4. 1 rue Olivier de Clisson.
▯ 40 54 01 90. **◯** noon–2:30pm
Tue–Sun, 8–9pm Tue–Sat. **▯◉▯ ▯**
▯ ▯ ▯ ▯ ★ ▯ AE, MC, V.
Ⓕ Ⓕ Ⓕ

Local produce is used for the inventive dishes served in this restaurant. Try the Vendéen duck with figs or the poached fish with spices, and leave space for their delectable desserts.

FONTENAY-LE-COMTE

Auberge de la Rivière

Road map B4. Velluire. **▯** 51 52
32 15. **◯** 12:5–2pm Tue–Sun, 8–
9:30pm Tue–Sat (summer: daily). **▯◉▯**
▯ ▯ ▯ ▯ MC, V. **Ⓕ Ⓕ**

Sited near the northern end of the Marais Poitevin, 11 km (7 miles) southwest of Fontenay-le-Comte, this *auberge* offers country comfort

and delicious cooking. The fish dishes are especially good, as are the langoustines (small crayfish).

ILE D'YEU

La Marée

Road map A4. 27 rue Pierre-Henry,
Port-Joinville. **▯** 51 58 41 33. **◯**
noon–2pm daily, 7–9pm daily
(closed 20 Nov–10 Jan). **▯◉▯ ▯ ▯** V.
Ⓕ Ⓕ See also **Where to Stay**, p207.

La Marée, the restaurant of the Flux Hôtel, specializes in fish and seafood dishes. For dessert, try a *tartilaise*, the Ile d'Yeu prune tart.

MAILLEZAIS

Le Collibert

Road map B5. Rue Principale.
▯ 51 87 25 07. **◯** noon–3pm
Tue–Sun, 7:30–10pm Tue–Sat
(Easter–mid-Sep daily). **▯◉▯ ▯ V**
▯ ▯ AE, MC, DC, V. **Ⓕ Ⓕ Ⓕ**

Situated in the Marais Poitevin at the entrance to La Venise Verte, this restaurant is highly regarded for its regional buffet and versions of local specialities.

MORTAGNE-SUR-SÈVRE

Hôtel de France

Road map B4. Pl du Docteur Pichat.
▯ 51 65 03 37. **◯** 12:15–2pm
Sun–Fri, 7:30–9pm Mon–Fri. **▯◉▯ ▯**
V ▯ ▯ ▯ AE, MC, DC, V. **Ⓕ**

A cheerful atmosphere and good food awaits diners at this 400-year-old coaching inn. There are two restaurants: the classic La Taverne, and the slightly cheaper La Petite Auberge. Rooms are available to those wishing to stay overnight.

NANTES

La Taverne de Maître Kanter

Road map B3. 1 pl Royale. **▯** 40 48
55 28. **◯** noon–2am daily. **▯◉▯ ▯**
▯ ▯ ▯ AE, MC, DC, V. **Ⓕ**

Part of a chain, this Alsatian tavern excels with its *choucroute* (sauerkraut), cold meats and beers. It serves food until 2am.

La Cigale

Road map B3. 4 pl Graslin.
▯ 40 69 76 41. **◯** 8–12:30am
daily. **▯◉▯ ▯ ▯ ▯ ▯** V. **Ⓕ Ⓕ**

The interior of this Belle Epoque brasserie *(see p190)* is decorated with glazed tiles and gilding. The quality of the cuisine is also exceptional, featuring a wide choice of fresh seafood and fish.

Torigaï

Road map D3. Ile de Versailles.
▯ 40 37 06 37. **◯** noon–2pm,
7:30–10pm Mon–Sat. **▯◉▯ ▯ ▯**
▯ ▯ AE, MC, V. **Ⓕ Ⓕ Ⓕ Ⓕ**

On an island in the River Erdre, in a conservatory full of exotic plants, sample the unique blending of Oriental and French cooking. For wine lovers, there is a five-course "Muscadet" set menu, each course served with a different Muscadet.

OULMES

L'Escargot Vendéen

Road map B5. 29 rue Georges
Clémenceau. **▯** 51 52 49 00.
◯ noon–2:30pm daily, 7–10pm
Wed–Mon. **▯◉▯ ▯ V ▯ ▯**
▯ MC, V. **Ⓕ**

This elegant restaurant is set in a restored old building. It is a good place to try local dishes, such as *mojettes du marais* (haricot beans served with local ham); *escargots* (snails) cooked in red wine and bacon; eels or frogs legs.

LES SABLES D'OLONNE

Beau Rivage

Road map A4. 40 promenade
Georges Clemenceau. **▯** 51 32 03
01. **◯** 12:30–2pm Tue–Sun, 7:30–
9:30pm Tue–Sat (May–Oct: daily). **▯◉▯**
▯ V ▯ ▯ ▯ AE, MC, DC, V.
Ⓕ Ⓕ Ⓕ Ⓕ

This pretty restaurant is located on the beach promenade. Diners can watch boats sailing in and out of the harbour as they eat. Local fish is the speciality.

ST-LYPHARD

Auberge de Kerhinet

Road map A3. Kerhinet. **▯** 40 61
91 46. **◯** 12:15–3pm Thu–Tue, 7:15–
11pm Thu–Mon (Jul–Aug: daily). **▯◉▯**
▯ V ▯ ▯ ▯ AE, MC, DC, V.
Ⓕ Ⓕ See also **Where to Stay**, p207.

This hotel restaurant is decorated with old photographs and farm tools. Typical local fish specialities include *anguilles au rocquefort* (eel with Rocquefort), using fresh eels from the Lac de Grand-Lieu.

SHOPS AND MARKETS

SHOPPING FOR SPECIALITIES of the Loire Valley is always a pleasure, and the region's towns and cities also offer many opportunities to purchase the goods that France is famous for – fashion accessories and clothes, kitchenware, porcelain and crystal, and particularly food. Specialist shops are everywhere, and

Bourges shop sign

visiting the region's open-air and indoor food markets gives the visitor a wonderful opportunity to buy a vast range of local produce and culinary specialities. This section provides guidelines on shopping in the Loire Valley, and pages 222–3 show some of the best regional foods, wines and other specialist goods available.

Chocolates on display in La Livre Tournois, a *confiserie* in Tours

OPENING HOURS

SMALL FOOD SHOPS in the Loire region open early – around 7:30 or 8am – and close at around 12:30 for lunch, then reopen at about 3:30 or 4pm until 7 or 8pm.

Other small shops are open from roughly 2 to 6:30 or 7pm on Mondays, 9am to noon and 2 to 6:30 or 7pm, Tuesday to Saturday. Small supermarkets generally take quite a long lunch break, but department stores and large supermarkets do not close for lunch. Sales are traditionally held in late-June and January.

Open-air food markets take place one, two or three mornings a week, often including Sundays, while the large indoor food markets *(les halles)* are usually open from Tuesday to Saturday for the same hours as small food shops. This guide lists the market days for each town featured.

SPECIALIST SHOPS

DESPITE THE mushrooming of supermarkets and large superstores, small specialist shops have continued to

thrive in France, and they add enormously to the pleasure of shopping trips. Food shops in particular often specialize in a single theme. *Boulangeries* sell fresh bread, but they may be *boulangeries-pâtisseries*, which means that tempting cakes and pastries will also be on offer. *Traiteurs* sell prepared dishes, while *épiceries* are small grocers. *Crémeries* specialize in dairy products, *fromageries* sell only cheese and *charcuteries* specialize in cooked and cured meats with a few prepared, cold dishes. An *épicerie fine* focuses on high-class groceries and is a good source of gifts to take home, such as local mustards or vinegars in attractive jars or bottles.

An *alimentation générale* (general food store) may have a self-service system. In small villages, this is sometimes the only shop, although fresh bread will always be available either there or from the local café. A travelling van also supplies fresh bread in some regions.

Cleaning products are bought in a *droguerie*, hardware from a *quincaillerie*, books from a *librairie* and stationery (much of which is particularly stylish in France) from a *papeterie*.

The area has some specialist shops that focus on a single product, such as umbrellas or walking sticks, chess sets or stamps, or in a single field such as militaria or natural history books. Their owners are usually extremely knowledgeable about their particular subject, and they enjoy sharing it if you show an interest. Antique shops *(magasins d'antiquités)* tend to be very pricey. Head instead for a *brocante* (bric-à-brac shop), or try hunting for bargains in local flea markets.

TASTING AND BUYING WINE

THE LOIRE VALLEY is famous for its wines and the region is scattered with producers. Signs beside the road saying *"dégustation"* mean that a "tasting" is held in the vineyard. It is important to remember that the local *vigneron* will expect a modest purchase of a few bottles after you have drunk several experimental glasses. However, in Saumur it is possible to tour the *chais* (the wine growers' own cellars) with the minimum of sales pressure. Best of all, visit the *Maisons du Vin* in most major towns, where the literature, information and often free tastings are very helpful and interesting.

Sign for a charcuterie

HYPERMARKETS AND CHAIN STORES

SUPERSTORES and the larger hypermarkets *(hyper-marchés)* are usually situated on the outskirts of towns, often as part of a *centre commercial* (shopping complex) that may also include small boutiques, a DIY outlet and a petrol station. Many of these big stores belong to the Auchan, Carrefour or Continent chains.

The old-style *grand magasin,* or department store, found in the region's towns has generally either been converted into a series of boutiques or taken over and modernized by the up-market Nouvelles Galeries or Printemps national chains. These chic stores are good for clothes, accessories and perfumes. The popular Monoprix and Prisunic stores are worth visiting if you are looking for inexpensive stationery, lingerie and cosmetics. Many of them also have a reasonably priced food department.

A flower-seller and customer at the village market in Luynes

MARKETS

OPEN-AIR FOOD markets are one of the delights of the Loire Valley. Their offerings are mouth-watering: mounds of succulent vegetables, *charcuterie* specialities, goats' cheeses and plump poultry and game. Of this excellent fare, most is produced locally, often in small-scale market gardens owned and worked by the stall-holder. Produce that has

Fresh local produce on sale in the market in Saumur's place St-Pierre

been grown locally is labelled *pays.* Look out for unusual specialities, such as the strangely-shaped squashes and pumpkins that appear in autumn, wild mushrooms and flavoured honeys. Honey stalls often sell honey-flavoured confectionery and honey soap, too. Spice and herb stalls are also interesting, providing a wealth of gift ideas. Some markets have stalls selling clothes or shoes and leather goods. Look out also for local craft work.

Flea markets *(marchés aux puces)* are regular events in many towns and are often held in small towns and villages in countryside districts during the summer holiday season.

VAT REBATES

SINCE THE ADVENT of the Single European Market, rebates of value-added tax *(taxe à la valeur ajoutée* or *TVA)* are only available to those not resident in a European Union country. They apply only to purchases totalling at least F2,000 in a single shop and taken out of the country within six months. The form you receive on purchase must be handed to the customs officer as you leave France. The reimbursement usually goes directly to your bank. Some articles are not eligible for rebates. In stores frequented by foreign tourists, staff are familiar with the paperwork that is involved.

Local goats' cheese for sale in Amboise market

What to Buy in the Loire Valley

THE BEST BUYS IN THE LOIRE tempt the eye as well as the stomach. A gourmet's paradise, the food shops and open-air markets of the region attract visitors with their delicious scents and sights. Local producers are justifiably proud of their goods and pack them with respect, in attractive crates or pottery jars. But gourmet treats are not the only local goods worth looking for. The region has long been famous for its china from Gien and for the fabric and lace of the Touraine, evocative of the remarkable history of the Loire.

A beautifully wrapped package of sweets

CONFECTIONERY

Local confectionery specialities make good gifts to take home, especially when they are so prettily packaged. The region is well-known for its wide range of sweets, which are available from tearooms and specialist confectioners, and many towns also have their own mouth-watering treats.

Forestines from Bourges

Macaroon biscuits from Cormery

Pruneaux fourrés, prunes stuffed with marzipan

Chocolates resembling traditional slate tiles

Fruit-flavoured sweets

SOUVENIRS

The châteaux and museums of the Loire Valley have well-stocked shops that sell an array of appealing souvenirs. In addition to the usual booklets and posters, many sell gifts with an historical theme, such as replica playing cards or tapestries. Wine bought direct from a local vineyard is another special souvenir (see pp30–31).

Playing cards with historical figures

Wine made at Chenonceau

THE FLAVOURS OF THE LOIRE

It is impossible to visit the Loire without being amazed by the abundance of delicious food. Much comes perfectly packaged for travelling. Near the game-filled forests of the Berry, you can buy jars and tins of pâtés and terrines. Goats' cheeses are moulded into a variety of shapes, and the firmer varieties travel successfully. Heather honey from Berry's heathland and wine vinegars from Orléans are also specialities of the region.

Confiture de vin, jelly made from wine

Poulain chocolate made in Blois

Pickled samphire

Goats' cheese

Cotignac, quince jelly from Orléans

Sea salt from Guérande

Crémant de Loire, sparkling wine

LOCAL CRAFTS

Traditional crafts survive throughout the Loire Valley, and you can often visit craftsmen and women at work in their studios. Many towns in the region have long been renowned for their craft specialities, such as Malicorne for its lattice-work faïence, Villaines-les-Rochers for its baskets or Gien for its china.

Pottery from La Borne in Berry

Gien china side plate

Wicker basket from Villaines

Dinner plate from Gien

ACTIVITIES IN THE LOIRE VALLEY

A HOLIDAY IN THE Loire Valley can combine the cultural highlights of visits to the spectacular châteaux with enjoyment of the region's wealth of natural environments. The gentle terrain and beautiful forests are perfect for exploration on foot, horseback or mountain bike, and the clear waters of the lakes and rivers – not to mention the spectacular Atlantic coastline – are enticing spots for swimming or boating. Here is a selection of just a few of the activities on offer in the region. For more information contact the departmental *Loisirs-Accueil* offices *(see p227)*, which focus on leisure activities, or the local tourist offices in towns and villages.

WALKING

THE LOIRE VALLEY is renowned for its many accessible and scenic walks, which are called *Randonnées (see pp26–7)*. Although these routes are clearly signposted, it is a good idea to carry a Topo-Guide, which are only available in French but do contain maps, a description of the itinerary, details of sites of architectural or natural interest to be found along the route, an estimate of the time it will take you to complete the walk and the addresses of local hotels, restaurants, hostels and camp sites. Most Topo-Guides cost around F100. There is also a one-volume Topo-Guide describing the GR3 between Orléans and Guérande. A complete list of walks in the Loire Valley is available from the **Fédération Française de la Randonnée Pédestre**.

You will never be more than a day's walk away from a town or village where you will be able to find food and accommodation, so it is not necessary to carry a large amount of equipment, but, as always, you should wear good, strong walking shoes. Remember that some paths can be damp and muddy during the spring and autumn.

CYCLING

THE GENERALLY flat landscape of the Loire Valley makes it perfect for cyclists. Because many of the châteaux are so near to each other, it is easy to visit several by bicycle in only a few days. Mountain bike enthusiasts will enjoy riding the clearly signposted paths through the region's forests and nature reserves.

Motorways and a few other major roads are forbidden to cyclists, and these are clearly marked: the sign has a white background with a red border and a cyclist in the middle. Cycle lanes, when they exist, are compulsory. Bicycles must have two working brakes, a bell, a red rear reflector and yellow reflectors on the pedals, as well as a white front light and a red rear light after dark. It is also advisable to wear a helmet and to carry a few essential spare parts in case of breakdown. While bicycle shops are common in the region, foreign spare parts may not be available.

It is possible to hire touring bicycles and mountain bikes throughout the region. Local tourist offices will be able to provide you with a list of cycle hire centres. The SNCF *(see p242)* also runs a *Train et Vélo* service, which offers cycles for hire at some train stations in the region.

Transporting your bicycle on local trains is free in most cases, although on major train routes the SNCF requires you to register your bicycle and will levy a small charge. The booklet *Guide du Train et du Vélo*, available at train stations and from the SNCF, gives more information on transporting bicycles by train.

A number of local tourist offices have organized itineraries for cyclists and will provide comprehensive route maps. In the central Loire Valley, a group of hoteliers and camp sites are members of *Vélotel-Vélocamp*. This means that they are particularly friendly to cyclists and can arrange bicycle hire, organize local itineraries and provide you with a picnic lunch on request.

The **Fédération Française de Cyclo-Tourisme** is the umbrella organization for more than 2,800 cycling clubs in France. They are able to provide advice, local contacts and a number of cycling itineraries in the region if you write to them well in advance.

Cycling, one of the most pleasant ways to see the Loire Valley

A riverside pony trek in the beautiful Vendée region

HORSE RIDING AND PONY TREKKING

HORSE LOVERS will enjoy a visit to the National Riding School in the important equestrian town of Saumur, where the world-famous Cadre Noir riding team perform in regular displays *(see p83).*

The forests of the Loire Valley, with their well-maintained networks of trails and well-marked bridle paths, are ideal for riding. Topo-Guides are as useful for riders as they are for walkers.

Experienced riders can hire horses by the hour, half-day or day from numerous stables in the region. A sign reading *Loueur d'Equidés* means that horses are for hire without an instructor. If you prefer to be accompanied when riding, you should search out an *Ecole d'Equitation* or a *Centre Equestre* (riding school).

Many stables also offer longer treks on horseback, called *randonnées,* which last between a weekend and a week. Small groups are accompanied on the trek by an experienced guide, and accommodation is usually in quite basic hotels or hostels, although some luxury tours are also available.

The rental of old-fashioned horse-drawn caravans is becoming increasingly popular in the Loire Valley. Travellers sleep in the carriage overnight and journey at a slow, leisurely pace during the day. Generally caravans come in two sizes: the smaller one carries four adults or two adults and three children; the other carries six to eight people. There are also larger, open wagons, driven by a guide, that are used for group excursions of up to 15.

FISHING

THE RIVERS of the Loire Valley are teeming with freshwater fish, including bream, bullhead, carp, grey mullet, perch, pike, roach, shad and zander. There are also trout in some of the faster-running tributaries of the Loire.

Freshwater fish

To fish in private waters, you must make arrangements with the owner. To fish in state-controlled waters, you must buy a permit, which is available from many tackle shops and tourist offices. Applicants must provide proof that they are a member of an angling association at home and pay a fishing tax.

There are two kinds of fishing tax: the basic tax covers fishing with worms in rivers that do not have trout runs; the special tax covers spinning, fly-fishing, and fish-bait fishing in all rivers, including those with trout. You cannot fish more than half an hour before sunrise or after sunset. There are set seasons for certain fish and limits on their size.

The **Conseil Supérieur de la Pêche**, which supervises all fishing in France, uses the tax money to promote and improve fishing conditions. It also publishes a helpful, free booklet, *Fishing in France,* which explains the regulations and includes a map giving useful information about all the French rivers. Ocean fishing is free from any tax as long as you do not use nets, although there are restrictions on the equipment a boat can carry. *Fishing in France* also has information on fishing from boats and underwater fishing.

Fly-fishing on the tranquil River Loir

GOLF

EVIDENCE of the growing popularity of golf in France can be seen throughout the Loire Valley, which has many beautiful and challenging courses. Some of the region's golf courses, such as the Golf du Val de l'Indre, located near Châteauroux in Berry, and La Bretesche in Missillac in the Loire-Atlantique, are set in the grounds of châteaux.

In the Loiret, four courses around Orléans have joined up to provide a golf pass that combines greens fees for the different courses and the added option of accommodation in nearby two- or three-star hotels. For more information, contact the *Loisirs-Accueil* office or the tourist office of the Loiret.

The booklet *The Western Loire Golf Courses*, available from the tourist office in Nantes *(see p231)*, includes a Golf Passport – play on five courses in the western Loire and the greens fee on the sixth is free. The comprehensive brochure also suggests top-class accommodation within easy reach of the courses.

BOATING AND WATER SPORTS

BECAUSE THE Loire Valley is criss-crossed with beautiful rivers, most visitors cannot resist the temptation to take at least one boat trip. A wide variety of short excursions is available from riverside *ports de plaisance* (marinas) throughout the Loire region, and in general they do not require advance reservations.

The marshes of the Marais Poitevin *(see pp182–5)* are best viewed from its canal network in a *barque* (the traditional, flat-bottomed boat).

One option is to base your entire visit on the water by renting a house-boat or a cruiser for a period of a few days or for one or two weeks. Boats of different sizes and styles are available, from old-fashioned canal boats to sophisticated modern cruisers. Most prices are for round trips and include bedding, kitchen equipment and full training, and it may also be possible to rent bicycles or canoes, or to make a one-way *(simple)* trip. Further information is available from the main tourist offices.

If you are looking for a more adventurous way of enjoying the region's rivers, try canoeing or kayaking. It is best to take a guided tour from one of the clubs based along the river. Although the river may look calm, there can be dangerous undercurrents and obstacles.

Kayaking on the River Mayenne

There are good activity centres beside many of the rivers and lakes in the Loire Valley, and there may also be facilities for renting pedaloes, canoes and yachts – some centres even offer water-skiing. A good number of the Atlantic coastal resorts also have facilities for renting windsurfers – Les Sables d'Olonne *(see p181)* was host to the world wind-surfing championships in 1988.

Swimmers should stay in the approved areas. While the sand banks may look inviting, there are risks from strong currents and shifting sands. Further information on water safety is given on pages 234–5.

Windsurfing at La Tranche-sur-Mer on the Atlantic Coast

THE LOIRE FROM THE AIR

ONE OF THE most luxurious and unusual ways to see the Loire Valley is from a hot-air balloon (*montgolfière* in French). There are daily flights during the summer, weather permitting, from the towns of Nantes, Tours and Amboise.

One company, called **France Montgolfière**, will put together custom excursions, combining a balloon trip with a return on mountain bikes, a wine-tasting or a gourmet picnic.

You can also arrange to take a tour in a helicopter or a light aircraft within the region. In addition to major airports at Tours and Nantes, there are a number of other smaller airfields throughout the Loire Valley. The tourist offices will be able to give you complete information. Flying lessons are also available at many of these centres.

Ballooning over Le Plessis-Bourré in Anjou

DIRECTORY

SERVICES LOISIRS-ACCUEIL

Cher
10 rue de la Chappe,
18014 Bourges.
☎ 48 70 74 75.

Eure-et-Loir
19 pl des Epars,
28002 Chartres.
☎ 37 36 90 90.

Indre
1 rue St-Martin,
36003 Châteauroux.
☎ 54 22 91 20.

Indre-et-Loire
38 rue Augustin-Fresnel,
37171 Chambray-lès-Tours.
☎ 47 48 37 27.

Loire-Atlantique
Comité Départementale
du Tourisme (CDT)
2 allée Baco,
44000 Nantes.
☎ 51 72 95 30.

Loiret
8 rue d'Escures,
45000 Orléans.
☎ 38 54 83 83.

Loir-et-Cher
5 rue de la Voûte du
Château,
41005 Blois.
☎ 54 78 55 50.

Maine-et-Loire
Pl Kennedy,
49021 Angers.
☎ 41 23 51 51.

Mayenne
84 av Robert Buron,
53018 Laval.
☎ 43 53 18 18.

Sarthe
Hôtel du Département,
2 rue des Maillets,
72072 Le Mans.
☎ 43 81 72 72.

Vendée
8 pl Napoléon,
85000 La Roche-sur-Yon.
☎ 51 05 45 28.

WALKING

**Fédération
Française de la
Randonnée
Pédestre**
64 rue de Gergovie,
75014 Paris.
☎ 45 45 31 02.

CYCLING

**Fédération
Française de
Cyclo-Tourisme
(FFCT)**
8 rue Jean-Marie-Jégo,
75013 Paris.
☎ 44 16 88 88.

HORSE RIDING

**Association
Nationale pour le
Tourisme Equestre
(ANTE)**
170 quai de Stalingrad,
92130 Issy-les-Moulineaux.
☎ 45 54 29 54.

PONY TREKKING

**Fédération des
Randonneurs
Equestres**
16 rue des Apennins,
75017 Paris.
☎ 42 26 23 23.

FISHING

**Conseil Supérieure
de la Pêche**
134 av de Malakoff,
75016 Paris.
☎ 45 01 20 20.

GOLF

**Fédération
Française de Golf
(FFG)**
69 av Victor-Hugo,
75016 Paris.
☎ 45 02 13 55.

SAILING AND WINDSURFING

**Fédération
Française de Voile**
55 av Kléber,
75016 Paris.
☎ 45 53 68 00.

CANOEING AND KAYAKING

**Ligue Pays de la
Loire de Canoë-
Kayak (LPLCK)**
75 av du Lac de Maine,
49000 Angers.
☎ 41 73 86 10.

THE LOIRE FROM THE AIR

**France
Montgolfières**
La Ribouilère,
41400 Monthou-sur-Cher.
☎ 54 71 75 40.

SURVIVAL
GUIDE

PRACTICAL INFORMATION

IN THE LOIRE VALLEY, as else
where in France, the peak
holiday period is from mid-
June to the end of August. The
area is very well prepared to
meet the practical needs of its
many visitors, however, providing accommodation ranging
from top hotels and private
châteaux to small camp sites, as well as
a selection of excellent restaurants.

**National logo for
tourist information**

Because of the profusion of places of
great historical, aesthetic or natural
interest, ranging from stunning châteaux
and cathedrals to windswept Atlantic
beaches and wild marshlands, it is a

good idea to draw up a list of
priority visits before you travel.
You should also check that the
places you plan to visit are not
closed for seasonal breaks or
for restoration work. Before
you leave home, the French
Government Tourist Offices
are invaluable sources of information. The local tourist information
offices in most towns in the region offer
advice on the spot.

With a wide variety of activities available, the Loire Valley has something to
offer all its visitors. The following tips will
help you make the most of your visit.

**Tourist information office in
Fontenay-le-Comte**

TOURIST INFORMATION

MOST LARGE TOWNS have a
tourist information office,
known either as the *Syndicat
d'Initiative* or the *Office de
Tourisme*. This guide provides
the address and telephone
number of the tourist office
in each town featured in its
pages. In smaller towns the
town hall *(hôtel de ville)* will
offer information. Tourist
offices supply free maps,
advice on accommodation
(which can include booking
hotels) and information on
regional recreational and
cultural activities, such as
festivals. The main branches
are listed opposite. You can
also obtain details in advance
from French Government
Tourist Offices before leaving
your own country.

OPENING TIMES

GENERALLY, most shops and
banks open from 8 or
9am until noon, and from 2 or
3pm until 6pm, Tuesday to
Saturday *(see pp220–21 and
pp236–7)*. Opening hours
vary with the size of town.
Many shops and banks are
closed on Mondays
and also close
for lunch daily,
although big
department
stores, super-
markets, tourist
offices and some
sights may remain
open all the time.
Restaurants may
close for one day a
week, so it is best to
check before setting
off *(see pp208–19)*. Off
season, some seaside resorts,

**Brochures for sights
in the Loire Valley**

as well as many châteaux and
smaller museums, close down.
Telephone to check, as some
hotels and restaurants shut for
several months of the year.

SIGHTSEEING

IN FRANCE, MANY museums
close for lunch – normal
opening hours are
between 9am
and noon and
from 2pm until
5:30pm. They
usually also close
for one day each
week: national
museums close on
Tuesdays and
municipal museums
on Mondays. Several
museums also close
throughout the
month of November. Opening
hours tend to vary according

Tables outside a café in Les Sables d'Olonne

Entertainment at a festival in Luçon

to season. Generally, most museums are open for longer hours between May and September.

Museum admission charges range from F10 to F40. Passes for more than one museum or monument are rare. Normally, you will need to buy separate tickets for each sight within a town.

There are usually some discounts available for students who have valid International Student Identity Cards (ISIC) *(see p233)* or the French *carte jeunes.* Anyone aged under 18 or over 65 can also be eligible for a reduction in price. Most museums offer discounted or free entry for everyone on Sundays.

Churches and cathedrals are open every day but may shut during lunch. While admission is normally free, small charges are sometimes levied to visit cloisters, belltowers, crypts and chapels.

National logo for the disabled

DISABLED ACCESS

ALTHOUGH IN SOME of the Loire Valley's medieval villages, narrow streets can make it difficult for disabled travellers to get around, wheelchair access in the area is generally good. Many châteaux and museums offer special services and facilities for disabled visitors, which staff are happy to explain;

CHATEAU DE CHENONCEAU *Propriété Privée* **Entrée pour 1 personne** 369230

Entrance ticket to Chenonceau

however, it is advisable to telephone and check about access before your visit.

Access to hotels and restaurants has been improved in many cases to accommodate disabled customers. Information specific to the area is available from town halls or from regional tourist offices. Parking spaces reserved for vehicles that have disabled permits are marked with a special sign. For more information about facilities for the disabled before departure, contact the International Relations Department of the **Comité National pour la Réadaptation des Handicapés**.

ENTERTAINMENT INFORMATION

THERE ARE SEVERAL sources of entertainment information in the Loire Valley. Magazines and brochures listing forthcoming events are available at tourist information offices as well as in many hotels and camp sites. Both newsagents *(maisons de la presse)* and tobacconists' shops *(tabacs)* sell newspapers and magazines. Local papers can also provide details of festivals and sporting events as well as the weather forecast.

Sign for a tobacconist

VISAS

THERE ARE NO French visa requirements for citizens of the European Union. Tourists from the United States or New Zealand who are staying in France for less than three months need not apply for a visa. After three months, a *visa de long séjour* is required. Visitors from Australia, Canada and other countries should request visa information from the French authorities in their own country before departure.

TAX-FREE GOODS

IF YOU ARE resident outside the European Union you can reclaim the TVA (VAT or sales tax) on French goods if you spend more than F2,000 in one shop, obtain a *détaxe* receipt and take the goods out of the country within six months. Ask for a *détaxe* form when making your purchases (*see p221*), hand it in at customs when leaving the country and the refund will be sent on to you, usually via your bank.

Exceptions for *détaxe* rebate are food and drink, medicines, tobacco, cars and motorbikes, although tax reimbursements are allowed for bicycles bought in France.

DUTY-FREE LIMITS

UNTIL 31 June 1999, French limits for any goods that are bought in duty-free shops and imported by European Union nationals to France are as follows: 5 litres of wine, and either 2.5 litres of alcohol over 22º proof (that is, all spirits) or 3 litres of alcohol less than 22º proof; 75 g of perfume; 1 kg of coffee; 200 g of tea; and up to 300 cigarettes.

Non-European Union nationals are allowed to import 2 litres of wine, and a litre of spirits or 2 litres of alcohol 22º proof or less; 50 g of perfume; 500 g of coffee and 100 g of tea, as well as a maximum of 200 cigarettes.

French perfumes, available duty-free

Visitors under 17 are not allowed to import or export duty-free tobacco or alcohol, even if it is intended as a gift.

DUTY-PAID LIMITS

THERE ARE no longer any restrictions on the quantities of duty-paid and VAT-paid goods you are allowed to take from one European Union country to another, as long as the goods are for your own use and are not intended for resale. Customs officers may ask you to prove that the goods are for your personal use if they exceed the suggested amounts: 10 litres of spirits, 90 litres of wine, 110 litres of beer and 800 cigarettes.

IMPORTING OTHER GOODS

IN GENERAL, personal goods (such as a car or a bicycle) may be imported to France duty-free and without any paperwork as long as they are obviously for personal use and not for resale. The *Bon Voyages* brochure, which is available from the **Centre des Renseignements des Douanes**, clarifies this. At the border, customs officers are also able to give advice and information, although this is likely to be in French.

For regulations covering the import and export of plants between countries within the European Union, consult your own customs office before you leave home.

An ISIC international student card

STUDENT INFORMATION

STUDENTS who hold a valid International Student Identification Card (ISIC card) can benefit from discounts of between 25 and 50 per cent when they produce the card at museums, theatres, cinemas and also at many public monuments. The region's principal universities are in Nantes and Tours. Other large universities are located in the towns of Le Mans, Angers, Laval, Orléans and La Roche-sur-Yon.

In Orléans and Nantes, the **Centre Régional d'Information Jeunesse** (CRIJ) offices offer a great deal of useful information about student life and can also provide a list of inexpensive accommodation for young people.

ETIQUETTE

IT IS IMPORTANT to respect the French rituals of politeness, which apply in the Loire Valley just as much as they do everywhere else in the country.

Friends greeting each other with two or three kisses

When you are introduced to someone, it is correct to shake hands with them. In shops, you should be prepared to say *bonjour* to the assistant before asking for what you want, and then *merci* when you receive your change and finally *au revoir, bonne journée* (goodbye, have a nice day) when you depart. The usual greeting among friends of either sex is generally two or three kisses on the cheek.

Throughout the Loire Valley region, and particularly in the smaller communities, all efforts by English speakers to make enthusiastic use of their French, however limited, and to show a real interest in the area will be met with encouragement by the local people.

LOIRE VALLEY TIME

THE LOIRE VALLEY is one hour ahead of Greenwich Mean Time (GMT). France is in the same time zone as Germany, Italy, Spain and other western European countries.

Standard time differences between the Loire Valley and some major cities of the world are as follows: London: minus 1 hour; New York: minus 6 hours; Dallas: minus 7 hours; Los Angeles: minus 9 hours; Perth: plus 7 hours; Sydney: plus 9 hours; Auckland: plus 11 hours; and Tokyo: plus 8 hours. These can vary according to local summer alterations to the time.

The French use the 24-hour clock (they do not use the am and pm system): after midday, just continue counting 13, 14 and so on to provide the 24-hour clock time. For example, 1pm = 13:00.

CONVERSION CHART

Imperial to metric

To convert	Multiply by
Inches to centimetres	2.54
Feet to metres	0.3
Yards to metres	0.91
Miles to kilometres	1.6
Ounces to grams	28
Pounds to kilograms	0.45
Pints to litres	0.6
Gallons to litres	4.5

Metric to imperial

To convert	Multiply by
Centimetres to inches	0.4
Metres to feet	3.3
Metres to yards	1.09
Kilometres to miles	0.6
Grams to ounces	0.04
Kilograms to pounds	2.2
Litres to pints	1.8
Litres to gallons	0.22

French two-pin electrical plug

ELECTRICAL ADAPTORS

THE VOLTAGE in France is 220 volts. The plugs on French electrical appliances have two small round pins; the heavier-duty appliances have two large round pins. Some up-market hotels offer built-in adaptors for shavers only.

Multi-adaptors, which are useful because they have both large and small pins, can be bought at most airports before departure. Standard adaptors can be purchased from most department stores.

RELIGIOUS SERVICES

ALTHOUGH THE MAJOR religion in the region is Catholicism, the Loire Valley also has many Protestant churches, and some Jewish synagogues and Islamic mosques, particularly in the larger towns. These reflect the religious diversity of modern French society.

DIRECTORY

CUSTOMS INFORMATION

Paris
Centre des Renseignements des Douanes,
23 bis rue de l'Université.
[40 24 65 10.

Orléans
Centre de Dédouanement,
Rte N20, Saran.
[38 73 48 75.

Nantes
Renseignements Douaniers,
15 quai Ernest Renaud.
[40 73 52 15.

STUDENT INFORMATION

Orléans
CRIJ Région Centre,
5 blvd de Verdun.
[38 78 91 78.

Nantes
CRIJ des Pays de la Loire,
28 rue du Calvaire.
[51 72 94 50.

YOUTH HOSTELS

Angers
Centre D'Accueil du Lac de Maine,
49 av du Lac de Maine.
[41 22 32 10.

Bourges
Auberge de Jeunesse
22 rue Henri Sellier.
[48 24 58 09.

Le Mans
Auberge de Jeunesse
23 rue Maupertuis.
[43 81 27 55.

Nantes
Résidence Sonacotra
Julienne David,
85 pl Menetrier.
[40 93 28 30.

Orléans
14 fbg Madeleine.
[38 62 45 75.

Tours
Parc Grandmont,
Av d'Arsonval.
[47 25 14 45.

PLACES OF WORSHIP

Catholic
La Cathédrale St-Etienne,
Pl de la Cathédrale,
Bourges.

La Cathédrale Notre-Dame,
Pl de la Cathédrale,
Chartres.

La Cathédrale St-Gatien,
Pl de la Cathédrale,
Tours.

La Cathédrale St-Pierre-et-
St-Paul,
Pl St-Pierre,
Nantes.

Protestant
Temple Protestant,
5–7 rue du Musée,
Angers.
[41 48 06 07.

Eglise Protestante,
21 rue de Cheverus,
Laval.
[43 53 74 90.

Jewish
Synagogue,
4–6 bd Paixhans,
Le Mans.

Synagogue,
14 rue Robert de
Courtenay,
Orléans.
[38 62 16 62.

Islamic
Mosquée,
Av Rembrandt,
Le Mans.

Grande Mosquée de Tours,
18 rue Lobin, Tours.
[47 66 38 03.

Personal Security and Health

O N THE WHOLE, the Loire Valley is a safe place for visitors: take normal precautions, such as keeping an eye on your possessions at all times, and avoid isolated and unlit urban areas at night. If you fall ill during your stay, pharmacies are an excellent source of advice. Consular offices can offer help and advice in an emergency. In the case of a serious medical problem, call the emergency services.

Policeman   **Fireman**

PERSONAL PROPERTY

I N BIG CITIES, try not to carry conspicuous valuables with you and only take as much cash as you think you will need. Traveller's cheques are the safest method of carrying large sums of money. You should always make sure you are covered by an adequate insurance policy.

In major towns, the multistorey car parks are kept under surveillance by video cameras. Parking there will reduce the threat of car crime and avoid the greater risk of parking in an illegal space and being towed away to a police pound.

In the event of a theft, go to the nearest police station, or *gendarmerie*, with your passport or other identity papers (and vehicle registration and insurance documents, if relevant). The report process (a *PV* or *procès-verbal*) may take time, but you will need a full police statement for any insurance claim. If your passport is stolen, contact the police and your nearest consulate.

Ambulance

Fire engine

Police car

PERSONAL SAFETY

V IOLENT CRIME is rare in the Loire Valley, although random incidents are sometimes reported. If travelling late at night, it is a good idea, especially for women, to remain within busy, well-lit areas and to be careful about talking to, or accompanying, strangers. If you are involved in a dispute or car accident, avoid confrontation. In potentially difficult situations, try to stay calm and speak French if you can, as your efforts may diffuse the situation.

LEGAL ASSISTANCE

I F YOUR INSURANCE policy is comprehensive, including a service in France such as Europ Assistance or Mondial Assistance, they will be able to help with legal advice on claims, such as accident procedure. If not, you should call your nearest consulate office and ask their advice.

INTERPRETERS

I F YOU REQUIRE an interpreter, telephone the Société Française des Traducteurs Professionels or contact them via Minitel *(see p239)*.

BEACH AND RIVER SAFETY

M OST OF THE BEACHES on the Atlantic coast are guarded in the summer by lifeguards *(sauvetuers)*. There are a number of good family beaches, where bathing is not generally dangerous. However, a system of coloured flags tells bathers whether it is safe to swim. Green flags mean that bathing is permitted and is safe. Orange flags warn that bathing may be dangerous and usually only part of the beach is guarded. The guarded area is marked out by flags, beyond which you should not swim. Very dangerous conditions (high waves, shifting sands and strong undercurrents) are denoted by red flags, which mean that any bathing is strictly forbidden. Many of the region's beaches also display the blue flags used throughout the European Union as a sign of cleanliness.

A green flag shows the sea is safe for bathers

The River Loire and its tributaries also tempt summer bathers, but beware of the treacherous currents and shifting sands. It is safest to stick to established bathing areas.

MEDICAL TREATMENT

ALL EUROPEAN UNION nationals are entitled to French social security coverage, but treatment must be paid for in cash and hospital rates vary. Reimbursements may be claimed if you have obtained an E111 form from a post office in the UK before leaving. The claims process can be lengthy, so it is best to purchase your own insurance. The law obliges non-EU nationals to carry medical insurance, taken out in the visitor's home country before departure. In case of medical emergencies, call the SAMU (ambulance) or the *Sapeurs Pompiers* (fire service), who offer a first aid and ambulance service.

French pharmacists are able to diagnose minor health problems and to suggest appropriate treatment. Pharmacies can be recognized by the green cross sign outside their shops.

PUBLIC TOILETS IN THE LOIRE VALLEY

Modern automatic toilets are now found in many towns in the Loire Valley. Do not let children under ten use these alone as the automatic cleaning function can be dangerous.

Even when using the toilets in cafés or restaurants where you are a customer, you should take some change with you, as there is often a small charge or you may be expected to leave a tip for the cleaner. Traditional *pissoirs* and keyhole toilets, still found in more rural areas, are not always very clean. Toilet facilities are provided on the *autoroute* at drive-in rest areas every 20 km (12 miles).

1 Put the amount indicated in the slot.

2 Press the button to open the sliding door.

3 The light shows vacant or engaged.

DIRECTORY

EMERGENCY NUMBERS

Ambulance (SAMU)
📞 15.

Fire (Sapeurs Pompiers)
📞 18.

Police (Gendarmerie)
📞 17.

TRANSLATION SERVICES

Société Française des Traducteurs Professionels
📞 Minitel 3616 SFTRAD.
Paris 📞 48 78 43 32.

HOSPITAL EMERGENCIES

Angers
Centre Hospitalier,
4 rue Larrey.
📞 41 35 36 37.

Bourges
Centre Hospitalier,
34 rue Gambon.
📞 48 68 40 00.

Le Mans
Centre Hospitalier du Mans,
194 avenue Rubillard.
📞 43 43 43 43.

Nantes
Centre Hospitalier,
place Alexis Ricordeau.
📞 40 08 33 33.

Orléans
Centre Hospitalier Régional,
1 rue Porte Madeleine.
📞 38 51 44 44.

Tours
Hôpital Bretonneau,
2 boulevard Tonnelé.
📞 47 47 47 47.

CONSULATES AND EMBASSIES

Australia
4 rue Jean Ray, 75015 Paris.
📞 40 59 33 00.

Canada
35 av Montaigne,
75008 Paris.
📞 44 43 29 00.

UK
16 rue d'Anjou, 75008 Paris.
📞 42 66 91 42.

Banking and Local Currency

IN THE LOIRE VALLEY, as elsewhere in France, the banks, along with American Express and Thomas Cook, usually offer the best rates of exchange. Privately-owned *bureaux de change* are common in tourist areas, especially around the châteaux, but tend to have more variable rates. Take care to check the commission and minimum charges before you complete a transaction. Travellers' cheques are the safest form of money. Credit cards and some ATM (automatic teller machine) cards can be used to withdraw money, but you may be charged by the card issuer for this service.

BANKING HOURS

BANKS IN BIG TOWNS are usually open from 9am to noon and from 2 to 6pm, Tuesday to Saturday. They often close on Mondays. Over public holiday weekends, they may be shut from Friday noon until Tuesday morning. Opening hours can be more limited in smaller towns.

USING BANKS

THERE IS NO LIMIT to the amount of money you may bring into France, but if you want to take more than F50,000 back to the UK, you should declare it on arrival. Most banks have a *bureau de change*, offering the best exchange rates but also charging commission. Even in more remote areas, many banks now have ATMs that take cards in the Visa/Carte Bleue or Eurocard/MasterCard groups, as well as some cashpoint cards. To take out money, you need to tap in a PIN (Personal Identification Number). The ATMs' instructions are given in French, English and German.

It is also possible to withdraw up to F2,000 each day on Visa or MasterCard at the foreign counter of any bank where the Visa or MasterCard sign is displayed. You will need your passport to make any transaction over a bank counter in France.

Keypad to check your PIN

TRAVELLER'S CHEQUES AND CREDIT CARDS

TRAVELLER'S CHEQUES can be obtained from American Express, Thomas Cook or your bank, building society or some post offices. American Express cheques are widely accepted in France, and Amex offices exchange them without charging commission.

In France, Visa/Carte Bleue and Eurocard/MasterCard are the most common credit cards, while American Express cards are not always accepted.

French credit and debit cards are now smart cards *(cartes à puce)*. Retailers are equipped with machines that read smart cards and older magnetic strips. If your card cannot be read in the smart card slot, you will be told you have a *puce morte*. Ask the cashier to put the card through the *bande magnétique* (magnetic reader). You may also have to tap in your PIN and press the green key *(validez)* on a small keypad.

EUROCHEQUES

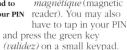

Eurocheque logo

EUROCHEQUES, available from most banks, act as normal cheques and can be written in any European currency. Banks and post offices can also cash them. In France, the limit on each cheque is F1,400 but several can be written to cover a larger sum. Cheques are guaranteed by a Eurocheque card, for which you pay an annual fee.

CURRENCY

THE FRENCH UNIT of currency is the franc. It is generally indicated by the letter F or by FF, to distinguish it from the Belgian franc and the Swiss franc, written BEF and FS respectively. There are 100 centimes to the franc, but their value is so insignificant that 1-centime coins are no longer in circulation. The amount of centimes in a price is separated from the amount of francs by a comma rather than by a decimal point.

Banknotes
French banknotes come in F20, F50, F100, F200 and F500 denominations. They increase in size in proportion to their value. Although the F50 and F500 note shown here are both new designs, the old notes will remain legal tender for the next decade.

F500 note

F200 note

F100 note

F20 note

F50 note

Coins
Coins (shown here actual size) come in the following denominations: 5, 10, 20 and 50 centimes; F1, F2, F5, F10 and F20. The 5-, 10- and 20-centime coins are brass. The 50-centime, F1, F2 and F5 coins are silver-alloy.

F20

F10

F5

F2

F1

50 centimes

20 centimes

10 centimes

5 centimes

Communications

Sign for public telephone

FRENCH TELECOMMUNICATIONS are among the most advanced in the world. The national agency is France Télécom, while postal services are run by La Poste. Public telephones are well distributed throughout the Loire Valley. Most take a telephone card *(télécarte)*, which can be purchased at local shops. Post offices, or *bureaux de postes*, are identified by the blue-on-yellow La Poste sign. Road signs may still say PTT, as La Poste was formerly known. Foreign newspapers are available in most large towns, and some TV channels broadcast English-language programmes.

Mail boxes throughout France are a distinctive yellow

USING A PHONECARD TELEPHONE

1 Lift the receiver and wait for the dialling tone.

2 Insert the *télécarte* with the arrow side facing up.

3 The screen displays the number of units still available, then gives you instructions to key in the phone number.

4 Key in the phone number and wait to be connected.

5 If you want to make another call, do not replace the receiver: simply press the green follow-on call button.

6 Replace the receiver after the call. When card re-emerges, remove it.

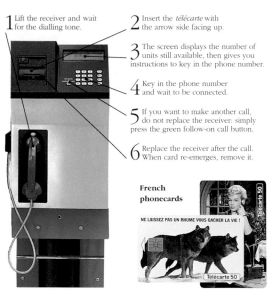

French phonecards

NE LAISSEZ PAS UN RHUME VOUS GACHER LA VIE !

Télécarte 50

SENDING A LETTER

POSTAGE STAMPS *(timbres)* are sold at La Poste singly or in *carnets* of ten. Common postage stamps are also sold at tobacconists. There are eight different price zones for international mail.

Post office hours vary. The minimum hours are around 9am to 5pm from Monday to Friday with a two-hour lunch break from noon to 2pm. On Saturdays they are open from 9am until noon. In larger towns, the main post office may remain open on weekdays from 8am until 7pm.

Letters and parcels can be sent worldwide. Letters are dropped into yellow mail boxes, which often have three slots – one for the town you are in; one for the surrounding *département* (the Loire Valley is divided into eleven *départements*, each with its own postcode); and one for other destinations *(autres destinations)*.

For a small collection fee, you can also receive or send mail care of post offices in France *(poste restante)*. The sender should write the recipient's name in block letters, followed by "Poste Restante", then the postcode and the name of the town to which the letter is to be sent.

TELEPHONING IN FRANCE

NEARLY ALL French public phone boxes now take telephone cards *(télécartes)*. A few are still coin-operated, taking F1, F2, F5 and F10 coins. Telephone cards, sold in units of either 50 or 120, can be bought at post offices, tobacconists and some newsagents. Pay-phones in cafés are coin-operated and take a minimum charge of F2.

The Home Direct call service, or *pays direct*, enables you to make a call via the operator in your country, paying by telephone chargecard, credit card or by reversing the charges. In some cases, you

can also call a third country (with AT&T, for example). Reverse charge calls are known as *PCV*.

Most phone boxes are able to receive incoming calls. The box telephone number is displayed above the telephone unit. Main post offices offer long distance calling facilities from booths, or *cabines*. You pay at the counter after the call. This system is considerably cheaper than making an international call from a hotel, as hotels tend to add a large surcharge to the bill. The Minitel electronic telephone directory can be used free in post offices (*see* How to Key in to Minitel).

Standard issue stamps and a small book of stamps called a *carnet*

OTHER SERVICES

At POST OFFICES you can also consult telephone directories *(annuaires)*, cash Eurocheques and send or receive money orders *(mandats)*. You can also make use of fax and telex services.

A huge amount of information is available when you use the Minitel electronic directory, which is rapidly replacing paper directories. The service is free of charge and can be found at many post offices.

TELEVISION AND RADIO

The subscription channel Canal+ broadcasts CBS American evening news at 7am daily. Sky News and CNN are available in many hotels. The Franco-German channel ARTE broadcasts programmes and films from all over the world, often in the original language with French subtitles.

The BBC monthly magazine *Worldwide* gives the details for the BBC World Service.

HOW TO KEY IN TO MINITEL

Minitel provides a vast range of services through a screen and keyboard connected to the telephone line.

To use the system, press the telephone symbol and enter the Minitel number and code. For directory information, press the telephone symbol and key in 11. When beeping starts, press *Connexion/Fin*. Specify the service or name of supplier required. Enter town or area and press *Envoi* to start. To disconnect, press *Veille* or *Connexion/Fin*. Charges payable are then displayed on the screen.

THE DÉPARTEMENTS OF THE LOIRE VALLEY

France is divided into 96 *départements*. Each *département* has its own two-digit number, and this is the first number of the postcode for any address in the *département*. If the postcode has three zeros at the end, the address lies within the *département's* main town.

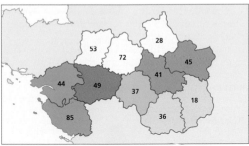

Département	Postcode	Main Town
Cher	18	Bourges
Eure-et-Loir	28	Chartres
Indre	36	Châteauroux
Indre-et-Loire	37	Tours
Loir-et-Cher	41	Blois
Loire-Atlantique	44	Nantes
Loiret	45	Orléans
Maine-et-Loire	49	Angers
Mayenne	53	Laval
Sarthe	72	Le Mans
Vendée	85	La Roche-sur-Yon

FOREIGN NEWSPAPERS

In MOST MAIN towns, English-language newspapers such as the *International Herald Tribune*, the *Guardian* and the *Financial Times* are often available for sale on the day of issue. Most other English newspapers as well as Swiss, Italian, German and Spanish titles are sold on the day of publication during the summer months and the on day after issue in the low season. The *European* is published on Fridays.

A range of the newspapers available in the Loire Valley

USEFUL DIALLING CODES

- From 18 **October 1996**, all French numbers will need ten rather than eight digits. For the northwest (including the Loire Valley) prefix the number with 02; Ile de France: 01; northeast: 03; southeast: 04; southwest: 05.
- To **call France**, dial: from the UK: 00 33; from Australia: 00 11 33. Omit the initial 0 of the French area code.
- For **operator service**, dial 13.
- For **international information**, dial: Germany: 16 12; other European countries: 16 13; rest of world: 16 14.
- For **Home Direct** calls, dial 19, then dial 00.
- To make direct **international calls**, dial 00 first.
- The **country codes** are: Australia, 61; Canada and USA, 1; Eire, 353; New Zealand, 64; UK, 44.

TRAVEL INFORMATION

FORMING A BROAD BAND about 110 km (70 miles) south of Paris and stretching from the centre of France in the east to the Atlantic coast in the west, the Loire Valley is relatively well served by international motorway and rail links. The city of Nantes has an international airport with

Road sign to Nantes airport

flights serving many major European cities. For travelling across the region, the TGV (see pp242–4) is swift, and the motorail journey from Paris to Nantes, taking 3 hours, 40 minutes, is effortless and avoids motorway tolls. The motorways are excellent but can become crowded in mid-summer.

ARRIVING BY AIR

NANTES-ATLANTIQUE airport has flights to most major European and Mediterranean cities, and Montreal and Toronto. There are restaurants, bars, newsagents and a gift shop at the terminal, as well as a bank with a *bureau de change* (open during normal banking hours, *see p236*), and an information desk, which will make hotel reservations if necessary.

Parents travelling with young children and baggage can ask for help from airport staff, and there are fully equipped baby-changing facilities. Wheelchair access around the building is good, and assistance getting on and off the plane is available for disabled passengers .

Taxis to the town centre cost around F120 (more at night and on Sundays). Airport buses to the centre are timed to coincide with most flight arrivals. Car-hire companies at the airport are Avis, Budget, Citer, Eurodollar, Europcar, Eurorent and Hertz.

AIRLINE DETAILS

AIR CLUB (handled by the travel agency Nouvelles Fontières) and Air Transat (book through travel agents) operate charter flights from Nantes to Canada (Montreal on Tuesdays and Thursdays; Toronto on Tuesdays and Fridays). From the UK, Brit Air flies twice daily from London Gatwick to Nantes,

with an extra flight per day in July and August. Air Inter has six domestic flights per day from Paris to Nantes.

From other international departure points to Nantes, it is necessary to change planes in Paris. Passengers transferring in Paris or London to a connecting flight can ask to have their baggage sent on to Nantes when they check in. There are no direct flights to France from Australia or New Zealand, but Qantas Airways connects with British Airways and Air France in London.

Airport trolley slot machine

FARES AND DEALS

AIRLINE FARES to Nantes are at their highest over the Easter period and in the peak season in July and August. Different airlines, however, may have slightly different peak periods, so check with the airlines or an agent to find out which fares will apply when you travel.

For flights only, Advance Purchase Excursion fares (APEX) are relatively inexpensive but they have to be booked well in advance. They cannot be changed or cancelled without a penalty and contain minimum and maximum stay clauses. Note that children often travel

The interior of Nantes-Atlantique Airport

more cheaply than adults. The price of a standard fare ticket is often cheaper if your visit includes at least one Saturday overnight stay.

Competition between the airlines means that there are some very attractive deals on offer, both for charter and regular scheduled flights. It is worth taking the time to look around for the best deals.

If you book a cheap deal with a discount agent, check that the agent belongs to a recognized regulatory body. This may guarantee that you will get a refund if the agent should cease trading. Do not part with the full fare until you have seen the ticket. Check with the relevant airline to ensure that your seat has been confirmed, and reconfirm your return journey.

FLY-DRIVE AND FLY-RAIL PACKAGE HOLIDAYS

AIR FRANCE and the French railways offer combined fares for flight and train. You fly into Paris and then catch the train south. Very good deals are available to Angers, Nantes and Tours. There are also companies offering tailor-made package holidays in the Loire Valley with flight, car hire and accommodation all included in the cost.

A Boeing 737 jet belonging to the national airline, Air France

FLIGHT TIMES TO NANTES

ON LONG-HAUL flights you will need to change planes in Paris or London. Approximate flight times between major cities are as follows:

London: 1 hour, 25 minutes.
Paris: 50 minutes.
Toronto: 7 hours, 30 minutes.

SAFETY IN THE AIR

PASSENGERS should make sure that their baggage is securely fastened and tagged and not left unattended at the airport. Never look after or check in baggage for somebody else. You are likely to be asked whether

you are carrying any electrical goods, and it is advisable to keep these to a minimum.

If you are travelling with very young children, advise the airline as soon as possible in order to reserve a "skycot". If a child is not to occupy a separate seat, a special seat belt should be provided.

Pregnant women should check in advance with the airline to ensure they will be allowed to fly: most airlines have a cut-off date of 36 weeks. Between 28 and 36 weeks it is necessary to have a letter from your doctor stating that you are healthy enough to travel, and giving your estimated delivery date.

You should inform the airline in advance if you have any specific dietary needs.

DIRECTORY

AIRPORT INFORMATION

Nantes-Atlantique Airport
📞 40 84 80 00.
Distance to town:
12 km (8 miles).
Transport to town:
bus, taxi.

AIRLINE TELEPHONE NUMBERS

For dialling codes for numbers in France see pp238–9.

Air Canada
UK 📞 (0181) 759 2636.
Paris 📞 44 55 52 00.

Air France
UK 📞 (0181) 742 6600.
Paris 📞 44 08 22 22.

Air Inter
Paris 📞 47 23 59 58.

Air UK
UK 📞 (0181) 745 7321.
Paris 📞 44 56 18 14.

Brit Air
UK 📞 (01293) 502 044.
France 📞 98 62 10 22.

British Airways
UK 📞 (0181) 759 2525.
France 📞 05 12 51 25.

Delta
UK 📞 (0800) 414 767.
Paris 📞 47 68 92 92.

Qantas Airways
UK 📞 (0345) 747 767.
Paris 📞 44 55 52 00.

DISCOUNT TRAVEL AGENCIES

Loire Valley
Nouvelles Frontières
Angers 📞 41 88 41 41.
Bourges 📞 48 24 54 07.
Le Mans 📞 43 84 42 96.
Nantes 📞 40 20 24 61.
Orléans 📞 38 53 75 00.
Tours 📞 47 64 64 50.

UK
Campus Travel
52 Grosvenor Gardens,
London
SW1W OAG.
📞 (0171) 730 3402.

Nouvelles Frontières
11 Blenheim Street,
London
W1Y 9LE.
📞 (0171) 629 7772.

TAILOR-MADE PACKAGE HOLIDAYS

Air France Holidays
Gable House, 18–24,
Turnham Green Terrace,
London
W4 1RF.
📞 (0181) 742 3377.

Allez France Holidays
27 West Street,
Storrington
RH20 4DZ.
📞 (01903) 742 345.

Cresta Holidays
Tabley Court, Victoria
Street,
Altringham,
Cheshire.
WA14 1EZ
📞 (0161) 927 7000.

Getting Around by Train

TRAVELLING TO THE LOIRE VALLEY by train is fast and efficient. The French state railway, the Société Nationale des Chemins de Fer Français (SNCF), is one of Europe's best equipped and most comfortable. The train journey from Paris to Nantes or to Tours is very quick – the TGV *(Train à Grande Vitesse)* takes only 2 hours and 10 minutes to Nantes, and 75 minutes to Tours. With the Eurostar high-speed service running through the Channel Tunnel, travel to the Loire Valley from the UK is faster than before.

Automatic ticket machine

MAIN ROUTES

THE MAIN TRAIN routes to the Loire Valley from Northern Europe pass through Paris. The TGV network links the port of Calais with Paris Gare du Nord station. From there, passengers must transfer to Gare Montparnasse, before continuing their journey on the TGV Atlantique to the main towns in the Loire region. Corail express trains to Nantes also leave from Gare Montparnasse, while Corail express trains to all other Loire Valley destinations leave from Gare d'Austerlitz. Tickets from London to all the Loire Valley towns, travelling via the Eurostar, hovercraft or ferry, are available from British Rail International and SNCF offices. From southern Europe, trains run to Nantes from Madrid in Spain (with a journey time of 16 hours) and Milan in Italy (with a journey time of 14 hours, 30 minutes).

Within the Loire Valley, the route along the River Loire via Nantes, Angers and Orléans is popular, so it is best to reserve tickets in advance on this and other *Grandes Lignes*.

BOOKING IN THE UK

FRENCH RAILWAYS have UK postal and telephone contacts. Reservations made in the UK may be difficult to change in France, due to different computer booking systems. If you need to alter your return date you may have to pay for another reservation or, with Motorail, you will have to buy another ticket and then claim a refund on your return.

BOOKING IN FRANCE

TICKET COUNTERS at all the stations are computerized. There are also automatic ticket and reservation machines (with English instructions) on the concourse of main stations. If you have a credit card with a PIN, you can check times and fares and make reservations using the Minitel system *(see p239)*. For travel by TGV, a ticket reservation is necessary, but can be made as little as five minutes before the train leaves. Ticket prices for all trains rise considerably at peak times, and reservations are compulsory during public holidays. The SNCF's international ticket and reservation system is connected by computer to most European travel agents and stations, allowing direct booking on services throughout Europe.

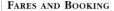

SNCF logo

FARES AND BOOKING

TICKETS BOOKED in France using as SNCF discount card are subject to supplements specified by the *calendrier voyageurs*, a red, white and blue division of the calendar. Red days are peak-time travel and blue is for the cheapest services. Many of the discounts offered (up to 60 per cent) are available on "blue" days only.

SNCF issues a *carte vermeil* for the over-60s, a *carte couple* for couples sharing an address, and a *carte Kiwi* for up to four people travelling with a child. There are also Carissimo fares available for those under 26, and Joker fares for journeys booked in advance and holiday return trips of more than 1,000 km (600 miles). Ask for details at **SNCF**.

Rail passes bought outside the country for use in France include Eurodomino tickets, which allow three, five or ten days' travel within a month. Eurotrain passes, for those under 26, last two months.

Specialist agencies, such as **Travel Cuts**, offer Inter-Rail cards, which allow a month's unlimited travel in France and 25 other European countries, excluding the country in which the pass is bought.

The ticket office at Chartres railway station

TIMES AND PENALTIES

TIMETABLES change twice a year, and leaflets for main routes are free. Trains in France are almost always on schedule. You must time-punch (composter) your ticket in the orange machine at the platform entrance or pay a penalty on the train

MOTORAIL

MOTORAIL SERVICES (trains autos) carry cars, motor-bikes and passengers to Paris overnight from Bologna or Milan in Italy (once or twice a week in the summer months only, with a journey time of 14 hours, 30 minutes). There are also daily services from Madrid in Spain (the journey takes 16 hours) and in the summer only from Düsseldorf (16 hours, 30 minutes) via Frankfurt (journey takes 13 hours). From Paris, a motorail service runs to Nantes about once a week, except in the summer, when there is one train per day from Gare Montparnasse; the journey takes 3 hours and 40 minutes. Information and bookings are available via French Railways in London or from any SNCF station in France. There are no motorail connections with the UK, although the "Le Shuttle" service carries cars and their passengers from Folkestone to Calais through the Channel Tunnel.

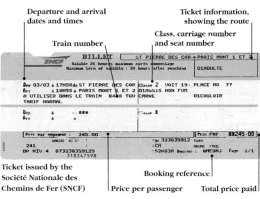

Departure and arrival dates and times

Train number

Ticket information, showing the route

Class, carriage number and seat number

Ticket issued by the Société Nationale des Chemins de Fer (SNCF)

Booking reference

Price per passenger

Total price paid

TGV RAIL SERVICE

Trains à Grande Vitesse, or high-speed trains, travel at up to 300 km/h (185 mph). Their speed and comfort make them relatively expensive. You must always reserve a seat in advance, which costs between F40 and F140, depending on your destination and on the time and date of your journey.

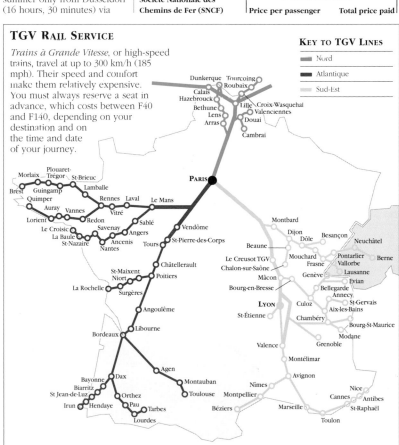

KEY TO TGV LINES

Nord
Atlantique
Sud-Est

A high-speed TGV arriving at the station in Tours

MAIN LINE STATIONS

Nantes has two main line stations, Gare Sud and Gare Nord, which are within walking distance of each other. All TGV services go to Gare Sud, near the new Palais des Congrès. All other trains go to Gare Nord.

In Tours, most trains arrive at the suburban station of St-Pierre-des-Corps, from which a shuttle train *(navette)* takes passengers on to the town centre station in ten minutes.

A similar shuttle service operates in Orléans, where many main line trains arrive at Les Aubrais station, 3 km (2 miles) outside the town centre. In both cases, the price of the shuttle is included in the cost of the ticket, and shuttles are timed so that they coincide with main line services. The departure time given on your ticket is the time at which the shuttle leaves the town centre and not the main line station.

EUROSTAR

Eurostar's striking yellow-and-white trains currently run 15 services per day between London's Waterloo International Station and the Gare du Nord in Paris. Each train has first- and second-class compartments, with the option of a waiter-service meal in first class. You can also buy refreshments from a trolley service or in the buffet car. The journey takes 3 hours. You must book tickets in

advance and check in at least 20 minutes before the departure time. To book, contact French Railways' Rail Shop or ring the Eurostar bookings line.

LE SHUTTLE

Le shuttle carries cars and coaches and their passengers through the Channel Tunnel in 35 minutes. Tickets can be bought in advance from travel agents or by calling the Le Shuttle Customer Service Centre, but it is also possible to purchase a ticket for the next train when you arrive at the terminals in Folkestone or Calais. There are up to four trains an hour during peak times in the summer, and a minimum of one an hour at night. The terminals at each end have a range of restaurants and duty-free shops. Before boarding Le Shuttle you go through passport and customs controls for both countries. This means you drive straight onto the motorway when you arrive at the other side.

The station forecourt in Tours

Getting Around by Road

FRANCE IS A MOTORIST'S PARADISE, and the main route to the Loire Valley is via an excellent, if expensive, autoroute (motorway) network. There are many beautiful roads in the Loire region, particularly those running along the banks of the rivers. Popular routes, especially the Atlantic coastal roads and the roads leading between the châteaux, can be busy in high season, but are clearer at other times of year.

WHAT TO TAKE

IF YOU ARE TAKING your own car to the Loire Valley, it is advisable to obtain a green card (a free extension of an existing policy from some insurers). Without it you only have third-party coverage in France, regardless of whether you have comprehensive cover in your own country. The AA, RAC and Europ Assistance also offer special policies. It is compulsory to take the original registration document for your car, a current insurance certificate and a valid driving licence. You should also carry a passport or identification card. A sticker showing the country of registration should be displayed close to the rear number plate. The headlights of right-hand drive cars must be adjusted – kits for this are available at most ports. You must also carry a red warning triangle. Other recommended accessories include spare headlight bulbs, a first-aid kit and a fire extinguisher.

GETTING TO THE LOIRE VALLEY

UNLESS YOU ARE PREPARED TO take minor roads south from the western Channel ports through Normandy and Brittany, travellers from the UK and northern Europe will have difficulty avoiding Paris.

From Calais and Boulogne the A26 and A1 motorways lead to Paris and skirt the city centre, connecting with the southern A10 for Orléans, Blois and Tours and with the A11 for Chartres, Le Mans, Angers and Nantes. Avoid the Paris rush hour if you can.

From western Spain, take the A8 from San Sebastian to Bayonne, then the N10 to Bordeaux and the A10 to Tours and Orléans. From the eastern Spanish coast you can reach Bordeaux on the A7 and A61 and A62 passing via Narbonne and Toulouse. From Italy take the A7 and A8 or the A43 to Lyon, which is where the A72 and A71 head north to Bourges and Orléans. From anywhere in Germany, the quickest way to get to the Loire Valley is via Paris.

In high season, the motorways get crowded and, if you have time, it may be worth taking more minor (and more attractive) roads. Try not to travel over the first and last weekends in July and August, when thousands of French and foreign holiday-makers are on the roads.

USING THE AUTOROUTE TOLL

When you join an autoroute, take a ticket from the machine. This identifies your starting point on the autoroute. You do not pay until you reach an exit tollbooth. Charges are made according to the distance travelled and the type of vehicle.

Motorway Sign
These signs indicate the name and distance to the next tollbooth. They are usually blue and white; some show the various tariff rates for cars, motorbikes, caravans and large trucks.

Tollbooth with Attendant
When you hand in your ticket at a staffed tollbooth, the attendant tells you the cost of your journey (péage) on the autoroute and the price will be displayed. You can pay with coins, notes, credit cards or with a Eurocheque in French francs. A receipt is issued on request.

Automatic Machine
On reaching the exit tollbooth, insert your ticket into the machine and the price of your journey will be displayed in French francs. You can pay either with coins or by credit card. The machine will give change and can issue a receipt.

CAR HIRE

IT IS WORTH contacting a number of car-hire firms before you go, as there are often special offers if you pre-pay. In France, **Rent-a-Car** is good value. Other options include Fly-drive packages, and the train and car-hire deals from the SNCF, with collection from main stations.

For more than three weeks, the best option may be TT Leasing, the short-term purchase and buy back service offered by Citroën, Peugeot and Renault.

Three of the most widely available car-hire firms in the Loire Valley

RULES OF THE ROAD

REMEMBER to drive on the right. The *priorité à droite* rule also applies, which means that you must give way to any vehicle coming out of a side turning on the right, unless signposting indicates otherwise. However, the *priorité à droite* rule no longer applies at roundabouts, so give way to cars already on the roundabout.

Seat belts are compulsory for both front and back seats. Overtaking when there is a single solid centre line is heavily penalized.

Be aware that instant fines are issued for speeding and drink-driving.

No entry for any vehicles

One-way system

VOUS N'AVEZ PAS LA PRIORITÉ

Give way at roundabouts

Right of way ends, give way to right

One of the motorways in the Loire Valley region

FAST THROUGH ROUTES

THERE ARE three main motor-ways in the Loire Valley: the A11 *(L'Océane)* from Nantes to Chartres via Angers; the A10 *(L'Aquitaine)* from Tours to Orléans via Blois; and the A71 from Orléans to Bourges. There are police stations at motorway exits.

COUNTRY ROUTES

ONE OF THE pleasures of touring the Loire Valley is turning off the main routes onto small country roads. The RN and D (*Route Nationale* and *Départementale*) roads are often a good alternative to motorways.

The *Bison futé* ("crafty bison") signs will indicate alternative routes to avoid heavy traffic, and are par-ticularly helpful during the French holiday periods, which are appropriately known as the *grands départs*. The worst weekends are in mid-July, and at the beginning and end of August when the French holidays start and finish.

SPEED LIMITS

THE SPEED LIMITS in the Loire Valley are as follows:
• **Toll motorways** 130 km/h (80 mph) in dry weather, 110 km/h (68 mph) when it rains;
• **Dual carriageways and non-toll motorways** 110 km/h (68 mph), 100 km/h (60 mph) in the rain; 50 km/h (30 mph) in towns;
• **Other roads** 90 km/h (56 mph), 80 km/h (50 mph) in the rain;
• In **towns** 50 km/h (30 mph).
• In **fog**, 50 km/h (30 mph).

MAPS

THE BEST GENERAL maps of the Loire Valley are the yellow Michelin regional maps (No. 232 for the Pays de la Loire and No. 238 for Centre Val de Loire) at a scale of 1:200 000. **IGN** *(Institut Géographique National)* maps are more detailed.

Town plans are usually provided free by local tourist offices. In large towns you may need a more detailed map, and these are published by Michelin or **Plans-Guides Blay**. In the UK, **Stanfords** in London is famous for its range of maps.

Some of the available maps of the Loire Valley

PETROL

PETROL *(essence)* is relatively expensive in France, especially on autoroutes. Large supermarkets and hypermarkets sell petrol at a discount. A map issued by French Government Tourist Offices *(see p231)* indicates the cheaper petrol stations situated up to 2 km (just over a mile) from motorway exits.

Many petrol stations in France are self-service (*libre*

service), but if an attendant is on duty, it may be helpful to know that *faire le plein* means "to fill up the tank".

The grades of petrol to be found at most stations are premium *(super)*, regular *(essence)* and unleaded *(sans plomb)*. Diesel *(gas-oil)* is also common and is the cheapest fuel on sale in France. LPG gas is also available, often at stations on motorways.

An *borodateur*, or pay-and-display parking meter

PARKING REGULATIONS

Parking in the large towns is strictly regulated. If you are illegally parked, you may be towed away instantly to the police pound and face a fine of up to F1,000. Loire Valley towns now have pay-and-display machines *(borodateurs)*. Many towns and villages offer free parking from noon to 2pm – ticket machines will automatically allow for this.

Even if you are legally parked, it is possible that you will find yourself hemmed in when you return: the French usually honk their horns to attract the guilty party.

COACH AND BUS TRAVEL

Although the journey time to Nantes from London with Eurolines is almost 14 hours, compared to a 75-minute flight, the coach trip does cost less than half the price of the flight, which makes it good value. Coaches also depart from London to Tours from Tuesday to Friday, and there is a twice-weekly service to Nantes and Angers, changing at Tours. In the

summer, the services are more frequent.

Local bus services in the region are good. In towns it is usually possible to take a bus from a rail station to the centre, and in the country-side, services are quite frequent and reliable.

There are also bus links between major tourist sites, as well as day trips to several châteaux, which are organized locally by some private coach companies.

For more information on bus routes and timetables, contact local town halls or tourist information offices.

TAXIS

Prices vary from one part of the region to another. The charges, predictably, are highest in the busy tourist areas. The pick-up charge is usually around F15, and F4 or more for every kilometre. An extra charge will be made for any luggage. All taxis must use a meter *(compteur)*. Hailing a taxi is not custom-ary in the Loire Valley – you must go to a taxi rank or book by phone.

A taxi meter showing a 14-franc fare, or *prix à payer*

HITCHHIKING

Hitchhiking is legal in France, although officially frowned upon. You will be cautioned by the police if you are hitching on motorways. **Allostop** can put you in touch with cars travelling in France and Europe. After paying an initial fee, which is determined by the length of the trip, hitchhikers pay the driver a maximum of 20 cen-times per kilometre, which includes petrol costs and motorway tolls. The organ-ization keeps records of drivers' and hitchhikers' details for security reasons.

General Index

Acknowledgments

Dorling Kindersley would like to thank the following people whose assistance contributed to the preparation of this book.

Main Contributor
Jack Tresidder has been living and writing in France since 1992. A former newspaper journalist and theatre critic, he has edited and written books on art, cinema and photography as well as travel.

Editorial Consultant
Vivienne Menkes-Ivry.

Contributors and Consultants
Sara Black, Hannah Bolus, Patrick Delaforce, Thierry Guidet, Jane Tresidder.

Additional Photography
Tony Gervis, Jason Lowe, Clive Streeter.

Additional Illustrators
Robert Ashby, Graham Bell, Stephen Conlin, Toni Hargreaves, The Maltings Partnership, Lee Peters, Kevin Robinson, Tristan Spaargaren, Ed Stuart, Mike Taylor.

Cartography
Lovell Johns Ltd, Oxford, UK.

Technical Cartographic Assistance
David Murphy.

Proof Reader
Sam Merrell.

Indexer
Brian Amos.

Design and Editorial Assistance
Poppy Body, Sophie Boyack, John Grain, Richard Hansell, Matt Harris, Ciaran McIntyre, Emma O'Kelly, Zoe Ross, Alison Verity, Ingrid Vienings.

Special Assistance
Mme Barthez, Château d'Angers; M Sylvain Bellenger, Château de Blois; M Bertrand Bourdin, France Télécom; M Jean-Paul and Mme Caroline Chaslus, Abbaye de Fontevraud; M Joël Clavier, Conseil Général du Loiret; Mme Dominique Féquet, Office de Tourisme, Saumur; M Gaston Huet, Vouvray; Mme Pascale Humbert, Comité Départemental du Tourisme de l'Anjou; M Alain Irlandes and Mme Guylaine Fisher, Atelier Patrimoine, Tours; Mme Sylvie Lacroix and M Paul Lichtenberg, Comité Régional du Tourisme, Nantes; M André Margotin, Comité Départemental du Tourisme du Cher; M Jean Méré, Champigny-sur-Veude, Touraine; Mme Marie-France de Peyronnet, Route Jacques-Cœur, Berry; M R Pinard, l'Ecole des Ponts et Chaussées, Paris; Père Rocher, Abbaye de Solesmes; M Loïc Rousseau, Rédacteur, Vallée du Loir, M Pierre Saboureau, Lochois; M de Sauveboeuf, Le Plessis-Bourré; M Antoine Selosse and M Frank Artiges, Comité Départemental du Tourisme de Touraine; Mme Sabine Sévrin, Comité Régional du Tourisme, Orléans; Mme Tissier de Mallerais, Château de Talcy.

Photography Permissions
Dorling Kindersley would like to thank the following for their assistance and kind permission to photograph at their establishments: M François Bonneau, Conservateur, Château de Valençay; M Nicolas de Brissac, Château de Brissac; Caisse Nationale des Monuments Historiques et des Sites; Conseil Général du Cher; Marquis and Marquise de Contades, Château de Montgeoffroy; M Robert de Goulaine, Château de Goulaine; Mme Jallier, Office de Tourisme, Puy-du-Fou; Château de Montsoreau, Propriété du Département de Maine-et-Loire; Musée Historique et Archéologique de l'Orléanais; M Jean-Pierre Ramboz, Sacristain, Cathédrale de Tours; M Bernard Voisin, Conservateur, Château de Chenonceau and all other churches, museums, hotels, restaurants, shops and sights too numerous to thank individually.

Picture Credits
t = top; tl = top left; tc = top centre; tr = top right; cla = centre left above; ca = centre above; cra = centre right above; cl = centre left; c = centre; cr = centre right; clb = centre left below; cb = centre below; crb = centre right below; bl = bottom left; b = bottom; bc = bottom centre; br = bottom right; bla = bottom left above; bca = bottom centre above; bra = bottom right above; blb = bottom left below; bcb = bottom centre below; brb = bottom right below.

Every effort has been made to trace the copyright holders and we apologize in advance for any unintentional omissions. We would be pleased to insert the appropriate acknowledgments in any subsequent edition of this publication.

Works of art have been reproduced with the permission of the following copyright holders:
© ADAGP, Paris and DACS, London 1996: 77ca, 102tl, 150b; © DACS, London 1996: 48cla; © DACS, London and SPADEM, Paris: 104c

The publisher would like to thank the following individuals, companies and picture libraries for permission to reproduce their photographs:

Photo AKG, London: 48br, Bibliothèque Nationale 51crb; Catherine de Médicis anon 16th-century 109tl; Stefan Diller 49bl; Galleria dell' Accademia Saint Louis Bartolomeo Vivarini 1477 50cl; Louvre, Paris Charles VII Jean Fouquet c.1450 47tl; Musée Carnavalet, Paris George Sand Auguste Charpentier 1839 22c; National Gallery, Prague Self Portrait Henri Rousseau 1890 23b; Samuel H Kress Collection, National Gallery of Art Washington Diane de Poitiers in the Bath François Clouet c.1571 108cla; AllSport: Pascal Rondeau 59crb; Ancient Art and Architecture Collection: 22b, 50br, 51tl, 54tr, 55b; Archives du Loiret: 58clb.

Y Berrier: 77tl; Bibliothèque Nationale, Dijon: 149b; Bibliothèque Nationale, Paris: 52–3c; Bridgeman Art Library: Bibliothèque Nationale, Paris 47tc; British Library, London 46br, 52clb; Glasgow University Library 49br; Kress Collection, Washington DC 47tr; Kunsthistorisches Museum, Vienna 54br; Louvre, Paris François I Jean Clouet 44; Musée Condé, Chantilly 46bl, 135b; Prado, Madrid The Vision of St Hubert (detail) Jan Brueghal and Peter Paul Rubens 135t; Scottish National Potrait Gallery, Edinburgh Mary Queen of Scots in White Mourning François Clouet 23c; State Collection, France 54bl; Victoria

& Albert Museum, London 19tr, 54tl; Bridgeman Art Library/Giraudon: Château de Versailles 4br, 56cla, *Louis XIV as Jupiter Conquering La Fronde* anon 17th century 134tr; Galleria degli Uffizi, Florence 54cla; Louvre, Paris *Henry IV Receiving the Portrait of Marie de Médicis* Peter Paul Rubens 55tl, 74b; Musée des Antiquités Nationales, St-Germain 48cla; Musée des Beaux-Arts, Nantes *The Corn Sifters* Gustave Colbert 192b; Musée Condé, Chantilly 23t, 47bc, 47bl, 52tl, 93b, *Gabrielle d'Estrées in her Bath* French School 17th century 96c; Musée d'Orsay, Paris *Marcel Proust* Jacques-Emile Blanche c.1891–2 22tc; Musée de la Venerie, Senlis *Diane de Poitiers as Diana the Hunter* Fontainebleau School 16th century 55crb; British Museum 54–5; Michael Bussell's Photography: 29tl and br.

Cahiers Ciba: 77crb; Camera Press: 77tr; Cephas: Stuart Boreham 63bl; Hervé Champollion 63cra, 152tr; Mick Rock 27crb; Jean-Loup Charmet, Paris: 45b, 51b, 57cra; Château de Chamerolles: 137cbl; Château de Montgeoffroy: 71cl; Christie's Images, London: 53b; Bruce Coleman. NG Blake: 71bc; Denis Green 185cr; Udo Hirsch 185bl; Hans Reinhard 28br, 184bl; Uwe Walz 71bl, 71br, 185br; Comité Départemental du Tourisme du Cher: 25cra; Comité Régional du Tourisme, Nantes: 226t and b, JP Guyonneau 227tl, J Lesage 225tr; Comité du Tourisme de l'Anjou: 84b, JP Guyonneau 84c.

Diatotale: Château de Chenonceau 106t.

Editions Gaud: Château de Villandry *Jeune Infante* Pantoja de la Cruz 94tl; C Ferrath: 24br, 182tr, 183bl; ET Archive: 50bl, 100br; Mary Evans Picture Library: 9inset, 22tl, 53cl, 61inset, 151tl, 195inset, 227inset; Explorer: F Jalain 56cl.

Fédération Nationale de Logis de France: 197c; Fontenay-le-Comte Office de Tourisme: 230cl; Fontevraud Abbey: 41b, 87b; Fontgombault Abbey: Frère Eric Chevreau 147c.

Giraudon, Paris: 48tr and bl, 76tr and c, 135c; Archives Nationales, Paris 50tl; Bibliothèque Municipale, Laon 50–51cr; Château de Versailles *Louis XIII – Roi de France et de Navarre* after Vouet 47br, 56bl; Musée Antoine Lécuyer 134br; Musée Carnavalet, Paris 30tl, *Madame Dupin de Francueil* 109tr; Musée Condé, Chantilly 52br, 108b; Musée d'Histoire et des Guerres de Vendée, Cholet *Henri de la Rochejaquelein au Combat de Cholet le 17 Octobre 1793* Emile Boutigny 69cl; Musée de Tessé, Le Mans 166tr; Musée des Beaux-Arts, Blois 169crb; Musée du Vieux Château, Laval 160b (all rights reserved); Telarci 51cla; Victoria & Albert Museum, London 95tl; Gîtes de France: 199ct; La Goélette: JJ Derennes *The Three Graces* Charles-André Van Loo 106br.

Sonia Halliday Photographs: 53tl; Robert Harding: 37br; Paolo Koba 17br; Sheila Terry 102b; D Hodges: 167b; Kit Houghton: 38c; Hulton-Deutsch Collection: 46tr, 111tc, 134cla.

Image Bank: 34clb; David W Hamilton 32; Image de Marc 14b, 90c, 103b, 117b; Inventaire Général: Musée du Grand-Pressigny 48cla, 104c.

Jerrican/Berenguier: 11bl.

Frank Lane Picture Agency: R Wilmshurst 74t.

Mairie de Blois: J-Philippe Thibaut 42b; Mansell Collection: 30b; T Mezerette: 26t, 27tl; Musées d'Angers: 16t, 51clb, 57crb, 77cra; Collection Musée d'Art et d'Histoire de Cholet: 57b, Studio Golder, Cholet *Jacques Cathelineau* Anne-Louis Girodet-Trioson 1824 187b; Musée d'Arts Décoratifs et Musée du Cheval, Château de Saumur: 82cr; Musée des Beaux-Arts de Rennes: Louis Deschamps *Bal à la Cour des Valois* 109cbr, Musée des Beaux-Arts, Tours: *Vue Panoramique de Tours en 1787* Pierre-Antoine Demachy 8–9; P Boyer *Christ in the Olive Grove* Andrea Mantegna 114b; Musée de Blois: J Parker 126c, 127br; Musées de Bourges: Musée des Arts Décoratifs, Hôtel Lallemant *Concert Champêtre Instrumental* French-Italian School 150t; Musée Dobrée, Nantes: 55clb, 191tl; Collection Musée Estève © ADAGP/DACS: Dubout *Samsâra* Maurice Estève oil on canvas 150b; Courtesy, Museum of Fine Arts Boston: *Valley of the Petite Creuse* Claude Monet 1889 oil on canvas Bequest of David P Kimball in Memory of his Wife, Clara Bertram Kimball (© 1995. All rights reserved) 147br; Musée Historique d'Orléans: 48clb; Musées du Mans: 166c; Musée des Marais Salants, Batz-Loire-Atlantique: G Buron 179cr; Collection du Musée de la Marine de Loire, Châteauneuf-sur-Loire (Loiret): 33bc.

NHPA: Manfred Danegger 185cl; M Garwod: 79b; BA Janes 28tl; Helio & Van Ingen 29bl, 182tl; Andy Rouse 29c; R Sorensen and JB Olsen 184br; Robert Thompson 29tr; National Motor Museum, Beaulieu: 57tr.

Parc Naturel Régional du Poitevin: 185tr; John Parker: 1c, 18bc, 24bl, 25tl, 35crb, 36crb, 37cla and cl, 38bl, 51cra, 54clb, 55cra, 58tl, 63br, 72tl, 73c, 75bc, 87tc, 95bc, 106cla, 107cb, 110bl, 111br, 115c, 116tr, 117cr, 121br, 126cl, 127bl, 128tl, 130tl and bl, 131tc and bc, 132tl, cl, clb and br, 133tc, cr, bc and br, 144tr, 170br, 171br, 220cl; Photographers' Library: 28cla; 159b; 199b.

Réunion des Musées Nationaux, Paris: Château de Versailles *Château de Chambord* PD Martin (© Photo RMN) 134crb; Rex Features/Sipa Press: Riclafe 59tr, Tall 58bl; Route Historique Jacques Cœur: 16b; David Rowley: 83b.

The Science Museum/Science & Society Picture Library, London: 56br; Science Photo Library/CNES: 11tr; Spectrum Colour Library: 137cr; Tony Stone Worldwide: 63tl and tr, Charlie Waite 154t.

Telegraph Colour Library: Jean-Paul Nacivet: 24cla; TRH Pictures: 58tr.

Ville d'Amboise: Musée de la Poste 33cb; Roger-Viollet: 52bl, Bibliothèque Nationale 56clb, 137tr, Musée d'Orléans *Entrée de Jeanne d'Arc à Orléans* Jean-Jacques Scherrer 137br.

J Warminski: 79t; C Watier: 67t, 70b; Wildlife Matters: 94tr, 95c and br.

Front endpaper: all commissioned photography.

Jacket: all commissioned photography with the exception of Bruce Coleman: front bl.

Phrase Book

IN EMERGENCY

Help!	Au secours!	oh se**koor**
Stop!	Arrêtez!	aret-**ay**
Call a	Appelez un	apuh-**lay** uñ
doctor!	médecin!	med**sañ**
Call an	Appelez une	apuh-**lay** oon
ambulance!	ambulance!	oñboo-**loñs**
Call the	Appelez la	apuh-**lay** lah
police!	police!	poh-**lees**
Call the fire	Appelez les	apuh-lay leh
brigade!	pompiers!	poñ-**peeyay**
Where is	Où est le	oo ay luh
the nearest	téléphone le	tehleh**fon** luh
telephone?	plus proche?	ploo **prosh**
Where is the	Où est l'hôpital	oo ay l'**opee**tal luh
nearest hospital?	le plus proche?	ploo **prosh**

COMMUNICATION ESSENTIALS

Yes	Oui	wee
No	Non	noñ
Please	S'il vous plaît	seel voo **play**
Thank you	Merci	mer-**see**
Excuse me	Excusez-moi	exkoo-**zay** mwah
Hello	Bonjour	boñ**zhoor**
Goodbye	Au revoir	oh ruh-**vwar**
Good night	Bonsoir	boñ-**swar**
Morning	Le matin	ma**tañ**
Afternoon	L'après-midi	l'apreh-**meedee**
Evening	Le soir	swar
Yesterday	Hier	eeyehr
Today	Aujourd'hui	oh-zhoor-**dwee**
Tomorrow	Demain	duh**mañ**
Here	Ici	ee-**see**
There	Là	lah
What?	Quel, quelle?	kel, kel
When?	Quand?	koñ
Why?	Pourquoi?	poor-**kwah**
Where?	Où?	oo

USEFUL PHRASES

How are	Comment	kom-moñ
you?	allez-vous?	tal**ay** voo
Very well,	Très bien,	treh byañ,
thank you.	merci.	mer-**see**
Pleased to	Enchanté de	oñshoñ-**tay** duh
meet you.	faire votre	fehr votr
	connaissance.	kon-ay-**sans**
See you soon.	A bientôt.	Ah byañ-**toh**
That's fine.	Voilà qui est	vwalah kee ay
	parfait	par**fay**
Where is/are...?	Où est/sont...?	oo ay/soñ
How far	Combien de	kom-**byañ** duh
is it to...?	kilomètres	keelo-**metr**
	d'ici à...?	d'ee-**see** ah
Which	Quelle est la	kel ay lah **deer**-
way to...?	direction pour...?	ek-**syoñ** poor
Do you speak	Parlez-vous	par-**lay** voo
English?	anglais?	oñg-**lay**
I'm sorry.	Excusez-moi.	exkoo-**zay** mwah

I don't	Je ne	zhuh nuh kom-
understand.	comprends pas.	**proñ** pah
Could you	Pouvez-vous	poo-**vay** voo
speak slowly	parler moins	par-**lay** mwañ
please?	vite s'il vous plaît?	veet seel voo play

USEFUL WORDS

big	grand	groñ
small	petit	puh-**tee**
hot	chaud	show
cold	froid	frwah
good	bon	boñ
bad	mauvais	moh-**veh**
enough	assez	as**say**
well	bien	byañ
open	ouvert	oo-**ver**
closed	fermé	fer-**meh**
left	gauche	gohsh
right	droite	drwah
straight on	tout droit	too drwah
near	près	preh
far	loin	lwañ
up	en haut	oñ oh
down	en bas	oñ bah
early	de bonne heure	duh bon **urr**
late	en retard	oñ ruh-**tar**
entrance	l'entrée	l'on-**tray**
exit	la sortie	sor-**tee**
toilet	les toilettes, les WC	twah-let, vay-**see**
free, unoccupied	libre	leebr
free, no charge	gratuit	grah-**twee**

MAKING A TELEPHONE CALL

I'd like to	Je voudrais	zhuh voo-dreh
place a long-	faire un	fehruñ
distance call.	interurbain.	añter-oorbañ
I'd like to	Je voudrais	zhuh voo**dreh**
make a	faire une	fehr oon **syoñ**
reverse charge	communication	komoonikah-
call.	PCV.	peh-seh-veh
I'll try again	Je rappelerai	zhuh rapel-
later.	plus tard.	**eray** ploo tar
Can I leave a	Est-ce que je peux	es-**keh** zhuh puh
message?	laisser un	leh-**say** uñ
	message?	meh**sazh**
Hold on.	Ne quittez pas,	nuh kee-**tay** pah
	s'il vous plaît.	seel voo play
Could you	Pouvez-vous	poo-**vay** voo
speak up a	parler un peu	par-**lay** uñ puh
little please?	plus fort?	ploo for
local call	la communication	komoonikah-
	locale	**syoñ** low-**kal**

SHOPPING

How much	C'est combien	say kom-**byañ**
does this cost?	s'il vous plaît?	seel voo play
I would like ...	je voudrais...	zhuh voo-**dray**
Do you have?	Est-ce que	es-**kuh** voo
	vous avez?	zav**ay**

English	French	Pronunciation
I'm just looking.	Je regarde seulement.	zhuh ruh**gar** suhl**moñ**
Do you take credit cards?	Est-ce que vous acceptez les cartes de crédit?	es-**kuh** voo zaksept-**ay** leh kart duh kreh-**dee**
Do you take traveller's cheques?	Est-ce que vous acceptez les chèques de voyage?	es-**kuh** voo zaksept-**ay** leh shek duh vwa**yazh**
What time do you open?	A quelle heure vous êtes ouvert?	ah kel urr voo zet oo-**ver**
What time do you close?	A quelle heure vous êtes fermé?	ah kel urr voo zet fer-**may**
This one.	Celui-ci.	suhl-wee-**see**
That one.	Celui-là.	suhl-wee-**lah**
expensive	cher	shehr
cheap	pas cher, bon marché	pah shehr, boñ mar-**shay**
size, clothes	la taille	tye
size, shoes	la pointure	pwañ-**tur**
white	blanc	bloñ
black	noir	nwahr
red	rouge	roozh
yellow	jaune	zhohwn
green	vert	vehr
blue	bleu	bluh

TYPES OF SHOP

antique shop	le magasin d'antiquités	maga-**zañ** d'oñteekee-**tay**
bakery	la boulangerie	booloñ-**zhuree**
bank	la banque	boñk
book shop	la librairie	lee-**brehree**
butcher	la boucherie	boo-**shehree**
cake shop	la pâtisserie	patee-**sree**
cheese shop	la fromagerie	fromazh-**ree**
chemist	la pharmacie	farmah-**see**
dairy	la crémerie	krem-**ree**
department store	le grand magasin	groñ maga-**zañ**
delicatessen	la charcuterie	sharkoot-**ree**
fishmonger	la poissonnerie	pwasson-**ree**
gift shop	le magasin de cadeaux	maga-**zañ** duh ka**doh**
greengrocer	le marchand de légumes	mar-**shoñ** duh lay-**goom**
grocery	l'alimentation	alee-moñta-**syoñ**
hairdresser	le coiffeur	kwa**fuhr**
market	le marché	marsh-**ay**
newsagent	le magasin de journaux	maga-**zañ** duh zhoor-**no**
post office	la poste, le bureau de poste, le PTT	pohst, booroh duh pohst, peh-teh-teh
shoe shop	le magasin de chaussures	maga-**zañ** duh show-**soor**
supermarket	le supermarché	soo pehr-**marshay**
tobacconist	le tabac	tabah
travel agent	l'agence de voyages	l'azhoñs duh vwayazh

SIGHTSEEING

abbey	l'abbaye	l'abay-**ee**
art gallery	le galerie d'art	galer-**ree** dart
bus station	la gare routière	gahr roo-tee-**yehr**
cathedral	la cathédrale	katay-**dral**
church	l'église	l'ayg**leez**
garden	le jardin	zhar-**dañ**
library	la bibliothèque	beeb**leeo**-tek
museum	le musée	moo-**zay**
railway station	la gare (SNCF)	gahr (es-en-say-ef)
tourist information office	les renseignements touristiques, le syndicat d'initiative	roñsayn-**moñ** too-rees-**teek**, sandee-ka d'eenee-syat**eev**
town hall	l'hôtel de ville	l'oh**tel** duh veel
private mansion	l'hôtel particulier	l'oh**tel** partikoo-**lyay**
closed for public holiday	fermeture jour férié	fehrmeh-**tur** zhoor fehree-**ay**

STAYING IN A HOTEL

Do you have a vacant room?	Est-ce que vous avez une chambre?	es-kuh voo-**zavay** oon shambr
double room	la chambre à deux personnes	shambr ah duh pehr-**son**
with double bed	avec un grand lit	avek un gronñ lee
twin room	la chambre à deux lits	shambr ah duh lee
single room	la chambre à une personne	shambr ah oon pehr-**son**
room with a bath, shower	la chambre avec salle de bains, une douche	shambr avek sal duh bañ, oon doosh
porter	le garçon	gar-**soñ**
key	la clef	klay
I have a reservation.	J'ai fait une réservation.	zhay fay oon rayzehrva-**syoñ**

EATING OUT

Have you got a table?	Avez-vous une table libre?	avay-**voo** oon tahbl leebr
I want to reserve a table.	Je voudrais réserver une table.	zhuh voo-**dray** rayzehr-**vay** oon tahbl
The bill please.	L'addition s'il vous plaît.	l'adee-**syoñ** seel voo **play**
I am a vegetarian.	Je suis végétarien.	zhuh swee vezhay-**tehryañ**
Waitress/ waiter	Madame, Mademoiselle/ Monsieur	mah-**dam**, mah-demwah**zel**/ muh-**syuh**
menu	le menu, la carte	men-**oo**, kart
fixed-price menu	le menu à prix fixe	men-**oo** ah pree feeks
cover charge	le couvert	koo-**vehr**
wine list	la carte des vins	**kart**-deh vañ
glass	le verre	vehr
bottle	la bouteille	boo-**tay**
knife	le couteau	koo-**toh**
fork	la fourchette	for-**shet**

English	French	Pronunciation
spoon	la cuillère	kwee-**yehr**
breakfast	le petit déjeuner	puh-**tee** deh-**zhuh**-nay
lunch	le déjeuner	deh-**zhuh**-nay
dinner	le dîner	dee-**nay**
main course	le plat principal	plah prañsee-**pal**
starter, first course	l'entrée, le hors-d'œuvre	l'oñ-**tray**, or-duhvr
dish of the day	le plat du jour	plah doo zhoor
wine bar	le bar à vin	bar ah vañ
café	le café	ka-**fay**
rare	saignant	**say**-noñ
medium	à point	ah **pwañ**
well done	bien cuit	byañ **kwee**

Menu Decoder

French	Pronunciation	English
l'agneau	l'anyoh	lamb
l'ail	l'eye	garlic
la banane	ba**nan**	banana
le beurre	burr	butter
la bière	bee-**yehr**	beer
la bière à la pression	bee-**yehr** ah lah pres-**syoñ**	draught beer
le bifteck, le steack	beef-**tek**, stek	steak
le bœuf	buhf	beef
bouilli	boo-**yee**	boiled
le café	kah-**fay**	coffee
le canard	kan**ar**	duck
le chocolat	**shoko**-lah	chocolate
le citron	see-**troñ**	lemon
le citron pressé	see-**troñ** press-**eh**	fresh lemon juice
les crevettes	kruh-**vet**	prawns
les crustacés	**kroos**-ta-**say**	shellfish
cuit au four	kweet oh foor	baked
le dessert	deh-**ser**	dessert
l'eau minérale	l'oh **meeney**-ral	mineral water
les escargots	leh zes-kar-**goh**	snails
les frites	freet	chips
le fromage	from-**azh**	cheese
le fruit frais	frwee freh	fresh fruit
les fruits de mer	frwee duh mer	seafood
le gâteau	gah-**toh**	cake
la glace	glas	ice, ice cream
grillé	gree-**yay**	grilled
le homard	om**ahr**	lobster
l'huile	l'weel	oil
le jambon	zhoñ-**boñ**	ham
le lait	leh	milk
les légumes	lay-**goom**	vegetables
la moutarde	moo-**tard**	mustard
l'œuf	l'uf	egg
les oignons	leh zonyoñ	onions
les olives	leh zo**leev**	olives
l'orange	l'oroñzh	orange
l'orange pressée	l'oroñzh press-**eh**	fresh orange juice
le pain	pan	bread
le petit pain	puh-**tee** pañ	roll
poché	posh-**ay**	poached
le poisson	pwah-**ssoñ**	fish
le poivre	pwavr	pepper
la pomme	pom	apple

French	Pronunciation	English
les pommes de terre	pom-duh tehr	potatoes
le porc	por	pork
le potage	poh-**tazh**	soup
le poulet	poo-**lay**	chicken
le riz	ree	rice
rôti	row-**tee**	roast
la sauce	sohs	sauce
la saucisse	soh**sees**	sausage, fresh
sec	sek	dry
le sel	sel	salt
la soupe	soop	soup
le sucre	sookr	sugar
le thé	tay	tea
le toast	toast	toast
la viande	vee-**yand**	meat
le vin blanc	vañ **bloñ**	white wine
le vin rouge	vañ **roozh**	red wine
le vinaigre	vee**naygr**	vinegar

Numbers

	French	Pronunciation
0	zéro	zeh-**roh**
1	un, une	uñ, oon
2	deux	duh
3	trois	trwah
4	quatre	katr
5	cinq	sañk
6	six	sees
7	sept	set
8	huit	weet
9	neuf	nerf
10	dix	dees
11	onze	oñz
12	douze	dooz
13	treize	trehz
14	quatorze	ka**torz**
15	quinze	kañz
16	seize	sehz
17	dix-sept	dees-**set**
18	dix-huit	dees-**weet**
19	dix-neuf	dees-**nerf**
20	vingt	vañ
30	trente	tront
40	quarante	karoñt
50	cinquante	sañk**oñt**
60	soixante	swas**oñt**
70	soixante-dix	swasoñt-**dees**
80	quatre-vingts	katr-**vañ**
90	quatre-vingts-dix	katr-vañ-**dees**
100	cent	soñ
1,000	mille	meel

Time

English	French	Pronunciation
one minute	une minute	oon mee-**noot**
one hour	une heure	oon urr
half an hour	une demi-heure	oon duh-mee urr
Monday	lundi	luñ-**dee**
Tuesday	mardi	mar-**dee**
Wednesday	mercredi	mehrkruh-**dee**
Thursday	jeudi	zhuh-**dee**
Friday	vendredi	voñdruh-**dee**
Saturday	samedi	sam-**dee**
Sunday	dimanche	dee-**moñsh**